ADDRESSES AND SPEECHES.

Robt. C. Winthrop.

ADDRESSES

AND

SPEECHES

ON VARIOUS OCCASIONS,

FROM 1869 TO 1879.

BY

ROBERT C. WINTHROP.

BOSTON:

LITTLE, BROWN, AND COMPANY.

1879.

CAMBRIDGE:
PRESS OF JOHN WILSON AND SON.

TO THE HONORABLE

HUGH BLAIR GRIGSBY, LL.D.,

PRESIDENT OF THE VIRGINIA HISTORICAL SOCIETY, AND CHANCELLOR OF THE COLLEGE OF WILLIAM AND MARY IN VIRGINIA,

This Volume

IS INSCRIBED WITH THE CORDIAL REGARD AND RESPECT OF HIS OLD FRIEND,

THE AUTHOR.

PREFACE.

I AM not unmindful that "Memoirs" or "Miscellanies" might have been a more popular title for this book. But, as I have already allowed two volumes to be published under the title of "Addresses and Speeches," — one in 1852, containing the record of my public service, and the other in 1867, — it is too late to seek a more attractive designation for the third volume. The three volumes must, therefore, take their chance, for such consideration as may be accorded to them, under a common name.

The contents of the present volume partake largely of the character of the period through which we have been passing during the last ten years. That period has included the Two Hundred and Fiftieth Anniversary of the Landing of the Pilgrim Fathers at Plymouth, and the Centennial Commemoration of our National Independence. The Historical Addresses connected with these events are the most substantial papers in these pages, and those which I should have been least willing to spare from any collected edition of my literary productions.

I have been glad, however, to associate with them many briefer papers, which may help to illustrate the lives of distinguished men or valued friends, and to preserve the record of interesting events or important Institutions.

A single page, or even a single paragraph, may sometimes suffice to supply a date, recall a name, or prolong a memory, not within ready recollection or easy research. Meantime, my duties as President of the Massachusetts Historical Society, and of the Trustees of the Peabody Education Fund, have given me occasion, more often than could have been wished, for Notices of men whose lives and deaths were of public and permanent interest.

Let me only add that in this volume, as in both of those which have preceded it, there has been no attempt to reconstruct what had already been composed or uttered, but that, in conformity with the views I have always entertained as to what was due to the truth of history, every thing has been printed here as it was originally prepared or spoken.

ROBERT C. WINTHROP.

BROOKLINE (BOSTON),
15 November, 1878.

CONTENTS.

EX-GOVERNOR CLIFFORD.

LORD STANHOPE.

WILLIAM LAMBARDE.

THE EVACUATION OF BOSTON.

THE SANDERS THEATRE.

CENTENNIAL ORATION.

PEABODY EDUCATION FUND.

COLONEL THOMAS ASPINWALL.

THE UNVEILING OF THE STATUE OF DANIEL WEBSTER.

OLYMPIA MORATA.

EMORY WASHBURN.

WEDNESDAY EVENING CLUB.

QUINCY AND MOTLEY.

THE ORIGIN AND PROGRESS OF THE PEABODY EDUCATION TRUST.

GEORGE T. DAVIS.

THIERS.

THE EARL OF ST. GERMANS.

THE BOSTON PUBLIC LATIN SCHOOL.

THE PEABODY MUSEUM OF AMERICAN ARCHÆOLOGY AND ETHNOLOGY.

GENERAL THEOLOGICAL LIBRARY.

WILLIAM C. BRYANT.

SEMI-CENTENNIAL OF THE CLASS OF 1828.

TWO HUNDRED AND FIFTIETH ANNIVERSARY OF ENDICOTT'S ARRIVAL AT NAUMKEAG.

BENJAMIN F. THOMAS.

APPENDIX.

MASSACHUSETTS AND ITS EARLY HISTORY.

INTRODUCTORY TO A COURSE OF HISTORICAL LECTURES AT THE LOWELL INSTITUTE, 5 JANUARY, 1869.

AN Introductory Lecture, my friends, like an overture to an oratorio or an opera, has, proverbially, a wide scope; and I shall avail myself, with your indulgence, of the largest privileges of my position. It is no affectation in me, however, to say to you at the outset, that I have little hope of satisfying even the reasonable requisitions of the service which has been assigned me. I am conscious, indeed, of coming here this evening to offer an apology, rather than to deliver an historical lecture. Most gladly would I have prepared myself to do something worthy of such an occasion, and of such an audience as I see before me. Most gladly would I have prepared myself, had it been in my power, to deliver something suitable to the position which I am called to occupy here, as the President of the old Historical Society of Massachusetts, — the oldest historical society in our country, — which, for more than three-quarters of a century, has devoted itself to the illustration of the Colonial history of New England, publishing more than forty volumes of invaluable historical materials, which ought to be in the library of every town and village of New England, but which, I am sorry to say, have had fewer patrons, or certainly fewer purchasers, than they deserved and needed.

Most gladly, too, would I have prepared myself, had it proved to be possible, to say something appropriate and proportionate to the great theme of that series of lectures which I am privileged to introduce, — the historical merits and virtues of the founders and builders-up of this old Puritan Commonwealth, — not second, certainly, to any Commonwealth beneath the sun, for the influence it has exerted upon the welfare of the world, and the examples it has afforded for the admiration and imitation of mankind. Such a theme, I am sensible, deserves and demands the best treatment of which any of us are capable. The praises of the New England Fathers should not be feebly uttered. To preface a course of lectures on such a subject, and by such lecturers as are to succeed me, by any vapid commonplaces, or any mere vaporing and boastful panegyrics, were like putting up a lath-and-plaster portico to some stately Doric temple, or a façade of stucco upon some solid mausoleum of marble or porphyry. Better let the structure be, without any façade at all, — as the grand Cathedral of Florence, with that majestic dome which so roused the emulation of Michel Angelo, has stood for so many centuries, — than impair its grandeur, and offend its majesty, by any cheap or incongruous frontispiece. There was nothing of *sham* in the character or the conduct of those with whom our lectures are to deal; and nothing of *sham* should be associated with their commemoration.

Why, then, am I here at all, — seeing that I must needs be so reckless of my own rede, and do only what I feel to be so far short of my own conception, at least, of what is due to the occasion? The answer to this question, my friends, will supply me with a subject, and will furnish the substance of the apology which I am here to offer you.

Allow me, at the outset, to recall the circumstances under which I first heard of these lectures. It was about the end of last January, just as I was leaving the pleasant city of Nice, recently included in the Empire of France, that I received a kind letter from my valued friend, Dr. George E. Ellis, — the original proposer of these lectures, and without whom they would not and could not have been undertaken, and who is himself to address you next Friday evening on the "Aims and Purposes of the Founders of the Massachusetts Colony," — a letter announcing that such a course was in process of arrangement between Mr. Lowell and himself, and suggesting the hope that I might return home in season for its opening or its close. I had just taken leave of our grand Admiral Farragut, who, throughout that eventful circumnavigation from which he has recently returned, made friends for his country as well as for himself, wherever he went; and the carriage was already at the door, which was to bear me along that magnificent Corniche road, — on the very brink of the Mediterranean, — of which any one who has ever been over it will require no description, while to those who are still strangers to its marvellous attractions and its magic beauty, no words of others, certainly not of mine, could convey any adequate conceptions of them. I drove along this incomparable road during three days of delicious weather, and on the fourth day entered that superb city which a grander Admiral even than Farragut might well have been proud to claim as his birthplace, — Christopher Columbus, a native of Genoa. A noble monument to Columbus, recently finished, surmounted by a striking statue of him, and adorned by a series of bas-reliefs illustrating the strange, eventful story of his life, — from which, I need hardly say, the Discovery of America was not wholly omitted, — greeted us at the gates, with the simple inscription in Italian, "To Christopher Columbus from his Country;" and, as I gazed upon it with admiration, I could not help feeling that it was not there alone that a monument and a statue were due to his memory, but that upon the shores of our own hemisphere, too, there ought to be some worthy memorial of the discoverer of the New World. I could not help feeling, indeed, how fit it would be, if we could have at New York,[1] or in Boston, or at Washington, or at Worcester, — under the auspices of our excellent American Antiquarian Society, which has taken the supposed date of Columbus's discovery as the date of its own anniversary, — an exact reproduction of this admirable monument at Genoa, so that hemisphere should seem to

[1] I am glad to say that, only six weeks after the delivery of this lecture, a colossal statue of Columbus, by an accomplished American artist (Miss Emma Stebbins), which is described as "grand in its conception and beautiful in its execution," was presented to the Commissioners of the Central Park at New York, by the Hon. Marshall O. Roberts, an eminent and munificent merchant of that city, and is immediately to be added to the decorations of that noble park.

respond to hemisphere in a common tribute to the heroic and matchless old navigator. It would be some sort of atonement, I thought, on the part of America, — tardy and inadequate, indeed, but better than nothing, — for having allowed the name of another, however meritorious, to usurp the place to which his name was so pre-eminently entitled in the geographical nomenclature of the globe.

No one, however, who observes the course of things in our own land, if not in other lands, in regard to monuments and statues, can be surprised that the claims of Columbus should have been postponed. Shakspeare has portrayed the whole philosophy of the matter, in that most impressive passage which he has put into the mouth of the not altogether reticent Ulysses of ancient Greece. You all remember it: —

> "Time hath, my lord, a wallet at his back,
> Wherein he puts alms for oblivion,
> A great-sized monster of ingratitudes:
> Those scraps are good deeds past; which are devour'd
> As fast as they are made, forgot as soon
> As done: . . . . .
> One touch of nature makes the whole world kin, —
> That all, with one consent, praise new-born gawds,
> Though they are made and moulded of things past;
> And give to dust, that is a little gilt,
> More laud than gilt o'er-dusted.
> The present eye praises the present object."

How true is it, my friends, here and elsewhere, now as in Shakspeare's time, that the man who discovered a continent, or founded a great commonwealth, is postponed to some living hero, or to him who died but yesterday! For a time the heroes of our Revolution crowded out all commemoration both of the Pilgrim and of the Puritan Fathers. Then came the heroes of a later war with England to crowd out the Revolutionary patriots. Next followed the heroes of the conquest of Mexico. More recently, the heroes and martyrs of our late civil war have absorbed all our sympathies and all our means. It is not unnatural; nor is it a subject for reproach or complaint, or for any thing but satisfaction. We grudge no tribute, certainly, however costly, to those heroic young lives which were offered up so nobly for the recent rescue of the National Union. Yet it may be hoped that a day will still come, when America may have time to look back, even as far as Columbus; and, coming down through the various stages of her early colonial settlement, and her later constitutional government, may provide some fit memorials of the men to whom she has owed her rise and progress. It may be hoped that a day will come, when Massachusetts may have leisure to examine that "wallet of oblivion at the back of Time," and to rescue from it some names and deeds of her own earlier and later history, which she would not willingly let die. It may be hoped that a day will come, when our own city may have time to review her roll of honor, and may realize that no Campo Santo, or Santa Croce, or Père la Chaise, or Westminster Abbey, of the Old World, contains dust more precious, or more worthy of commemoration, than that which lies almost unmarked in some of her own ancient graveyards. I will mention but a single name; that of the great minister of our first Puritan church, in honor of whose intended coming our city is said to have been called:— we sent, indeed, over the Atlantic, not many years since, a considerable sum of money to repair the little chapel of his noble church in Boston, Lincolnshire, Old England; but there is nothing to tell the passer-by, unless he stoops over the mouldering stone with the microscope of an Old Mortality, where, in the Boston of New England, have reposed for two centuries the ashes of JOHN COTTON.

But the statue of Columbus was not the only thing I saw in Genoa, which awakened reflections and associations connected with my own land. I did not fail to grope my way through the old Historic Hall, with its double row of original portrait statues of the old Genoese nobles, formerly known as the Bank of St. George, but now desecrated to the use of the dingiest department of what, I should hope and believe, is the dingiest custom-house in the world. Heaven forbid, thought I, that any historic hall of my own land should ever suffer such a profanation! Yet when I remembered how inadequately cared for our own Faneuil Hall, and still more our own old State House, had often been; and how much of their sanctity and of their safety had been sacrificed in years past, if they were not still, to any and every purpose which might increase the rents, and add a few more hundreds of dollars to a treasury from which so much goes out from year to year for more than doubtful expenditures, — I was less emboldened to indulge in any wholesale strictures upon other cities. But better, a thousand-fold better, let me say in passing, that all such structures, whether in Genoa or in Boston, should be razed to the ground at once, and live only as they are photographed on the hearts of those who have held them sacred, than that they should be left cumbering the ground and blocking the highway, only to signalize the more conspicuously that indifference and irreverence towards the noblest scenes and associations of a glorious past, which have been engendered by the rush and crush of modern improvement and modern traffic.

But pardon me, my friends, for such a digression, and bear with me kindly as I roll rapidly again along the Riviera, resting at mid-day on the lofty hill at Rota, which commands so wonderful a view, and reaching Sestri di Ponente just in season to enjoy one of those indescribable Italian sunsets. The necessity of an early start, the next day, not only secured us an opportunity of witnessing what Jeremy Taylor had so vividly in mind when he quaintly recommended to the readers of his "Holy Living," that they should sometimes "be curious to see the preparations which the sun makes, when he is about to quit his chamber in the East;" but enabled us also to reach the summit of the last mountain on our route, in season to look down upon the lovely harbor of Spezia, just as the day-star was once more sinking beneath the blue waters of the Mediterranean, and casting those ineffable roseate hues upon the snow-capped Apennines in the distance, while at the same instant a full-orbed moon was rising majestically from behind them. A more delightful and inspiring view it has hardly entered into the imagination of poet or painter to conceive. Shall I be forgiven, however, for saying that there was an added beauty to that view, — to American eyes, certainly, — when we descried in the harbor below us, safely riding at anchor, and surrounded by its companions of the squadron, and surmounted by the stars and stripes, the same noble propeller, bearing the name of the "Great Bostonian," — Franklin, — which we had left at Nice, and which had come round there that very day? I do not envy the apathy of any American, young or old, who can suddenly find himself face to face, in a foreign land, with the flag of his country, flying from the masthead of one of its noblest frigates, and symbolizing more especially the personal presence and authority of an admiral who himself went into action lashed to a mast-head, — I do not envy, I say, the composure of one who can confront that flag, under such circumstances, without emotion; or, who would not consider any prospect, which sun and moon and azure waves and snow-capped hills combined can make up, as beautified and glorified by such an additional feature.

The next morning, I found myself in the train with Farragut and his party, and went on with them to Pisa, where we all ascended "the tower which leans and leans and leans, but never falls." On the following day, I was where I could read the inscription on the ancient residence of Americus Vespucius; and where I was led to wish again, as I had more than once wished before, that Boston would follow the example of Florence, and so inscribe its local history on the names of its streets, and the walls of its houses, that it might be read by every boy and girl on their way to school.

But what, you may well ask, my friends, what has all this to do with the course of historical lectures which I am here officially to introduce? What has it all to do even with the apology which I proposed to offer you? Not so much, perhaps, with either as might be wished, yet by no means so little as some of my hearers may at first be disposed to think. For as I drove along that magnificent road, during those five or six days of superb weather, when sun and moon and each particular star would seem to have shed their selectest influence upon our pathway — and be it always borne in mind, that one may as well look for the beauties of a landscape while passing through a tunnel, as attempt to form any idea of the grandeur of the Corniche by traversing it in a fog or a storm, — as I drove along that marvellous road which, too soon, I fear, is to be abandoned for the greater despatch and economy of an already half-finished railroad, the letter of my friend Dr. Ellis, announcing these lectures, and which had been opened as I entered the carriage, was fresh in my mind and frequently in my hand. I read it certainly more than once, or twice, or thrice ; and the subject to which it referred kept strangely blending itself with all I was observing and enjoying, entering unbidden alike into my thoughts by day and my dreams by night. As I gazed, at one moment, on the glorious sea at my side, and marked the matchless blueness of its waters; and at another, on the gorgeous hues of sunrise, or of sunset, around and above me, fulfilling, as hardly anywhere else is so completely fulfilled, the exquisite idea of the Psalmist, — "Thou makest the outgoings of the morning and the evening to rejoice;" — as I contemplated the varied luxuriance of the climate and the soil, where, on those last days of January and first days of February, the vine and the olive were still wearing their leafy honors side by side, and oranges and lemons still ripening on the branches, and the rose and the sweet pea still blooming on the walls and in the gardens; — as I inhaled that balmy air which made it a luxury to breathe; — as I turned to the thousand forms of beauty and of grandeur which greeted me from the distant hills and mountains, the Maritime Alps or Ligurian Apennines, with their robes of ice and diadems of snow: — all the while, old Massachusetts and its history and its Historical Society, and this very course of Lowell lectures, were still uppermost, or undermost, or somewhere in the midst of my thoughts, — sometimes in the way of comparison and sometimes of contrast, sometimes of yearning and sometimes, I do confess, of dread.

I could not help feeling, of course, that whatever else my native State might have to boast of, she had nothing in the way of sea, or sky, or soil, of climate or of scenery, to be compared for an instant with what I was beholding. I could not help contrasting the genial temperature and glowing atmosphere which I was enjoying, with the bleak winds and deep snows and drenching storms and freezing cold, which my fellow-citizens at home must have been at that moment enduring. And while I was thus meditating and musing, the fire kindled, and I found myself seriously asking myself, whether I would permanently exchange, were it in my power to do so, such sea and sky and soil, as we have here in New England to-day, for those of southern France or central Italy; and suddenly I found myself resolving, that if I should reach my home safely and in season, and should be called on to take either an opening or a closing part in this course of lectures, — ignorant as I was, what other subjects might be left open to me, — I would give my reasons for saying no, — emphatically *no*, — to this question; and would devote my little hour to some thoughts on the influences upon the character and career of our earlier and our later people, and on the supreme results to our history as a Commonwealth, of that very soil and climate about which we are so often disposed to complain, and of which my letters from home were at that moment saying, "that it was feared the Gulf Stream had changed its current, and that we might soon be looking out for polar bears and other arctic curiosities!" And soon the subject and its treatment began to expand and shape itself in my mind. I bethought me that Massachusetts, too, had a sea of her own, — an historical sea, if I may so speak; that, indeed, she had risen out of the sea; that she could not have been Massachusetts had she not been founded on the coast. And I followed that coast around, on the map of my memory, from the farthest point of Cape Cod, to which Captain John Smith, — one of the pioneers of New England exploration, of whom my friend Hillard has given us so good a Life, and who himself deserves a statue or a monument somewhere along shore, — attempted to affix the name of King James; round to the extremest verge of Cape Ann, to which the same bold, though erratic — I had almost said vagabond — navigator essayed to give the portentous and not altogether musical title of Cape Tragabigzanda. I found myself pausing in this survey, as you will not doubt, to mark the spot in Provincetown Harbor, where, in the cabin of the "Mayflower," the first written Constitution known to the history of the world, was drawn up, agreed upon, and signed. I found myself pausing again, as you will not doubt, to mark the spot in Plymouth Harbor, where the Pilgrim Fathers left the "Mayflower" at that terrible wintry season, and landed on that consecrated rock. I found myself pausing once more, you may be sure, to mark the spot in the gentler waters which wash that charming Beverly shore in the harbor of Salem, where the

"Arbella," with the charter of Massachusetts, and its governor and company, came to anchor ten years later. Nor did I altogether forget the little islands on which Bartholomew Gosnold had landed and built a house, before Puritan or Pilgrim, or even John Smith, had ventured within our bay. And then there came over me a more vivid impression than ever before, of all which that bay, with the great ocean of which it is an inlet, had done for the character and enterprise and industry of our people, from those early days to this. I bethought me of those whale-fisheries, of which it had been the cradle and the nursery, and which elicited that well-remembered and magnificent tribute of Edmund Burke, in his speech on conciliation with America, — a tribute, which, at the end of nearly a hundred years, cannot be read without stirring our blood like a trumpet, and which is worthy of being read and re-read, as a piece of glorious prose which neither Macaulay nor Milton often, if ever, surpassed: —

"Look at the manner in which the people of New England," said Burke, "have of late carried on the whale-fishery. Whilst we follow them among the tumbling mountains of ice, and behold them penetrating into the deepest frozen recesses of Hudson's Bay and Davis's Straits, whilst we are looking for them beneath the arctic circle, we hear that they have pierced into the opposite region of polar cold, that they are at the antipodes, and engaged under the frozen serpent of the South. Falkland Island, which seemed too remote and romantic an object for the grasp of rational ambition, is but a stage and resting-place in the progress of their victorious industry. Nor is the equinoctial heat more discouraging to them, than the accumulated winter of both the poles. We know that whilst some of them draw the line and strike the harpoon on the coast of Africa, others run the longitude, and pursue their gigantic game along the coast of Brazil. No sea but what is vexed by their fisheries. No climate that is not witness to their toils. Neither the perseverance of Holland, nor the activity of France, nor the dexterous and firm sagacity of English enterprise, ever carried this most perilous mode of hardy industry to the extent to which it has been pushed by this recent people; a people who are still, as it were, but in the gristle, and not yet hardened into the bone of manhood."

I bethought me, too, of the cod fisheries which our bay had nourished and cherished, until they became at one time so far the very staple of our Commonwealth, that their emblem, — as I have the best reason for remembering, — was suspended, where it still hangs, over the chair of the presiding officer of the representatives of the people in our legislative halls. I bethought me, again, of the mercantile marine it had built up, until Salem became one of the great seats of the East-India trade; and Captain Robert Gray, of Boston, discovered the Columbia River; and Boston itself rose to be the third, — as it not long ago was, I know not where it stands now, — while New Bedford was hardly less than the fifth, in the commercial tonnage of the Union. Nor, certainly, did I fail to remember what our bay and our sea had done for the national navy, and the thousands of gallant tars it had supplied for fighting their country's battles on the ocean, — whether under Bainbridge and Lawrence and Chauncey and Hull and Decatur, in those days when George Canning declared, in the House of Commons, that "the spell of British invincibility on the ocean was at last broken;" or in these latter days of not inferior glory, under Porter and Rodgers and Winslow and Foote and Farragut. Was this a sea, I asked myself, to be disowned, or abandoned, or exchanged for any other sea beneath the sun? It was no Mediterranean, indeed. It did not run between vine-clad hills and romantic villages; and one could hardly sail an hour upon it, in a straight course, without leaving capes and headlands and snug harbors behind him, and going out to buffet with the big rollers and swelling billows of the vast Atlantic, with nothing but the sea and the sky, and the God above the sky, to witness the encounter. But, for this very reason, it was a sea to impart the bravery it demanded; to stimulate the adventure it invited; and to breed and educate, as it has bred and educated, a race of hardy and intrepid mariners, taking to the water, — as Dr. Palfrey once so happily said, — as naturally as so many ducks to a pond; whose enterprise and exploits have supplied, and are still destined to supply, the theme of solid history, as well as of brilliant romance, to the end of time; mariners of New England, who are as worthy of being famous in song and story, as those mariners of Old England, whose memories are embalmed in the immortal song of Campbell.

And then I bethought me of the climate of Massachusetts,

which had so marvellously co-operated with the sea, in giving vigor and energy and hardihood to our people. True, we had no Januarys or Februarys like those I was experiencing. True, our winters were almost always long and dreary and dreadful, and our summers too often brief and scorching. A glorious autumn we might generally boast of, kindling our forests into a thousand glories, as the inexorable Frost-King blazes his pathway through the valleys and along the hill-sides, in colors such as never adorned the train of any other earthly monarch: but we have had recent experience that even this cannot be counted on; while as to spring, — why, if our poet Bryant had seen fit to vie with Thomson, — as I think he might have done, — and to depict the Seasons of New England, he could have done nothing but include spring in a parenthesis!

Yet, would I alter all this? Would I, if the wand of Prospero, to lay or lift a tempest, were in my hand, exchange even our Boston east wind, eager and nipping as it is, for some sweet but treacherous south, breathing, indeed, over a bank of violets, but bringing in its track the lassitude, the self-indulgence, the aversion to labor, the inaptitude for liberty, the incapacity for self-government, or for sustained and manly effort of any sort, which characterize so many of the inhabitants of those sunny climes through which I was then passing? Admit that our east wind may have imparted not a little of its harsh and acrid quality to the tempers of those who first weathered it, which has not been wholly eradicated, which perhaps never can be eradicated, from the tempers of their descendants; for I am disposed to think, that the acrid quality of the climate was, in part at least, primarily responsible for creating that "acrid spirit of the times," which Longfellow tells us, at the close of one of his graceful New England tragedies, "corroded the true steel" of one of the earliest and bravest of the old Puritan leaders. But what other climate could have given them the muscle, the grit, the gristle, as Burke called it, the strong right arms, and the stern and dauntless souls, which enabled them to endure the deprivations of a wilderness, and to subdue a soil which would have repelled and defied all feebler hands or hearts?

And, next, I bethought me of that soil: what a soil it was,

here in New England, what a soil it is still, compared with that then beneath my feet! And I remembered but too vividly the dreary and desolate look of a Massachusetts landscape for six or seven months of the year, not only without fruit or flowers, like those which were on all sides around me, but without a spire of grass or a leaf on the trees. But I remembered, too, a little dialogue which I had once heard from the lips of Edward Everett. Would that those lips had language still, and could repeat it, in their own inimitable way, once more! He was accompanying Henry Clay, during the month of April, I think it was in the year 1833, through the county of Middlesex, which Mr. Everett then represented in Congress, on a visit to Lowell. "Everett," exclaimed Mr. Clay, "in Heaven's name, what do your constituents live on? I see nothing hereabouts capable of supporting human life, or animal life of any sort." "Why, Mr. Clay," replied Everett, "don't you see that tree in the middle of yonder field there?" "Yes, I do," said Mr. Clay; "and a very small and miserable specimen of a tree it is; there is not a leaf or a bud on it; it looks dead already, and hardly fit for firewood." "Ah!" said Mr. Everett (in playful resentment of an old impertinence to a neighboring New-England State), "it makes capital wooden nutmegs!"

Yes, my friends, the barrenness of our ground has made our brains fertile; and even the invention which built up Lowell, has owed not a little of its stimulus to the sterility of the surrounding acres. The willing and luxuriant harvests of other latitudes are, indeed, unknown to us; but who shall complain of a soil which has so enforced industry; which has so quickened and sharpened the wits; which has so nourished independence and freedom; which has presented no temptation to make woman a yoke-fellow with the brutes, exhibiting her, like those I saw around me, subjected to the hardest labors of the field; and which, above all, — far, far above all, — has so repelled and repudiated from its culture every form of human servitude! Boast as we will, and as we well may, of the influence of free schools and free governments in moulding and training the characters and careers of New England men, — and my friend, Mr. Emerson, will tell you all about that, when his turn to lecture comes, —

we must not forget that there are influences underlying and overlying all these, — the influences of the earth beneath us and of the sky above us. One of the most popular of Old England's poets, even in the very piece in which he proposed to illustrate the influence of education and government upon mankind, — a piece which, though fragmentary and unfinished, is not unworthy to stand beside his own exquisite Elegy in a Country Churchyard, — has given expression to this idea in some noble lines: —

> "Not but the human fabric from the birth
> Imbibes the flavor of its parent earth;
> As various tracts enforce a various toil,
> The manners speak the idiom of their soil.
> An iron race the mountain-cliffs maintain,
> Foes to the gentler genius of the plain."

One might almost imagine, indeed, that Gray had New England, and New-England men, distinctly in his mind, when he adds: —

> "For where unwearied sinews must be found
> With side-long plough to quell the flinty ground,
> To turn the torrent's swift-descending flood,
> To brave the savage rushing from the wood, —
> What wonder if, to patient valor train'd,
> They guard with spirit what by strength they gain'd!"

And you all remember that good, dear, pious Mrs. Barbauld has condensed the whole thought into one of the grandest couplets in all poetry: —

> "Man is the nobler growth our realms supply,
> And souls are ripened in our northern sky."

Yes, my friends, we of New England, after all, may well thank Heaven that our Pilgrim Fathers landed upon nothing softer than a rock,[1] and that the Puritan founders of Massachusetts were not persuaded, — as Oliver Cromwell endeavored to persuade them, and would fain have forced them, had he dared to try it, — to abandon their flinty glebe for the rich mould of the tropics. It is not enough for us to be grateful, that the region

[1] An accomplished and classical friend has reminded me that Herodotus (the old father of History), at the end of his last book (Calliope), makes Cyrus say: "Φιλέειν γὰρ ἐκ τῶν μαλακῶν χώρων μαλακοὺς ἄνδρας γίνεσθαι."

to which they so firmly adhered, was not a region exposed to such inundations as have recently devastated so many of the fields and villages of Switzerland, and made such a claim upon the sympathy and succor of all who have witnessed the glories of the Alps, and the simple virtues of those who inhabit them. It is not enough for us to be grateful, that the clime to which they clung so tenaciously, is not a clime subject to such convulsions as have recently swallowed up whole cities on our own hemisphere; and the mere liability to which is itself sufficient to unnerve and demoralize even those who may escape all actual damage to person or property. It is not enough for us to be grateful, that the bay around which they nestled and clustered, had no smouldering volcano on its right hand or on its left, threatening at every outbreak, like Vesuvius or Ætna at this moment, to overwhelm all within its reach with a torrent of burning lava. It is not enough for us to be grateful, that the land and the sea which they refused so obstinately to abandon or exchange, were free alike from the corrupting and distracting influences of mines of silver or of gold, and of fisheries of coral or of pearl; though I may not forget that, in these latter years, some of our not very distant hills have occasionally been suspected of gold, and that a few exquisite pearls have actually been found, in the streams near Sandwich, not far from where the Pilgrims landed. But, beyond and above all this, may we not well thank God, as we review our history, even for that springless climate, of short summers and long winters, of late and early frosts, of sharp and sudden vicissitudes, which has demanded, from first to last, the steady and sturdy struggle of intelligent freemen for existence and for bread? May we not well thank God for a soil, from which no North-western Ordinance or Missouri Compromise, no Wilmot Proviso or Constitutional Amendment, was ever needed to shut out slavery; and for a temperature which has braced up our children to a manly, vigorous, independent, self-sustaining, and self-relying exercise of their own thews and sinews and brains in every field of useful labor or worthy enterprise?

Who is not willing to unite with me in exclaiming, in this sense at least, — Let Massachusetts be "left out in the cold" for ever, with nothing but ice and granite for her natural exports, rather than have all the manhood melted and thawed out of her children, as it was out of so many of those whom I saw by the way-side, too limp for any thing but to bask in the sun and beg? Who can say that upon a different soil, and under other skies, even New-England principles, as we call them, would have been proof against the temptation of establishing, or at least permanently tolerating, domestic institutions which have been so fatal elsewhere, and which it has cost at last such a deluge of blood and treasure to abolish? Who can say that if the pilot of the Pilgrims, to whom, justly or unjustly, treachery has sometimes been imputed, had conducted the Mayflower nearer to the Southern Cross, instead of steering her ever by that blessed North Star; and if the Massachusetts colony had followed in their wake, — we, their descendants, might not at this moment be suffering, as so many of our brethren elsewhere are suffering, from the destitution and desolation, directly or indirectly brought upon ourselves, by a vain struggle, in the interests and under the influence of slavery, to overthrow that National Government, and rend asunder that Constitutional Union, which it is now our pride and glory to have defended and preserved for our children?

Such, my friends, were some of the thoughts, on the influence of soil and climate upon the character and history of New England, which came swarming through my mind as I whirled along that magnificent Corniche road last winter, with the letter of my friend Dr. Ellis in my hand. Such were the leading ideas of the lecture I then conceived, and proposed to prepare deliberately, if I should be called on to prepare any thing, for this occasion; and which I thought might be worked up into a not altogether inappropriate Introductory to such a course. But a thousand unforeseen circumstances of foreign travel, and of domestic and personal experience, soon occurred to obliterate the whole subject from my mind; and I returned home, not long ago, without ever thinking of it again, and without a note on which I could rely for reviving and reconstructing the train of ideas. And all that I have been able to do, since my return, has been to recall thus hastily the associations of time and place, to gather up the tangled threads wherever I could lay hold of them in my memory, and to present to you thus crudely, what I would so gladly have elaborated, illustrated, and perfected. If, however, by throwing myself into the gap, — as I have done, at the last moment, and at the imperative call of others, — I shall have prepared the way for the instructive and well-considered and eloquent discourses which I know are to follow, my hour will not have been spent in vain; and you, I am sure, will all pardon me for so desultory and discursive an utterance.

I must not let you go, however, without reverting, in a few closing remarks to the original purpose of these lectures, and to the general objects of the Society under whose auspices they have been undertaken. There is something remarkable, and more than remarkable, — there is something quite wonderful, I think, — about the way in which the history of this old Commonwealth of ours, and the history of New England, of which it was the capital colony, have been preserved, cared for, and "treasured up as for a life beyond life," from the very outset of their career. Not only are we spared the pains of seeking the story of our origin in myths and fables, in traditions and legends, like the people of so many other lands, but we may find it written out for us at the moment, by those who could tell us all that they saw, and a most important part of which they were.

Hardly had the Pilgrims landed at Plymouth in 1620, before William Bradford, who was so soon to succeed the lamented Carver as their governor, began to collect the original letters and papers, which, ten years afterwards, he commenced "piecing up at times of leisure," to use his own phrase, until he had completed a connected and careful account of the first twenty-seven years of that pioneer plantation. This invaluable work, — after remaining in manuscript for more than two hundred years, known only by a few citations which had been made from it by later writers, who had enjoyed the privilege of consulting it, — after having disappeared from all view, and eluded all search, for more than half a century; and after having been lamented over like one of the lost books of Livy, — to us, if not to the world at large, a thousand times more precious than the whole of Livy, — was at last discovered in 1855, on the other side of the Atlantic Ocean, in the library of the Bishop of London at Fulham, and was printed for the first time, by this Society, in 1856, from an exact copy made for the purpose, under the faithful editorship of our present accomplished Recording Secretary, Mr. Charles Deane.

On the other hand, the Massachusetts Company proper, with their charter, had not left their final anchorage at the Cowes, near the Isle of Wight, in 1630, before the governor of that colony — John Winthrop — had made the first entry in a journal or history, which he continued from day to day, and from year to year, until his death in 1648–9. That work, too, remained in perishable manuscript for a century and a half. The original was in three volumes; the first two of which were printed, for the first time, at Hartford, in 1790, from an inaccurate copy, which had been commenced by Governor Trumbull, with a preface and dedication by the great lexicographer, Noah Webster, who subsequently confessed that he had never even read the original manuscript. It remained for one whom we now recognize, since the death of our veteran Quincy, as the venerable senior member of our Society, and its former President, — James Savage, — to decipher and annotate and edit the whole; for lo! in 1816, the third volume, of which nothing had been seen or heard for more than sixty years, turned up in the tower of the Old South Meeting-house! The Rev. Thomas Prince, the pastor of that church, who kept his library in that tower, and is known to have had all three of the volumes in 1755, died without returning this third volume to the family of the author, from whom I have the best reason to think they were all borrowed. And so in 1825–6, one hundred and ninety-five years after that first entry, on that Easter Monday, while the "Arbella" was "riding at the Cowes," these annals of the first nineteen years of the Massachusetts colony were published in a correct and complete form. But as if to illustrate the risks to which they had been so long exposed, and to signalize the perils they had so providentially escaped, one of the original volumes was destroyed by a memorable fire in Court Street, before Mr. Savage had finished the laborious corrections and annotations to which he had devoted himself.

Here, then, we find the striking fact of the two governors of the two originally independent colonies of Plymouth and Massachusetts Bay, which afterwards, in 1691, were combined in a single Commonwealth, — the two men who were the leading witnesses of all that occurred, and the leading actors in all that was done, — preparing careful histories of the rise and progress of each, and leaving them in manuscript at their death: Those manuscripts we find remaining unprinted, uncopied, and seemingly uncared for, during a period of a century and a half and two centuries respectively; exposed to all and more than all the common accidents which wait upon ancient papers, — the moth, the bookworm, the damp, the flames, — owing to the unsettled and troubled condition of the colonies, from time to time, and almost all the time: — For instance, when the British cavalry occupied the Old South Church, as a riding-school and a stable, in 1775, and took Governor Winthrop's old house, which stood next, for firewood, both of these precious manuscripts were in the tower, where Prince had left them; and both were doomed, to all human eyes, to be used as kindling; but they were really destined for another sort of kindling: — Both of them we find reappearing in the end, — substantially every leaf of them; — one of them, and a large part of the other, turning up at last where they would least have been looked for, or have been imagined to be; and both of them waiting, — waiting, as it were, for the fulness of time, — to be published, as they have been, by those most capable of appreciating them and doing them justice!

What is there in the curiosities of secular literature more striking? Surely, we may say, so far as Massachusetts history is concerned, "There's a divinity that shapes our ends, rough-hew them how we will." But this is but the beginning of the story. While these original and more authentic accounts of the infant Commonwealth were still scarcely known to exist beyond the family circle of their authors, — as early as 1654, — Edward Johnson, one of the intensest of Puritans, publishes in London, his "Wonder-working Providence of Sion's Saviour in New England," which, though written in a most inflated and bombastic style, and full of blunders and doggerel, contains many most important and valuable facts, and is worthy of being remembered as the first printed book of New England history. A beautiful edition of it, with a valuable Introduction, has recently been published by Mr. W. F. Poole, the late faithful Librarian of the Boston Athenæum. Then came Nathaniel Morton, a nephew of Governor Bradford, with his "Memorial of Plymouth Colony," abounding, also, in important references to the Massachusetts Colony proper, published originally at our Cambridge in 1669, and republished in 1826, under the admirable editorship of another former President of this Society, — the late excellent Judge Davis.

And now "draws hitherward, — I know him by his stride," — the giant of New-England early literature, — the marvellous and marvel-loving Cotton Mather, with a voracity for every thing relating to our colonial condition and history as insatiate as his own vanity; seeking and searching for something new and strange, like those men of ancient Athens whom Paul depicted; of a credulity which swallowed every thing which was told him, and a diligence which digested almost every thing which he swallowed; and publishing, in London, in 1702, after a prodigious amount of strugglings and wrestlings, of prayers and fastings, of visions by day and dreams by night, a huge folio volume, entitled "Magnalia Christi Americana," or, as the titlepage has it, "The First book of the New-English History, reporting the Design where*on*, the Manner where*in*, and the People where*by*, the several colonies of New England were planted, by the endeavour of Cotton Mather;" — containing a monstrous mass of information and speculation, of error and gossip, of biography and history, of italics and capitals, of classical quotations, Latin and Greek, and of original epitaphs, Latin and English, in prose and in verse, which, as old Polonius said of Hamlet's actors, "either for tragedy, comedy, history, pastoral, pastoral-comical, historical-pastoral, tragical-comical, scene individable or poem unlimited," has hardly a parallel in the world! Let me not seem to disparage or undervalue Cotton Mather, — a perfect Dr. Pangloss, as he was in many particulars, — for with all his foibles and all his faults, all his credulity and all his vanity, it cannot be denied that he did a really great work for New England history. The lives of our Worthies could not have been written without him; while his "Essay to do Good" is known to have given the earliest incentive to the wonderful career of New England's most wonderful son, — Benjamin Franklin.

Passing rapidly now over Church's "King Philip's War," first printed in 1716, of which a beautiful edition has recently been added to "the New-England Library" by the Rev. Henry Martyn Dexter; and John Dunton's "Letters from New England," in 1686, just printed for the Prince Society, from the original manuscript in the Bodleian Library, under the careful editorship of Mr. W. H. Whitmore, — we come next, in order of date, to the "Chronological History of New England" by the accurate and indefatigable Thomas Prince himself, whose first volume was published in 1736; and who, in 1755, began a second volume, of which only three serial numbers were printed before his death, in 1758. Then we have the valuable historical "Summary" of Dr. William Douglas, published in Boston, in numbers, the first of them in 1746–7; and the whole two volumes of which were completed in 1751.

And now appears upon the scene, as an historian of Massachusetts, another of her colonial governors, whose name was so identified, justly or unjustly, with the Stamp Act, and others of those acts of British oppression which drove us to rebellion, and through rebellion to independence, that it long was held in too much of passionate abhorrence to allow of any justice being done to any thing he did or said or wrote; but who, take him for all in all, did as much for the history of this his native State, and did it as well, as any man who has lived before or since. Let us not fail to do justice to his memory in this respect. Governor Hutchinson's first volume was published in 1764. The second volume, almost ready for the press, was in his house in Garden-Court Street, on the 26th of August, 1765, when it was so shamefully sacked and pillaged by a mob. Hutchinson, as the mob approached, was engaged in bearing to a place of safety a beloved daughter who had refused to quit his side, and was thus compelled to abandon his precious papers to their fate. Every thing was destroyed, or thrown out of the windows; and the scattered pages of this second volume of his history were left lying in the street for several hours in a soaking rain. But thanks to the care and pains of the Rev. Andrew Eliot, one of the servants, then and always, of the good God to whom we owe the marvellous preservation of those other and earlier manuscripts of those other and earlier governors, all but eight or ten sheets were collected and saved ; and so much of them was still legible that, in spite of the muddy footprints of the Vandals who had trampled on them, the author was able to supply the rest, transcribe the whole, and publish it in 1767. Still a third volume, hardly less valuable than either, and written with an almost judicial fairness and a wonderful freedom from prejudice, considering the treatment he had received, remained in manuscript for half a century after his death in 1780, and was only rescued from perdition, and published in 1828, through the persevering efforts of Mr. Savage, and other members of our Society.

I must not forget that still another governor of Massachusetts, James Sullivan, the first President of our Society, early devoted his leisure from professional and public labors to the preparation of a history of his native Province of Maine, — then a part of Massachusetts, — and published it in 1795. I must not forget the excellent account of that great epoch in Massachusetts history, commonly called "Shays's Rebellion," published in 1788 by George Richards Minot, the father of our venerable William; and followed, in 1798 and 1803, by two substantial volumes of the history of the province, from 1748 to 1765. I must not forget either the really great work of one who was so long our Corresponding Secretary, and whose accomplished son — who so well illustrates the idea of ancient mythology, "one power of physic, melody, and song" — is announced among the lecturers of our course; I mean the "American Annals" of the late Dr. Abiel Holmes, published in 1805, and abounding in dates and facts of Massachusetts and New England, as well as of National, interest. Still less must I forget the elaborate History of New England, by the Rev. William Hubbard, an early minister of Ipswich, completed in manuscript as long ago as 1682, but which it remained for this Society, with the patronage of the Legislature of Massachusetts, to publish for the first time as lately as 1815.

Time would fail me, or certainly your patience would be

exhausted, my friends, were I to attempt to speak, as I ought to speak, of all the more recent contributions and contributors to the historical illustration of our Commonwealth, and of New England; of the Rev. John Eliot, and of Alden Bradford; of Dr. Felt's Ecclesiastical History, and Governor Washburn's Judicial History; of Drake's comprehensive and elaborate History of Boston; of Quincy's Harvard University; of Young's Chronicles of Plymouth and of Massachusetts, and of the Records of those old Colonies, edited by our worthy Mayor, Dr. Shurtleff; of Mr. Savage's Genealogical History of New England; of Tudor's James Otis; of Richard Frothingham's Siege of Boston, and Life of Warren; of Sabine's Fisheries and Loyalists; of Dr. Holland's Western Massachusetts, and General Schouler's Massachusetts in the late Civil War, with its admirable portrait of the lamented Andrew, and its vivid presentment of many of the stirring scenes through which we have so lately passed; of the Life and Letters of John Adams by his distinguished grandson; of Barry's Massachusetts; of Bancroft's Colonial Period; of Upham's recent and most interesting History of Witchcraft; and of Palfrey's consummate and crowning work on New England, which may fitly complete the calendar, and which is worthy, I need not say, of far more than any mere passing commendation of mine.

I have omitted, I doubt not, in this running catalogue, many names which deserve to be mentioned; and I have said nothing of what has been done so well, in their Collections and Registers, by our sister societies of other States, and by kindred associations in our own State; or of the numerous town histories, and church histories, which have been so faithfully written. But I have said enough to recall to your remembrance the fact, that while New England has furnished not a few able and brilliant historians and biographers for some of the great political and literary epochs of other lands, ancient and modern, and for some of the great statesmen of other parts of our own land, — in our lamented Prescott and Sparks and Felton, and in our living Ticknor and Motley and Parkman and Kirk, — her own history has by no means been neglected; but that there has been a most striking succession of men, — many of them governors, judges, ministers, counsellors, men of renown, famous in their generation, — who have been moved, as by a common impulse, to keep the record of New England, and of Massachusetts in particular, and to illustrate the history of their rise and progress; some of whose works, like those of William Bradford and John Winthrop and Thomas Hutchinson, have come down to us under circumstances of almost romantic interest; and all of which together can hardly fail to leave the impression on a thoughtful mind, — I will not admit that it need be a superstitious mind, — that for good or for evil, for encouragement or for warning, for our glory or for our shame, that history was not destined to be lost to mankind.

But I could not be forgiven, — I could not forgive myself, — were I to close without an allusion to one other name, which I have purposely reserved to the last, — the name of the Rev. Dr. Jeremy Belknap, the recognized founder of our Society, whose History of New Hampshire, in three volumes, published in 1784, 1791, and 1792, and his two volumes of early American biography, published in 1794 and 1798, are full of importance to the work of which I have been speaking. Under his lead, our Society was organized in 1791, — to gather up the fragments, that nothing be lost, — composed of ten members, at the outset, increased to thirty, and afterwards to sixty in all, and now limited to a hundred members throughout the Commonwealth. Beginning their career upon the most economical scale; ordering their Treasurer, Judge Tudor, to buy "twelve Windsor green elbow-chairs, a plain pine table, painted, with a drawer and lock and key, and an inkstand;" and with no resources but an assessment of two dollars a year upon each member, — they proceeded to collect papers and pamphlets and books, and to publish, scrap by scrap, as an appendix or a preamble to a magazine called "The American Apollo," whatever original manuscripts, relating to New England, they were able to pick up, the very first of these scraps having been published on the 6th of January, 1792, just seventy-six years ago to-morrow. In these latter years, the liberal and noble benefactions of Samuel Appleton and Thomas Dowse and George Peabody have added greatly to their library and to their funds, and have enabled them to go on with their work more conspicuously and more confidently. But the enormous cost of printing and the inadequate sale of their volumes are serious impediments to their progress; and this very course of lectures has been arranged, as a labor of love on the part of the members, not without at least a secondary view to eking out the insufficiencies of our treasury.

Forty-five volumes of Collections and Proceedings have already been printed, — many of them containing papers of unspeakable importance and interest; and some of them throwing a light upon the formation of our institutions, the establishment of our towns and schools, and the inner life of the earlier and later settlers of New England, which can be found nowhere else. Other papers of equal interest and value are awaiting the press. Without any very large addition to our resources, if it were only secured before some of our members, now in my eye, but whose names I forbear to mention, shall have lost the taste and the faculty for this sort of labor, our valuable manuscripts might be printed, and placed beyond the reach of accident as fast as is desirable. And it is easy to suggest a legitimate and effectual mode of relief, — in the wider circulation and sale of our Collections, — if we could only accomplish its adoption. We cannot hope, indeed, that our volumes will find any great number of purchasers or readers, in competition with the illustrated poems or sensation novels, of which the tenth or the twentieth thousand are advertised in successive months. But there are more than three hundred towns in Massachusetts. In the public or social libraries of every one of them, there ought to be a complete set, or as complete a set as is still possible, of these Historical Collections. Everywhere we observe liberal men, residents or natives of these towns, founding, or endowing, or aiding these public libraries. If we could find enough of such liberal men, who, severally or jointly, would be responsible for placing sets of these Collections in only one-half of the town libraries, — and I know not what more appropriate New-Year's present could be made by any one to the place of his nativity, or of his winter or summer residence, — I should feel the greatest confidence, that we and our successors could go on, without let or hindrance, to continue the story of this noble Commonwealth in all its earlier, and in all its later, relations to

New England and to the nation at large, — "nothing extenuating, nor setting down aught in malice," but giving the truth, the whole truth, and nothing but the truth, after the manner and example of those who have preceded us.

It is a work, my friends, which, you will all agree with me, ought not to be left incomplete. We owe it to the memory of our fathers, that no authentic account of their lives and labors should be lost. We owe it to our children, that the great examples of piety and purity, of endurance and enterprise, of wisdom and patriotism and heroism, with which our earlier and our later annals abound, should be handed down to them in all the exactness of contemporaneous records. We owe it to ourselves not to be behindhand, at this day of our prosperity and abundance, in doing our share towards completing a history, which so many good and great men, under so many disadvantages and discouragements, have labored at so lovingly and so successfully, and which would almost seem to have been watched over from the beginning by a higher than human Power.

CENTRAL BUREAU OF CHARITY.

ADDRESS AT THE OPENING OF THE NEW ROOMS OF THE BOSTON PROVIDENT ASSOCIATION IN THE BUREAU OF CHARITY, 19 MAY, 1869.

WE hold our annual meeting to-night, my friends, for the first time in this new Temple of Charity; and our Association is the first, I believe, which has enjoyed the privilege of using the hall in which we are assembled, for the purposes of a public anniversary. It is eminently appropriate that it should be so. It was from the managers of this Association, nearly twelve years ago, that the original memorial to the City Council proceeded, which has led at last to the erection of this edifice. As one of those managers then and now, and as one who may be permitted to remember and to acknowledge the authorship of that memorial,[1] I cannot but feel the greatest satisfaction at the accomplishment of our design.

We owe our first acknowledgments to the City Council, who sanctioned our plans and made such liberal appropriations for their completion. We owe our acknowledgments, next, to the Overseers of the Poor, under whose auspices the building was undertaken and finished. We owe our acknowledgments, also, to many of our fellow-citizens, who liberally contributed to the private subscription required by the City Council before the work was entered upon; and especially to one, whose anonymous offer of $5,000 at the outset gave such encouragement to our enterprise.[2]

[1] Winthrop's Addresses and Speeches, Vol. II. p. 361.

[2] Note at the end of this Address, p. 33.

Nor can we forget on this occasion the deep interest taken in the plan by the late excellent Dr. James Jackson, who had suggested something of a kindred character many years before, and who expressed to me, not long before he was overcome with the infirmities of age, his earnest hope that he might live to see the work accomplished.

We have here a substantial and commodious structure; in a situation as central and as accessible as could reasonably have been desired for such a purpose; with an admirable arrangement of apartments, and with all the conveniences necessary to their occupation. Already the principal charitable agencies of our city are in full possession of these apartments, in perfect correspondence and sympathy with each other; pursuing the different departments of their common labor side by side, and gladly aiding each other by mutual contributions of information and advice. The Overseers of the Poor, whose cares and counsels I was permitted to share for three years under their new organization, and to whose zeal and fidelity I can bear personal and cordial testimony; the Society for Industrial Aid and the Prevention of Pauperism; and our own Provident Association, — the three organizations whose spheres of action are widest, and whose operations were designed to be co-extensive with the limits of our city, — are here in the principal stories. A branch of the Boston Dispensary is in the basement, with the office of the City Physician adjoining it. We should all have eagerly welcomed our friends of the Howard Benevolent and the Young Men's Benevolent Associations, had they found it consistent with their more limited objects to accept the apartments offered to them. But we can hardly regret that rooms have been left for more than one association of benevolent ladies, and for more than one agency of the funds for the relief of the Soldiers of the late war. The ladies, indeed, were foremost in taking possession of the rooms allotted to them; and their presence here gave the earliest pledge, and the earliest assurance, of success to the experiment of thus concentrating the leading charitable organizations of a whole city beneath a single roof.

In immediate connection with these agencies stands the new building for what is known by the name of the Temporary

Home, with every accommodation for supplying temporary food for the hungry, and temporary shelter for the houseless ; where any destitute and not absolutely unworthy persons may find a breakfast, or a dinner, or a night's lodging, until they can look about them for employment or permanent relief. And I know of nothing which is calculated to afford more real satisfaction to a benevolent heart, than to know that there is now in our city, easily accessible at all hours of the day or night, and of every day and night of the year, an ample and commodious edifice, where any one, young or old, of either sex, who is really in distress for food or shelter, and who is not ashamed or afraid to apply for them, may find admission and succor. I do not forget that the Rev. Dr. Wells, of St. Stephens, and Dr. Andrew Bigelow, and our venerable friend, Father Cleveland, and other good men, have done something, have done much, in this way heretofore, and that this very Institution has been in operation, as an experiment and on a small scale, for several years past. But I think we shall all lie down on our own pillows with more comfort, when some wintry storm is howling about our windows, now that we are assured that if any poor person, man or woman, boy or girl, by any accident or any rashness, has wandered away too far from home or friends, and is exposed to the rigor of the elements or to perils a thousand-fold worse, — a safe and comfortable refuge will always be open, and always within reach.

Let the Institution be thoroughly known, and let it be carefully and rigidly guarded against abuse, — as I am convinced it will be, under the direction of the Overseers of the Poor, and with the aid of an honest and vigilant Police, — and the results will be as abundant in satisfaction to the community generally, as they cannot fail to be in comfort and safety to the poor.

Indeed, my friends, all that is wanted, if any thing be wanted, to make this Charity Bureau, with the Temporary Home annexed to it, a complete success, is to have its character and its locality fully known to the rich and to the poor, and to have a generous support and confidence accorded to it by all. It might well be worth while to have placards at some of the corners of the streets, and on some of the lamp-posts, so as to be illuminated at night, — "Bureau of Charity and Temporary Home, corner of Chardon and Hawkins Streets," — so that every wayfarer might read it readily. And no householder of our city should be without cards of reference to the establishment, always at hand for delivery to those who call. Let it be everywhere understood that here, under a common roof, are to be found the agencies for relieving all who are really in want, — whether the want be of employment, of food, of fuel, of clothing, or of lodging; and let all applicants for charity be directed to this building.

We do not propose that any one should drive the beggar away from his own door, if he comes there, or pass him by in the street, if he appeals for succor. We would not have the old text disregarded, even though it be apocryphal, — "Never turn thy face from any poor man; and then the face of the Lord shall not be turned away from thee." But let us all agree that, instead of throwing away our small sums, or our large sums, on every one or any one who presents an appearance of poverty, to be squandered in drink or vicious indulgence, and to encourage pauperism, beggary, and imposture, we will simply and kindly say to each and all alike, as they approach us, "Go to the Bureau of Charity in Chardon Street, and, in one or other of the offices there, you will be relieved, if you require and deserve it." And then let the small sums or the large sums, which might have been given upon mere impulse or importunity, be sent to our treasuries here.

Why, my friends, if one-half of the money which has gone heedlessly into the pockets of street-beggars and vagrants, whether with papers or without papers, during the last twenty years, could have been collected into the coffers of the Associations now gathered under this roof, in proportion to their respective expenditures, I hazard little in saying that we should have required but few other contributions. We must put a final stop to street-begging. We must ferret out and expose all imposture. We must make a broad line between the honest and deserving poor and the profligate professional beggars, who strive to get the means of living in idleness and vice by imposing on the sympathies of the benevolent. This is the design of the noble

Building we inaugurate to-night; and may we not well call upon our whole community, — upon the rich and the poor, upon all who require help, and upon all who are able and willing to do something for the relief of their less favored neighbors, — to unite in assuring success to this first systematic attempt to organize, concentrate, and economize the charities of our city? With the blessing of God, and the cordial co-operation of our fellow-citizens, Boston may have, as the recent Annual Report of the Overseers of the Poor has predicted, "a more perfect system of public charity than any other large city in the world." Let us invoke that blessing, and that co-operation, and let us look confidently to the result.

In regard to our own particular Association, my friends, I need say little on this occasion. Organized in 1851, it has now been in active operation for eighteen years. The amount expended for charities in 1853 was but little over $6,000. The amount expended for charities in 1867–8 was nearly $16,000. The reports of the Executive Committee and of the Treasurer, which will presently be submitted to you, will inform you as to the operations and expenditures of the year just ended. Meantime, however, let me say distinctly that we need larger contributions than we have ever yet been able to procure, in order to accomplish all the good of which our organization is capable; and let me add that I think we have a right to demand them. We need, and ought to have, a greater number of annual subscribers, in small sums and in large sums. Not a few of our largest original contributors have passed away; and others must come forward to fill their places, if our labors are to continue successful.

I do not believe that Boston would willingly allow such an Association as this, with its organization so carefully arranged, and with all the experience it has acquired, to fail for want of means. Nor do I think it can fairly be expected of our managers to turn beggars themselves, and to solicit from house to house the amount which is necessary for the relief of the poor. Our treasury at this moment is, indeed, almost exhausted; but I cannot doubt that this very Building will be the means of awakening a fresh interest in our operations; that all who are not indifferent to the condition of the poor will take pains to inform themselves of what we have done and of what we are doing; that they will not only visit our office and satisfy themselves as to our system of registration, examination, and relief, but will voluntarily inquire, from time to time, into the condition of our resources, and not wait for solicitation before contributing liberally to our funds. If the amount allowed by our visitors to a poor woman or a poor family sometimes seems small, let it always be remembered that we give to the full extent of the means placed at our disposal. Indeed, it has frequently happened, in the course of the fifteen years during which I have presided over the Association, that our expenditures have greatly exceeded our receipts, and that we have been compelled to begin a new year with the discouraging work of providing for a large arrearage.

This ought not so to be; and I cannot conclude without an earnest appeal to our whole community, to see to it that the treasury of this Association is seasonably replenished from year to year.

NOTE.

[The following communication to the "Boston Daily Advertiser" of Nov. 16, 1865, which immediately called forth the anonymous offer of $5,000 for the proposed Building, belongs now to the history of the Charity Bureau, and may rightfully claim a place in this volume, as from the same pen with its other contents. Meantime, while this page is passing through the press, the death of GEORGE O. HOVEY, Esq., an eminent merchant of Boston, removes the seal of secrecy, and authorizes the public mention of his name, as having, in response to this appeal, made so large a contribution to the work.]

A NEW BUILDING WANTED IN BOSTON.

WE have many noble edifices in our city. We have schoolhouses admirably arranged and of appropriate architecture. We have churches, commodious, and some of them handsome. We have warehouses, not a few of which are unsurpassed in our own or in any other land. We have a Public Library capacious enough for all present needs, and with land enough in reserve to allow of enlargement to the full measure of future wants. We have jails and hospitals and houses of industry, strikingly adapted to the objects for which they were erected. A new Horticultural Hall has just been completed, worthy of the excellent Association to whose uses it is dedicated. And, more recently still, a noble City Hall has been thrown open, whose proportions are in keeping with the character of a liberal and munificent community. One more building remains to be erected; perhaps more than one, but certainly one. It need not be expensive. It ought not to be ostentatious. A plain, simple, substantial structure is all that is wanted. Its uses will give it a sufficient attraction. Its object will be its best ornament. It is that Bureau of Charity, or Central Relief Building for the Poor, which has been so earnestly recommended by the Overseers of the Poor under their new organization. It is a building where all the charities of the city may be concentrated; where the Overseers of the Poor and the Provident Association and the Society for the Prevention of Pauperism, and any and all other associations which may be willing to unite, may have convenient and contiguous offices, and may keep up a system of relief and registration which shall be common to all. It is a building to which every poor person may be directed, with the assurance that in some one of its offices the wants of the deserving and the destitute will be relieved. It is a building to be kept open at all hours of every day, so that there shall be no excuse for begging in the street or applications at the door. It is a building where imposture cannot escape detection, while honest poverty will never fail of assistance or employment. Such a structure will do more to systematize and economize the administration of our public and private charities than any thing which could be devised. And never was there a greater call for economizing and systematizing our charities than now. The restoration of peace and the return of those who have been engaged in the war cannot fail to bring to our doors an immense number of new applicants for aid. The high prices of provisions and fuel and clothing greatly enhance the difficulty of dealing with them. The prospect of a visitation of the cholera, too, demands the most careful provision for the poor, who may not only be its victims themselves, but may communicate it to their neighbors. Every thing calls for system and economy in the administration of our charities. Let there be a single Bureau, in a central but retired situation, where the public and private charities of the city may be dispensed, and where a complete registration of all deserving and all undeserving cases may be open to the inspection of such as are interested in the subject. This is substantially the scheme recommended by the managers of the Provident Association seven or eight years ago, and which the venerable Dr. Jackson had urged upon the City Government many years previously. It has recently been urged afresh by the new board of Overseers of the Poor, and the authorities of the city have given it their sanction. The City Council have passed an order pledging the municipal government to proceed with the work whenever the sum of thirty thousand dollars shall have been subscribed from private sources, and the Overseers of the Poor have presented an appeal to our fellow-citizens for this amount. One or two liberal subscriptions have already been tendered in response to this appeal, but the principal part of the sum is still to be contributed. We cannot doubt that, when the question is understood, the funds will be forthcoming. It is contemplated to unite with this building a new Temporary Home for the Poor, where meals and a night's lodging may be supplied in cases of immediate distress, and where foundlings may be provided for until they are permanently adopted or otherwise disposed of. The experiment of such a Home has been most successfully tried under the direction of the Overseers of the Poor. But the building in

Charles Street is insufficient, and the lease of it will soon expire, to be renewed at a greatly increased rent. We trust that a substantial edifice for these purposes will not be much longer wanting to the catalogue of our public buildings, but that a Bureau of Charity, or Central Relief Building, will be placed at the disposition of the Overseers of the Poor, without further delay than is necessary for its erection.

We subjoin a list of the Overseers of the Poor, any of whom would doubtless be glad to receive and acknowledge any contributions for this object: —

Robert C. Winthrop,	Francis E. Parker,
Thomas C. Amory,	William B. Spooner,
James L. Little,	Loring Lothrop,
John W. Warren,	Joseph Buckley,
Joel Richards,	George S. Hale,
Ebenezer Atkins,	Martin Griffin.

GEORGE PEABODY.

EULOGY PRONOUNCED AT THE FUNERAL OF GEORGE PEABODY, AT PEABODY, MASSACHUSETTS, 8 FEBRUARY, 1870.

While I have been unwilling, my friends, wholly to decline the request of your Committee of Arrangements, or to seem wanting to any service which might, perchance, have gratified him, whom, in common with you all, I have so honored and loved, — I have still felt deeply, and I cannot help feeling, at this moment, more deeply than ever before, that any words of mine, or of others, might well have been spared on this occasion.

The solemn tones of the organ, the plaintive notes of the funeral chant, the consoling lessons of the Sacred Scriptures, the fervent utterances of prayer and praise, — these would have seemed to me the only appropriate — I had almost said, the only endurable — interruptions of the silent sorrow which befits a scene like this.

Even were it possible for me to add any thing, worth adding, to the tributes on both sides of the ocean, which already have well-nigh exhausted the language of eulogy, — the formal phrases of a detailed memoir, or of a protracted and studied panegyric, would congeal upon my lips, and fall frozen upon the ears and hearts of all whom I address, in presence of the lifeless form of one, who has so long been the support, the ornament, the dear delight, of this village of his nativity.

We cannot, indeed, any of us, gather around these cherished remains, and prepare to commit them, tenderly and affectionately, to their mother earth, without a keen sense of personal affliction and bereavement. He was too devoted and loving a brother; he was too kind and thoughtful a kinsman; he was too genial and steadfast a friend, not to be missed and mourned by those around me, as few others have ever been missed and mourned here before. I am not insensible to my own full share of the private and public grief which pervades this community.

And yet, my friends, it is by no means sorrow alone, which may well be indulged by us all at such an hour as this. Other emotions, I hazard nothing in saying, far other emotions besides those of grief, are even now rising and swelling in all our hearts, — emotions of pride, emotions of joy, emotions of triumph.

Am I not right? How could it be otherwise? What a career has that been, of which the final scene is now, at length, before us! Who can contemplate its rise and progress, from the lowly cradle in this South Parish of old Danvers — henceforth to be known of all men by his name — to the temporary repose in Westminster Abbey, followed by that august procession across the Atlantic, whose wake upon the waters will glow and sparkle to the end of time, growing more and more luminous with the lapse of years, — who, I say, can contemplate that career, from its humble commencement to its magnificent completion, without an irrepressible thrill of admiration, and almost of rapture?

Who, certainly, can contemplate the immediate close of this extraordinary life without rejoicing, not only that it was so painless, so peaceful, so happy in itself; not only that it was so providentially postponed until he had been enabled, once more, to revisit his native land, to complete his great American benefactions, to hold personal intercourse with those friends at the South for whose welfare the largest and most cherished of those benefactions was designed, and to take solemn leave of those to whom he was bound by so many ties of affection or of blood, — but that it occurred at a time, and under circumstances, so peculiarly fortunate for attracting the largest attention, and for giving the widest impression and influence, to his great and inspiring example?

For this, precisely this, as I believe, would have been the most gratifying consideration to our lamented friend himself, could he have distinctly foreseen all that has happened, since he left you a few months since. Could it have been foretold him, as he embarked, with feeble strength and faltering steps, on board his favorite "Scotia" at New York, on the 29th of September last, not merely that he was leaving kinsfolk and friends and native land for the last time, but that hardly four weeks would have elapsed, after his arrival at Liverpool, before he should be the subject of funeral honors, by command of the Queen of England, and should lie down, for a time, beneath the consecrated arches of that far-famed Minster, among the kings and counsellors of the earth; — could it have been foretold him that his acts would be the theme of eloquent tributes from high prelates of the Church, and from the highest Minister of the Crown, and that Great Britain and the United States — not always, nor often, alas! in perfect accord — should vie with each other in furnishing their proudest national ships to escort his remains over the ocean, exhibiting such a funeral fleet as the world, in all its history, had never witnessed before; — could all this have been whispered in his ear, as it was catching those last farewells of relatives and friends, — he must, indeed, have been more than mortal, not to have experienced some unwonted emotions of personal gratification and pride.

But I do believe, from all I have ever seen or known of him, — and few others, at home or abroad, have of late enjoyed more of his confidence, — that far, far above any feelings of this sort, his great heart would have throbbed, as it never throbbed before, with gratitude to God and man, that the example which he had given to the world, — by employing the wealth which he had accumulated, during a long life of industry and integrity, in relieving the wants of his fellow-men wherever they were most apparent to him; in providing lodgings for the poor of London; in providing education for the children of our own desolated South; in building a Memorial Church for the parish in which his mother had worshipped; in founding or endowing institutes and libraries and academies of science in the town in which he was born, in the city in which he had longest resided, and in so many other places with which, for a longer or a shorter time, he had been connected, — that this grand and glorious example, of munificence and beneficence, would thus be so signally held up to the contemplation of mankind, in a way not only to commend it to their remembrance and regard, but to command for it their respect and imitation. This, I feel assured, he would have felt to be the accomplishment of the warmest wish of his heart; the consummation of the most cherished object of his life.

Our lamented friend was not, indeed, without ambition. He not only liked to do grand things, but he liked to do them in a grand way. We all remember those sumptuous and princely banquets, with which he sometimes diversified the habitual simplicity and frugality of his daily life. He was not without a decided taste for occasional display, — call it even ostentation, if you will. We certainly may not ascribe to him a pre-eminent measure of that sort of charity which shuns publicity, which shrinks from observation, and which, according to one of our Saviour's well-remembered injunctions, "doeth its alms in secret." He may, or he may not, have exercised as much of this kind of beneficence as any of those in similar condition around him. I fully believe that he did. We all understand, however, that

> "Of that best portion of a good man's life,
> His little, nameless, unremembered acts
> Of kindness and of love,"

there can be no record except on high, — or in the grateful hearts of those who have been aided and relieved. That record shall be revealed hereafter. The world can know little or nothing of it now.

But any one must perceive, at a glance, that the sort of charity which our lamented friend illustrated and exercised was wholly incompatible with concealment or reserve. The great Trusts which he established, the great Institutions which he founded, the capacious and costly Edifices which he erected, were things that could not be hid, which could not be done in a corner. They were, in their own intrinsic and essential nature, patent to the world's eye. He could not have performed these noble acts in his lifetime — as it was his peculiar choice to do, and as it will be his peculiar distinction and glory to have done — without suffering himself "to be seen of men;" without being known, and recognized, and celebrated as their author. He must have postponed them all, as others have done, for posthumous execution; he must have refrained from parting with his millions until death should have wrested them from a reluctant grasp, — had he shrunk from the notoriety and celebrity which inevitably attend upon such a career.

He did not fail to remember, however, — for he was no stranger to the Bible, — that there were at least two modes of doing good commended in Holy Writ. He did not forget that the same glorious Gospel, nay, that the same incomparable Sermon on the Mount, which said, "Let not thy left hand know what thy right hand doeth," said, also, "Let your light so shine before men, that they may see your good works, and glorify your Father which is in heaven." This, this might almost be regarded as the chosen motto of his later life, and might, not inappropriately, be inscribed as such on his tombstone.[1]

Certainly, my friends, his light has shone before men. Certainly, they have seen his good works. And who shall doubt that they have glorified his Father which is in heaven? Yes, glory to God, glory to God in the highest, has, I am persuaded, swollen up from the hearts of millions in both hemispheres, with a new fervor, as they have followed him in his grand circumnavigation of benevolence, and as they have witnessed, one after another, his multifold and magnificent endowments. And his own heart, I repeat, would have throbbed and thrilled, as it never thrilled or throbbed before, with gratitude to God and man, could he have foreseen that the matchless example of munificence, which it had been the cherished aim of his later years to exhibit, would be rendered, as it has now been rendered, so signal, so inspiring, so enduring, so immortal, by the homage which has been paid to his memory by the princes and poten-

[1] The text of Scripture, with other words from Mr. PEABODY's own lips, given on the next page, were soon afterwards inscribed, by direction of Dean Stanley, on the pavement of Westminster Abbey, where the remains had rested.

tates, as well as by the poor, of the Old World, and by the Government and the whole people of his own beloved Country.

I have spoken of the exhibition of this example, as having been the cherished aim of his later years; but I am not without authority for saying that it was among the fondest wishes of his whole mature life. I cannot forget, that, in one of those confidential consultations with which he honored me some years since, after unfolding his plans, and telling me substantially all that he designed to do, — for almost every thing he did was of his own original designing, — and when I was filled with admiration and amazement at the magnitude and sublimity of his purposes, he said to me, with that guileless simplicity which characterized so much of his social intercourse and conversation, "Why, Mr. Winthrop, this is no new idea to me. From the earliest years of my manhood, I have contemplated some such disposition of my property; and I have prayed my Heavenly Father, day by day, that I might be enabled, before I died, to show my gratitude for the blessings which He has bestowed upon me, by doing some great good to my fellow-men."

Well has the living Laureate of England sung, in one of his latest published poems, —

"More things are wrought by prayer
Than this world dreams of."

That prayer, certainly, has been heard and answered. That noble aspiration has been more than fulfilled. The judgment of the future will confirm the opinion of the hour; and History, instead of contenting herself with merely enrolling his name, in chronological or alphabetical order, as one among the many benefactors of mankind, will assign him — unless I greatly mistake her verdict — a place by himself, far above all competition or comparison, first without a second, as having done the greatest good for the greatest number of his fellow-men, — so far, at least, as pecuniary means could accomplish such a result, — of which there has thus far been any authentic record in merely human annals.

It would afford a most inadequate measure of his munificence, were I to sum up the dollars or the pounds he has distributed;

or the number of persons whom his perennial provisions, for dwellings or for schools, will have included, in years to come, on one side of the Atlantic or the other. Tried even by this narrow test, his beneficence has neither precedent nor parallel. But it is, as having attracted and compelled the attention of mankind to the beauty, the nobleness, the true glory of living and doing for others; it is, as having raised the standard of munificence to a degree which has almost made it a new thing in the world; it is, as having exhibited a wisdom and a discrimination in selecting the objects, and in arranging the machinery, of his bounty, which almost entitle him to the credit of an inventor; it is, as having, in the words of the brilliant Gladstone, "taught us how a man may be the master of his fortune, and not its slave;" it is, as having discarded all considerations of caste, creed, condition, nationality, in his world-wide philanthropy, regarding nothing human as alien to him; it is, as having deliberately stripped himself in his lifetime of the property he had so laboriously acquired; delighting as much in devising modes of bestowing his wealth, as he had ever done in contriving plans for its increase and accumulation; literally throwing out his bags like some adventurous aëronaut, who would mount higher and higher to the skies, and really exulting as he calculated, from time to time, how little of all his laborious earnings he had at last left for himself; it is, as having furnished this new and living and magnetic example, which can never be lost to history, never be lost to the interests of humanity, never fail to attract, inspire, and stimulate the lovers of their fellow-men, as long as human wants and human wealth shall coexist upon the earth, — it is in this way, that our lamented friend has attained a pre-eminence among the benefactors of his age and race, like that of Washington among patriots, or that of Shakspeare or Milton among poets.

I do not altogether forget those Mæcenases of old, whom philosophers and poets have so delighted to extol. I do not forget the passing tribute of the great Roman orator to one of the publicans of his own period, as having displayed an incredible benignity in amassing a vast fortune, not "as the prey of avarice, but as the instrument of doing good." I do not forget the founders of the Royal Exchange in London, and of the noble hospital in Edinburgh; the princely merchant of Queen Elizabeth's day, or the "Jingling Geordie" of England's first King James. I do not forget how strikingly Edmund Burke foreshadowed our lamented friend, when he said of one of his own contemporaries: "His fortune is among the largest, — a fortune which, wholly unencumbered as it is, without one single charge from luxury, vanity, or excess, sinks under the benevolence of its dispenser. This private benevolence, expanding itself into patriotism, renders his whole being the estate of the public, in which he has not reserved a *peculium* for himself, of profit, diversion, or relaxation." I do not forget the Baron de Monthyon, of France, whose noble benefactions are annually distributed by the Imperial Academy, and whose portrait has been combined with that of our own Franklin on a medal commemorative of their kindred beneficence. I recall, too, the refrain of an ode to a late munificent English Duke, on the erection of his statue at Belvoir Castle, which might well have been sung again, when Story's statue of our friend was so gracefully unveiled by the Prince of Wales, —

> "Oh, my brethren, what a glory
> To the world is one good man!"

Nor do I fail to remember the long roll of benefactors, dead and living, of whom our own age, and our own country, and our mother country, — New England and Old England, — may so justly boast. But no one imagines that either Caius Curius, or Sir Thomas Gresham, or George Heriot, or Sir George Savile, or any Duke of Rutland, or Monthyon, or Franklin, or Smithson, or any of the later and larger benefactors of our own time or land, can ever vie in historic celebrity, as a practical philanthropist, with him whom we bury here to-day.

Think me not unmindful, my friends, that, for the manifestation of a true spirit of benevolence, two mites will suffice as well as untold millions, — a cup of cold water, as well as a treasure-house of silver and gold. Think me not unmindful, either, of the grand and glorious results, for the welfare of mankind, which have been accomplished by purely moral or religious influences; by personal toil and trust, by the force of Christian character and example, by the exercise of some great gifts of intellect or eloquence, by simple self-devotion and self-sacrifice, without any employment whatever of pecuniary means; — by missionaries in the cause of Christ, by reformers of prisons and organizers of hospitals, by Sisters of Charity, by visitors of the poor, by champions of the oppressed; by such women as Elizabeth Fry and Florence Nightingale, and such men as John Howard and William Wilberforce; or, to go further back in history, by men like our own John Eliot, the early apostle to the Indians, or like that sainted Vincent de Paul, whose memory has been so justly honored in France for more than two centuries. But philanthropy of this sort, I need not say, stands on a somewhat different plane, and cannot fairly enter into this comparison.

It is enough to say of our lamented friend, as we have seen and known him of late, that in him were united — as rarely, if ever, before — the largest desire and the largest ability to do good; that his will was, at least, commensurate with his wealth; and that nothing but the limited extent of even the most considerable earthly estate prevented his enjoying the very antepast of celestial bliss: —

> "For when the power of imparting good
> Is equal to the will, the human soul
> Requires no other heaven."

And now, my friends, what wonder is it, that all that was mortal of such a man has come back to us, to-day, with such a convoy, and with such accompanying honors, as well might have befitted some mighty conqueror, or some princely hero? Was he not, indeed, a conqueror? Was he not, indeed, a hero? Oh! it is not on the battle-field, or on the blood-stained ocean, alone, that conquests are achieved and victories won. There are battles to be fought, there is a life-long warfare to be waged, by each one of us, in our own breasts, and against our own selfish natures. And what conflict is harder than that which awaits the accumulator of great wealth! Who can ever forget, or remember without a shudder, the emphatic testimony to the character of that conflict, which was borne by our blessed Saviour, — who knew what was in man better than any man knows it for himself, — when He said, "How hardly shall they that have riches enter into the kingdom of God;" and when he bade that rich young man sell all that he had and distribute to the poor, and then come and follow him!

It would be doing grievous injustice to our lamented friend, were we to deny or conceal that there were elements in his character which made his own warfare, in this respect, a stern one. He was no stranger to the love of accumulation. He was no stranger to the passion for gaining and saving and hoarding. There were in his nature the germs, and more than the germs, of economy and even of parsimony; and sometimes they would sprout, and spring up, in spite of himself. Nothing less strong than his own will, nothing less indomitable than his own courage, could have enabled him, by the grace of God, to strive successfully against that greedy, grudging, avaricious spirit, which so often besets the talent for acquisition. In a thousand little ways, you might perceive, to the last, how much within him he had contended against, how much within him he had overcome and vanquished. All the more glorious and signal was the victory! All the more deserved and appropriate are these trappings of triumph with which his remains have been restored to us! You rob him of his richest laurel, you refuse him his brightest crown, when you attempt to cover up or disguise any of those innate tendencies, any of those acquired habits, any of those besetting temptations, against which he struggled so bravely and so triumphantly. Recount, if you please, every penurious or mercenary act of his earlier or his later life, which friends have ever witnessed, — if they have ever witnessed any, — or which malice has ever whispered or hinted at, — and malice, we know, has not spared him in more ways than one, — and you have only added to his titles to be received and remembered as a hero and a conqueror.

As such a conqueror, then, you have received him from that majestic turreted Iron-clad which the gracious Monarch of our motherland has deputed as her own messenger to bear him back to his home. As such a conqueror, you have canopied his funeral car with the flag of his Country; — aye, with the flags of both his countries, between whom I pray God that his memory may ever be a pledge of mutual forbearance and affectionate regard! As such a conqueror, you mark the day and the hour of his burial by minute-guns, and fire a farewell shot, it may be, as the clods of his native soil are heaped upon his breast.

We do not forget, however, amidst all this martial pomp, how eminently he was a man of peace; or how earnestly he desired, or how much he had done, to inculcate a spirit of peace, national and international. I may not attempt to enter here, to-day, into any consideration of the influence of his specific endowments, at home or abroad, American or English; but I may say, in a single word, that I think history will be searched in vain for the record of any merely human acts, recent or remote, which have been more in harmony with that angelic chorus, which, just as the fleet, with this sad freight, had entered on its funeral voyage across the Atlantic, the whole Christian World was uniting to ring back again to the skies from which it first was heard, — any merely human acts, which while, as I have said, they have waked a fresh and more fervent echo of "Glory to God in the highest," have done more to promote "Peace on earth and good-will towards men."

Here, then, my friends, in this home of his infancy, where, seventy years ago, he attended the common village school, and served his first apprenticeship as a humble shop-boy; — here, where, seventeen years ago, his first large public donation was made, accompanied by that memorable sentiment, "Education: a debt due from present to future generations;" — here, where the monuments and memorials of his affection and his munificence surround us on every side, and where he had chosen to deposit that unique enamelled portrait of the Queen, that exquisite gold medal, the gift of his Country, that charming little autograph note from the Empress of France, that imperial photograph of the Pope, inscribed by his own hand, and whatever other tributes had been most precious to him in life; — here, where he has desired that his own remains should finally repose, near to the graves of his father and mother, enforcing that desire by those touching words, almost the last which he uttered, "Danvers,—Danvers,—don't forget,"—here let us thank God for his transcendent example; and here let us resolve, that it shall neither fail to be treasured up in our hearts, and sacredly transmitted to our children and our children's children, nor be wholly without an influence upon our own immediate lives. Let it never be said that the tomb and the trophies are remembered and cherished, but the example forgotten or neglected.

I may not longer detain you, my friends, from the sad ceremonies which remain to be performed by us; yet I cannot quite release you until I have alluded, in the simplest and briefest manner, to an incident of the last days, and almost the last hours, of this noble life, which has come to me from a source that cannot be questioned. While he was lying, seemingly unconscious, on his death-bed in London, at the house of his kind friend, Sir Curtis Lampson, and when all direct communication with him had been for a time suspended, it was mentioned aloud in his presence, in a manner, and with a purpose, to test his consciousness, that a highly valued acquaintance had called to see him; but he took no notice of the remark. Not long afterwards, it was stated, in a tone loud enough for him to hear, that the Queen herself had sent a special telegram of inquiry and sympathy; but even that failed to arouse him. Once more, at no long interval, it was remarked that a faithful minister of the Gospel, with whom he had once made a voyage to America, was at the door;[1] and his attention was instantly attracted. That "good man," as he called him with his latest breath, was received by him, and prayed with him, more than once. "It is a great mystery," he feebly observed, "but I shall know all soon;" while his repeated Amens gave audible and abundant evidence that those prayers were not lost upon his ear or upon his heart. The friendships of earth could no longer soothe him. The highest honors of the world,— the kind attentions of a Sovereign whom he knew how to respect, admire, and

[1] Rev. Thomas Nolan, D.D., then Rector of St. Anne's, Brunswick Square, London.

love, — could no longer satisfy him. The ambassador of Christ was the only visitor for that hour.

Thus, we may humbly hope, was at last explained and fulfilled for him that mysterious saying of one of the ancient prophets of Israel, which he had heard many years before, as the text of a sermon by one whom he knew and valued;[1] which had long lingered in his memory, and which, by some force of association or reflection, had again and again been recalled to his mind, and more than once, in my own hearing, been made the subject of his remark: "And it shall come to pass in that day, that the light shall not be clear nor dark; but it shall be one day which shall be known to the Lord, not day, nor night; but it shall come to pass, that at evening time it shall be light."

At evening time, it was, indeed, light for him. And who shall doubt, that, when another morning shall break upon his brow, it shall be a morning without clouds, — all light, and love, and joy, — for "the glory of God shall lighten it, and the Lamb shall be the light thereof"!

And so I bid farewell to thee, brave, honest, noble-hearted friend! The village of thy birth weeps, to-day, for one who never caused her pain before. The "Flower of Essex" is gathered at thy grave. Massachusetts mourns thee as a son who has given new lustre to her historic page; and Maine, not unmindful of her joint inheritance in the earlier glories of the parent State, has opened her noblest harbor, and draped her municipal halls with richest, saddest robes, to do honor to thy remains. New England, from mountain-top to farthest cape, is in sympathy with the scene, and feels the fitness that the hallowed memories of "Leyden" and "Plymouth"[2] — the refuge and the rock of her Pilgrim Fathers — should be associated with thy obsequies. This great and glorious Nation, in all its restored and vindicated union, partakes the pride of thy life and

[1] Rev. Dr. Lothrop, Pastor of Brattle-Square Church, Boston.

[2] The "Leyden" was the flag-boat of Admiral Farragut, who commanded the U. S Monitors assembled at Portland to receive the funeral fleet, and the "Plymouth" was the U. S. Ship which accompanied the English Iron-clad.

the sorrow of thy loss. In hundreds of schools of the desolated South, the children, even now, are chanting thy requiem and weaving chaplets around thy name. In hundreds of comfortable homes, provided by thy bounty, the poor of the grandest city of the world, even now, are breathing blessings on thy memory. The proudest shrine of Old England has unlocked its consecrated vaults for thy repose. The bravest ship of a navy "whose march is o'er the mountain waves, whose home is on the deep," has borne thee as a conqueror to thy chosen rest; and, as it passed from isle to isle, and from sea to sea, in a circumnavigation almost as wide as thy own charity, has given new significance to the memorable saying of the great funeral orator of antiquity: "Of illustrious men the whole earth is the sepulchre; and not only does the inscription upon columns in their own land point it out, but in that also which is not their own, there dwells with every one an unwritten memorial of the heart."

And now, around thee are assembled, not only surviving schoolmates and old companions of thy youth, and neighbors and friends of thy maturer years, but votaries of Science, ornaments of Literature, heads of Universities and Academies, foremost men of Commerce and the Arts, ministers of the Gospel, delegates from distant States and rulers of thy own State, — all eager to unite in paying such homage to a career of grand but simple Beneficence, as neither rank nor fortune nor learning nor genius could ever have commanded. Chiefs of the Republic, representatives and more than representatives of Royalty,[1] are not absent from thy bier. Nothing is wanting to give emphasis to thy example. Nothing is wanting to fill up the measure of thy fame.

But what earthly honor — what accumulation of earthly honors — shall compare for a moment with the supreme hope and trust which we all humbly and devoutly cherish at this hour, that when the struggles and the victories, the pangs

[1] H. R. H. PRINCE ARTHUR, and H. B. M.'s Minister Plenipotentiary, Sir EDWARD THORNTON, were among those from a distance who were present on the occasion.

and the pageants, of time shall all be ended, and the great awards of eternity shall be made up, thou mayest be found among those who are "more than conquerors, through Him who loved us"!

And so we bid thee farewell, brave, honest, noble-hearted Friend of Mankind!

PEABODY EDUCATION FUND.

ADDRESS AT THE ANNUAL MEETING OF THE TRUSTEES, AT WASHINGTON, 15 FEBRUARY, 1870.

GENTLEMEN OF THE BOARD OF TRUSTEES OF THE PEABODY EDUCATION FUND:

WHEN the day of our Annual Meeting was fixed at Baltimore in January of the last year, we were not without some hope that our munificent Founder might be personally present here with us at this meeting; and we were encouraged in this hope when so many of us met him last summer at the special meeting, which was held at his request, at Newport. But God has ordered it otherwise; and my first duty, in taking the chair, to-day, is to announce to the Board, officially, an event, of which you are all, as individuals, but too well informed.

Mr. Peabody died in London on the 4th of November last; and his remains, after reposing for a time in Westminster Abbey, have been entombed, agreeably to his own desire, in the cemetery of his native town in Massachusetts.

Our meeting, which was appointed for the 20th of January, has been deferred until now, as you know, in order to allow those of us who were able to do so, to be present at his funeral. Having been called on to deal publicly with his character and general career, on that occasion, I shall leave it to others of our number, to-day, to pay to his memory such tributes of personal gratitude, respect, and affection as they may think appropriate to this meeting.

I may be pardoned, however, if, before inviting such expressions from any of those around me, I pass rapidly in review the proceedings of this Board, so far as we have gone, during the life which has now closed; for the purpose of recalling to your thoughts all that our lamented friend has done for the great cause which he has committed to our charge, and of communicating to you, almost from his own lips, the hopes and wishes which he cherished to the last in regard to our future course.

The full term of three years has just expired since this Board was originally organized. The letter of Mr. Peabody announcing the endowment and creating the Trust bears date "Washington, Feb. 7, 1867."

That memorable and noble letter, after referring to "the educational needs of those portions of our beloved and common country which have suffered from the destructive ravages, and the not less disastrous consequences, of civil war," contained the following passage, which furnishes the key-note of his whole design, and which must ever give a controlling direction to all our proceedings: —

"I feel most deeply, therefore, that it is the duty and privilege of the more favored and wealthy portions of our nation to assist those who are less fortunate; and, with the wish to discharge, so far as I am able, my own responsibility in this matter, as well as to gratify my desire to aid those to whom I am bound by so many ties of attachment and regard, I give to you, gentlemen, most of whom have been my personal and especial friends, the sum of one million of dollars, to be by you and your successors held in trust, and the income thereof used and applied in your discretion for the promotion and encouragement of intellectual, moral, or industrial education among the young of the more destitute portions of the Southern and South-western States of our Union; my purpose being that the benefits intended shall be distributed among the entire population, without other distinction than their needs and the opportunities of usefulness to them."

On the day following the date of this letter, ten of our number, — whom, at Mr. Peabody's request, I had invited to meet him in this city, — assembled at Willard's Hotel; and there, in presence of Mr. Peabody himself, accepted the obligations prescribed by his letter, and inaugurated the work committed to us. Our proceedings on that occasion, however, were purely preliminary and formal.

On the 19th of March following, the Board held their first business meeting, in the city of New York, and devoted four days, in company with Mr. Peabody, to the consideration and adoption of the plans which have since been carried out. Those plans were ultimately embodied in the three following resolutions, which were unanimously adopted by the Board: —

"1. *Resolved*, That, for the present, the promotion of Primary or Common-School Education, by such means or agencies as now exist or may need to be created, be the leading object of the Board in the use of the fund placed at its disposal.

"2. *Resolved*, That, in aid of the above general design, and as promotive of the same, the Board will have in view the furtherance of Normal-School Education for the preparation of teachers, as well by the endowment of scholarships in existing Southern institutions, as by the establishing of Normal Schools, and the aiding of such Normal Schools as may now be in operation, in the Southern and South-western States; including such measures as may be feasible, and as experience shall dictate to be expedient, for the promotion of education in the application of Science to the industrial pursuits of human life.

"3. *Resolved*, That a General Agent, of the highest qualifications, be appointed by the Board, to whom shall be intrusted, under an Executive Committee, the whole charge of carrying out the designs of Mr. Peabody in his great gift, under such resolutions and instructions as the Board shall from time to time adopt."

Under this last resolution, our friend, Dr. Sears, then President of Brown University, Rhode Island, was unanimously appointed the General Agent of the Board; and his letter accepting the appointment bears date the 30th of the same month. With that acceptance, the practical work committed to us may fairly be considered as having commenced.

How extensive and how successful that work has been, can only be ascertained by a careful perusal of Dr. Sears's reports.

Three of those reports are already in print, in the published proceedings of the Board, — the first of them presented at the meeting of the Trustees in Richmond, Virginia, on the 21st of January, 1868; the second presented at a meeting of the Trustees in New York, on the 16th of July, 1868; and the third presented at the meeting of the Trustees held at Baltimore, on the 21st of January, 1869.

I may say for myself, gentlemen, — and I am sure I may say for you all, — that we had enjoyed no adequate opportunity for fully appreciating the labors which have thus far been performed, and the results which have thus far been accomplished, by our General Agent, until these three reports, in connection with all the proceedings of the Board, were recently printed together for the use of the Trustees. And I should be wanting to my own feelings, and to my responsibilities both to the living and the dead, — as the organ at once of Mr. Peabody and of this Board, — if I failed to give some formal and public expression to the gratification, and, I must say, the astonishment, I have experienced, on a deliberate examination of those reports. The Report which is to cover the whole of the past year is still to be presented, and we shall soon have the satisfaction of listening to it. But I could not but feel, as I recently finished a second or a third reading of those which are already in print, that, if they had included a period twice, or even thrice, that which they do include, they would have afforded ample evidence of extraordinary diligence, of ardent devotion, of consummate practical wisdom, and of signal success.

This, I know, was the feeling of our lamented founder and friend. You all remember, that, on the first day of July last, our Board held a special meeting at Newport, Rhode Island, at the immediate request of Mr. Peabody. He had informed me confidentially, before I took leave of him in London, in the previous summer, that he intended to visit his native country again, God willing, during the present year; and that he should then make a considerable addition to our Fund. He was then strong and hopeful, and had great confidence that he might live at least ten years longer. But his health soon afterwards began to decline; and, as the next spring opened, he was led to entertain serious apprehensions that he might not live even until another year. After a careful consultation with his medical advisers, he suddenly resolved to come over at once, and complete his designs.

On the very day of his arrival in Boston, he informed Dr. Sears, Governor Clifford, and myself, who had met him at the station, and accompanied him to the hospitable home of his friend, Mr. Dana, that the first desire of his heart, and that which he had crossed the Atlantic especially to gratify, was to meet our Board once more, and to increase our means for carrying on the great work in which we were engaged. He met us accordingly at Newport, and added a second million of dollars to our cash capital, besides adding largely to the deferred securities which he had included in the original donation; all of which, he had the fullest faith, would, at no very distant day, become productive.

In the letter addressed to us, communicating this second princely gift, he used the following language: —

"I have constantly watched with great interest and careful attention, the proceedings of your Board, and it is most gratifying to me now to be able to express my warmest thanks, for the interest and zeal you have manifested in maturing and carrying out the designs of my letter of trust, and to assure you of my cordial concurrence in all the steps you have taken.

"At the same time, I must not omit to congratulate you, and all who have at heart the best interests of this educational enterprise, upon your obtaining the highly valuable services of Dr. Sears, as your General Agent, — services valuable, not merely in the organization of schools, and of a system of public education; but in the good effect which his conciliatory and sympathizing course has had, wherever he has met or become associated with the communities of the South, in social or business relations.

"And I beg to take this opportunity of thanking, with all my heart, the people of the South themselves, for the cordial spirit with which they have received the Trust, and for the energetic efforts which they have made, in co-operation with yourselves and Dr. Sears, for carrying out the plans which have been proposed and matured for the diffusion of the blessings of education in their respective States."

This letter of Mr. Peabody concluded as follows: —

"I do this with the earnest hope and in the sincere trust, that, with God's blessing upon the gift and upon the deliberations and future action of yourselves and your General Agent, it may enlarge the sphere of usefulness already entered upon, and prove a permanent and lasting boon, not only to the Southern States, but to the whole of our dear country, which I have ever loved so well, but never so much as now in my declining years, and at this time (probably the last occasion I shall ever have to address you) as I look back over the changes and the progress of nearly three-quarters of a century. And I pray that Almighty God will grant to it a future as happy and noble in the intelligence and virtues of its citizens, as it will be glorious in unexampled power and prosperity."

This second letter has, indeed, proved to be, as he himself anticipated, his last letter to this Board. But more than one of us have enjoyed opportunities, at a still later day, of ascertaining his views and feelings in regard to our course. Our General Agent, as you know, spent many weeks in immediate attendance upon him, at the White Sulphur Springs, in Virginia, during the months of August and September last, and was in daily conversation and consultation with him as to our plans of proceeding. He will not fail to give us the results of those interviews. And I may add, that I was myself with him for several hours of the last three or four days before he finally embarked for Liverpool. And nothing, certainly, could have been more emphatic than his expressions, on these occasions, not only of interest in all we were doing, and of approbation of all we had done, but of earnest desire and confidence that we should adhere firmly to the policy and the plans which had thus far been adopted and pursued.

The Common-School education of the children of the South, "without other distinction than their needs and the opportunities of usefulness to them," and with such incidental encouragement and support of Normal Schools as might secure an adequate supply of competent teachers, — this was the simple but grand design of Mr. Peabody, in establishing the Trust committed to us; and he did not fail to enforce that design upon us in his latest conversations, as well as in his earlier public letters.

He understood perfectly, that this design was not to be carried out by buying any thing, or by building any thing. He saw clearly that the purchase of lots, and the erection of school-houses, for the children of so many States, would exhaust our funds long before our legitimate work could be commenced. He was fully persuaded, that the best way in which his munificent donation could be employed, under existing circumstances, for the greatest good of the greatest number, was by sending out our Agent, as a sort of Missionary of Education, with all the annual interest of our Fund at his command, to help those who were willing to help themselves; to eke out the insufficiencies of local appropriations; to provide in succession for the immediate temporary wants of particular communities; and, above all that mere money could do, to give them the advantage of the largest information, the highest practical wisdom, and the longest personal experience, in the work of education. He perceived that this was precisely what we had done, and he was more than satisfied.

He did not fail to understand that other kinds of education, besides that of Common Schools, were in need of encouragement in the Southern States. He would gladly have had aid afforded to their Industrial Schools, whenever it were practicable. He knew, too, that there were young men of the highest promise there, whom recent events had deprived of the means of entering on a collegiate course. He was not insensible to their claims. Nor was he without an earnest hope that his example might call forth some benefactor, for that precise exigency, from among those, in the Southern States themselves, whose fortunes have been comparatively unimpaired. But his own Fund he evidently considered as pledged, for the present, to "the young of the entire population," until some change of circumstances should render a change of policy expedient, or until, at the end of thirty years, it should be devoted to other purposes.

And now, gentlemen, having had the benefit of his advice, his approbation, his cheering assistance and encouragement, for these three initiatory years of our work, we are called to enter upon a new term without him. It is a loss which we shall all deeply feel; and which will be felt hardly less deeply, I think, by those who shall succeed us, when our places shall in turn become vacant. His wise counsels, his lofty and generous aims, his genial and magnetic presence, can never be forgotten by those of us who have personally enjoyed them; nor will they ever fail to inspire us with a determination to discharge the obligations we have assumed at his hands, in the spirit in which they were imposed upon us.

Let us hope that his memory, and his great commission, may be held equally sacred by all who shall come after us; and that the faithful administration of this noble Trust, as long as it shall last, may fulfil all those wishes, which, living and dying, he so ardently cherished, for the prosperity and welfare of the Southern States, and for the harmony and happiness of our whole beloved Country.

A GLANCE AT THE CHANGES OF TWENTY-FIVE YEARS.

SPEECH AT THE SEMI-CENTENNIAL ANNIVERSARY OF THE BOSTON MERCANTILE LIBRARY ASSOCIATION, IN THE MUSIC HALL, BOSTON, 11 MARCH, 1870.

I AM most glad to remember, Mr. President, at this late hour of the evening, in view of all that has been already said and sung, and in view of what remains to be sung too, — for I had rather you would lose every thing that is in these poor notes of mine than that we should lose a single note of that charming music of which we have already enjoyed so much, — I repeat, sir, that I rejoice to remember, in view of all this, that I have rendered myself responsible this evening only for a few, a very few, informal words. Absent from home, as I have been for many weeks past, and uncertain almost to the last hour whether I could be here at all, it would have been quite out of my power to fulfil any larger expectations, even had I ever authorized them.

But, indeed, my friends, you have not come together to-night to listen to any long or labored addresses from any one. The occasion is rather one for congratulation and emotion, than for instruction or argument. The interesting sketch of the rise and progress of this Association, which we have all heard with so much pleasure from the lips of its past and present Presidents; the encouraging and excellent words of His Excellency the Governor, the Mayor, and the President of the Board of Trade; the charming solos of our Boston contralto,[1] and the noble

[1] Miss Adelaide Phillips.

choruses of this ancient and honorable Musical Association,[1] — always ready to lend its aid upon every worthy occasion of commemoration, whether of the living or the dead, and whose existence dates back at least five years behind and beyond the date of the original organization of this Association, even to the close of that war with England, in 1815, which, I pray God, — in spite of all the animosities and irritations and indignation which truculent "Alabamas" or remorseless "Bombays" may have occasioned, — may still and always stand recorded in history as our *last* war with the old Mother Country; — these words from so many distinguished persons, these choruses from so many noble voices, I am sure have been quite enough to gratify and satisfy you all, and I might well ask to be excused myself, even from the few off-hand words which I have somewhat rashly promised and somewhat hastily prepared.

And yet, Mr. President, I would not willingly have been wholly absent or wholly silent upon this occasion. The Governor has come to speak for our beloved Commonwealth. The Mayor has come to represent the good old city of Boston. My eloquent friend, Mr. Rice, is here to respond for that Board of Trade over which he so worthily presides. For myself, ladies and gentlemen, I am here only as the representative of the Past. But I feel that it is fit that the Past should not be left wholly unrepresented on such an occasion.

I have not forgotten that anniversary of yours twenty-five years ago, to which allusion has been repeatedly made this evening. The associations and memories of that evening have clustered thickly, and I must say sadly, about me, as I have prepared myself to address you to-night. Though I had then already represented my native city for at least five years in the Congress of the United States, I was still comparatively a young man; and the honor of being selected as your orator for that special celebration was not likely to be lost upon me. It was not lost upon me; and I am glad of the renewed opportunity to express my gratitude for that and for many other compliments which have been paid me by your Association. But I look

[1] The Handel and Haydn Society.

around me in vain, my friends, this evening, for the men who were then the pride and the strength of our community, and not a few of whom surrounded me on that occasion as your friends and as my own friends. The Lawrences, — the princely Abbott, and the kind, generous, amiable Amos, of whom you have already given so pleasant an anecdote to-night; the Appletons, — "Nathan, the Wise," whose opinion at this hour upon any question of finance or currency, I hazard nothing in saying, would be sought for more eagerly than that of any man living, and would have been placed almost in comparison with that of any of our own earliest and greatest statesmen, such as Alexander Hamilton or Albert Gallatin; Samuel Appleton, the benevolent, and the excellent William; the noble-hearted old Colonel — I hardly need add the name of Perkins to any one who knew him, — who was one of your earliest and largest benefactors; William Sturgis, Josiah Bradlee, and Robert G. Shaw; Theodore Lyman, who presided at your original organization just fifty years ago to-night; Samuel A. Eliot and Martin Brimmer; the venerated Quincy; Choate, Everett, Webster; all of whom took so warm an interest in the welfare of your Association, and did so much to animate and sustain it by liberal deeds or eloquent words: — I look for them — I had almost said I look for their like — in vain. I see, it may be, some of the sons who have risen to honor; but of the fathers, not one is left, save in those proud and precious memories of the good and great, which can never die. The very Hall in which that celebration was held has long ago been levelled to the ground, and its name is hardly remembered by the present generation.[1]

Yet of what account, after all, my friends, are changes like these, in the men or in the places of our city, compared with those marvellous changes in the condition of the world, and more particularly of our part of the world, which have signalized that second quarter of a century which your Association has now completed! Who can ever review the grand procession of events abroad and at home, during that most eventful period, without an almost bewildering amazement?

I remember well, that, in that twenty-fifth Anniversary Ad-

[1] The Odeon.

dress,[1] I endeavored to enforce and illustrate the idea that Commerce was the great antagonist of war, and war, as my friend Mr. Rice has just said, the ruthless destroyer of Commerce; and I ventured to express a hope, that, through the prevailing influence of the mercantile spirit, — if of nothing higher or nobler, — the martial spirit of the world might at last be exorcised or held in check. But when has the world ever seen such wars as those which have raged successively and almost continuously since that time on both sides of the ocean? Mexican wars, — I know not how many of them, — the Crimean war, the Italian war, the Prussian war, the Abyssinian war, and our own stupendous and incomparable Civil War, — these are but a part of the catalogue! Meantime, however, my friends, what glorious triumphs have been witnessed, in spite of those wars, or, in some cases, as their immediate attendants or results, — triumphs of science and triumphs of art as well as triumphs of arms, and, above all for us, and for the whole world if it did but know it, the great and final triumph of the American Union! And then, my friends, add to such a consideration the successful application of ether to relieve pain; the Ocean Telegraph; the apparition of Monitors upon the sea; the Pacific Railroad; the Suez Canal; the Chinese Mission, so sadly interrupted by the death of our lamented Burlingame; the grand benefactions and grander example of your late honorary member, George Peabody; and greater, a thousand-fold greater, than all, the final disappearance of African Slavery from our land, — a consummation which I do not forget that the poet of that twenty-fifth Anniversary — my good friend Mr. Waterston, who is with us here to-night — ventured to pray for in rhyme, but which the wildest rhapsodist would hardly have dared at that day to predict in sober prose as within "the prospect of belief" for a hundred years still to come. What quarter of a century has there been in the past, in all the past, since the coming of our Lord, — what quarter of a century can be anticipated in the future, in all the future, till our Lord shall come again, — so filled and crowded with wonderful events?

Let me not call them, my friends, merely wonderful events,

[1] Winthrop's Addresses and Speeches, Vol. I. pp. 39–69.

but, as our Puritan Fathers would have called them, let me say Wonderful Providences; and let me no longer delay the singing of the chorus which is to close these exercises,[1] — the only chorus which is adequate to express the emotions which belong to the contemplation of the events which have crowded the quarter of a century since your last great celebration by any reverential, I had as well said by any reflecting, mind.

[1] Handel's "Hallelujah Chorus."

VERPLANCK AND FROTHINGHAM.

REMARKS AT A MEETING OF THE MASSACHUSETTS HISTORICAL SOCIETY, APRIL 14, 1870.

YOU are aware, gentlemen, that this is our Annual Meeting; but, agreeably to usage, we proceed with our regular monthly business before entering on the more formal routine of Annual Reports and Elections. Before we pass, however, to any thing of a merely business character, it is fit that I should remind you that, since we met last, two names on our rolls have ceased to be the names of living members. One of them is the name of an Honorary Member, who was the contemporary and associate of Irving and Paulding and Sands and Cooper and Bryant of New York. The other is the name of a Resident Member, who was the associate and friend of our own Prescott and Everett and Sparks and Ticknor, and of others whom I see around me.

The name of the Honorable GULIAN C. VERPLANCK, LL.D., has stood, for several years past, first in the order of seniority on our Honorary Roll. He was elected on the 27th of January, 1820, — more than fifty years ago. He died in the city of New York, his native place, on the 18th of March last, in the eighty-fourth year of his age.

Mr. Verplanck was a graduate of Columbia College, and a lawyer by profession. His life was, however, mainly devoted to politics, literature, and works of public usefulness. He was a representative in the Legislature of New York as early as 1814; and, after several years' service in that capacity, he was elected a representative in Congress in 1825, and was a conspicuous and valuable member of the National Councils for eight years. He subsequently served for some years in the Senate of his native State.

His labors, however, during this period, were by no means confined to political subjects. In 1818, he delivered a lecture before the New York Historical Society, on "The Early European Friends of America," which attracted much attention and passed through several editions. In 1821, he was chosen to a Professorship on "The Evidences of Christianity," in the General Episcopal Seminary established at New York, and not long afterwards published a collection of essays on "The Nature and Uses of the various Evidences of Revealed Religion." In 1825, he published a work, well known to the Bar, on the "Doctrine of Contracts." In 1827, he was associated with the late Robert C. Sands and with William C. Bryant in publishing one of the earliest of our American Illustrated "Annuals," called the "Talisman," of which three volumes were issued in successive years, and afterwards all republished, with the names of the authors, in 1833. During the same year, Mr. Verplanck published a volume of his collected "Discourses and Addresses on Subjects of American History, Arts, and Literature." Many other Discourses and Addresses were delivered by him in subsequent years; and between the years 1844 and 1847 he published an edition of Shakspeare, in three volumes, with illustrations and annotations, which gave ample evidence of his taste and accomplishments as an editor and interpreter of the immortal dramatist.

About this same year, 1847, the Board of Emigration Commissioners was established in New York, for the protection of foreigners when first arriving on our shores, and Mr. Verplanck was immediately elected its President, — an office which he continued to hold and discharge with great zeal and energy until his death. He was connected, too, with many other boards and bodies of a charitable or religious character, and rendered valuable service to them all.

Nor did his literary labors entirely cease but with his life. Besides the annual reports which he prepared for fifteen years on the subject of emigration, and which were published in a volume in 1861, his "Twelfth Night at the Century Club," in 1858, and his Address on the opening of the New Tammany Hall on the 4th of July, 1868, — when he was eighty-two years old, — afford ample evidence that neither mind nor pen nor tongue had lost their cunning. He was active and vigorous and genial to the last. He seemed to have something of the strength and hardiness of one of those noble trees which adorn the park of the old manor house on the Hudson in which he passed his summers.[1] His leaf did not wither. His ruddy countenance and flowing silver locks have more than once recalled to me our own Leverett Saltonstall, the elder, as we knew him here a quarter of a century ago, and he could hardly have recalled a more cherished friend. Like him, he was a man whose warmth of heart and kindness of manner and earnestness of purpose endeared him to all who knew him, and he will be remembered by them all as a man whom it was a privilege to know.

The Reverend NATHANIEL LANGDON FROTHINGHAM, D.D., died in this city on the 4th inst., in the seventy-seventh year of his age. Among the large congregation which attended his funeral, on the 6th inst., at the First Church, of which he was so long the pastor, were the officers and many of the members of this Society; and an admirable eulogy was delivered on that occasion by one whom we are glad to count among our immediate associates.[2]

Dr. Frothingham was elected a member of our Society in 1843; and, until his infirmities confined him to his house, his presence at our meetings was as punctual as it was welcome. He took a warm interest, and sometimes a prominent part, in our proceedings. His impressive tribute to our lamented Prescott, and his charming verses when "The Crossed Swords" were transferred from Prescott's library to our own, cannot be forgotten by any one who had the good fortune to hear them. Nor shall we soon forget, I am sure, his last appearance among

[1] Winthrop's Addresses and Speeches, Vol. II. p. 347.

[2] Rev. F. H. Hedge, D.D.

us, but a few years since, when, his sight having already failed him, he was led into these rooms by a devoted son, and paid an off-hand but touching tribute to the eloquence of the late Rev. Dr. Hawks, of New York, whose death had been on that morning announced.

Of Dr. Frothingham, as a preacher, it hardly becomes me to speak. I may be permitted to say, however, that of the only two sermons which I can remember as ever having heard from his lips, the texts of both, and the treatment of those texts, are as distinct in my memory, after a lapse of more than thirty, it may be more than forty, years, as if I had listened to them yesterday.

And this leads me naturally to the very few remarks upon his character and career which I shall venture to make in presence of so many of those who have been associated with him as classmates at school or at college, as pastors of sister churches, or, it may be, as parishioners of his own church, or as life-long friends and associates in theological or literary pursuits. To them it peculiarly belongs to bear testimony to his virtues and his accomplishments.

Whether as preacher, as scholar, or as poet, — for in all these relations he has enjoyed a high distinction in our community, — there was a force and felicity in his style, a picturesqueness of conceit and imagery, a fervor and glow of thought and diction, which made all his utterances impressive and memorable. He spoke and wrote from the fulness of a warm heart and an earnest, noble spirit. Deeply imbued with a scholarship and a learning which had rendered him familiar with the best productions both of ancient and modern literature, his acquisitions only served to give richness and variety to the illustration of topics of which his own heart and mind were full. He occupied himself with no elaborate disquisitions or abstruse philosophies, but poured forth from time to time, from a rich storehouse of memory or imagination, sometimes in prose and oftener of late in verse, such words and thoughts as befitted the hour or the occasion. His heart seemed always intent upon the events which he witnessed, and always in sympathy with the joys or sorrows of those around him.

He had the strongest appreciation for the beautiful and the noble, in every form in which they are manifested to the sense or the soul, — in nature, in art, in music, in literature, in action, in character. It has happened to me to be with him in Rome, among the glorious remains of classic art; and in Switzerland, also, amid some of those wonderful scenes of pure, original, majestic nature. Frequently, too, some years ago, I have chanced to walk with him, at his favorite hour, and along his favorite path, across our own beautiful Common, towards the setting of an autumn sun. Everywhere he was filled with rapture for whatever was grandest or loveliest in the works of God or of man, and few men have known better how to give expression to such emotions. Not a few of his verses, whether original or translated, have lifted the hearts of hearers and readers, as they have lifted his own heart, in hours of trial or of devotion; and some of them cannot fail to have a permanent place in the occasional poetry, religious or secular, of our land.

I will not attempt to speak of the resignation and fortitude with which he bore the heavy load of personal deprivation and suffering, under which he has been withdrawn from us for some years past. It would seem, to any one who has been privileged to visit him during these days of darkness, as if he must have caught the full spirit of a stanza of one of those inspiring German hymns, which he has translated with so much feeling and beauty:

"Be brave, my heart! and weary
  Grow never in the strife:
The peace of God will cheer ye
  With trust and strength and life.
Be vigorous, not complaining,
  And every effort bend:
This very day, at waning,
  May see the conflict end."

Happily for him, the conflict has at last ended; and it only remains for us to do justice to his memory.

JOHN PENDLETON KENNEDY.

TRIBUTE TO THE MEMORY OF MR. KENNEDY, AT A MEETING OF THE MASSACHUSETTS HISTORICAL SOCIETY, SEPTEMBER 8, 1870.

It is with no little personal sorrow that I announce the death of my cherished friend, the Honorable John Pendleton Kennedy, who was elected a Corresponding Member of this Society in 1858. I am sure the Society will indulge me, this morning, in dwelling at some length on the character and career of one who had far higher claims than any friendship or affection of mine could give him to the regard and respect of his contemporaries.

Mr. Kennedy was born on the 25th of October, 1795, in the city of Baltimore; where his father, of Irish origin, who died early, was then a prosperous merchant. His mother, who lived to see her son — and he was her eldest — at the height of his reputation as an author and statesman, was a daughter of Philip Pendleton, of Berkeley County, Virginia, of a family distinguished by the virtues and accomplishments of more than one of its members. Graduated at Baltimore College in 1812, he soon selected the law as his profession. But our war with England was just then at its commencement; and his pursuits were interrupted by the excitements of the period, and by the perils to which his native city was peculiarly exposed. With his friend, the late Mr. George Peabody, he volunteered and served as a private at the battles of Bladensburg and North Point; and with him, not many years ago, received from the United States the bounty land awarded to that service.

Admitted to the Baltimore Bar in 1816, he practised with success for several years, at a period when that Bar was adorned by such men as William Pinckney and William Wirt and the late Chief-Justice Taney; with more than one of whom he was sometimes associated as junior counsel in important causes, and with all of whom he was on terms of personal friendship. His taste for literary life, however, soon came in conflict with that for legal studies; and as early as 1818 he had become joint editor, with his accomplished friend, the late Peter Hoffman Cruse, of a little fortnightly serial, in prose and verse, under the title of "The Red Book." This little work was continued for two or three years, and its contents subsequently collected into two volumes.

And now the attractions of political service and public employment threatened to draw him away both from literature and from law. He was induced to take an active part in the Presidential campaign of 1820; and in the same year was elected a member of the House of Delegates of Maryland. In that body he rendered conspicuous service for several years; a part of the time as Speaker, and always as an intelligent and earnest advocate of measures for improving the financial condition and restoring the credit of the State.

In 1823, he accepted an appointment from President Monroe, as Secretary of our Legation to Chili; and I have heard him describe most humorously his first interview with the late John Quincy Adams, — then Secretary of State, of whom in later years he enjoyed the intimate acquaintance and friendship, — when he called on Mr. Adams at the State Department for his instructions, preparatory to embarking for his post. "Instructions!" said Mr. Adams. "The only instructions I have to give you at present are these;" and reaching up, with the aid of a chair, to a high shelf, or pigeon-hole, in his book-case, he handed him a carefully prepared description and drawing of the uniform which our Legations abroad were then required to wear, — not yet discarded as inconsistent with Republican principles, — and told him to provide himself accordingly. Mr. Kennedy's youthful aspirations for diplomacy were not stimulated, or altogether satisfied, by this view of what was expected of him; and, before it was too late, he obtained leave to resign the appointment.

His interest in public affairs, however, continued unabated; and, in the intervals of professional labor, he prepared and published a number of political essays, which attracted a wide and marked attention. Having warmly espoused the views of Henry Clay — of whom not long afterwards he became one of the most trusted and valued friends — on the subject of American Industry, he wrote and printed, in 1830, an elaborate and masterly reply to Mr. Cambreleng's memorable Report on Commerce and Navigation, which had a general circulation throughout the country; and in the following year he rendered eminent service, by tongue and pen, at a National Convention of the friends of Manufacturing Industry, held in the city of New York.

But it soon appeared that his more purely literary labors had by no means been abandoned or suspended, and that he was destined to make no common mark — for that period, certainly — in a line of literature in which our own honored Founder, Dr. Jeremy Belknap, had led the way in 1792, by his American tale, "The Foresters;" and in which Charles Brockden Brown and Washington Irving and James Fenimore Cooper had since been so conspicuous.

In 1832, Mr. Kennedy published his first novel, under the name of "Swallow Barn, or a Sojourn in the Old Dominion;" a work which produced a decided impression, and which received high commendations from the pen of Edward Everett, in the "North American Review," the only vehicle at that time of well-considered literary criticism in our part of the country. Its sketches of Virginia life and manners, including a very notable chapter on Slavery, entitled "The Quarter," furnish the best picture we have even now of that section of the Union at the period to which they relate, and possess not a little of historical interest and permanent value. This, too, may be said, even more emphatically, of his second novel, "Horse-Shoe Robinson, a Tale of the Tory Ascendency," published in 1835; of which the scene was laid in the Carolinas, during our Revolutionary struggle, and of which the hero was drawn from the life, — the incidents of his remarkable career having been derived from his own lips by Mr. Kennedy himself, while he was residing at the South for the benefit of his health, in 1819.

A third novel, "Rob of the Bowl; a Legend of St. Inigoes," in which there is much historical matter connected with the religious commotions in Maryland, in the time of the second Lord Baltimore, was published by him in 1838; and in 1840 he produced, in a fourth volume, under the title of "The Annals of Quodlibet," a humorous and satirical account of the Presidential campaign in which he was at that moment a prominent actor, with an almost dramatic presentment, under fictitious names, of scenes which had actually occurred within the range of his own observation and experience.

Mr. Kennedy had now, however, become a member of Congress, having been chosen as one of the Representatives of the Baltimore District in 1838, and having been re-elected in 1841 and 1843. His services at Washington were of the highest value and importance; and particularly those which he rendered as Chairman of the Committee on Commerce in the Twenty-seventh Congress. Having been associated with him as his second on that Committee, as well as in the intimacies of a common table and of apartments under a common roof, I can bear personal testimony to the diligence and ability which he brought to the public business. His Reports on subjects connected with our Commercial System, and particularly on our proposed Reciprocity Treaties, were elaborate and exhaustive; and his speeches were forcible and eloquent. I cannot forget that we were together, too, on that Committee, when, not without hesitation and distrust, the first appropriation was reported to enable Mr. Morse to try the experiment, between Washington and Baltimore, of that Magnetic Telegraph which now covers our continent, and encircles the earth. Though the Report was written and presented by another hand, it owed much of its success, both in Committee and in the House, to the earnest support of Mr. Kennedy.

In 1844, he published a very striking little volume, called "A Defence of the Whigs," which became almost a hand-book of politicians, and which contains an admirable vindication of the party with which he was always connected as long as it existed. But that party had but a precarious and fitful supremacy in Baltimore; and at the next election, in 1845, he failed of a majority, and was never again returned to Congress. The following year, however, found him again in the Chair of the House of Delegates at Annapolis, having been elected once more to the Legislature of Maryland, after an interval of five and twenty years, with a view to an important juncture in the affairs of his native State.

This service rendered, Mr. Kennedy once more quietly resumed his literary labors, and, as the result of them, published, in 1849, an excellent biography, in two octavo volumes, of the eminent lawyer and statesman, William Wirt, — one of the purest and best of the public men of his day, upon whom Mr. Kennedy had delivered a Eulogy, immediately after his death, in 1834. This work — in which the author sedulously avoided all personal display, and allowed Mr. Wirt to exhibit himself to the best advantage in his own brilliant public addresses and lively familiar correspondence — was recognized everywhere as a valuable contribution to American Biography, and to the history of the times; and no better book of its kind could have been placed in the hands of the young men of the United States, to whom it was dedicated.

Meantime and previously, Mr. Kennedy had delivered not a few occasional Discourses, mostly of an historical character: one, in 1835, before the American Institute of New York; another, in the same year, before the Faculty of Arts and Sciences of the University of Maryland, in which he had been appointed Professor of History, and of which he was the Provost for many years before his death; and a third, in 1845, before the Maryland Historical Society, of which he was Vice-President, on the Life and Character of George Calvert, the first Lord Baltimore, which involved him in a sharp controversy with several of the Roman Catholics of Maryland, to whom he made an elaborate rejoinder, exhibiting great ability and research. His Address, too, before the Maryland Institute, in 1851, published with engraved illustrations of the old town of Baltimore, as it was just a hundred years before, was replete with valuable local descriptions and details.

In 1852, on the resignation of Governor Graham of North Carolina, who had been appointed Secretary of the Navy by President Fillmore, on his succession to the Presidency after the lamented death of General Taylor, Mr. Kennedy was called to preside over the Navy Department of the United States; and continued a member of the Cabinet, of which his friends Mr. Webster and Mr. Everett were successively the chiefs, until the change of Administration, in March, 1853. This was the period of some of our most interesting Naval Scientific Expeditions: that of Commodore Perry to Japan; and that of Dr. Kane to the Arctic Ocean, in search of Sir John Franklin, for which Mr. Kennedy prepared the instructions, and gave to it the most effective encouragement. His name was accordingly given by Dr. Kane to one of the channels which he discovered, and was inscribed on his map of the Arctic Regions.

The visit of Mr. George Peabody to his native land in 1856, and his noble endowment of the Peabody Institute in Baltimore, where, as a young banker, he had for some years resided, afforded Mr. Kennedy a new subject of interest, and opened to him a new field of useful labor. He was at once selected by Mr. Peabody, as the Chairman of the Board of Trustees for his great gift to the Baltimore Institute; and I have the best authority for knowing how earnestly he entered upon and pursued the work of organization committed to him, and how highly and gratefully his services were appreciated by Mr. Peabody to the last.

The darkest days of our country were now rapidly approaching. Mr. Kennedy was never, I believe, an owner of slaves, nor even a supporter or apologist for slavery. But, on the other hand, he had never co-operated or sympathized with the extreme Abolitionists of the North, and had always united in measures for securing to his own, and the other Southern States, the rights in regard to this institution which were expressed or implied in the Constitution of the United States, as he understood its provisions. No Northern man, however, could have been more averse than he was to the extension of slavery into new territories. He was, moreover, a devoted lover of the Union, and held in abhorrence all ideas either of peaceable or forcible secession or nullification. Living in a Border State, where the personal and party feuds which preceded and followed the outbreak of the Rebellion were so violent and bitter, and upon which at one time it seemed as if the whole brunt of the battle might fall, his first hopes undoubtedly were, as were those of many of his friends farther North, that some arrangement or adjustment might be devised, with a view to prevent the fratricidal strife, and avert the full horrors of Civil War. He was in complete accord with the great Boston Memorial to that effect, which, under the lead of Mr. Everett, and in company with others of all parties, I had a share in the privilege of bearing to Congress in January, 1861. In this spirit, he published, a few weeks before the first fatal blow had been struck, a pamphlet entitled "The Border States; their Power and Duty," which presented the great questions before the country with boldness and signal ability, and appealed to the Border States to interpose, by some separate concerted action, for the settlement of all issues in dispute, and for the ultimate preservation of the Union. Reviewed in the light of subsequent developments and of final results, this appeal would probably be regarded with less approbation than it was at the time of its publication. But even then, as it soon proved, the time for discussion had passed, and little remained but to resist force by force. In that contest, Mr. Kennedy's influence and efforts were strongly and unqualifiedly on the side of the Government and the Union, and no coldness of friends, or dangers from enemies, could deter or daunt him.

During the progress of the War, he communicated a series of Letters to the "National Intelligencer," under the assumed name of "Paul Ambrose," in which he ably discussed "the principles and incidents of the Rebellion as these rose to view in the rapid transit of events;" which were collected and published in a volume, with his own name, in 1865. This was the last work which he gave to the public; and he soon afterwards embarked for Europe, in the hope of reinvigorating his somewhat shattered health.

It was not his first visit abroad. He had crossed the Atlantic twice before, and was no stranger to some of the best of English and European society. In those visits, he had renewed the intimacy with Thackeray and Dickens which he had enjoyed while they were in America, and had formed many other friendships with the literary men of France and England. During his last tour, he was selected by Mr. Seward as one of the United States Commissioners, at the grand Exposition of the Industry of all Nations in Paris, and in that capacity rendered valuable services; especially as one of the small select Commission, under the Presidency of Prince Napoleon, to which the subject of a uniform Decimal Currency was referred.

Mr. Kennedy had more than once contemplated giving to the press his "Notes of Travel," of which he has left many manuscript volumes, carefully composed and revised, which may still, I trust, furnish the material of a posthumous publication.

On his last return home, in October, 1868, he presided at a great Republican Mass Meeting in Baltimore; and made an earnest and eloquent appeal to the South to acquiesce cordially in the results of the War, and to unite "in that new pathway which Providence has ordained to be the line of our future march to the highest destiny of nations." This was his last public word.

In looking back on the life which has been thus rapidly sketched, and comparing his capacities for usefulness with his actual career, one cannot but feel how much has been lost to the best service of the country, in his case as in too many others, by the accidents of politics, and the caprices of parties. As a Senator, or as a Diplomatist, he would have done eminent honor to the nation at home or abroad; and he seemed particularly suited, by his abilities, his accomplishments, and his tastes, for prolonged and continuous service in spheres like these. But it was not in his nature to seek them, and it was not his fortune to enjoy them. I may be pardoned for recalling, in such a connection, those striking lines of Coleridge: —

"How seldom, Friend! a good great man inherits
Honor or wealth, with all his worth and pains!
It sounds like stories from the world of spirits
If any man obtain that which he merits,
Or any merit that which he obtains.

. . . .

> Goodness and greatness are not means, but ends!
> Hath he not always treasures, always friends,
> The good great man? — three treasures, love, and light,
> And calm thoughts, regular as infant's breath;
> And three firm friends, more sure than day and night, —
> Himself, his Maker, and the angel Death."

Mr. Kennedy, as a man, was greater and better than all his books. One certainly looks in vain in all that he wrote or did for the full measure of those gifts and acquirements of mind and heart, that learning and wisdom, that wit and humor, that whole-souled cordiality and gayety and kindness, which shone out so conspicuously in the intimacies of daily intercourse. A truer friend or more charming companion has rarely been found or lost by those who have enjoyed the privilege of his companionship and friendship; and among those may be counted not a few of our most distinguished authors and statesmen. A delightful week which I passed under his roof, many years ago, gave me an opportunity of witnessing the esteem and affection in which he was held by my only fellow-guest, Washington Irving, — whose Life, indeed, contains more than one letter to him, beginning, "Dear Horse Shoe," and ending "Geoffrey Crayon."

Though far advanced in his seventy-fifth year, and though he had occasionally suffered not a little of late from severe physical infirmities, Mr. Kennedy was naturally of so genial and joyous a temper, and sympathized so warmly with the young and gay, that the idea of his being an old man had hardly yet occurred to any one but himself. In the eyes of those around him, he seemed to have nothing of age except its experience and its mellowness. He was not insensible himself, however, to the approach of the inexorable hour. In a letter which I received from him not many weeks ago, — one of the last of a series running through a term of more than thirty years, — he said to me with more of sadness than I had ever known him to write, certainly in regard to himself: "It is but small consolation to me — when I look at my letter-file, and see three or four of your letters asking for a word of recognition — to argue my good intentions, and my infirmity of hand, for that silence which I daily resolve to break; for it is so persistently followed by a new delinquency, in the breach of my resolve, as to bring me nothing better than a new regret. But I know you will pardon these habitual shortcomings, — like the good and trusty friend you have always been, — and indulge me in that constrained silence, which is, in truth, only the sign and warning of one more inevitable, that comes with gentle step and, I trust, a friendly message to make it welcome."

A few weeks more at Saratoga Springs, by the advice of his physician, and a few weeks afterwards at Newport, where he had fixed his summer residence for several years past, completed his earthly career. A hidden malady was developed, which, after two days of agony, patiently and bravely borne, and one day of tranquil slumbers, released him to his rest. I may not omit to add that, in a blessed interval of wakefulness and ease, he eagerly renewed those pledges of Christian faith which he had often given in health, and was able to take leave of those dearest to him, as he said, "In perfect peace of mind and body."

He died at Newport, on the 18th of August; and his remains were at once removed to his native city, to repose in the neighboring Green Mount Cemetery, at the dedication of which he had delivered the Address, in 1839.

Mr. Kennedy left no children. His wife, who, with her sister, has rendered his home for more than thirty years so dear and delightful to himself, and so attractive to his friends, is a daughter of the late Edward Gray, Esq., of Baltimore, one of the worthiest and most respected merchants of that city; of whom Irving, on hearing of his death in 1856, wrote thus, in words which I can indorse with all my heart: "To be under his roof, at Baltimore, or at Ellicott's Mills, was to be in a constant state of quiet enjoyment to me. Every thing that I saw in him, and in those about him; in his tastes, habits, mode of life; in his domestic relations and chosen intimacies, — continually struck upon some happy chord in my own bosom, and put me in tune with the world and with human nature."

Mr. Kennedy received the Honorary Degree of Doctor of Laws from Harvard University in 1863; and had been, for some years, an Associate Fellow of the American Academy of Arts and Sciences.

TWO HUNDRED AND FIFTIETH ANNIVERSARY

OF THE

LANDING OF THE PILGRIMS.

AN ORATION DELIVERED AT PLYMOUTH, DECEMBER 21, 1870.

THERE can be no true New England heart which does not throb to-day with something of unwonted exultation. There can be no true American heart, I think, which has not found itself swelling with a more fervent gratitude to God, and a more profound veneration for the Pilgrim Fathers, as this morning's sun has risen above the hill-tops, in an almost midsummer glory, and ushered in, once more, with such transcendent splendor, this our consecrated Jubilee.

When we reflect on the influence which has flowed, and is still flowing, in ever fresh and ceaseless streams, from yonder Rock, which two centuries and a half ago was struck for the first time by the foot of civilized, Christian man; when we reflect how mightily that influence has prevailed, and how widely it has pervaded the world, — inspiring and aiding the settlement of Massachusetts, and, through Massachusetts, of all New England, and, through New England, of so large a part of our whole wide-spread country, and thus, through the example of our country and its institutions, extending the principles of civil and religious freedom to the remotest regions of the earth, leaving no corner of Christendom, or even of Heathendom, unvisited or unrefreshed, — we should be dead, indeed, to every emotion of gratitude to God or man, were we not to hail this Anniversary as one of the grandest in the calendar of the Ages.

We are here, my friends, to celebrate the Fifth Jubilee of what is now known emphatically, wherever the history of New England, or the history of America, is read, as "The Landing." No other landing, temporary or permanent, upon our own or upon any other shore, can ever usurp its title, or ever supersede or weaken its hold upon the world's remembrance and regard.

There have been other landings, I need hardly say, which have left a proud and shining mark on the historic page: — landings of discoverers; landings of conquerors; landings of kings or princes, called by right of restoration or revolution to take possession of time-honored thrones; landings of organized Colonies, from large and well-appointed fleets, on conspicuous coasts, to occupy territories opened and prepared, in some degree, for human habitation.

Not such was the Landing which we commemorate to-day. Not such the event which has rendered this shortest day of all the year so memorable for ever in the annals of human freedom. It was the landing of a few weary and wave-worn men from a single ship, — nay, from a single shallop, — on a bleak and desolate shore, amid the storms and tempests of a well-nigh arctic winter, with none to welcome, none even to witness it. I might, indeed, be almost pardoned for saying, that the sun itself stood still in the heavens to behold it! But there were, certainly, no other witnesses, save those witnesses to each other's constancy and courage who were themselves the actors in the scene, and that all-seeing omnipresent God, who guided and guarded all their steps.

Turn back with me to that epoch of the winter solstice, just two hundred and fifty years ago, and let us spend at least a portion of this flying hour in attempting to recall the precise incidents which then occurred on the spot on which we are assembled, with some of their immediate antecedents and consequences. There have been, and will be, other occasions for boasting, if any one desires to boast, of what New England has accomplished, directly or indirectly, for herself or for mankind, in later times. There have been, and will be, other opportunities for a general glorification of New England principles, New England achievements, New England inventions and discoveries, past or present, remote or recent. We recognize them all to-day, — all, at least, that are worthy of being recognized at all, — as the legitimate result and development of this day's doings. We count and claim the progress of our country, in its best and worthiest sense, as the "Pilgrims' Progress;" — as the grand and glorious advance upon a line of march in which they were the pioneers, and for which they, in their own expressive phrase, literally as well as metaphorically, were the instruments "to break the ice for others."

To them the honors of this day are due. To their memories this Anniversary is sacred. Once in fifty years, certainly, we may well refresh our remembrance of what they did and suffered, and still more of the aims and ends of all their doings and sufferings. It is an old story, it is true; but there are some old stories which are almost forgotten into newness. There are some old stories which are actually new to every rising generation, and of whose real interest and nobleness thousands of young hearts receive their first vivid impression from what may be said or done on some occasion like the present. There are some old stories, too, of which even those who hold them in fondest and most familiar remembrance are never weary; and the appetite for which no repetitions can ever cloy, or even satisfy. There are some old stories, let me add, — and this is eminently one of them, — around which a haze, or it may be a halo, of legend and romance is gradually allowed to gather and thicken with the lapse of years, and which require and demand to be set forth afresh, from time to time, in their true simplicity and grandeur.

But there is no longer an excuse for doubt or uncertainty as to any substantial statement relating to the Pilgrim Fathers. Tradition, legend, romance, can find "no jutty, frieze, buttress, nor coigne of vantage, for their pendent bed and procreant cradle," in that solid structure of fact and truth which has recently been built up, — let me rather say, which has recently been discovered and unveiled, in all the simple beauty of its original proportions, — by the loving students and diligent investigators of Pilgrim history.

It is, indeed, a peculiar advantage of all young countries like our own, that, originating in a period of written and printed records, they may trace back the current of their career to its primal source and spring, without leaving room for any intermixture of myth or fable. Yet written or even printed records may disappear, or be overlooked and forgotten for a time, — awaiting such a search and such a scrutiny as Grote and Niebuhr, and Merivale and Mommsen, have recently brought to the history of Greece or Rome; or as Froude, even more remarkably, has just given to the history of England's Queen Elizabeth.

Even such a search and such a scrutiny have of late been applied to the history of the little band whose landing we are here to commemorate, and most richly have they been rewarded. Since the last Jubilee of the Pilgrims was celebrated, fifty years ago, — when that grand discourse of New England's grandest orator and statesman summoned the attention of the world so emphatically to their sublime but simple story, — antiquarians at home and abroad, pious and painstaking students, American travellers in foreign lands not forgetful of their own, one and all, have seemed inflamed with a new zeal to subject that story to the closest examination; to sift out from it every thing conjectural and legendary; and to investigate the Pilgrim track, footstep by footstep, wherever it could be found, in the Old World as well as in the New. Nothing has been too minute or trivial to elude their search; nothing too seemingly inscrutable to repel or discourage their pursuit; nothing too generally credited to satisfy their eagerness for positive proof and authentic verification. As the marvellous growth of that majestic perennial, of which the Mayflower supplied the seed, has been developed and displayed, with all its myriad leaves for the healing of the nations, and all its magic branches for sweetening so many bitter fountains, and all its rich and varied fruits for ourselves and for mankind, they have been more and more incited to trace back that seed to its native bed; to analyze with almost chemical exactness its smallest seminal principles; and to ascertain precisely by what culture, and by what hands, it was made so to take root upon a rock, and to bud and blossom and bear so abundantly in a wilderness.

We owe these laborious investigators a deep debt of gratitude, and it is fit that we should not forget them, this day, as we avail ourselves of their researches. I need but name the late admirable Judge Davis, whose excellent edition of "Morton's Memorial" led the way in the later illustrations of Pilgrim history. I need but name the late Reverend Dr. Alexander Young, whose "Chronicles of Plymouth" ought to be fresh in the memory of every son and daughter of the old Colony. But let me recall more deliberately a venerable antiquary of Old England, whom it was my good fortune to meet at the breakfast-table of the celebrated historian Hallam, nearly a quarter of a century ago, — the late Reverend Joseph Hunter; who, having diversified his routine of service, in her Majesty's Public Record Office, by tracts illustrative of the great triumphs of his own country in arms and in literature, — triumphs by the sword of Henry V. at Agincourt, and triumphs by the pens of Shakspeare and Milton in the fields of epic or dramatic poetry, — turned to the Pilgrims of Plymouth, and to the Puritans of Massachusetts, for the latest and best themes of his unwearied investigations. To him we primarily owe it that we can follow back that little band, to which the name of Brownists had been contemptuously given, to the very hive from which they first swarmed, — that little circle in Yorkshire and Nottinghamshire, and not far from Lincolnshire, around which he so fitly inscribed the legend, "Maximæ gentis incunabula," — the cradle of the greatest nation. By the light of his antiquarian torch, we are able to fix the precise locality and surroundings of the old Manor Place of Scrooby, — formerly a palace of the Archbishops of York, and which had often been the residence of at least one of them, "that he might enjoy the diversion of hunting" in the neighboring chase of Hatfield; which was occupied as a refuge for many weeks by the great lord Cardinal Wolsey, when, having "ventured in a sea of glory, but far beyond his depth," he had at last been left, "weary and old with service, to the mercy of a rude stream," which was for ever to hide him; and which, not many years afterwards, Henry the Eighth himself had selected for a resting-place, during one of his Royal progresses to the North;—but which, half a century later, had become the home of one, whose occupation of it, even for an hour, would have given it a celebrity and a sanctity in our remembrance and regard, which neither Archbishops, nor Cardinals, nor Kings, could have imparted to it in a lifetime.

There, in that "manor of the Bishops," of which, alas! hardly a fragment is now left, lived WILLIAM BREWSTER,—one of the noblest of the men whom we are here to commemorate, and not unworthy to be named first of all, on such an occasion as this. Educated at the University of Cambridge, and having served as the faithful Secretary of the accomplished Davison,—Queen Elizabeth's Ambassador in Holland, and afterwards one of her Secretaries of State,—until Davison's too prompt and implicit obedience to the orders of his Royal Mistress in the matter of poor Mary, Queen of Scots, had afforded a pretext for discarding him,—Brewster had retired with disgust from the pomps and vanities, the caprices and cruelties, of the Court, and had given himself up to religious meditation and study. Deeply impressed with the corruptions and superstitions, the prelatical assumptions and tyrannies, of the English Church, as it then existed, in those earlier transition stages of the Reformation, he had united himself with one of the little bodies of Separatists from that communion, and soon became "a special help and stay to them." At his house,—this very "manor of the Bishops," which Mr. Hunter helped us to identify,—we learn that the members of the church of which the sainted Robinson was the pastor, the church of our Plymouth Pilgrims, "ordinarily met on the Lord's Day; and with great love he entertained them when they came, making provision for them to his great charge; and continued so to do while they could stay in England."

Our mother country has many spots within her dominions which are dear to the hearts of the lovers of religious and of civil liberty in both hemispheres:—The plain of Runnymede, the Lollard's Tower, the Tower of London, the Martyrs' Monument at Oxford, the glorious Abbey of Westminster, the grand Cathedrals in almost every county; — but I know of none more worthy of being visited with pious reverence, by every American traveller certainly, than that old original site of Brewster's residence in Nottinghamshire; nor one which more deserves to be marked, not indeed by any ostentatious or sumptuous structure, out of all keeping with the plain and frugal character of those who have made it memorable for ever, but by some appropriate monument, a chapel or a school-house, erected by the care and at the cost of the sons and daughters of New England. We all remember that John Cotton's chapel at Old Boston was restored, not many years ago, by the contributions of a few of the generous sons of New Boston. The place where Robinson and Brewster gathered that first Pilgrim Church is certainly not less worthy of commemoration.

But it is not only the residence of Brewster which the researches of good Mr. Hunter, the very Nimrod of Antiquaries, have revealed to us. There, within that charmed circle — the cradle of the greatest nation — he helped us to discover a birthplace, which owing to a blundering misprint had so long baffled the most eager search; the birthplace of one who might almost contest with Brewster himself the right to be named first at any commemoration of the Pilgrim Fathers, — their Governor for thirty years, their Historian, their principal writer both in prose and verse, and second to no one of them, from first to last, in the fidelity and devotion with which he sustained and illustrated their principles. There, within that same charmed circle, of which the little market town of Bawtry is the centre, and the greater part, if not the whole, of which is now the property of one whose recent title, as a peer, has not obliterated our remembrance of his name as a poet, and who may be recalled with the more pleasure at this hour as one of the few among the English nobility who sympathized with the North in our late war for the Union, — there, in the record book of the little church of Austerfield, still standing, has been found the distinct entry, "William, son of William, Bradfourth, baptized the XIXth day of March, Anno Dñi 1589."

I hold in my hand a photographic picture of that ancient

edifice, and one, too, of the registered entry of Bradford's baptism, given me two or three years ago by Lord Houghton, — Monckton Milnes that was, — now Lord of the Manor, I believe, — and which I would gladly deposit in your Pilgrim Museum, if they are not there already.[1]

The font from which Bradford was christened, and the altar-rails at which his parents doubtless kneeled — for he must have been baptized according to the rites, and by a pastor, of the Church of England — are still preserved. But neither pastor nor parents could have dreamed, as the infant boy winced, perhaps, from the coldness of that sprinkled water, and shrunk, it may be, from the signing with the sign of the cross upon his tiny forehead, how sturdy and uncompromising a hater he was to become, in his mature life, of all mere forms and shows and ceremonies of religion; and, at the same time, how earnest and ardent and devoted a lover and upholder of the great truths and doctrines of which these were but the outward and visible signs.

Bradford and Brewster, if I mistake not, are the only two of our Pilgrim leaders, who can be distinctly identified with that little church at Scrooby, of which the venerable Richard Clifton and the zealous John Robinson were the associated pastor and teacher, and out of which came this first permanent settlement of New England. Bradford, indeed, was but a boy in age, at that early period, — hardly more than sixteen years old, an orphan boy, — and must have been like a son to Brewster, who was thirty years his senior; but he was a boy who seems to have known "little more of the state of childhood but its innocency and pleasantness," and who was capable, even then, of rendering no feeble aid and comfort to his maturer leader and friend. Together they braved persecution. Together they bore the taunts and scoffs of neighbors and relatives. Together they embraced exile. Together they were cast into prison at old Boston in Lincolnshire. Together, after a brief separation, — for Bradford was liberated first on account of his youth, — they found refuge in Holland. Together they embarked in the Mayflower. Together they were associated for three and

[1] They were deposited accordingly.

twenty years, — for Brewster lived in a vigorous old age till 1643, — in establishing and ruling the Pilgrim plantation here at New Plymouth.

Brewster and Bradford, the Æneas and Ascanius of our grand Pilgrim Epic, — I might better have said, the Paul and Timothy, or be it Titus, of our New England, Plymouth, Separatist Church, — both of them laymen, but both of them, by life and word, by precept and example, showing forth the great doctrines of Christ, their Saviour, with a power and a persuasiveness which might well have been envied by any pastor or preacher or lordly prelate of that or any other day: — For ever honored be their names in New England history and in New England hearts! Alas! that no portrait of either of them is left, — if, indeed, in their simplicity and modesty, they would ever have allowed one to be taken, — so that their image, as well as their names and their example, might be held up to the contemplation of our country and of mankind for endless generations!

But the little church of which they were members was able, as we know, to maintain its precarious and perilous existence at Scrooby, for hardly more than a single year, certainly for not more than two years. It could find indeed no safe refuge or resting-place in Old England; and having heard that in the Low Countries, as they were then called, there was freedom, or at least toleration, for differences of religious faiths and forms, its members resolved to fly from persecution and establish themselves in Holland. I will not attempt to describe the perils they encountered, and the sufferings they endured, in that flight; — the separations of children from parents, and of wives from husbands; the arrests and examinations, the fines and imprisonments, to which so many of them were subjected; the "hair-breadth 'scapes" of one large party of them during a tempestuous voyage of fourteen days, in crossing the German Ocean, in an almost sinking ship. The whole story is familiar to you. It is enough that we find them all at last safely in Amsterdam, where they are free to enjoy their pure and simple worship, and where they remain quietly for another year.

Not a trace is left of their residence in that then mighty mart, almost a second Venice; born of the sea, "built in the very lap of the floods, and encircled in their watery arms;" and claiming the whole ocean, from the Baltic to the Levant, not only as the field of its enterprise, but almost as its own rightful inheritance and domain. Not a trace of them is left there. We only know that, finding they were in danger of being involved in contentions about women's dresses and men's starched bands, and other such vital matters, which had sprung up in another little church of English Separatists which had fled there before them, and thus of being robbed of that harmony and peace which they prized above all earthly things, and which they had abandoned home and kindred and country to enjoy, — they thought it best to remove once more, and establish themselves at the neighboring inland city of Leyden.

It was a great epoch in Dutch history, when the Pilgrims took up their abode in Holland, and began to habituate themselves to its "strange and uncouth" customs and language. It was the precise period at which, as the close and consummation of "the most tremendous war for liberty ever waged," our own Motley has terminated his admirable account of "The United Netherlands," — to begin it again, we trust, at no distant day, and then to show us precisely what was going on in that interesting country while our Fathers were witnesses and partakers of its fortunes. Within a year after they reached Amsterdam, and the very year they removed to Leyden, the grand twelve years' truce between Spain and her revolted Colonies had been negotiated and ratified. Those Colonies had now virtually established their freedom and independence. Olden Barneveldt and Prince Maurice had reconciled their animosities and rivalries for a time; and the great Republic — henceforth, though not for ever, to be known and recognized as the United States of the Netherlands — was enjoying internal as well as external peace and rest, after a fearful struggle of forty years' duration.

It is a charming coincidence, certainly, that the coming of the Pilgrims was thus simultaneous with the commencement of that blessed truce, which was destined, too, by its own limitation, to last during the precise period of their stay there. One might almost picture the bow of peace and promise, lifting itself in all its many-colored glories, and overarching that blood-stained soil, to welcome the little band of fugitives for conscience' sake to their temporary repose, and to assure them that war should crimson its fields no more while they should bless it with their presence!

At Leyden, they find, as Bradford says, "a fair and beautiful city, and of a sweet situation, but made more famous by the University wherewith it is adorned, in which of late had been so many learned men." That was, certainly, a noble University, erected as a monument to the heroism of those who had fought and fallen in the dreadful siege which the city had endured so grandly in 1574,—erected in the same spirit in which our Memorial Hall has recently been founded at Cambridge by the Alumni of Harvard. Famous professors, and famous scholars also, it had indeed enjoyed. The learned Arminius had died just as the Pilgrims arrived there, but his teachings and doctrines were left to be the subject of endless disputation. The marvellous Joseph Scaliger, too, had died the same year; but his not less marvellous pupil, Hugo Grotius, was only at the outset of his great career, having published his Latin Tragedy, "The Suffering Christ," the very year of their arrival at Amsterdam, and his "Mare Liberum" the year of their removal to Leyden.

The youthful Bradford may not, perhaps, have been much in the way of taking note or notice of what was going on at this great seat of learning, as, in default of other means of support, he had put himself as an apprentice to a French Protestant, and was acquiring the art of dyeing silk. But Brewster had found employment as a tutor to some of the youth of the city and the University, and was teaching them the English language by a grammar of his own construction; while, at the same time, he had set up a printing-press, and "was instrumental in publishing several books against the hierarchy, which could not obtain a license in England." To him the University and its learned professors, and all their proceedings and lectures, must have been as familiar as they were interesting. His revered friend and pastor, Robinson, moreover,—as we learn from the researches of an accomplished and lamented New England scholar and traveller, — the late Mr. George Sumner, — was formally admitted to the privileges of a member or subject of the University four or five years after his arrival at Leyden. By the investigations of Mr. Sumner, too, and of a late American Minister at the Hague, the Hon. Henry C. Murphy, we have been enabled to identify the very spot, in the Cathedral Church of St. Peter, where the precious remains of this holy man, whose memory is so dear to New England, were at least temporarily deposited; while the record of that burial has also most happily helped us to fix the exact place of his residence as long as he lived there. In that residence, — and not in any church edifice, for they had none, — there is the best reason for thinking that the Pilgrims worshipped; and thanks to the pious pains of the Rev. Henry Martyn Dexter, of Boston, whose labors in the cause of Pilgrim history I may find further cause for acknowledging, a plate has been affixed to the walls of the building which now stands on that site, inscribed, "On this spot lived, taught, and died, JOHN ROBINSON, 1611–1625."

I cannot forget that I lingered in Leyden, for some hours, two or three years ago, for the single purpose of visiting that site, and the place of the grave of him who made it so memorable for ever; but I could find no one at hand to point either of them out for me; and, but for the record of Mr. Sumner and the inscription of Dr. Dexter, I might have missed all that there is there to recall the memory of the Fathers of New England. For, indeed, this is all, — the place of a temporary grave and the site of a dwelling long ago levelled to the ground, — this is absolutely all which can be identified of the Pilgrims' home at Leyden for eleven years. Yet no New Englander, I think, can visit that city on an early autumn or a late summer's day, and behold the ancient buildings on which their eyes must have been accustomed to look; and gaze on the countless canals, and on the flowing river, on the bosom of which they must so often have sailed, and on the banks of which they must so often have rested; and drink in that soft, hazy, golden sunshine, which one of the great masters of that region, — Cuyp, — not far from the very time and place at which they were enjoying it, was engaged in making the chief charm of not a few of his most exquisite landscapes, — without being conscious of the inspiration of the scene; nor without feeling and acknowledging that there is, and will for ever be, a magnetic sympathy between Leyden and Plymouth Rock, which no material batteries or tangible wires are needed to kindle and keep alive.

Leyden must indeed have been, as we know it was, most dear to the hearts of the Pilgrim Fathers. There they found rest and safety. There, to use their own language, they enjoyed "much sweet and delightful society and spiritual comfort together in the ways of God," and "lived together in peace and love and holiness." But there, too, they were joined by not a few of those who who were to be most serviceable and most dear to them in their future experiences and trials.

There they were joined by JOHN CARVER, of whom we know enough for his own glory, and for his perpetual remembrance among men, in knowing almost nothing except that he was counted worthy to be chosen the first Governor of the little band, and that he died, here at Plymouth, after a brief career, in the faithful discharge of that office.

There ROBERT CUSHMAN joined them, who, in spite of some infirmities of temper and some infelicities of conduct, and though at one time he seemed to have "put his hand to the plough and to have looked back," and was missing from the group whose advent we celebrate to-day, came over not long afterwards, reinstated in the confidence of those with whom he had been so prominently associated at Leyden; delivered, in the Common House of the Plantation, that memorable sermon on Self-Love, the first printed sermon of New England, if not of our whole continent; and, after a perhaps premature return home, continued to watch carefully over the interests of the Pilgrims in England, writing letters remarkable alike for the beauty of their style and for the prudence of their counsel; and was lamented by Bradford, when he heard of his death in 1624, as "a wise and faithful friend."

There they were joined by MILES STANDISH, the intrepid soldier and famous captain of New England; who, having served on the side of the Dutch in the armies of England in the war against Spain, and having now been released by the great truce from further campaigning in the Old World, united himself with the Pilgrims, and, though not a member of their church, followed their fortunes, and fought their battles gallantly to the end. A little man himself, — hardly more than five feet high, — the grand army with which he performed "his most capital exploit" was probably the smallest which was ever mustered for a serious conflict in the annals of human warfare, — only eight men besides their leader. But, "in small room large heart inclosed," he had acquired, not perhaps from Cæsar's Commentaries, his favorite study, but certainly from some other source, a knowledge which some ruthless warriors of the present day have failed to exhibit, — the knowledge where to stop, as well as when to strike; and, having secured a signal victory, he brought home in safety every man whom he carried out. Honor to Miles Standish, "the stalwart captain of Plymouth," of whose restrained wrath, when the Puritan influence had come in to temper the profanity for which there was a proverbial license in Flanders, our charming Longfellow would seem to have caught the very accent and cadence, when he says of it, —

> "Sometimes it seemed like a prayer, and sometimes it sounded like swearing;"

and whose threefold accomplishments he so tersely sums up, when he describes him as doubting

> "Which of the three he should choose for his consolation and comfort,
> Whether the wars of the Hebrews, the famous campaigns of the Romans,
> Or the artillery practice, designed for belligerent Christians."

A higher tribute to the fidelity, vigilance, and courage of the old Plymouth captain could hardly have been paid, than when the late venerable Judge Davis, — a Plymouth man, and full of the original Plymouth spirit, — not many years before his death, unwilling to be wanting to the volunteer patrol service, in Boston, on some occasion of real or imaginary peril, made solemn application to our old Massachusetts Historical Society for the use of one of his reputed — albeit somewhat rusty — swords, and walked the midnight round with that for his trusty and all-sufficient companion!

But there, too, at Leyden, they were joined, — by the accidents of travel, as it would seem, — in 1617, by one of the very noblest of our little band, who was soon associated most leadingly and lovingly with all their spiritual as well as temporal concerns; their Governor for three years, when Bradford had "by importunity got off;" the narrator and chronicler of not a few of the most interesting passages of their history; the leader of not a few of their most important enterprises; a man of eminent activity, resolution, and bravery; who did not shrink from offering himself as a hostage to the savages, while a conference was held and a treaty made with one of their barbarous chieftains; who did not shrink from imprisonment, and the danger of death, in confronting, as an agent of Plymouth and Massachusetts, the tyrannical Archbishop Laud; who earned a gentler and more practical title to remembrance as the importer of the first neat cattle ever introduced into New England; an earnest and devoted friend to the civilization of the Indian tribes and their conversion to Christianity; the chief commissioner of Oliver Cromwell in his warlike designs upon an island, which our own hero President has so recently attempted to secure by peaceful purchase: — EDWARD WINSLOW, — the only one of the Pilgrim Fathers of whom we have an authentic portrait; whose old seat of Careswell, at Marshfield, was the chosen home of Webster; and whose remains, had they not been committed to the deep, when he died so sadly on the sea, at the close of his unsuccessful expedition to St. Domingo, would have been counted among the most precious dust which New England could possess.

Leyden must indeed have been dear to the Pilgrims, as the place where so many of these leading spirits first entered into their association, and first pledged their lives and fortunes to the sacred enterprise.

But Leyden, and the whole marvellous land of which it was at that day one of the most interesting and enlightened cities, had a charm for our Forefathers far above all mere personal considerations. It was a land to which the great German poet, dramatist, and historian, Schiller, in his "Revolt of the Netherlands," gave the noblest testimony, in saying that "every injury inflicted by a tyrant gave a right of citizenship in Holland." It was a land to which that quaint old Suffolk County essayist, Owen Felltham, paid a still higher tribute when he described it as "a place of refuge for sectaries of all denominations." "Let but some of our Separatists be asked," said he, with evident reference to our English exiles of whom he was a contemporary, "let but some of our Separatists be asked, and they shall swear that the Elysian Fields are there." "If you are unsettled," says he in another place, "if you are unsettled in your religion, you may try here all, and take at last what you like best. If you fancy none, you have a pattern to follow of two that would be a church by themselves."

Yes, that was exactly it, — "a Church by themselves;" and there, in that church by themselves, our Pilgrim Fathers first tasted the sweets of civil and religious freedom, and enjoyed that liberty to worship God, according to the dictates of their own consciences, which to them was worth every sacrifice and above all price. There, too, just as they removed from Amsterdam to Leyden, the extraordinary sound was heard, — from the lips of a Roman Catholic, and in behalf of his Roman Catholic brethren, — of an appeal for liberty of conscience which was never surpassed by the founders of Rhode Island, Maryland, or Pennsylvania. "Those," said President Jeannin, most forcibly and eloquently, on taking leave of the States General, "those cannot be said to share any enjoyment from whom has been taken the power of serving God according to the religion in which they were brought up. On the contrary, no slavery is more intolerable, nor more exasperates the mind than such restraint. You know this well, my Lords States; you know, too, that it was the principal, the most puissant cause that made you fly to arms and scorn all dangers, in order to effect your deliverance from this servitude. You know that it has excited similar movements in various parts of Christendom, and even in the kingdom of France, with such fortunate success everywhere as to make it appear that God had so willed it, in order to prove that religion ought to be taught and inspired by the movements which come from the Holy Ghost, and not by the force of man."

We know not precisely how far the ears of the Pilgrims may have been regaled, and their hearts encouraged and strengthened, by this grand appeal from so unaccustomed a source. Brewster, who, as we have seen, had been in the Low Countries before, as Secretary to the English Ambassador, may hardly have been ignorant of it. But, at all events, it affords most significant testimony to the spirit of religious liberty which pervaded the land in which such words at that period could have been uttered; and, coming from the lips of a Romanist, it must have put to shame any Protestant bigotry or intolerance, if any such were lurking there, which might have restrained the full freedom of our English exiles. Dr. Belknap, in his American Biography, may, perhaps, have anticipated events in stating, as he does, that Robinson himself, about this time, after a friendly conference with one upon whose name he had recently made a petulant pun, in an angry controversy, — changing it reproachfully from Ames to *Amiss*, — relaxed the rigor of his Separatism; published a book, allowing and defending the lawfulness of communicating with the Church of England; "allowed pious members of the Church of England, and of all the reformed churches, to communicate with his church; and declared that he separated from no church, but from the corruptions of all churches." But the statement was substantially true of a later period, if not of this. The book, he adds, gained him the title of a Semi-Separatist, and was so offensive to the rigid Brownists of Amsterdam that they would scarcely hold communion with the Church of Leyden.

But, alas! more serious dissensions than these were soon to agitate again that whole united Republic, and to involve it in a crime of which all the multitudinous seas which surround it could hardly wash out the stain. The successor to the chair of Arminius in the University of Leyden — Vorstius — had not only stirred up "hearts of controversy" in his own land by teaching and preaching the peculiar doctrines of his master, but had roused the special indignation of the Royal theological polemic and titular Defender of the Faith across the channel, — that same James I., who a few years before had cut short a conference with the Puritan leaders, at Hampton Court, by declaring that "he would make them conform or he would harry them out of the land," and who, in this respect certainly, had been as good as his word. The recent assassination of his glorious fellow-sovereign, Henry IV. of France, had revived and quickened his antipathy not to Roman Catholics only, but to all religionists who did not agree with himself; and he had the insolence now to demand that the obnoxious Professor of Leyden should be dismissed from his chair and banished from the States, —leaving it, also, to their "Christian wisdom" whether he should not be burned at the stake for "his atheism and blasphemies." The States were compelled to comply, and did most humiliatingly comply, with this demand; but the banishment of Vorstius only the more inflamed the theological strife which raged throughout their dominions. Prince Maurice and Olden Barneveldt were again at each other's throats; the former as the leader of the Calvinist party, and the latter as the leader of the Arminians, with Grotius as his second. And, incredible as it seems to us at this hour, the controversy was only terminated by one of the most infamous judicial murders which pollute the annals of mankind; taking its loathsome place in the calendar of crime by the side of the execution of Sir Walter Raleigh, the year before, and of Algernon Sydney and Lord William Russell half a century later. On the 13th of May, 1619, Olden Barneveldt, the noble patriot and benefactor, second to no one among the founders of the Republic and the authors of its liberties, was condemned to death and beheaded at the Hague; while Grotius was sentenced to perpetual imprisonment, — from which, however, the ingenuity of his wife happily released him at the end of two years.[1]

I would gladly have found some allusion to these monstrous outrages in some of the journals or letters of the Pilgrims. Occurring, as they did, during the very last year of their residence there, I would gladly believe that some abhorrence of such crimes may have mingled with their motives for seeking another place of refuge. Although their religious sympathies

[1] The full story of Olden Barneveldt and Hugo Grotius was charmingly told, a few years afterwards (1874), by our accomplished historian Motley, whose death is, at this moment, the subject of so much sorrow at home and abroad.

were strongly with the Calvinist party, and their pastor, Robinson, had disputed publicly against the doctrines of Arminius, putting his antagonist Episcopius, the Arminian Professor, to "an apparent nonplus," as Bradford tells us, "not once only, but a second and third time, before a great and public audience, and winning a famous victory for the truth," and "much honor and respect for those who loved the truth," — yet he and Brewster and Bradford and Winslow must have shrunk with horror from this atrocious murder. There is good reason for believing that Brewster, indeed, left Leyden with his family not many weeks afterwards; and I will not doubt that such events increased the eagerness of them all once more to change the place of their habitation, and hastened their negotiations with the merchant adventurers in London.

But their purpose of quitting Holland had been conceived nearly two years before this terrible tragedy was enacted. As early as the autumn of 1617, Robert Cushman and John Carver had been sent as their agents to attempt an arrangement for their removal to America with the Virginia Company in London; and in 1618 the Church of Leyden — with a view to removing the objections, and conciliating the favor of the King and others — had adopted those memorable Seven Articles, first published in 1856 by our accomplished historian Bancroft, in which the authority of his Majesty and of his Bishops is acknowledged, with an unqualified assent "to the confession of faith published in the name of the Church of England and to every article thereof." The adoption of these "Seven Articles," and the appeals addressed to Sir Edwin Sandys and others by Brewster and Robinson, at length elicited an assurance that "both the King and the Bishops had consented to wink at their departure."

"Conniving at them and winking at their departure" were all the assurances they could wring from Royalty. "To allow or tolerate them by his public authority, under his seal, they found it would not be." And though the Virginia Company were strongly desirous to have them go to America under their auspices, and willing to grant them a patent with as ample privileges as they could grant to any one, the feuds and factions in the council of the Company occasioned such delays that no patent was sealed until the 9th of June, 1619; and, after all the labor and cost of procuring it, it was never made use of. An agreement, however, was entered into with Thomas Weston and other merchant adventurers; the Mayflower was hired to await them at Southampton; the Speedwell was bought to take them over to England, and keep them company afterwards; a day of solemn humiliation was spent, — after a parting sermon from Robinson, who was to remain behind with half the members of his church, — "in pouring out prayers to the Lord with great fervency mixed with abundance of tears," and so they proceeded to Delft Haven; and after another most touching parting scene, all kneeling in prayer and taking leave of each other, "with mutual embraces and many tears," the sail was hoisted, and with a prosperous wind they came in a short time to Southampton. There they found "the bigger ship come from London, lying ready, with all the rest of their company." A few days more are occupied in dealing with their agents and the merchant adventurers; a noble farewell letter from Robinson is received and read; and once more they set sail. A leak in the Speedwell compels them to put in at Dartmouth, and then again, after they had gone above a hundred leagues beyond Land's End, to put back to Plymouth, and to abandon the Speedwell altogether. At last, "these troubles being blown over, and now all being compact together in one ship, they put to sea again with a prosperous wind;" and on the 16th day of September, 1620, Old England is parted from for ever. The Mayflower, and its one hundred and two passengers, have entered on the voyage, which is to end not merely in founding a more memorable Plymouth than that which they left behind, but in laying the corner-stone of a mightier and freer Nation than the sun in its circuit had ever before shone upon.

England at the moment took no note of their departing. Her philosophers and statesmen and poets had not quite yet begun to appreciate the losses which religious persecution was entailing upon her. Lord Bacon, indeed, "the great Secretary of Nature and all learning," as Izaak Walton called him, had already foreshadowed the glory which was to be gained by some of his Suffolk and Lincolnshire neighbors, when, in one of his celebrated essays, he assigned the first place, "in the true marshalling of the degrees of sovereign honor," to the "*conditores imperiorum*, — the founders of States and Commonwealths."[1] But it was more than ten years afterwards before the saintly Herbert published those noted lines, which the Vice-Chancellor of Cambridge had so much hesitation about licensing: —

> "Religion stands on tiptoe in our land,
> Readie to passe to the American strand."

And it was nearly ten years later still, when John Milton, in his treatise "Of Reformation in England," exclaimed, "What numbers of faithful and free-born Englishmen, and good Christians, have been constrained to forsake their dearest home, their friends and kindred, whom nothing but the wide ocean, and the savage deserts of America, could hide and shelter from the fury of the bishops! Oh, sir, if we could but see the shape of our dear mother England, as poets are wont to give a personal form to what they please, how would she appear, think ye, but in a mourning weed, with ashes upon her head, and tears abundantly flowing from her eyes, to behold so many of her children exposed at once, and thrust from things of dearest necessity, because their conscience could not assent to things which the bishops thought indifferent!"

But the time was to come when England was to make signal recognition of this memorable Exodus. Little did they imagine, — those pious, humble, simple-hearted men and women, as they stood on the deck of their little bark of only one hundred and eighty tons' burthen, and looked wistfully upon their native shores receding from their moistened eyes, — little did they imagine that the scene of that embarkation, before two centuries and a half had passed away, should not only be among the most cherished ornaments of the Rotundo of the American Capitol, but should be found, as it is found this day, among the most conspicuous frescoes in the corridors of the Parliament Houses of Old England. Still less could the haughty Monarch and the

1 Bacon's Essays, No. LV.

bigoted Prelates, who had reluctantly been induced "to connive and wink at their departure," have dreamed, that such a picture should ever be warranted and welcomed by their successors, as one of the appropriate scenes for inspiring and for warning them, as they should sweep along, through the grand galleries of State, to their places on the throne or the Episcopal bench, in that gorgeous Chamber of the temporal and spiritual Lords of Great Britain.

But this would not be the only souvenir of the Pilgrim Fathers which might suffuse the cheeks of a Bancroft, a Wren, or a Laud, could they be permitted to revisit the scenes of their old prelatical intolerance and arrogance.

The suburban residence of the Bishop of London at Fulham has many charms. Its velvet lawn, its walks upon the Thames, its grand old oaks and cedars of Lebanon, its fine historical portraits, its rare library, its beautiful modern chapel, and, above all, its antique hall, recently restored, — in which the cruel Bonner and the noble Ridley may have successively held their councils during the struggles of the Reformation, and where Bancroft and Laud may have concerted their schemes of bigotry and persecution,[1] — render it altogether one of the most interesting places near London, and hardly less attractive than Lambeth itself. I have been privileged to visit it on more than one of those delicious afternoons of an English June, when the apartments and the grounds were thronged by all that was most distinguished in the society of the Metropolis, assembled to pay their respects to one whose exalted character, and earnest piety, and liberal churchmanship, and unsparing devotion to the humblest as well as the highest duties of his station, have won for him universal esteem, respect, and affection, and who has recently been called by the Queen to the Primacy of all England.[2] But I need hardly say, that to an American, or certainly to a New England eye, there was nothing in all the treasures of art, or of antiquity, or of literature, which that palace contained, — nothing in all the loveliness of its natural scenery and surround-

[1] See Note at the end of this Oration, p. 133.

[2] Archibald Campbell Tait, late Bishop of London, now Archbishop of Canterbury.

ings, nothing in all the historical associations of the spot, nothing in all the beauty and accomplishments and titled or untitled celebrity of the company gathered beneath the roof or scattered upon the lawn, — which could compare for a moment with the interest of an old manuscript volume, which strangely enough had found its way there, of all places in the world, and which had rested for three quarters of a century almost unidentified and unrecognized on its library-shelves. You will all have anticipated me when I say that it is the long-lost manuscript volume, of which but a small portion had ever been printed or copied, written by the hand of William Bradford himself, and giving the detailed story of the Pilgrim Fathers from their first gathering at Scrooby down to the year 1647.

My valued friend, Mr. Charles Deane, to whom, above almost all others, we are indebted for throwing light upon the early history of New England, in the edition of this volume which he so admirably prepared and annotated for the Collections of the Massachusetts Historical Society, has sufficiently described the circumstances of its discovery. When the glad tidings first reached us, I did not fail to sympathize with those who felt that a more rightful as well as more congenial and appropriate place for such a manuscript might be found on this side of the Atlantic. But after a little more reflection, and after we had secured an exact and complete transcript of it for publication, I could not help feeling that there was something of special fitness and felicity in its being left precisely where it is. There let it rest, as a remembrancer to all who shall succeed, generation after generation, to that famous See and its charming palace, of the simple faith, the devoted piety, the brave obedience to the dictates of conscience, of those who led the way in the colonization of New England, and who endured so heroically the persecutions and perils which that great enterprise involved!

How it would have gratified the honest heart of Bradford himself, could he have known where his precious volume should at length be found, and in what estimation it should be held after it was found! How it would have delighted him to know that instead of being set down in some "Index Expurgatorius," or burned at St. Paul's Cross, as compounded of heresy and blasphemy, — as it would have been by those who dwelt or congregated at Fulham at the time it was written, — it should be sacredly guarded among the heirlooms of the palace and its successive occupants! How much more it would have delighted him to know that so much of the simplicity and liberality of form and faith which it portrayed and inculcated, would be cherished and exemplified by more than one of those under whose official custody it was in these latter days to fall!

Few persons, I presume, will doubt that had the Church of England, between 1608 and 1620, been what it is to-day, and its Bishops and Archbishops such in life and in spirit as those who have recently presided at London and Canterbury, Brewster and Bradford would hardly have left Scrooby, and the Mayflower might long have been employed in less interesting ways than in bringing Separatists to Plymouth Rock. As that church and its prelates then were, let us thank God that such Separatists were found! An Episcopalian myself, by election as well as by education, and warmly attached to the forms and the faith in which I was brought up; believing that the Church of England has rendered inestimable service to the cause of religion in furnishing a safe and sure anchorage in so many stormy times, when the minds of men were "tossed to and fro, and carried about with every wind of doctrine;" and prizing that very prayer-book, — which was disowned and discarded by Bradford and Brewster, and by Winthrop, too, — as second only to the Bible in the richness of its treasures of prayer and praise; I yet rejoice, as heartily as any Congregationalist who listens to me, that our Pilgrim Fathers were Separatists.

I rejoice, too, that the Puritan Fathers of Massachusetts, who followed them to these shores ten years afterwards, — though, to the last, they "esteemed it their honor to call the Church of England their dear mother, and could not part from their native country, where she specially resideth, without much sadness of heart and many tears," were, if not technically and professedly, yet to all intents and purposes, Separatists, also; — Semi-Separatists at least, as Robinson himself was called when he wrote and published that book which so offended the Brownists. I rejoice that the prelatical assumptions and tyrannies of that day were resisted. The Church of England would never have been the noble church it has since become, had there been no seasonable protest against its corruptions, its extravagant formalism, and its overbearing intolerance. The earliest Separatists were those who separated from Rome; and when something more than a disposition was manifested to return towards Rome, in almost every thing except the acknowledgment of its temporal supremacy, another separation could not have been, ought not to have been, avoided. A serious renewal of such manifestations at this day, I need not say, would rend the Anglican Church asunder; and its American daughter would, under similar circumstances, deservedly share its fate. Pretensions of human infallibility need not be proclaimed by an Ecumenical Council in order to be offensive and abhorrent. It does not require a conclave of Cardinals to render assumptions and proscriptions and excommunications odious. Convocations and Conventions, and even Synods and Councils and Conferences, will answer just as well. When so much of the discipline of the English Church was devoted to matters of form and ceremony; when spiritualism was in danger of forgetting its first syllable, and of degenerating into an empty ritualism; when godly ministers were silenced for "scrupling the vestments," or for preaching an evening lecture, and men and women and children were punished for not bowing in the Creed, or kneeling at the altar, or for having family prayers under their own roof, — separation — call it Schism, if you will — was the true resort and the only remedy. For the sake of the church itself, but a thousand-fold more for the sake of Christianity, which is above all churches, it was needful that a great example of such a separation should be exhibited at all hazards and at any sacrifice. The glorious Luther, to whose memory that majestic monument has so recently been erected at Worms, had furnished such an example in his own day and land, and with relation to the church of which he had once been a devoted disciple. No name may be compared with his name in the grand calendar of Separatists. But our Pilgrim Fathers were humble followers in the same path of Protestantism, and thanks be to God that their hearts were inspired and emboldened to imitate his heroic course.

I would not seem too harsh towards those old prelates of the English Church, by whom Pilgrims or Puritans were persecuted. Sir James Mackintosh, I think, has somewhere said, that if the United Netherlands had erected a statue to the real author of all their liberties, it would have been to the Duke of Alva, whose abominable tyranny goaded the Dutch to desperation, and drove them into rebellion. I am not sure that, on this principle, New England might not well include Bancroft and Laud in her gallery of eminent benefactors. We must never forget, however, that almost all great movements are but the resultants of opposing forces; and that, in impressing upon them their final shape and direction, those who resist are hardly less effective than those who support and urge. Nor can it be forgotten that, in the turn of the wheel of England's fortunes, poor Laud was himself destined to persecution and martyrdom. It must have been a grim joke, when Hugh Peters and others proposed to send him over to New England for punishment, as his Breviate tells us they did; and it might be a matter for curious conjecture what would have happened to him, had he come here then. But the meekness and bravery and Christian heroism with which he bore his fate, when so wantonly and barbarously brought to the block, after four years of imprisonment in the Tower, are almost enough to make us forget that he was ever so haughty and insolent and cruel, and quite enough to extinguish all resentment of his wrongs.

But let me not longer delay to acknowledge, on this occasion, the deep debt which New England and our whole country owes to the Congregationalism which the Pilgrims established on our soil, and of which the very first church in America was planted by them here at Plymouth. My whole heart is in sympathy with the celebration of this Jubilee to be held in my native city, this evening, by the Congregationalists of our land. They would wrong themselves, indeed, as well as all who are not of their own communion, were they to celebrate it in any narrow, controversial spirit, and to turn a national into a merely denominational anniversary. But it would be doing them deep injustice to suggest or imagine such a thing. They have a right to celebrate it, and they will celebrate it, as a day whose associations and influences have far outreached every thing sectarian and every thing sectional, and which are as comprehensive as the land they live in, and as all-embracing as the Christianity they profess and cherish.

Few persons, if any, can hesitate to agree with them, that no other system of church government than Congregationalism could have been successful in New England at that day. No other system could have done so much for religion; no other system could have done so much for liberty, religious or civil. "The meeting-house, the school-house, and the training-field," said old John Adams, "are the scenes where New England men were formed." He did not intend to omit the town-house, for no one was more sensible than himself how much of New England education and character was owing to our little municipal organizations, and to the free consultations and discussions of our little town meetings. But he was right in naming "the meeting-house" first. Certainly, for the cause of religious freedom, no other security could have compared with the independent system of church government. Independent churches prepared the way for Independent States and an Independent Nation; and formed the earliest and most enduring barriers and bulwarks at once against hierarchies and monarchies.

That work fully and finally accomplished, and civil and religious freedom securely established, we may all be more than content, we all ought to rejoice, as we witness the association and the prosperous advancement, under whatever name or form they may choose to enroll themselves, of "all who profess and call themselves Christians," — studying ever, as Edward Winslow tells us the sainted Robinson studied, towards his latter end, "peace and union as far as might agree with faith and a good conscience." Let those who will, indulge in the dream, or cherish the waking vision, of a single universal Church on earth, recognized and accepted of men, whose authority is binding on every conscience, and decisive of every point of faith or form. To the eye of God, indeed, such a Church may be visible even now, in "the blessed company of all faithful people," in whatever region they may dwell, with whatever organization they may be connected, with Him as their head, "of whom the whole family in earth and heaven is named." And as, in some grand orchestra, hundreds of performers, each with his own instrument and his own separate score, strike widely variant notes, and produce sounds, sometimes in close succession and sometimes at lengthened intervals, which heard alone would seem to be wanting in every thing like method or melody, but which heard together are found delighting the ear, and ravishing the soul, with a flood of magnificent harmony, as they give concerted expression to the glowing conceptions of some mighty master, like him, the centennial anniversary of whose birthday has just been commemorated,[1] — even so, — even so, it may be, — from the differing, broken, and often seemingly discordant strains of sincere seekers after God, the Divine ear, upon which no lisp of the voice or breathing of the heart is ever lost, catches only a combined and glorious anthem of prayer and praise!

But to human ears such harmonies are not vouchsafed. The Church, in all its majestic unity, shall be revealed hereafter. The "Jerusalem, which is the mother of us all, is above;" and we can only humbly hope that, in the providence of God, its gates shall be wider, and its courts fuller, and its members quickened and multiplied, by the very differences of form and of doctrine which have divided Christians from each other on earth, and which have created something of competition and rivalry, and even of contention, in their efforts to advance the ends of their respective denominations. Absolute religious uniformity, as poor human nature is now constituted, would but too certainly be the cause, if it were not itself the consequence, of absolute religious indifference and stagnation.

Pardon me, fellow-citizens and friends, for a digression, — if it be one, — in which I may almost seem to have forgotten that I have been privileged to occupy this pulpit only for a temporary and secular purpose, and to have encroached on the prerogative of its stated incumbent; but coming here, at your flattering call, to unite in the commemoration of those whose

[1] Beethoven, born Dec. 17, 1770.

special distinction it was to have separated from the communion to which I rejoice to belong, I could not resist the impulse to give utterance to thoughts which are always uppermost in my mind, when I reflect on this period of New England history. I hasten now to resume and to finish the thread of that Pilgrim narrative which is the legitimate theme of my discourse.

I must not detain you for a moment by the details of that perilous voyage across the Atlantic, with its "many fierce storms, with which the ship was badly shaken and her upper works made very leaky; and one of the mainbeams in the midships bowed and cracked." I must not detain you by dwelling on that "serious consultation" in mid-ocean about putting back, when "the great iron screw which the passengers brought out of Holland" was so providentially found "for the buckling of the mainbeam," and "raising it into his place." All this is described in the journal of Bradford with a pathos and a power which could not be surpassed.

I must not detain you either by attempting to portray, in any words of my own, their arrival, on the 21st of November, within the sheltering arm of yonder noble Cape, — "the coast fringed with ice — dreary forests, interspersed with sandy tracts, filling the background;" — "no friendly light-houses, as yet, hanging out their cressets on your headlands; no brave pilot boat hovering like a sea-bird on the tops of the waves, to guide the shattered bark to its harbor; no charts and soundings making the secret pathways of the deep plain as a gravelled road through a lawn." All this was depicted, at the great second-centennial celebration of the settlement of Barnstable, by my lamented friend Edward Everett, with a grandeur of diction and imagery which no living orator can approach. They seem still ringing in my ear from his own lips, — for I was by his side on that occasion, and no one who heard him on that day can ever forget his tones or his words, as, "with a spirit raised above mere natural agencies," he exclaimed, — "I see the mountains of New England rising from their rocky thrones. They rush forward into the ocean, settling down as they advance, and there they range themselves, a mighty bulwark around the heaven-directed vessel. Yes, the everlasting God himself stretches out the arm of his mercy and his power in substantial manifestation, and gathers the meek company of his worshippers as in the hollow of his hand!"

Nor will I detain you for a moment on the simple but solemn covenant which the Pilgrim Fathers formed and signed in the cabin of the Mayflower on that same 21st of November, — the earliest "original compact" of self-government of which we have any authentic record in the annals of our race. That has had ample illustration on many other occasions, and has just been the subject of special commemoration by the New England Historic-Genealogical Society in Boston.

I turn at once to what concerns this day and this hour. I turn at once to that third exploring party which left the Mayflower — not quite blown up by the rashness of a mischievous boy, and still riding at anchor in Cape Cod harbor — on the 16th of December; and for whose wanderings in search of a final place of settlement our friend Dr. Dexter has supplied so precise a chronological table. I turn to those "ten of our men," with "two of our seamen," and with six of the ship's company, — eighteen in all, — in an open shallop, who, after spending a large part of two days "in getting clear of a sandy point, which lay within less than a furlong of the ship," — "the weather being very cold and hard," two of their number "very sick" and one of them almost "swooning with the cold," and the gunner for a day and a night seemingly "sick unto death," — found "smoother water and better sailing" on the 17th, but "so cold that the water froze on their clothes and made them many times like coats of iron;" who were startled at midnight by "a great and hideous cry," and after a fearful but triumphant "first encounter," early the next morning, with a band of Indians, who assailed them with savage yells and showers of arrows, and after a hardly less fearful encounter with a furious storm, which "split their mast in three pieces," and swept them so far upon the breakers that the cry was suddenly heard from the helmsman, "About with her, or else we are all cast away," found themselves at last, when the darkness of midnight had almost overtaken them, "under the lee of a small island, and remained all that night in safety," "keeping their watch in the rain."

There they passed the 19th, exploring the island, and perhaps repairing their shattered mast. The record is brief but suggestive: "Here we made our rendezvous all that day, being Saturday." But briefer still, and how much more suggestive and significant, is the entry of the following day! —

"10. (20) of December, on the Sabboth day wee rested."

I pause, — I pause for a moment, — at that most impressive record. Among all the marvellous concisenesses and tersenesses of a Thucydides or a Tacitus, — condensing a whole chapter of philosophy, or the whole character of an individual or a people, into the compass of a motto, — I know of nothing terser or more condensed than this; nor any thing which develops and expands, as we ponder it, into a fuller or finer or more characteristic picture of those whom it describes. "On the Sabboth day wee rested." It was no mere secular or physical rest. The day before had sufficed for that. But alone, upon a desert island, in the depths of a stormy winter; wellnigh without food, wholly without shelter; after a week of such experiences, such exposure and hardship and suffering, that the bare recital at this hour almost freezes our blood; without an idea that the morrow should be other or better than the day before; with every conceivable motive, on their own account, and on account of those whom they had left in the ship, to lose not an instant of time, but to hasten and hurry forward to the completion of the work of exploration which they had undertaken, — they still "remembered the Sabbath day to keep it holy." "On the Sabboth day wee rested."

It does not require one to sympathize with the extreme Sabbatarian strictness of Pilgrim or Puritan, in order to be touched by the beauty of such a record and of such an example. I know of no monument on the face of the earth, ancient or modern, which would appeal more forcibly to the hearts of all who reverence an implicit and heroic obedience to the commandments of God, than would an unadorned stone on yonder Clark's island, with the simple inscription, "20 Dec. 1620 — On the Sabbath day we rested." There is none to which I would myself more eagerly contribute.[1] But it should be paid for by the penny contributions of the Sabbath-school children of all denominations throughout the land, among whom that beautiful Jubilee Medal has just been distributed.

And what added interest is given to that record, what added force to that example, by the immediate sequel! The record of the very next day runs, — "On Monday we sounded the harbour and found it a very good harbour for our shipping; we marched also into the land, and found divers corn-fields and little running brooks, a place very good for situation; so we returned to our ship again with good news to the rest of our people, which did much comfort their hearts."

That was the day, my friends, which we are here to commemorate. On that Monday, the 21st of December, 1620, from a single shallop, those "ten of our men," with "two of our seamen," and with six of the ship's company, landed upon this shore. The names of almost all of them are given, and should not fail of audible mention on an occasion like this. Miles Standish heads the roll. John Carver comes second. Then follow William Bradford, Edward Winslow, John Tilley, Edward Tilley, John Howland, Richard Warren, Steven Hopkins, and Edward Dotey. The "two of our seamen" were John Alderton and Thomas English; and the two of the ship's company whose names are recorded were Master Copin and Master Clarke, from the latter of whom the Sabbath island was called.

They have landed. They have landed at last, after sixty-six days of weary and perilous navigation since bidding a final farewell to the receding shores of their dear native country. They have landed at last; and when the sun of that day went down, after the briefest circuit of the year, New England had a place and a name — a permanent place, a never to be obliterated name — in the history, as well as in the geography, of civilized Christian man.

[1] The inscription has since been made on the very rock, on Clark's Island, under the shadow of which they rested. I was privileged to select the place, in company with the Hon. E. S. Tobey, President of the Pilgrim Society, and the Hon. Thomas Russell, now United States Minister to Venezuela, having gone down to the island for the purpose, in the United States Revenue Cutter "Mahoning," on the 9th of August, 1871.

"They whom once the desert beach
Pent within its bleak domain, —
Soon their ample sway shall stretch
O'er the plenty of the plain!"[1]

I will not say that the corner-stone of New England had quite yet been laid. But its symbol and perpetual synonyme had certainly been found. That one grand Rock, — even then without its fellow along the shore, and destined to be without its fellow on any shore throughout the world, — Nature had laid it, — The Architect of the Universe had laid it, — "when the morning stars sang together, and all the sons of God shouted for joy." There it had reposed, unseen of human eye, the storms and floods of centuries beating and breaking upon it. There it had reposed, awaiting the slow-coming feet, which, guided and guarded by no mere human power, were now to make it famous for ever. The Pilgrims trod it, as it would seem, unconsciously, and left nothing but authentic tradition to identify it. "Their rock was not as our rock." Their thoughts at that hour were upon no stone of earthly mould. If they observed at all what was beneath their feet, it may indeed have helped them still more fervently to lift their eyes to Him who had been predicted and promised "as the shadow of a great rock in a weary land;" and may have given renewed emphasis to the psalm which perchance they may have recalled, — "From the end of the earth will I cry unto thee, when my heart is overwhelmed: lead me to the rock that is higher than I." Their trust was only on the Rock of Ages!

We have had many glowing descriptions and not a few elaborate pictures of this day's doings; and it has sometimes been a matter of contention whether Mary Chilton or John Alden first leapt upon the shore, — a question which the late Judge Davis proposed to settle by humorously suggesting that the friends of John Alden should give place to the lady, as a matter of gallantry. But the Mayflower, with John Alden, and Mary Chilton, and all the rest of her sex, and all the children, was still in the harbor of Cape Cod. The aged Brewster, also, was on board the Mayflower with them; and sorely needed must his

[1] Gray's "Fatal Sisters."

presence and consolation have been, as poor Bradford returned to the ship, after a week's absence, to find that his wife had fallen overboard and was drowned, the very day after his departure.

I may not dwell on these or any other details, except to recall the fact that on Friday, the 25th, they weighed anchor, — it was Christmas day, though they did not recognize it, as so many of us are just preparing to recognize it, as the brightest and best of all the days of the year; — that on Saturday, the 26th, the Mayflower, "came safely into a safe harbour;" and that on Monday, the 28th, the landing was completed. Not only was the time come and the place found, but the whole company of those who were for ever to be associated with that time and that place were gathered at last where we are now gathered to do homage to their memory.

I make no apology, sons and daughters of New England, for having kept always in the foreground of the picture I have attempted to draw, the religious aspects and incidents of the event we have come to commemorate. Whatever civil or political accompaniments or consequences that event may have had, it was in its rise and progress, in its inception and completion, eminently and exclusively a religious movement. The Pilgrims left Scrooby as a Church. They settled in Amsterdam and in Leyden as a Church. They embarked in the Mayflower as a Church. They came to New England as a Church; and Morton, at the close of the introduction to Bradford's History, as given by Dr. Young in his Chronicles, entitles it "The Church of Christ at Plymouth in New England, first begun in Old England, and carried on in Holland and Plymouth aforesaid." They had no license, indeed, from either Pope or Primate. It was a Church not only without a bishop, but without even a pastor; with only a layman to lead their devotions and administer their discipline. A grand layman he was, — Elder Brewster: it would be well for the world if there were more laymen like him, at home and abroad. In yonder Bay, it is true, before setting foot on Cape Cod, they entered into a compact of civil government; but the reason expressly assigned for so doing was, that "some of the strangers amongst them (*i.e.*, not Leyden men, but adventurers who joined them in England) had let fall in the ship that when they came ashore they would use their own liberty, for none had power to command them," or, as elsewhere stated, because they had observed "some not well affected to unity and concord, but gave some appearance of faction." They came as a Church: all else was incidental, the result of circumstances, a protection against outsiders. They came to secure a place to worship God according to the dictates of their own consciences, free from the molestations and persecutions which they had encountered in England; and free, too, from the uncongenial surroundings, the irregular habits of life, the strange and uncouth language, the licentiousness of youth, the manifold temptations, and "the neglect of observation of the Lord's day as a Sabbath," which they had so lamented in Holland.

We cannot be too often reminded that it was religion which effected the first permanent settlement in New England. All other motives had failed. Commerce, the fisheries, the hope of discovering mines, the ambition of founding Colonies, all had been tried, and all had failed. But the Pilgrims asked of God; and "He gave them the heathen for their inheritance, and the uttermost parts of the earth for their possession." Religious faith and fear, religious hope and trust, — the fear of God, the love of Christ, an assured faith in the Holy Scriptures, and an assured hope of a life of bliss and blessedness to come, — these, and these alone, proved sufficient to animate and strengthen them for the endurance of all the toils and trials which such an enterprise involved. Let it never be forgotten that if the corner-stone of New England was indeed laid by the Pilgrim Fathers, two centuries and a half ago to-day, it was in the cause of religion they laid it; and whatever others may have built upon it since, or may build upon it hereafter, — "gold, silver, precious stones, wood, hay, stubble," — God forbid that on this Anniversary the foundation should be ignored or repudiated!

As we look back ever so cursorily on the great procession of American History as it starts from yonder Rock, and winds on and on and on to the present hour, we may descry many other scenes, many other actors, remote and recent, in other parts of the Union as well as in our own, of the highest interest and importance. There are Conant and Endicott with their little rudimental plantations at Cape Ann and at Salem. There is the elder Winthrop, with the Massachusetts Charter, at Boston, of whom the latest and best of New England Historians, Dr. Palfrey, has said "that it was his policy, more than any other man's, that organized into shape, animated with practical vigor, and prepared for permanency, those primeval sentiments and institutions that have directed the course of thought and action in New England in later times." There is the younger Winthrop, not far behind, with the Charter of Connecticut, of whose separate Colonies Hooker and Haynes and Hopkins and Eaton and Davenport and Ludlow had laid the foundations. There is Roger Williams, "the Apostle of soul freedom," as he has been called, with the Charter of Rhode Island. There is the brave and generous Stuyvesant of the New Netherlands. There are the Catholic Calverts, and the noble Quaker Penn, building up Maryland and Pennsylvania alike, upon principles of toleration and philanthropy. There is the benevolent and chivalrous Oglethorpe, assisted by Whitefield and the sainted Wesleys, planting his Moravian Colony in Georgia. There is Franklin, with his first proposal of a Continental Union, and with his countless inventions in political as well as physical science. There is James Otis with his great argument against Writs of Assistance, and Samuel Adams with his inexorable demand for the removal of the British regiments from Boston. There are Quincy with his grand remonstrance against the Port Bill, and Warren, offering himself as the Proto-martyr on Bunker Hill. There is Jefferson with the Declaration of Independence fresh from his own pen, with John Adams close at his side, as its "Colossus on the floor of Congress." There are Hamilton and Madison and Jay bringing forward the Constitution in their united arms; and there, leaning on their shoulders, and on that Constitution, but towering above them all, is WASHINGTON, the consummate commander, the incomparable President, the world-honored Patriot. There are Marshall and Story as the expounders of the Constitution, and Webster as its defender. There is John

Quincy Adams with his powerful and persistent plea for the sacred Right of Petition. There is Jackson with his Proclamation against Nullification. There is Lincoln with his ever memorable Proclamation of Emancipation. And there, closing for the moment that procession of the dead, — for I presume not to marshal the living, — is George Peabody, with his world-wide munificence and his countless benefactions. Other figures may present themselves to other eyes as that grand Panorama is unrolled. Other figures will come into view as that great procession advances. But be it prolonged, as we pray God it may be, even "to the crack of doom," first and foremost, as it moves on and on in radiant files, — "searing the eyeballs" of oppressors and tyrants, but rejoicing the hearts of the lovers of freedom throughout the world, — will ever be seen and recognized the men whom we commemorate to-day, — the Pilgrim Fathers of New England. No herald announces their approach. No pomp or parade attends their advent. "Shielded and helmed and weapon'd with the truth," no visible guards are around them, either for honor or defence. Bravely but humbly, and almost unconsciously, they assume their perilous posts, as pioneers of an advance which is to know no backward steps, until, throughout this Western hemisphere, it shall have prepared the way of the Lord and of liberty. They come with no charter of human inspiration. They come with nothing but the open Bible in their hands, leading a march of civilization and human freedom, which shall go on until time shall be no more, — if only that Bible shall remain open, and shall be accepted and reverenced, by their descendants as it was by themselves, as the Word of God!

It is a striking coincidence that while they were just taking the first steps in the movement which terminated at Plymouth Rock, that great clerical Commission was appointed by King James, which prepared what has everywhere been received as the standard English version of the Holy Scriptures; and which, though they continued to use the Geneva Bible themselves, has secured to their children and posterity a translation which is the choicest treasure of literature as well as of religion. Nor can I fail to remember, with the warmest interest, that, at this moment, while we are engaged in this Fifth Jubilee Commemoration, a similar Commission is employed, for the first time, in subjecting that translation to the most critical revision; — not with a view, certainly, to attempt any change or improvement of its incomparable style and language, but only to purge the sacred volume from every human interpolation or error.

No more beautiful scene has been witnessed in our day and generation, nor one more auspicious of that Christian unity which another world shall witness, if not this, than the scene presented in Westminster Abbey, in the exquisite chapel of Henry VII., by that Revision Commission, in immediate preparation for entering on their great task, on the morning of the 22d of June last; — "such a scene," as the accomplished Dean Alford has well said, "as has not been enacted since the name of Christ was first named in Britain." I can use no other words than his, in describing it: "Between the latticed shrine of King Henry VII. and the flat pavement tomb of Edward VI. was spread 'God's board,' and round that pavement tomb knelt, shoulder to shoulder, bishops and dignitaries of the Church of England, professors of her Universities, divines of the Scottish Presbyterian and Free Churches, and of the Independent, Baptist, Wesleyan, Unitarian Churches in England, — a representative assembly, such as our Church has never before gathered under her wing, of the Catholic Church by her own definition, — of 'all who profess and call themselves Christians.'" It was a scene to give character to an age; and should the commission produce no other valuable fruit, that opening Communion will make it memorable to the end of time.

Yes, the open Bible was the one and all-sufficient support and reliance of the Pilgrim Fathers. They looked, indeed, for other and greater reformations in religion than any which Luther or Calvin had accomplished or advocated; but they looked for them to come from a better understanding and a more careful study of the Holy Scriptures, and not from any vainglorious human wisdom or scientific investigations. As their pastor Robinson said, in his farewell discourse, "He was confident the Lord had more truth and light yet to break forth out of his Holy Word."

Let me not seem, my friends, to exaggerate the importance to our country of the event which we this day celebrate. The Pilgrims of the Mayflower did not establish the earliest permanent English settlement within the territories which now constitute our beloved country. I would by no means overlook or disparage the prior settlement at Jamestown, in Virginia. The Old Dominion, with all its direct and indirect associations with Sir Walter Raleigh, and with Shakspeare's accomplished patron and friend, the Earl of Southampton, — with Pocahontas, too, and Captain John Smith, — must always be remembered by the old Colony with the respect and affection due to an elder sister. "I said an elder, not a better." Yet we may well envy some of her claims to distinction. More than ten years before an English foot had planted itself on the soil of New England, that Virginia Colony had effected a settlement; and more than a year before the landing of the Pilgrims, — on the 30th of July, 1619, — the first Representative Legislative Assembly ever held within the limits of the United States was convened at Jamestown. That Assembly passed a significant Act against drunkenness; and an Act somewhat quaint in its terms and provisions, but whose influence might not be unwholesome at this day, against "excessive apparel," — providing that every man should be assessed in the church for all public contributions, "if he be unmarried, according to his own apparel; if he be married, according to his own and his wife's, or either of their apparel." Such a statute would have been called puritanical, if it had emanated from a New England Legislature. It might even now, however, do something to diminish the dimensions, and simplify the material, and abate the luxurious extravagance, of modern dress. But that first Jamestown Assembly passed another most noble Act, for the conversion of the Indians and the education of their children, which entitles Virginia to claim pre-eminence, or certainly priority, in that great work of Christian philanthropy, for which our Fathers, with glorious John Eliot at their head, did so much, and for which their sons, alas! have accomplished so little, — unless, perhaps, under the new and noble Indian policy of the last twelve months. The political organization of Virginia was almost mature, while that of New England was still in embryo.

Again, I do not forget that the Pilgrims of the Mayflower built up no great City or Commonwealth. Within the first three months after their landing, one-half of their number had fallen victims to the rigors of the climate and the hardships of their condition; and at the end of ten years the whole population of the Colony — men, women, and children — did not exceed three hundred. They were but as a voice in the desert; but it was a glorious voice, and one which was destined to reverberate around the world, and ring along the ages with still increasing emphasis. Other Colonies, by the inspiration and encouragement of their example, soon succeeded them, and did the substantial work for which they only prepared the way; for which they, as they said themselves, were but "stepping-stones." The great "Suffolk Emigration" of 1630, — "The Governor and Company of the Massachusetts Bay," — coming over in eleven ships, with the whole government and its Charter, were the main founders and builders of the grand old Commonwealth, of which the Plymouth Colony, sixty years afterwards, became an honored part.

It is pleasant to remember how harmoniously and lovingly the two Colonies lived together. It is pleasant to remember that parting charge of John Cotton to the Massachusetts Company, at Southampton, "that they should take advice of them at Plymouth, and do nothing to offend them." I cannot forget, either, the cordial visit of Governor Bradford to Governor Winthrop in 1631; nor that Winthrop soon afterwards subjected himself to reproach for supplying the Pilgrims with powder, at his personal cost, in a moment of their urgent danger and distress. Still less can I forget that October day in 1632, when Governor Winthrop returned Bradford's visit, coming a large part of the way here on foot, and crossing the river on the back of his guide; and when Bradford and Brewster and Roger Williams and Winthrop, with John Wilson, the first pastor of Boston, were together on this spot, engaging in religious discourse, and partaking of the Sacrament together. That most impressive and memorable Communion was at once the harbinger and the pledge, the prediction and the assurance, of the peace and harmony, the co-operation and concord, which were long to prevail between the infant Colonies of New England.

True, there were some shades of difference in the religious sentiment and in the civil administration of the various plantations, as they were successively developed. The charges of intolerance, bigotry, superstition, and persecution, which there seems to have been a special delight, in some quarters, of late years, in arraying against our New England Fathers and founders, apply without doubt more directly to other Colonies, than to that whose landing we this day commemorate. The Pilgrims in their narrow retreat of rock and sand were but little disturbed by "intruders and dissentients," — as my friend Dr. Ellis has so well classified them, — and could afford to be less rigid in their admissions and exclusions. Their leaders, too, were perhaps of a somewhat more lenient and liberal temper than those who settled elsewhere. Let them have all the honor which belongs to them; and let censure and condemnation fall wherever it is deserved! I am not here to justify or excuse all the extravagances, superstitions, or persecutions of the Puritan Colonists. But still less am I here to pander to the prurient malignity of those who are never weary of prying into the petty faults and follies of our Fathers, and who seem to gloat and exult in holding them up to the ridicule and reproach of their children. As if those great hearts, whether of 1620 or 1630, had fled into the wilderness to assert and vindicate a broad, abstract, unqualified doctrine of religious liberty, or even of religious toleration, to which they had afterwards proved recreant themselves! As if the precarious circumstances of their condition — with savage foes watching to extirpate them, with famine ever staring them in the face, with disease and death menacing them in every shape and at every turn — did not constrain and compel them, in the earlier stages of their career, to adopt the principle of excluding from their community any and all who were bent upon introducing contention and discord, and of enforcing among themselves something of that stern martial rule which belongs to a besieged camp! Why, even Roger Williams himself was forced to introduce a right of exclusion, or non-admission, into his original articles of settlement at Providence!

We can never too often recall the language of the late venerable Josiah Quincy, — the last man of our day and generation — I had almost said of any day and generation — to palliate real bigotry or wanton intolerance, — when he said, in his masterly Discourse on the Second Centennial Anniversary of the Settlement of Boston in 1630: "Had our early ancestors adopted the course we at this day are apt to deem so easy and obvious, and placed their government on the basis of liberty for all sorts of consciences, it would have been, in that age, a certain introduction of anarchy. . . . The non-toleration which characterized our early ancestors, from whatever source it may have originated, had undoubtedly the effect they intended and wished. It excluded from influence, in their infant settlement, all the friends and adherents of the ancient monarchy and hierarchy; all who, from any motive, ecclesiastical or civil, were disposed to disturb their peace or their churches. They considered it a measure of 'self-defence.' And it is unquestionable that it was chiefly instrumental in forming the homogeneous and exclusively republican character for which the people of New England have, in all times, been distinguished; and, above all, that it fixed irrevocably in the country that noble security for religious liberty, the independent system of Church Government."

But whatever may have been the differences or disagreements of the first planters of Plymouth and Massachusetts Bay, of New Haven and of Connecticut, at the outset, we all know that in the summer of 1643 these four original Colonies established that noble New England Confederation, — the model and prototype of the Confederation of 1778, which "blended the many-nationed whole in one," and carried the thirteen American Colonies through the War of Independence, — whose grand and comprehensive preamble is alone an ample reply to all who would magnify one Colony at the expense of another: —

"Whereas we all came into these parts of America with one and the same end and aim, namely, to advance the Kingdom of our Lord Jesus Christ and to enjoy the liberties of the Gospel in purity with peace: And whereas in our settling (by a wise providence of God) we are further dispersed upon the Sea-coasts and Rivers than was at first intended, so that we cannot according to our desire with convenience communicate in one Government and Jurisdiction: And whereas we live encompassed with people of several Nations and strange languages, which hereafter may prove injurious to us or our posterity: And forasmuch as the Natives have formerly committed sundry insolences and outrages upon several plantations of the English, and have of late combined themselves against us: And seeing by reason of those sad distractions in England which they have heard of, and by which they know we are hindered from that humble way of seeking advice, or reaping those comfortable fruits of protection which at other times we might well expect: We therefore do conceive it our bounden duty without delay to enter into a present Consociation amongst ourselves, for mutual help and strength in all our future concernments: That as in Nation and Religion so in other respects we be and continue ONE, according to the tenor and true meaning of the ensuing Articles: Wherefore it is fully agreed and concluded by and between the parties or Jurisdictions above-named, and they jointly and severally do by these presents agree and conclude, That they all be and henceforth be called by the name of The United Colonies of New England."

The very next clause of this remarkable Ordinance provided as follows: "The said United Colonies for themselves and their posterities do jointly and severally hereby enter into a firm and perpetual league of friendship and amity for offence and defence, mutual advice and succour, upon all just occasions both for preserving and propagating the truth and liberties of the Gospel and for their own mutual safety and welfare." And another article provided for intrusting the whole management of the Confederation to two Commissioners from each of the four Jurisdictions, carefully adding, "all in Church fellowship with us," — thus leaving no shadow of doubt upon the point that it was a "Consociation" for religious as well as for political peace and unity.

Accordingly we find among the proceedings of the Commissioners at New Haven in 1646 — a meeting at which neither Bradford nor Winslow nor either of the Winthrops was present, but at which all of the four Colonies were fully represented, and to whose proceedings all of them ultimately subscribed — that most memorable Declaration as to the "Spreading nature of Error and the dangerous growth and effects thereof," "under a deceitful colour of liberty of conscience," which recommended, among other things, that "Anabaptism, Familism, Antinomianism, and generally all errours of a like nature," "be seasonably and duly suppressed;" and which concluded with that glowing prediction for New England: "If thus we be for God, he will certainly be with us; and though the God of the world (as he is styled) be worshipped, and by usurpation set upon his throne in the main and greatest part of America, yet this small part and portion may be vindicated as by the right hand of Jehovah, and justly called Emmanuel's land."

I do not forget that, in reference to the clause recommending the suppression of errors, the Plymouth Commissioners "desired further consideration;" but the whole Declaration is entered upon the Plymouth Records as agreed upon, and was ultimately subscribed alike by the Commissioners of all the Colonies.

I do not forget, either, that all New England was not included in that Confederation. All that there was of New Hampshire was indeed within the jurisdiction of Massachusetts. But we miss Rhode Island from the historic group. We miss Clarke and Coddington and Roger Williams from the roll of the Commissioners. It must be borne in mind, however, that it was not because the Plantations at Providence and the Islands were opposed to the Confederation or any of its articles, that they were not members of it. Both of them desired and solicited admission. "There was yet another, a fifth New England Colony," — said John Quincy Adams in 1843, — "denied admission into the Union, and furnishing, in its broadest latitude, the demonstration of that conscientious, contentious spirit, which so signally characterized the English Puritans of the seventeenth century, the founders of New England, of all the liberties of the British Nation, and of the ultimate universal freedom of the race of man. The founder of the Colony of Rhode Island," adds he, "was Roger Williams, a man who may be considered the very impersonation of this combined conscientious, contentious spirit."

Rhode Island may well afford to bear with equanimity any charges against the early contentiousness of her founders, in view of the glory which that very contentiousness has acquired for her on the page of history. "Roger Williams," says Bancroft, "was the first person in modern Christendom to assert in its plenitude the doctrine of the liberty of conscience, the equality of opinions before the law; and in its defence he was the harbinger of Milton, the precursor and superior of Jeremy Taylor." The man upon whose tombstone such an inscription, — even with some allowances for rhetorical exaggeration, — may be justly written, need fear no strictures to which other peculiarities of character or conduct may subject him. I have an hereditary disposition, too, to be not only just but tender towards his memory, for Williams and the Winthrops of old, in spite of all differences, were most loving friends from first to last. I would palliate not a particle of the persecution or cruelty which he suffered; from whatever source it may have proceeded, or by whomever it may have been prompted. There was an heroic grandeur in his endurance and fortitude; there was an unsparing self-devotion in his care for the Indians; there was a simplicity, sincerity, and earnestness in his whole career and character, — which must ever command our warmest sympathy and admiration.

But it would be gross injustice to our other New England Fathers, and especially to our Massachusetts Fathers, not to admit that the conduct of Williams, in some of its earlier manifestations, was too precipitate and turbulent to be compatible with the peace and safety of the infant Colonies, — denying, as Winslow says he did, the lawfulness of a public oath, refusing "to allow the colors of our nation," and holding forth the unlawfulness of the patent from the king; — while the condition and temper of the Plantations of Rhode Island — a State which we now so honor and love, and to which we owe more than one of our most valued citizens — were such, at that time, as to cause even the Plymouth rulers and elders to say: "Concerning the Islanders, we have no conversing with them, nor desire to have, further than necessity or humanity may require."[1]

But with the exception of these Rhode Island Plantations, which were still very small and scattered, New England was then one; one, not only as the multiplied States of our American Union are one at this day, for civil, political, and military purposes; but one, also, in a unity to which our Federal Constitution presents no counterpart; — one for the preservation and propagation of Religion; a Union for the defence and diffusion of pure, Protestant Christianity, such as the world had hardly ever witnessed before, and may hardly ever witness again. It was a grand Experiment, conceived and instituted for the glory of God and the welfare of man's estate. But a higher than human power had long ago emphatically declared, "My Kingdom is not of this world;" and the result gave abundant evidence that, on this Continent at least, the Temporal and Spiritual power were not destined to be wielded successfully by the same hands. Church and State were never meant to thrive together on American soil. It remains to be seen how long they are to thrive together anywhere.

I hasten to the conclusion of this discourse. I may not attempt to pursue the thread of Pilgrim history further on this occasion. We all know what New England has been doing since the days of that Confederation. We all know how her sons and her daughters, besides founding and building up noble institutions within her own limits, have sought homes in other parts of the country, near and remote, and how powerfully their influence and enterprise have everywhere been felt. It may safely be said that there is hardly a State, or county, or town, or village, on the Continent, in which New England men and women are not turning their faces towards Plymouth Rock to-day with something of the affectionate yearning of children towards an ancestral, or even a parental, home. We all know

[1] See communication of Charles Deane, LL.D., in Proceedings of the Massachusetts Historical Society, 1873, pp. 341–358, and the elaborate and exhaustive monograph, "As to Roger Williams," by the Rev. H. M. Dexter, D.D., 1876.

what contributions they have made to the cause of Education, of Learning, of Literature, of Science, and of Art. We all know what they have done for Commerce on the ocean, and for Industry on the land, vexing every sea with their keels, and startling every waterfall with their looms. We all know what examples of Patriotism and Statesmanship they have exhibited in every hour of Colonial or National trial. We do not fail to remember that New England led the march to Independence at Lexington and Concord and Bunker Hill, and that the bones of her sons were mingled with almost every soil on which the battles of the Revolution were fought. Still less can we forget with what alacrity and heroic self-sacrifice her bravest and best rushed forth, — so many of them, alas! never to return, — for the defence of the Union, in the great struggle which has so recently terminated.

But we are not here to-day to boast of our own exploits, or to deal with the events of our own day. It becomes us rather to remember our own shortcomings and our own unworthiness, in view of the sublime examples of piety, endurance, and heroic valor which were exhibited by those "holy and humble men of heart" by whom our Colonies were planted. We sometimes assume to sit in judgment upon their doings. We often criticise their faults and failings. There is a special proneness of late years to deride their superstitions and denounce their intolerance. And certainly we may well rejoice that the days of religious bigotry and proscription are over in our land. But is it not even more true at this hour, than when no less liberal a Christian than John Quincy Adams uttered the warning, thirty years ago, that the intensely religious feelings and prejudices of our infancy have not only given way to universal toleration, but "to a liberality of doctrine bordering upon the extreme of a faltering faith"? God forbid that our own religious freedom should ever be described as Gibbon described that of the age of Antoninus, from which he dates the decline and fall of the Roman Empire: "The various modes of worship," says he, "which prevailed in the Roman world were all considered by the people as equally true; by the philosophers as equally false; and by the magistrates as equally useful. And thus toleration produced not only mutual indulgence, but even religious concord." Such a spirit of toleration, — such religious liberty as that, — even in an age of Paganism, gradually led to the overthrow of the great Empire of the Old World. What else but overthrow can it accomplish in a Christian age for the great Republic of the New World?

May it not be wise and well for us all sometimes to reflect — and may I not be pardoned for concluding this discourse by summoning the sons and daughters of New England, here and everywhere, to reflect this day — what judgment would be pronounced upon us by our Pilgrim and our Puritan Fathers, could they be permitted to behold and to comprehend the grand expansion and development which we now witness of the institutions which they planted? Could they descend among us, at this moment, in bodily presence, and with organs capable of embracing at a glance a full perception and understanding of every thing which has been accomplished on this wide-spread continent, since they were withdrawn from these earthly scenes and entered into their rest, — what would they think, what would they say?

It is not difficult to imagine the surprise with which they would contemplate the existing condition of New England, and of the mighty nation of which it forms a part. It is not difficult to imagine the astonishment with which they would regard the great inventions and improvements of modern times. It is not difficult to imagine the eager and incredulous amazement with which Miles Standish, for instance, would listen to the click of a little machine, almost at his own old doorway, which could supply him daily and hourly with the latest phases of the big wars in Europe, which in his lifetime he could only have studied in bulletins, or broadsides, or "books of the news," not much less than half a year old.[1] It is not difficult to conceive the wonder of Edward Winslow, as he should see, or be told of, some noble ship traversing the wide Atlantic, from Land's End to Cape Cod, with undeviating regularity, without sails and against the wind, in far less time than he could have relied on crossing

[1] The American end of the French Cable was not far from the residence of Miles Standish, at Duxbury, Mass.

from one little island to another of the Caribbean Sea, before he sunk so sadly beneath its waters. It is not difficult to picture the bewilderment of Brewster and Bradford as they should listen to the rattling and whistling and thundering, by day and by night, of cars bringing more passengers than the whole population of Plymouth in their day, and more freight than would have sustained that whole population for a winter, not merely from Boston in not much more than an hour, but from the shores of the Pacific Ocean in not much more than a week! It is easy to conceive the consternation of them all, could they see this whole assembly, by an almost instantaneous flash of sunlight, grouped and pictured with an exactness which the most protracted labors of ancient or modern art could never have reached. It is easy to conceive their rapture should they witness the intensest physical agonies of the human frame charmed to sleep by the inhalation of the vapor of a few drops of ether. It is easy to understand how astounded they would be, not merely at learning that all those phenomena of the celestial bodies which had so often perplexed and alarmed them were now familiar to every school-boy; but at being specially informed that to-morrow there should be a great eclipse of the sun, total in some parts of the world though hardly visible here; and that Science, not satisfied with calculating, by the old processes of which they may have heard something before, the precise instants of its beginning and end, had equipped and sent out formal expeditions to many distant lands to observe and record all its phases and incidents!

We can readily suppose that such marvels as these would not be taken in by them without reawakening something of their old superstitious fear and awe; and we might expect to hear from their lips some exclamations, if not about "the old Serpent," certainly about "wonders and more wonders of the invisible world." But we need not resort to these miracles of science and art in order to illustrate the surprise and amazement with which our Fathers would contemplate the condition of their posterity. The mere extent, population, and power of our country, its great States, its magnificent cities, its vast wealth, its commerce, its crops, its industry, its education, its freedom,

— no longer a slave upon its soil, — all, all of all races, equal before the law, — what else could they desire to fill up the measure of our development, or of their own delight! What more could they possibly wish to complete and crown the vision of glory vouchsafed to them?

Ah, my friends, have you forgotten, or can you imagine that they would forget for an instant, the cause in which they came here? Can you believe that they would be so dazzled and blinded by the glare of mere temporal success and material prosperity, or by the grandeur of intellectual triumphs and scientific discoveries and philosophical achievements, as to lose sight and thought of that which animated — and, I had almost said, constituted — their whole mortal existence? Can we not hear them inquiring eagerly and earnestly, as they gaze upon all around them, "Is the moral welfare of the country keeping pace with its material progress? Has religion maintained the place we assigned it, as the corner-stone of all your institutions? Is the Bible, the open Bible, which we brought over in our hands, still reverenced of you all as the Word of God? Is the Lord's Day still respected and observed as a day of religious rest, as we observed it on that desolate island before our feet had stept upon yonder consecrated rock? Are your houses of worship proportionate to your population? Are there worshippers enough, Sunday by Sunday, to fill the houses which you have? Are there no temples of false prophets — no organized communities of licentiousness, under the color of religion — in your land? Are there none among you who 'seek unto them that have familiar spirits and unto wizards that peep and that mutter, — for the living to the dead'? Are you doing your full part in carrying the Gospel to the heathen? Or are you waiting until the heathen shall have come over into your inheritance, bringing their idols with them, to cheapen labor and to dilute your own civilization and Christianity? Are your schools and colleges still dedicated, as we dedicated at least one of them, 'to Christ and the Church'? Is there no fear that your science has been emboldened by its triumphant successes to overleap the bounds of legitimate investigation, putting Nature to the rack to wring from her, if it were possible, some denial, or some doubt, of that great Original, whom she has always rejoiced, and still rejoices, to proclaim? Is there no fear that your philosophy has been tempted to transcend the just 'limits of religious thought,' and to set up some material theory, or some self-styled positive system, which may seduce the deluded soul from its hope of immortality, and weaken, if not destroy, its sense of the need of a Saviour? Is there no fear that a sentimental, sensational, licentious literature is corrupting the tastes and sapping the morals of your children, and rendering the universal appetite for reading an almost doubtful blessing? Are your charities, public and private, numerous and noble as they are, altogether commensurate with your wealth? Or is the larger half of your surplus incomes absorbed in a cankering and debasing luxury, destructive alike to the physical, intellectual, and spiritual energy of all who indulge in it? Are integrity and virtue enthroned in your hearts and homes? Have they a recognized and undisputed sovereignty in the market-place and on the exchange? Or are vice and crime making not a few days dark, and not a few nights hideous, in your crowded cities? Is there purity and principle and honor in your public servants? Or are corruption and intrigue and fraud threatening to make havoc of your free institutions, rendering all things venal, and almost all things, except mere party disloyalty, venial, in your State and National Capitals?"

Such questions as these, I am conscious, if coming from any living lips, or, certainly, from any living layman's lips, might be jeered at as savoring of sanctimoniousness and fanaticism. I do not presume to ask them for myself; much less would I presume to answer them. Make what allowance you please for the rigid austerity and excessive scrupulousness of those for whom I am only an interpreter. But does any one deny or doubt that they are the very questions which would be asked first and most eagerly and most emphatically, by those whom we this day commemorate, and by those who were associated with them in founding and building up New England?

Can we not hear them, at this moment, solemnly warning us, lest, in the pride of our prosperity and greatness, "when our silver and our gold is multiplied, and all that we have is multiplied," our hearts be lifted up to say, each for himself, "My power and the might of mine hand hath gotten me this wealth," while the great lesson of our stewardship, to Him to whom we owe it all, is forgotten or neglected?

Can we not hear them, at this moment, solemnly warning us, lest, in the pride of our freedom and independence, we forget that "the liberty we are to stand for, with the hazard not only of our goods, but of our lives if need be," is "a liberty for that only which is good, just, and honest," and not a liberty to be used as a cloak of maliciousness and licentiousness?

Can we not hear them, at this moment, from yonder hill of graves, solemnly and affectionately warning us lest, in the pride of our science, while a thousand telescopes and spectroscopes are ready to be levelled, on the morrow, at the orb of day, — to reveal its chromosphere and its photosphere, to measure its tornadoes, to detect the exact nature of its corona, and to mark the precise instants of its partial or total obscuration, — the Sun of Righteousness, all unobserved, be dimmed and darkened in our own hearts, and an Eclipse of Faith be suffered to steal and settle over our land, whose beginning may be imperceptible, and its end beyond calculation?

Oh, let us hear and heed these warnings of the Fathers to the children, as they come to us to-day, enforced not only by all the precious memories of their faith and piety, their virtues and sacrifices and sufferings, but by all the lessons and experiences of the times in which we live! We need not look beyond the events of the single year which is just closing, — this *Annus Mirabilis*, compared with which that of Dryden and Defoe was without significance or consequence; a year more marvellous in its manifestations than almost any which has preceded it since the great year of our Lord, and from whose calendar no form of physical, political, or religious convulsion seems to have been wanting to startle and confound the nations; a year, whose Christmas, alas! is clouded and saddened by the continuance, in a land bound to us by memories not yet obliterated, of a conflict and a carnage which must fill every Christian heart with horror, and for the termination of which we would devoutly invoke the only Intervention which has not been, and which cannot be, rejected; — we need not, I say, look beyond the events of this single jubilee year of the Landing, to find evidence of the vanity of all human ambition and the impotence of all human power, and to see renewed and startling proof that while

> "A thousand years scarce serve to form a State,
> An hour may lay it in the dust."

Let us not be deaf to the warnings of the Fathers. Let us not be insensible to the lessons of the hour. Let us resolve that no National growth or grandeur, no civil freedom or social prosperity or individual success, shall ever render us unmindful of those great principles of piety and virtue which the Pilgrims inculcated and exemplified. Let us resolve that whatever else this Nation shall be, or shall fail to be, it shall still and always be a Christian Nation, in the full comprehensiveness and true significance of that glorious term, — its example ever on the side of Peace and Justice; its eagle, not only with the shield of Union and Liberty emblazoned on its breast, but, like that of many a lectern of ancient cathedral or modern church, abroad or at home, ever proudly bearing up the open Bible on its outspread wings! And then, as year after year shall roll over our land, as jubilee shall succeed jubilee, and our children and our children's children shall gather on this consecrated spot to celebrate the event which has brought us here to-day, those grand closing words of Webster fifty years ago — the only words worthy to sum up the emotions of an hour like this, and send them down all sparkling and blazing to the remotest posterity, — shall be repeated and repeated by those who shall successively stand where he then stood, and where I stand now, not with any feeble expectation or faltering hope only, but with that firm persuasion, that undoubting confidence, that assured trust and faith, with which I adopt and utter them as the closing words of another Jubilee discourse: —

"Advance, then, ye future generations! We would hail you, as you rise in your long succession to fill the places which we now fill, and to taste the blessings of existence where we are passing, and soon shall have passed, our own human duration. We bid you welcome to this pleasant land of the Fathers. We bid you welcome to the healthful skies and the verdant fields of New England. We greet your accession to the great inheritance which we have enjoyed. We welcome you to the blessings of good government and religious liberty. We welcome you to the treasures of science and the delights of learning. We welcome you to the transcendent sweets of domestic life, to the happiness of kindred and parents and children. We welcome you to the immeasurable blessings of rational existence, THE IMMORTAL HOPE OF CHRISTIANITY, AND THE LIGHT OF EVERLASTING TRUTH!"

NOTE.

(Page 100.)

THE following inscription in the Hall of the Bishop of London's Palace, at Fulham, was copied for me most kindly by my venerable friend the late Bishop McILVAINE, of Ohio: —

"This Hall, with the adjoining quadrangle, was erected by Bishop Fitzjames in the reign of Henry VII. on the site of buildings of the old Palace as ancient as the Conquest. It was used as the Hall by Bishop Bonner and Bishop Ridley, during the struggles of the Reformation, and retained its original proportions till it was altered by Bishop Sherlock in the reign of George II. Bishop Howley, in the reign of George IV., changed it into a private unconsecrated Chapel. It is now restored to its original purpose on the erection by Bishop Tait of a new Chapel of more suitable dimensions.

"A. D. 1866."

The Palace must have been occupied by Richard Bancroft, during whose intolerant policy the Pilgrims fled to Holland; as he was Bishop of London some years before becoming Archbishop of Canterbury. It must, also, have been occupied by Laud, from whose intolerance the Puritans suffered; as he, after serving as Bishop of St. David's, and of Bath and Wells, was translated to London in 1628, and continued in that See, exercising great influence over the ecclesiastical affairs of the realm, until he succeeded the more liberal Abbot as Primate of all England.

REPLY TO A COMPLIMENTARY TOAST

AT THE PILGRIM JUBILEE BANQUET, PLYMOUTH, DECEMBER 21, 1870.

MR. PRESIDENT, LADIES AND GENTLEMEN, — I am sure the whole company will agree with me on one point, at least; and that is that my voice has already been sufficiently heard on this occasion. I propose, therefore, to make my acknowledgments to you all for this kind and friendly greeting, and for the compliment expressed in the sentiment just offered, in a very few words.

I hope I may be allowed to take that compliment as the welcome assurance that I have not altogether disappointed my audience in the effort I have made to-day. You know, Mr. President, that it was with no little distrust and hesitation that I accepted the flattering invitation of your Committee. I could not forget whom I was to follow. That man encounters no easy or enviable responsibility who attempts to glean a field over which have successively swept the broad scythe of Daniel Webster and the golden sickle of Edward Everett. I am conscious of having followed them *longo intervallo*, in more senses of the words than one. I might, indeed, claim to have been at least one day ahead of them both: since we of this generation have learned that we are not quite so far behind our Fathers as we thought we were, and that the 21st and not the 22d of December, which they celebrated, is the true date of the Pilgrim Landing. But I confess to being a full half-century behind at least one of them in every other respect.

I was hardly of an age to be here with Webster fifty years ago. At any rate, I was not here. But I well remember how the fame of that grand Oration shook every school-bench in New England, and how soon it supplied the choicest pieces of declamation for every school-boy. No similar effort of any one else, or even of his own, has ever awakened such echoes of enthusiastic admiration from that day to this.

Four years afterward I was here; and I shall not soon forget that long, wintry stage-coach drive of ten or twelve hours each way, in company, I am glad to remember, with one of your own townsmen, who has long since been at the head of our Boston Bar,[1] and in company too, I believe, — for certainly we were here together, and rambled together over yonder graves of the Pilgrims, after dinner, — with the excellent pastor of our Boston Brattle Street Church,[2] who has been at my side again to-day. But still less can I forget how abundantly and superabundantly we were all rewarded for the fatigues and exposures of our journey by the magnificent discourse of Edward Everett. He was then — in 1824 — in the very prime of life, just entering on that career of secular oratory in which he had no rival, and has left no peer. Often as I heard him afterwards, I look back to that effort as unsurpassed in brilliancy, even by himself.

May I be pardoned, however, for adding that it was not only the vivid remembrance of what others had done here so gloriously which made me shrink from undertaking the task you assigned me? May I be pardoned for confessing that I was a little afraid of my own shadow? I could not quite forget that in the city of New York, at the call of the New England Society there, I had gone over the same ground thirty-one years ago to-morrow. I was then but little more than half as old as I am now, and had all the energy and ambition of youth. It was my very first Occasional Address anywhere, I believe; and I had spared no pains in its preparation. It was two hours and ten minutes in delivery; and I remember that at the end of its delivery my cherished and lamented friend, the late Bishop Wainwright, who had sat near me, called my attention to the fact, of which I

[1] Hon. Sidney Bartlett, LL.D.

[2] The Rev. Samuel K. Lothrop, D.D.

had been entirely unconscious, that my manuscript had been upside down during the whole time! I should not dare to trust my memory with such a load in these later years of my life. And, indeed, I despaired of being able to compose another address on the same subject half as good as that was; and I am by no means sure that I have done so. If it had not been long ago printed,[1] I should have been tempted to repeat it, and not have adventured upon a second treatment of the same precise theme.

But while I was pondering upon these and other discouragements and difficulties, I suddenly bethought me of that old Massachusetts Colony, with which you have so kindly associated me. I bethought me what a comfort, what a delight, it must have been to them on their arrival at Salem, in the first desolation of their condition, not only to find Endicott and Higginson on the spot awaiting them, but to know that Bradford and Brewster and Winslow were already established here at Plymouth, ready and eager to exchange, as they did exchange, the right hand of fellowship with them, and to afford them all the succor in their power. I bethought me of that noble first Governor, — John Winthrop, — whose blood to-day seems coursing through my veins in a fuller tide than ever before, and whose image seemed to rebuke me for hesitating an instant to speak in his name, as well as in my own, in honor of the Pilgrim Fathers. He reminded me, among other things, of the powder which he had himself furnished them, in a time of their distress and danger, at his own cost, and how gratefully it was received and acknowledged by them.[2] And so, Mr. President, while I was musing, the fire burned, and I resolved to speak with my tongue, as I have spoken to-day. I resolved, in a word, that I would not decline to supply to the descendants of the Pilgrims, for their occasion and at their call, such ammunition as I could muster, even should it be at my own cost, and to my own discomfiture; — feeling sure that they would make all proper allowances for the fact that others had already appropriated the essential ingredient for such a composition, — had

[1] Winthrop's Addresses and Speeches, Vol. I. p. 1.

[2] Life and Letters of John Winthrop, Vol. II. p. 97.

already well-nigh exhausted that Attic salt which is as necessary for an oration as saltpetre is for gunpowder.

But I have occupied far more of the time of this occasion than belongs to me; and I must not delay you longer, while so many others remain to be called on. Let me only say that as the Pilgrims gave me the earliest inspiration in the way of occasional oratory, I shall be more than content if they shall have afforded me the last. If I have had any faculty in dealing with such occasions as this, — and I am sensible how small it is, — I am ready to say to-day at Plymouth Rock, "*Hic cestus artemque repono.*" I can certainly say that I shall be present in the body at no other Pilgrim Jubilee. Let me hasten, then, to thank you and your Society, and all who have so kindly listened to me, for the distinguished compliment which has been paid me; and let me propose as a sentiment, —

The Sons and Daughters of New England: Wherever they may be gathered, and wherever they may be scattered, here and in every clime, now and to the end of time: May they never forget the Rock, nor ever fail to be true to the memory and the example of those who landed upon it!

SEARS AND TICKNOR.

REMARKS AT A MEETING OF THE MASSACHUSETTS HISTORICAL SOCIETY, FEBRUARY 9, 1871.

ON a humble tablet in the graveyard beneath our windows, at the top of which is inscribed, "John Winthrop, Governor of Massachusetts, died 1649," may also be read the inscription, "Ann Winthrop Sears, the wife of David Sears, died October 2d, 1789, aged 33." This lady was a lineal descendant, in the fifth generation, of the old first Governor, and was an elder sister of the late Lieut. Governor Winthrop, a former President of this Society. She left at her death one child, a son, of about two years old, who bore the name of his father, and of whose death, on the 14th of January last, we are now called to make mention.

Born on the 8th of October, 1787, and deprived thus early of maternal care, he received the best school education which those days could afford; entered the University at Cambridge at sixteen years of age, and was graduated with the Class of 1807. The only son of a rich father was not likely to engage very earnestly either in business pursuits or professional studies; and, after a brief course of legal reading, Mr. Sears married a daughter of the late Hon. Jonathan Mason, and proceeded to make a tour in Europe. The sudden death of his father, — "an eminent merchant and excellent citizen," to whose enterprise and virtues a funeral tribute was paid by the Rev. Dr. Gardiner, then the beloved Rector of Trinity Church, — devolved upon him, in 1816, the care of as large an estate as, probably, had ever passed into the possession of a single hand in New England. And thus, before he was quite thirty years of age, Mr. Sears was called to assume that responsible position among the very richest men of our city, which he has continued to hold for more than half a century.

Building for himself a costly and elegant mansion, fit for the exercise of those generous hospitalities which belong to wealth, he began early, also, to make plans for doing his share in those acts of public and private beneficence, which are the best part of every rich man's life. As early as 1821, a donation was made by him to St. Paul's Church, in this city, with whose congregation he was then associated, which has resulted in their possession of a valuable library, a site for their lecture room, and a considerable fund for charitable purposes; and this was followed, in succeeding years, by various provisions for other religious, literary, or charitable objects, which, while accomplishing valuable purposes at once, may not exhibit their full fruit for a long time to come.

The Sears Tower of the Observatory at Cambridge, built at his cost, gave the first encouragement to an establishment which has since been munificently endowed by others, and to whose permanent funds he was also a handsome contributor.

A stately rural chapel on the crowning ridge of yonder village of Longwood, — after the design of the church of his paternal ancestors at Colchester in Old England, — for which he had carefully prepared a form of service in correspondence with the peculiar views of his later life, and beneath which he had caused vaults to be constructed for the last resting-places of himself and those most dear to him, will stand as a monument of his aspirations after Christian union.

A spacious block of houses not far from it, destined ultimately for the dwellings of such as have seen better days, and an accumulating fund, under the control of the Overseers of the Poor of Boston, which has already added not a little, year by year, to the comfort and support of a large number of poor women, — the two already involving an amount of hardly less than $90,000, — will bear testimony to his thoughtful and well-considered benevolence.

We may not forget that our own Society owes to him the foundation of our little Historical Trust Fund, which, it was his hope, might be built upon by others, until it should have put us in a condition of greater financial independence.

Mr. Sears had often enjoyed such public honors as he was willing to accept, and had served his fellow-citizens acceptably as a Senator in our State Legislature; as an Overseer of the University; and as a member of the Electoral College at the very last Presidential election. He had occasionally mingled in the public discussions of the day, and an elaborate Letter which he addressed to the late John Quincy Adams, on the best mode of abolishing Slavery, while that was still a living question, will be particularly remembered among his contributions to the press. Living to the advanced age of eighty-four, it was only during the last year that his familiar form has been missing from the daily walks of our citizens. He will long be remembered by all who have known him, as one of those courteous and dignified gentlemen of the old school, of whom so few are now left to remind us of the manners and bearing of other days.

When the owner of great pecuniary wealth passes away, his possessions, whether divided among heirs or bequeathed to the public, are not lost. But when one is taken from us, whose whole life has been spent in amassing the treasures of literature and learning, there is nothing to supply the void, save as some part of those treasures may have been "embalmed for a life beyond life" in the written or printed page. Such a loss our community and the literary world have sustained in the death of Mr. Ticknor.

He was born in Boston on the 1st of August, 1791, and would seem to have been dedicated to letters from his childhood. He was graduated at Dartmouth College in 1807, at an age when boys, in these days, have hardly finished their schooling. During the next seven or eight years he was pursuing studies of many sorts in his native place, and he even proceeded far enough in legal preparation to be admitted to the Suffolk bar. But the modern languages and literature were destined to supply the field of his triumphs; and in 1815 he embarked for Europe, and entered systematically on the labors which were to be the crown of his life. Two years at Göttingen, and shorter terms successively at Rome, Madrid, Paris, and Edinburgh, made up the five years of study, observation, and travel, from which he returned to assume the newly established Professorship of Modern Languages and Belles Lettres at Harvard University.

His lectures, during fifteen years in this chair, served, as was well said by Prescott, "to break down the barrier which had so long confined the student to a converse with antiquity;" and "opened to him a free range among those great masters of modern literature, who had hitherto been veiled in the obscurity of a foreign idiom." But while he was thus employing his acquisitions for the instruction and inspiration of his immediate hearers, Mr. Ticknor was making the best preparation for the great work by which he was to be known to posterity; and, on the resignation of his Professorship, he at once entered upon that work. "The History of Spanish Literature" was first published in 1849; and a third American edition, enlarged and corrected, received his last hand as late as 1863. His charming biography of Prescott, partly prompted by a vote of our own Society, soon followed. By the first of these works, Mr. Ticknor secured for his name a permanent place in the libraries and literature of the world; by the latter he most gracefully entwined his own memory, in the hearts of thousands at home and abroad, with that of one who will be remembered with affection as well as pride by all who knew him.

I need say nothing of the inestimable services rendered by Mr. Ticknor in the organization of our Boston Public Library, to which, it is understood, he has ultimately bequeathed his own large and precious collection of Spanish and Portuguese books.

I need say nothing of the great number of eminent persons whose acquaintance and friendship he had enjoyed abroad and at home; or of the charms of his conversation and correspondence, during these latter years, when the mellowing touch of time had reached him.

Nor will I venture to anticipate what will be so much better said by others in reference to his personal virtues, his private charities, and his Christian principles.

Dying, in the eightieth year of his age, on the early morning of the 26th of January, and buried without parade, agreeably to his own request, at noon of the 28th, it was not alone the few friends who were privileged to follow his hearse who felt deeply, at that hour, how much of acquisition and accomplishment, what a fund of anecdote and reminiscence, what stores of rare learning and of rich experience, were buried with him.

And thus, within a fortnight of each other, have passed from among us the honored heads of two of our most conspicuous houses: — one of them distinguished for pecuniary wealth, yet not without the added charm of high culture and refinement; the other pre-eminent for intellectual wealth and accomplishments, yet not without the independence of an ample fortune; both natives of Boston; both only sons of prosperous and public-spirited merchants; both Christian gentlemen; both associated with the establishment or advancement of more than one of our most important institutions; both more than common friends of some of our most lamented statesmen and scholars. There were no homes, certainly, in which Prescott, to name no one else, was a more frequent and endeared visitor — I had almost said, inmate — than the two which now together have been left desolate.

Our own Society has its full share in this double bereavement; and I am sure we shall all concur in the adoption of the Resolution, which our Standing Committee have authorized and instructed me to submit: —

Resolved, By the Massachusetts Historical Society, that by the recent deaths of the venerable DAVID SEARS, a former Vice-President of the Society, and of GEORGE TICKNOR, one of the most eminent of American scholars and authors, our roll has been deprived of names which will ever be held in honored and grateful remembrance.

PEABODY EDUCATION FUND.

ADDRESS AT ANNUAL MEETING, AT PHILADELPHIA, FEBRUARY 15, 1871.

GENTLEMEN OF THE BOARD OF TRUSTEES OF THE PEABODY EDUCATION FUND:

BY a vote of the Board previous to our adjournment at Washington on the 17th of February last, it was decided that, with a view of holding our Annual Meetings as near as might conveniently be to the birthday of our munificent friend, the Founder of this great Trust, — whom we desire ever to hold in grateful remembrance, — we would meet on the third Wednesday of February every year, except when otherwise ordered. It was also voted that the Annual Meeting for the present year be held in this city of Philadelphia.

You may remember, too, that a Resolution was adopted expressing the expediency of holding a Special Meeting of the Trustees at Memphis, Tennessee, during the fourth week of October last; and adding, according to the record, "that the same be notified by the Chairman or Secretary, unless otherwise determined in the mean time." The language of this Resolution, though somewhat equivocal, was well understood and explained by those who advocated and adopted it, as designed to leave a discretion to the Chairman, after due consultation, by correspondence or otherwise, with the members of the Board, — as the time should approach, — to notify the meeting, or to abandon it, as circumstances should dictate. Such consultation was held in the early part of the summer; and it was found that, owing to the absence of several of our number in Europe, and to the engagements or ill-health of others, — and owing, too, to the extreme heat of the season, and the anticipation of a more than usual prevalence of autumn fever in the South-western States, — there was a general disposition that the meeting should be abandoned. Indeed, there was more than a probability that, if it were notified, we should find ourselves at Memphis without a quorum for business. I could not hesitate, under such circumstances, to withhold the notifications.

I take pleasure in saying that the kindest communications were received from the municipal authorities and Board of Education of Memphis, tendering us the hospitalities of the city, to which, in your behalf, I returned a grateful acknowledgment.

We are assembled here, then, to-day, after an interval of a full year, to receive the Annual Report of our General Agent, to examine our Treasurer's accounts, to make the needful appropriations for the year to come, and to attend to such other business as may be submitted for our consideration. Before proceeding, however, to business of any kind, it is fit that I should announce to you two vacancies in our Board: one of them resulting from illness and absence from the country, and contingent upon your acceptance of the resignation which I shall presently read; the other, final, absolute, resulting from a well-remembered and deeply lamented death.

The following letter from Edward A. Bradford, Esq., of New Orleans, one of our original number, was received by me about the middle of last June. It is due to him that it should be entered in full upon our records, and I incorporate it into these introductory remarks with that view: —

VILLA DÉSIRÉE, PAU, May 28, 1870.

MY DEAR MR. WINTHROP, — I fear I owe an apology, not for the present communication, but for deferring it so long. I left New York in October last, under medical advice, to pass the winter in the south of France. I was encouraged to hope that I should be able to return in the spring in improved health. But the winter was exceptionally severe, and left me so much reduced, that the spring, instead of bringing a renewal of strength, has brought only greater weakness and exhaustion, so that I am almost forbidden to hope for any future improvement.

Under these circumstances, I feel it to be my duty, as one of the Trustees of the Peabody Education Fund, to place myself at your disposal. I have been prevented by various causes from taking that part in the administration of this important Trust, which I hoped to take in the future, and which seemed especially incumbent on those of the Trustees who belonged to that section of the country which the Trust was created to benefit. I know how difficult it is to administer even so considerable a fund, in such a manner as to work out any apparent or recognized results in so vast a field; and I was the more anxious, on that account, to take my share of the duty and of the responsibility. I have therefore deferred this communication as long as possible, and I send it with regret even now. But I will not allow myself to obstruct a cause that I cannot serve. I do not remember whether the number of Trustees is limited or not, but in any case it may be desirable that my place should be filled by one who has the power (as well as the will) to be actively useful. You may, therefore, if you please, receive this as my resignation, or I will send my resignation in any other form that you may suggest.

Allow me to add, that I earnestly hope you may be able so to administer this Trust as to make it productive of all the good results that Mr. Peabody intended from it. Its creation was well-timed, and was the expression of a patriotism so comprehensive, and a munificence so surpassing, as to overpower all prejudice and silence all cavil. It has already, I think, had a good effect; and I trust that, by its silent but constant operation, it may continue to exert an increasing and expanding influence, in reviving and restoring, through all sections of our common country, that fraternal feeling, which in the beginning made the Union possible, and which alone can finally preserve it, or make it worth preserving.

I am, with great respect and regard, yours truly,

E. A. Bradford.

I lost no time in replying to this letter; informing Mr. Bradford that the question would remain open until this Annual Meeting of the Board, and expressing an earnest hope that his health might, in the mean time, be sufficiently restored to warrant the withdrawal of his resignation. A private letter received from him, within a few months past, indicates no change in his decision; and it is for you, therefore, to act upon his resignation as you may see fit.[1]

The death of our honored and beloved associate, ADMIRAL FARRAGUT, occurred on the 14th of August last; and this Board was represented at his funeral in Portsmouth, a few days afterwards, by Governor Clifford and myself. Many more of us, including the President of the United States, were present at the grand obsequies attending his final interment, in New York, on the 29th of September.

It would be quite out of place, on this occasion, for me to dwell on the heroic acts which signalized the career of our lamented friend, and which had won for him, from so many sources, the title of "the Nelson of our Navy." As Trustees, we have only known him after all his conflicts were past, all his victories achieved; and while, on the restoration of union and peace, at which no one rejoiced more than himself, he was enjoying the honor and renown which ever await a gallant and successful discharge of duty. He was with us at the first organization of our work in the city of New York, four years ago, and entered heartily into the plans of our Board for executing the noble Trust with which Mr. Peabody had honored us. Absent from the country for a year, during that memorable cruise of the "Franklin," he did not forget in foreign lands, and while he was the almost daily recipient of the most flattering attentions from the highest functionaries of Europe, the cause in which we were engaged. I remember well the eagerness with which he examined the first Report of our General Agent when I communicated it to him in Rome, just before he was summoned to a private audience by the Pope; and how deeply interested he was in every evidence of our successful progress. He was with us on his return, and would not allow his enfeebled health to interfere with a punctual attendance at our meetings.

Nor was he willing to plead his growing infirmities as an exemption from the honorable service which was soon afterwards assigned him by the President of the United States, on the

[1] Mr. Bradford died soon afterwards.

death of Mr. Peabody. Many of us were witnesses to the zeal which he exhibited, and the exposures which he encountered, while in command of the fleet designated for the reception of the remains of our venerated Founder, when they arrived on our shores in her Britannic Majesty's ship "Monarch." As we saw him standing on the Portland pier on that wintry day, baring his head to the storm as those remains were landed, we had sad forebodings that we were witnessing what might prove to be his last official service. And so it was. Returning to his home in New York after the ceremonies at Portland were completed, he found himself sufficiently refreshed by a week's rest to proceed with us to Washington to attend our last Annual Meeting; but we left him there, on our adjournment, confined to his bed, and with little hope that he would ever be well enough to meet with us again. Early in the summer he sought refuge from the noise and heat of New York, whither he had returned in the spring, and passed a few weeks of comparative comfort and repose at the Portsmouth Navy Yard, where he died.

I need not say a word in regard to the exalted place which the grand old Admiral had attained in the estimation and admiration of his country. The tributes which have already been paid to his memory are enough to perpetuate his fame, and to leave no doubt as to the hold he had acquired on the hearts of his fellow-citizens. But you would hardly pardon me if I did not give expression to the feelings of respect and affection with which he was regarded by his associates in this Board, and to the deep sense of personal loss which we experience in meeting for the first time without him. There was an unspeakable charm in the directness and simplicity of his character. One might almost have applied to him the words of the great Dramatist, —

> "He was as true as truth's simplicity,
> And simpler than the infancy of truth."

We were, indeed, often in danger of forgetting the unsurpassed, and almost unmatched, daring and heroism of the sailor, in the mild, modest, affectionate intercourse of the companion and friend. The one idea of his life seemed to be the faithful discharge of duty, — duty to his country, duty to his fellow-men, duty to his God. Wherever duty called him, according to his own conscientious convictions, there he was to be found, firm and fearless. The consolations of religion were not wanting for his hours of danger and of decline. He knew where to find "his Pilot" for the dark flood which he has now crossed. It is our privilege to remember him, not only as a gallant officer and a cherished friend, but as a Christian hero.

BOSTON PROVIDENT ASSOCIATION.

REPORT READ AT THEIR ANNUAL MEETING, MAY, 1871.

THE Managers of the Boston Provident Association once more respectfully submit their Annual Report to the members of the Association and to their fellow-citizens at large.

Twenty years have now elapsed since this Association was originally organized. Seventeen years are completed since it became an incorporated institution.

As we look back over our operations during so considerable a period, we find abundant cause for gratitude to God for the success which has attended our efforts in behalf of the poor. We commenced them in a small hired office, and without a dollar in hand for paying our rent or our salaries. Convenient and ample apartments are now supplied us by the City; and our invested funds have been gradually increased by private liberality, until the income is sufficient to defray a large part, if not the whole, of our incidental expenses. And while not a few of those who were foremost in our service have passed away, without witnessing our full success, others have always been ready to take their places, and to carry on, with zeal and efficiency, the great work in which we are engaged.

That work was at the outset, and still is, of a two-fold character: — First, to relieve in all suitable ways, and to the extent of our means, the really deserving poor of the whole city, without distinction of age or sex, of creed or nationality; and, Second, to put a stop, as far as possible, to street-begging, and to the imposture which so generally attends it.

No one at all acquainted with the history of pauperism in Boston can hesitate to admit that much, very much, has been accomplished in this secondary work of our society. The number of beggars in our streets has been greatly diminished by the system which we originated, and which we have steadily pursued; and if that system has not in this respect been completely successful, the failure must be attributed not so much to any imperfection of its own as to the refusal of many well-meaning but inconsiderate persons to co-operate with us in effecting so important a result.

If every one to whom application for relief or assistance, either in the street or at the door, would resolutely insist that such application should be the subject of investigation or inquiry, by some agent or visitor of our own or of some other charitable association, the wants of the really destitute and deserving would be speedily relieved, while all encouragement to the systematic beggary and imposture, which are among the prevailing vices of large cities, would be done away. Money enough would, in this way, be saved or diverted from the idle and fraudulent to add two-fold, if not ten-fold, to the means for assisting the meritorious and industrious poor; and all who are actually in want would soon be made to comprehend that for them, as for all others, honesty is not merely the best, but the only, policy.

Now that, under the auspices and at the urgent instance of this Association, a Central Bureau of Charity has been established, where the offices of almost all the principal charitable agencies of our city are to be found, side by side, under a common roof; to which every applicant for aid of any sort, and under any circumstances, may be directed, and where the needy, the sick, the unemployed, and such as are in immediate want of a meal or a night's lodging, may find relief, — there is no longer any excuse for those who continue practically to encourage idleness and imposture, by yielding to the importunity of such as make it a business to beg from door to door.

If all our fellow-citizens would keep tickets to the Charity Bureau always at hand, and would give them to all applicants for aid; and if they would send the sums of money, large or small, which they are willing to bestow on such cases, to the treasury of this or of some other kindred society, their own benevolent impulses would be indulged, and the best interests of the honest and deserving poor would be efficiently subserved.

It is any thing but true charity to give money indiscriminately to the sturdy beggars on our thoroughfares, to be spent in drink or profligacy. Nor is it always safe or often wise to trust to the representations contained in what may seem to be well-authenticated papers, even with numerous respectable signatures attached to them. The impostures practised through the means of such papers, often heedlessly signed, have been greatly multiplied of late; and not a few of those who have given credence to them have learned too late that they had only ministered to vice and fraud.

In the first great object of our Association, — the relief of the really destitute or needy, without respect of persons, — we may claim to have accomplished all which the contributions of our fellow-citizens have enabled us to attempt. The measure of our relief has been, of course, and must always be, proportionate to the means put into our hands. Those means have been annually increasing, as the operations of our Association have been extended, and as the confidence of the community in our work has been developed.

Our total receipts during the first year of our corporate existence were less than $6,000, and were considerably less than our expenditures for that year. Our resources in 1869–70 were more than $16,000, — though they still were less than our expenditures, and we were thus compelled to make up the deficiency by selling a part of our invested property.

While, therefore, we gratefully acknowledge the growing favor of our fellow-citizens, we cannot fail to add that our treasury has never received the full supplies which it requires for our work, and to which we believe it to be justly entitled.

In examining the list of our receipts during the last two years, we find the whole number of those who have contributed any thing to our resources has been only about six hundred and fifty, and of these about one-half have given sums ranging only from one to five dollars per annum.

Our main supplies have thus come from hardly more than three hundred persons, and a very large proportion of those supplies from not more than one hundred persons.

That in a great city like Boston, with so many wealthy and liberal inhabitants, only three hundred persons should have contributed more than five dollars each to the treasury of the only Association for the poor which is co-extensive with the whole city, and which recognizes no distinction of age, sex, creed, color, or nationality, would have seemed in the highest degree improbable. That only six hundred and fifty persons should have contributed at all to such an Association, would have seemed absolutely incredible. But the figures on our books establish these facts, and we state them because we are persuaded that they can only have resulted from inadvertence or accident.

May we not hope and trust that benevolent men and women, into whose hands this Report may fall, will see to it that their proportionate aid is not wanting to such a work in future? May we not hope and trust that those, especially, — if any such there still are, — who are disposed to complain of the smallness of our allowances for the poor, will ask themselves whether they have done their full share in encouraging us to make those allowances larger, or have even united in enabling us to do as much as we have thus far done?

We are not ignorant or unmindful of the fact that serious misunderstandings, in regard to our proceedings and our policy, have served to prejudice the minds of some of our fellow-citizens, and to prevent their hearty co-operation in our course.

It has sometimes been alleged that not only were our allowances to poor families limited to a meagre sum, but that they were restricted to a single quarter of the year; in a word, that we doled out a uniform pittance to all alike during the three winter months, and that there was the end of our operations.

Such statements are wholly unfounded. Our work is carried on without intermission through the whole year; and our visitors are instructed to relieve real want and suffering whenever and wherever they find them, and to the full extent which the circumstances of each individual case may require.

As a matter of fact, our allowances to different families, in the way of fuel and groceries, during the last two or three years, have ranged from less than five dollars to more than thirty dollars each; while, in addition to these allowances, a large quantity of shoes and clothing has been annually distributed among those who stood in need of them.

If, in connection with this material aid, we take into account the moral support afforded to the honest and industrious poor by the assurance of our visitors that, under no circumstances, shall they be left uncared for, and that their real needs shall always be supplied, — it may well be doubted whether we could do more, without subjecting our Association to the charge of encouraging an exclusive reliance on charity, instead of that self-reliance and that self-respect, which are the best securities against chronic pauperism.

Our Association has, indeed, always encountered, and must always expect to encounter, the hostility of professional beggars, — whose very occupation it is to prey on the sympathies of the community, and who shrink from being detected and exposed in their vagabond life. All such persons will protest that the Provident Association will do nothing at all for them, and will either refuse our tickets altogether, or will tear them up on the doorsteps. Some of these latter will afterwards pretend that they presented the tickets to our visitors or at our office, and were refused relief.

If those who are inclined to give credence to such representations would kindly call at our office themselves, or would send a note of inquiry to our General Agent, they would be abundantly satisfied that, except in some case of accident, no worthy application for aid has ever failed of attention.

The full details of our operations during the past year, and of our existing financial condition, will be found in the Tables annexed to this Report, and in the Annual Report of our Treasurer which precedes them. We may safely leave them to speak for themselves. . . . .

And thus, with gratitude for the past and confidence for the future, we once more commend our work to the blessing of Heaven and the favor of our fellow-citizens.

SIR WALTER SCOTT.

ADDRESS AT A MEETING OF THE MASSACHUSETTS HISTORICAL SOCIETY ON THE ONE HUNDREDTH ANNIVERSARY OF HIS BIRTH-DAY, AUGUST 15, 1871.

You have not failed to remark, gentlemen, that the centennial anniversary of the birthday of Walter Scott, which occurs to-day, has been thought worthy of distinguished commemoration on both sides of the Atlantic; and some of you may have observed, in examining the roll of our Corresponding and Honorary Members, which has just been prefixed to the new volume of our printed Collections, that Sir Walter's name was added to that roll on the 3d of January, 1822.

I know not whether our corresponding secretary of that day — the Rev. Dr. Holmes — was as careful in filing his official papers as his successors have been in later years. But it would be most interesting to see the letter, if there was one, in which Scott acknowledged and accepted the election. We could hardly have a more precious autograph. One would like to know how far the great poet and novelist appreciated such a tribute from a land with whose political condition he had but little sympathy, and of whose literary advancement he could then have formed no very exalted estimate. We should certainly be curious to hear, if it were still possible, precisely what was said at Abbotsford when our certificate of membership reached there, so long ago; and to learn whether it were thrown aside with indifference as of little account, or carefully treasured up among the welcome muniments of a world-wide fame. It must have borne the attest of a Lowell as well as of a Holmes;

but another generation was to pass away, and Scott himself to pass away with it, before either of those names, venerable as they both were at home, was to be associated with such distinction, in song or in story, as in our own day has given them a significance and a known value in lands beyond the sea.

Some of our young Americans of the highest promise, and who have long since fulfilled that promise and gone to their rest, had, however, already enjoyed the personal acquaintance of " the mighty minstrel of the North," as he was then called, and had given him some impression of American culture and American character. As early as 1817 Washington Irving had spent several delightful days with him; had sauntered with him up the haunted glen of old Thomas the Rhymer; had nestled under his plaid as a shelter from the rain, and had gathered in that rich store of reminiscences which lends such a charm to the sketch of Abbotsford in the "Crayon Miscellany."

Indeed, Irving had evidently found his way to Scott's heart, by his exquisite humor, as early as 1813; before even "Waverley" had witched the world, and while Sir Walter was only famous as a poet. The *fac-simile* of a letter is on our own files, which is full of interest in its relations both to its writer and its subject, and which I cannot forbear from reading in this connection. It is addressed to the late Henry Brevoort of New York, the intimate friend of Irving, who had sent a copy of "Knickerbocker" to Scott, who replied as follows: —

My dear Sir, — I beg you to accept my best thanks for the uncommon degree of entertainment which I have received from the most excellently jocose history of New York. I am sensible that, as a stranger to American parties and politics, I must lose much of the concealed satire of the piece; but I must own that, looking at the simple and obvious meaning only, I have never read any thing so closely resembling the style of Dean Swift as the Annals of Diedrich Knickerbocker. I have been employed these few evenings in reading them aloud to Mrs. S. and two ladies who are our guests, and our sides have been absolutely sore with laughing. I think too there are passages which indicate that the author possesses powers of a different kind, and has some touches which remind me much of Sterne. I beg you will have the kindness to let me know when Mr. Irving takes pen in hand again, for assuredly I shall expect a very great treat, which I may chance never to hear of but through your kindness.

Believe me, dear sir,

Your obliged humble serv't,

WALTER SCOTT.

No American author, certainly, has ever won a more enviable compliment than the one contained in this letter, dated "Abbotsford, 23 April, 1813," and postmarked "Melrose." What a picture for Sunnyside might have been made out of the scene which it describes, by Leslie, or Wilkie, or Stuart Newton! — Scott, surrounded by his wife and guests, reading Irving aloud night after night, comparing his style alternately with those of Swift and of Sterne, laughing over his humor till his sides were sore, and looking eagerly forward to more works from the same hand, as a treat of which he was loath to be deprived!

But Irving was not the only eminent American who had become known to Sir Walter before 1822. Our lamented associates, Edward Everett in 1818, and George Ticknor in 1819, had been partakers of his hospitality both in Edinburgh and at Abbotsford; and they have both contributed to Dr. Allibone's "Dictionary of Authors" most interesting accounts of their respective visits. It was perhaps at their suggestion that Scott's name was placed on our honorary roll.

But, however that may have been, we shall all agree that no worthier or nobler name has ever adorned it. In 1822, Scott was in the full enjoyment of his fame. No cloud had yet overshadowed his faculties or his fortunes. "Kenilworth" and the "Pirate" had just succeeded to "Ivanhoe," the "Monastery," and the "Abbot," in that marvellous series of historical romances which so absorbed and electrified the reading world for nearly twenty years. It may well be doubted whether so prolific and so magnetic a brain had existed since that of Shakspeare; or one which poured forth purer, richer, or more varied streams of entertainment and instruction for the delight and wonder of mankind.

It is possible that, in his modest estimate of his own powers, and in his ever-generous appreciation of the productions of others, he himself, had he lived till now, would have said of

Dickens, or of Thackeray, in connection with his own novels, what he did say of Byron in regard to his own poems: "He beat me out of the field in the description of the strong passions, and in deep-seated knowledge of the human heart; and so I gave up poetry for the time." Indeed, he actually expressed something of the same sort in his diary, on the death of Jane Austen, when he observed that "Edgeworth, Ferrier, and Austen had all given portraits of real society far superior to any thing vain man had produced of a like nature;" adding, in his most characteristic vein, this special tribute to Miss Austen: "That young lady had a talent for describing the involvements, feelings, and characters of ordinary life, which is to me the most wonderful I have ever met with. The big bow-wow I can do myself like any one going; but the exquisite touch which renders commonplace things and characters interesting, from the truth of the description and the sentiment, is denied to me."

How much stronger he would have made this admission, had he lived to read "David Copperfield" or "The Newcomes"!

We are hardly disposed to allow that any faculty was, as he says, "denied to him;" but it is certain that he seldom or never attempted to deal with the incidents of the "ordinary life," or the characters of the "real society," around him. His genius found a different sphere for its display. He was eminently an antiquarian; almost an archæologist; with a profound reverence for the past; with an intense relish for historical research; and with an attachment as patriotic and as passionate as that of Burns to the local traditions, the local tales and ballads, the local superstitions and scenery of his native land. These furnished the staple of his poetry and prose alike, and supplied both warp and woof for his magic embroidery. He sacrificed little to what in these days would be called the sentimental or the sensational. He certainly never pandered to licentiousness, sensuality, or scepticism. It was no flattery, when a venerable bishop of the church he loved told him at a banquet, — of which he divided the honors with the Duke of Wellington, — that "he could reflect upon the labors of a long literary life, with the consciousness that every thing he had written tended to the practice of virtue, and to the improvement of the human race." It was no self-delusion, when, at the very close of that life, he said of himself: "I have been perhaps the most voluminous author of the day; and it is a comfort to me to think that I have tried to unsettle no man's faith, to corrupt no man's principle." Let us all thank God for that record, and still more for the fact which it so justly embodies.

It were doing but half justice to the memory of Sir Walter, more particularly in connection with his membership of a Society like this, if allusion were made only to his poems and novels. We cannot forget how much both biography and history were indebted to him for those three quarto volumes of the Sadler State Papers, in 1809; for those thirteen ponderous tomes of Somers' Tracts, in 1812; for his "Border Antiquities of England and Scotland;" for those grand editions of Dryden and Swift; for those charming Lives and Memoirs of the British Novelists; for that elaborate and masterly treatment of a great period of French history in the Life of the First Napoleon; for those delightful sketches of French, and more especially of Scotch, history in the "Tales of a Grandfather;" and for that continuous stream of brilliant criticism which he contributed to the periodical reviews of his day.

Nor must we forget that all this gigantic literary labor was performed in the intervals of an exacting professional career, and of a social life full of obligations and distractions; performed so quietly and almost invisibly that hardly any one, save an occasional copyist or a publisher, knew what he was doing, or when he had time for doing any thing. And yet it was no exaggeration in Irving to say of him, that "his works have incorporated themselves with the thoughts and concerns of the whole civilized world, and have had a controlling influence over the age in which he lived." Nor can I help thinking that if Dickens and Thackeray could have lived — as we all might have hoped that they would live — to take the lead in this centennial commemoration of their illustrious exemplar, and had been called on, as experts, to say what were the two names which, upon the whole, had exercised the greatest and best, the most pervading and most permanent, influence upon English literature, down even to the day of their own lamented deaths, — they would have agreed in suggesting that the same initial letters would indicate them both; and would have concurred in assigning to Walter Scott, in that line of literature to which both belong, the place most nearly approaching — at however wide an interval — to William Shakspeare. For no one else, I think, — unless perchance for one of themselves, — would such an approximation be claimed; but it will be for posterity, when their centennials shall come round, and when contemporary opinions shall have been set aside or confirmed by maturer judgments, to pronounce upon their titles to pre-eminence. "*Commenta opinionum delet dies; naturæ* (or, as we may imagine Cicero saying in such a connection as this, *humani generis orbisque totius*) *judicia confirmat.*"

I may not conclude, gentlemen, without reminding you that by the favor of our ever-honored benefactor, the late Mr. Dowse, who had a most enthusiastic admiration for Scott, his noble library came to us accompanied by one of Chantrey's original marble busts of Sir Walter, which we can hardly prize too highly. Lockhart, in his admirable biography, tells us that "it was during his visit to London, in 1820, that Scott sat to Chantrey for the bust which alone preserves for posterity the cast of expression most fondly remembered by all who ever mingled in his domestic life." The final touches to the first marble copy were given during the following year, when Sir Walter had come to London to attend the coronation of George IV., and that original marble is now at Abbotsford. But the one which we possess, and which is the mute but well-nigh conscious witness of our homage to-day, is hardly less precious.

We have, too, before us — kindly contributed by their owners to lend additional interest to this occasion — the beautiful portrait of Scott painted by Leslie for our lamented associate, Mr. Ticknor, and another excellent head painted by Stuart Newton for the late Mr. Samuel Williams.

I leave it to others to call your attention more particularly to these interesting pictures, and I hasten to make way for them by offering, with the sanction of the Standing Committee of the Society, the following resolutions: —

Resolved, By the Massachusetts Historical Society, that, in view of the centennial celebration of the birthday of Walter Scott, on this 15th of August, 1871, we cannot forget that our predecessors, almost fifty years since, adorned our honorary roll with his name, and thus transmitted to us a peculiar privilege, if not a peculiar obligation, to unite in doing homage to his memory.

Resolved, That we look back with admiration and amazement upon a literary career so crowded with brave effort, and so crowned with brilliant achievement; which has left such enduring and ennobling influences on the literature of the world, and has supplied such pure and inexhaustible streams of entertainment and instruction for all generations.

Resolved, That our warmest sympathies are with all at Abbotsford, or elsewhere, who are engaged in this just tribute to the genius of one whose power over the human heart no distance of time or place can extinguish; and whose memory is cherished on every hill-side and in every valley of New England, as gratefully as by those who are privileged to tread his native heather.

BANQUET TO THE GRAND DUKE ALEXIS.

SPEECH FROM THE CHAIR, DECEMBER 10, 1871.

I AM deeply sensible, gentlemen, how high a distinction has been assigned to me this evening. I owe, at the outset, the most grateful acknowledgments to my friends and fellow-citizens here present, for counting me worthy to be their organ in welcoming to our banquet, to Boston, and to New England, the illustrious young stranger in whose honor we are assembled. There are, I am conscious, many, many others around me better fitted for such a service; far better fitted, I do not say by their age, but by their accomplishments and by their youth, — if His Imperial Highness, fresh from the classics, will pardon the familiarity of the allusion, — for playing Corydon to such an Alexis. But you have called me to the chair, gentlemen, and let me hasten to proceed with the discharge of its duties.

Our honored guest comes to us from a far distant land, which but few of us have had the good fortune to visit. But I hazard nothing in saying that all Americans who of late years have enjoyed that privilege, — and I have more than one of them in my eye at this moment, — have returned home not only full of gratitude for the kindness with which they were received, but full of admiration for the great works of internal communication and improvement, for the noble monuments and museums of art, for the grand academies of science and learning, and for all the accumulated evidences of progressive civilization, of social refinement, and of Christian culture, which they have witnessed there.

I shall not soon forget the enthusiasm — I had almost said the rapture — of my lamented friend, the heroic Farragut, when I met him on board the "Franklin" at Nice three or four years ago, as he recounted all that he had witnessed, and all that he had enjoyed, during that remarkable visit to Russia from which he had just returned. His portrait, by your favor, sir, is to find a place in the imperial palace at St. Petersburg. I think no small part of his heart had been left there long ago. Certainly, if that portrait could speak, if those lips had language, no other voice would be needed to express the admiration and gratitude which recent American visitors to Russia have so uniformly brought back with them.

Our honored guest comes to us from a region of rigorous and relentless cold, the mere mention of whose protracted and terrible winters is almost enough to freeze our blood; a land of whose brave and enduring soldiery our own Boston-born Franklin once said that they were habituated to march cheerfully up to their chins in snow, and then intrench themselves contentedly and comfortably in ice! It was the same Franklin, sir, whose heroic experiment with the kite, in drawing down a thunderbolt from the skies, was rendered but too memorable in St. Petersburg very soon afterwards, by costing the life of an enthusiastic young Russian philosopher who had ventured to repeat it. We have not forgotten, too, that a spacious palace of ice was among the playthings of a Russian Empress. It may be seen, indeed, to this very day, undissolved, defying the sunbeams, gorgeous and glittering still, in the crystal verses of a charming English poet.[1]

But who are we, my friends, that we should speak irreverently of a Russian winter? What have we had to boast of, in the way of milder or more genial temperature, since the Grand Duke's arrival? Surely, surely, if the noble frigate "Svetland" and its gallant consorts did not contrive, in some mysterious way, to bring over a huge cut, a monstrous cantle, of their own congealed climate with them, as we shrewdly suspect; or if the

[1] Cowper's "Task," Book V.

cold and the frosts and the icy winds of his native land did not harness themselves to his ocean car, like the Nereids of the old mythology, in token of their love and loyalty to a Prince of the blood; — if one of these be not the true solution of this exceptional season, then at least it must be admitted that our own American climate has made haste to put on an unaccustomed livery, and gone forth to meet him more than half way. The very elements seem to have bestirred themselves in sympathy with our earnest desires to make your Imperial Highness feel perfectly at home on American soil.

Once more, and more seriously, my friends, our illustrious guest has come to us from a country with whose forms and modes and shows of government our own cherished Republican system is in the widest and most glaring contrast. But shows are sometimes shams, and forms not always substance. It is enough for us to remember to-night, certainly, that, republicans though we are, the imperial rulers of Russia, from the earliest period of our national history, have been our most steadfast and unwavering friends. We rejoice to remember that over the relations of Russia and the United States not a cloud has ever gathered. We rejoice to remember that in all our struggles, remote and recent, abroad or at home, we have enjoyed the frank and avowed good-will of the Czar.

As long ago as 1781, during our first great struggle for national existence, the friendly mediation of the Empress Catherine, in company with the Emperor of Austria, was tendered in the cause of peace. Nor can I omit to allude to the interest which that great Empress soon afterwards manifested in procuring, though the Marquis de Lafayette, from our own Washington, — I have no title or epithet, sir, worthy to be coupled with that transcendent name, — in procuring, I say, from George Washington, a vocabulary of our Indian Tribes, with a primary view to her favorite idea of a universal dictionary; but not without a secondary reference to obtaining proof of some early and remote connection and communication between the northern parts of America and Asia, — between your aboriginal tribes and our own. She would gladly, I doubt not, have made us all out first cousins, at the farthest; and Washington was nothing loath to help her in doing so. I know not whether that vocabulary is still extant in the imperial archives at Moscow or St. Petersburg. If it be, we might well invoke your gracious intervention to secure a copy for our own philologists and antiquarians. But it was certainly procured and transmitted in 1788; and the language of Washington in transmitting it is too remarkable and too grand to be lost to such an occasion and such a presence as this: —

"I heartily wish," wrote Washington to Lafayette, "that the attempt of that singularly great character, the Empress of Russia, to form a universal dictionary may be attended with merited success. To know the affinity of tongues seems to be one step towards promoting the affinity of nations. Would to God the harmony of nations were an object that lay nearest to the hearts of sovereigns; and that the incentives to peace, of which commerce and facility of understanding each other are not the most inconsiderable, might be daily increased! Should the present or any other efforts of mine to procure information respecting the different dialects of the aborigines in America, serve to reflect a ray of light on the obscure subject of language in general, I shall be highly gratified. For I love" — said he, — "to indulge the contemplation of human nature in a progressive state of improvement and amelioration; and, if the idea would not be considered visionary and chimerical, I could fondly hope that the present plan of the great Potentate of the North might in some measure lay the foundation for that assimilation of manners and interests which should one day remove many of the causes of hostility from amongst mankind."

Noble sentiments from a noble soul, — worthy of being written in letters of gold on tablets of imperishable platinum from the mines of your own Ural Mountains, where all the world, and all the sovereigns of the world, might read them! But we need not go back to the days of Washington and the Empress Catherine for illustrations or evidences of the friendship and goodwill of Russia. We do not forget that, during our war of 1812, the mediation of the Czar was again proffered in our behalf; and that, though it was not accepted by Great Britain, it led to a direct negotiation between the two parties to the war, which terminated in the Treaty of Ghent. Nor can any of us require to be reminded of the warm and generous and welcome words of suggestion and sympathy which came to us from the present Emperor through Prince Gortschakoff, at a most critical period of our late struggle for the preservation of the American Union.

Most eagerly, therefore, and most gladly, have we availed ourselves of this first visit to our shores of a member of the imperial family of a country with which we have always been at perfect peace, and always on terms of cordial friendship, to manifest to him and to all the world our profound sense of the value of that friendship and that peace, and our earnest hope and trust that in the good providence of God they may be unbroken and undisturbed for ever. We seek, I need not say, we seek no entangling alliances against or in favor of any other nation. We do not forget the farewell warnings of the Father of his Country against passionate attachments or inveterate aversions. We cannot fail to remember that France was our earliest ally, and that we were most deeply indebted to her sympathy and succor in our struggle for Independence. Nor are we here to renounce or disregard our filial ties to Old England. We would not, if we could, conceal the heartfelt sympathy we all feel with the good Queen at this moment, in the overwhelming anxiety and agony which has so suddenly come upon her in beholding the young Prince, whose presence here eleven years ago was as graceful as it was welcome, on the verge of being swept away for ever from the reach of that sceptre which, to all human eyes, he was destined so soon to grasp and wield.[1]

We rejoice more than ever that a Treaty of Arbitration has already been negotiated and ratified, by which all questions between England and the United States are to be amicably arranged and finally settled. But with Russia we have had no questions to settle; no disputed boundaries; no sailors' rights or fishermen's wrongs; no premature recognitions; no violated neutrality. There may have been passages in her long-past history which we

[1] A telegram announcing the death of the Prince of Wales, of the fever from which he so happily recovered, had just been received.

deplore. There may be foreshadowings, false or true, of a future policy which we deprecate. Of what other nation may we not say the same? Might we not, must we not, confess as much even of our own? But the uniform fairness and constant friendliness which have characterized the course of Russia towards our beloved country in all our varying fortunes, prosperous and adverse, have made no light or transitory impression on the great American heart; and it would be strange, indeed, if we did not recall and adopt the memorable precept of the matchless poet: —

> "The friends thou hast, and their adoption tried,
> Grapple them to thy soul with hooks of steel."

Russia and the United States, ever at peace with each other, and with a cordial understanding that this peace is precious to them both and shall never be lightly put at peril, may furnish, at least, the first strong link in that golden chain of goodwill and concord which, we pray God, may at last encircle the earth, and bind together all the nations that dwell upon its surface!

His Imperial Highness, let me say once more, has come to us in the freshness of his early manhood to observe the condition of our country, to study the character of our institutions and of our people, and to witness for himself the workings of our great experiment of free government. But let me not call it an experiment. It is an experiment no longer. It has been tried for nearly a century, — tried successfully, tried triumphantly, and never found wanting. It will be the fault of ourselves and not of our institutions; it will be the insufficiency of our engineers, and not of the machinery, — if there shall be any failure hereafter.

Did I say that it had been tried for nearly a century only? Two centuries and a half are more than completed since the first written compact of self-government was signed in the cabin of the "Mayflower." Two hundred and forty years have elapsed since Massachusetts was planted and Boston founded. And it is a very striking fact for our remembrance on this occasion, that these events of our earliest New England history were so nearly coincident with the first accession to the throne, in the person of the Emperor Michael, of that Romanoff dynasty by which Russia has been advanced to all her existing importance and grandeur. When Michael assumed the imperial sceptre in 1613, the Virginia Colony had just established itself at Jamestown, and the Pilgrim Fathers had already fled to Holland on their way to Plymouth Rock. While we were still in our colonial infancy, Michael was succeeded by his young son Alexis, the first, and thus far the only, Emperor of that name, whose reign of more than thirty years was signalized by the most important improvements in the condition of his people, — by a Digest or Code Imperial which was long recognized as the common law of the realm; and by a wise and loving rule which won for him at his death the pre-eminent title of the "Father of his Country." But he was not only the father of his country; he was the father of a son, Peter the Great, whose romantic and marvellous career is familiar to every schoolboy in Christendom, and whose reign resulted in making Russia known and recognized for the first time throughout the world as one of the greatest powers of the earth.

Russia had, indeed, an earlier history. There are dim records and traditions of her existence — and, thank God, of her Christian existence — not far from the time when that Scandinavian Erik is said to have discovered our own land. And old Marco Polo, the Venetian voyager, speaks of her a few centuries afterwards in a single sentence, I believe, as a province of Northern Asia bordering on the region of darkness! But the real history of Russia begins with that Romanoff Dynasty, whose accession was so closely coincident with the very beginnings of American colonization and settlement. Russia and the United States may thus be almost said to have begun the march of empire together. We may almost be said to have entered simultaneously on those grand careers, eastern and western, along which both have gradually advanced, with varying fortunes, under circumstances as widely different as the skies above us, with very unequal steps, but with no steps backward, until we stand face to face this day, and recognize each other, and are recognized by all mankind, as two of the greatest nations on the globe.

One word more before I close. There is another coincidence,

and a still more striking and impressive one, in our most recent history. It is now hardly more than ten or eleven years since there was common to large masses of the population of both nations a deplorable condition of serfdom or slavery. We thank our God this night, in presence of each other, that from both lands that dark spot has disappeared for ever. In our own case, indeed, its disappearance could only be effected by our martyr President, as he himself saw and said, as the result of the contingencies and necessities of a protracted civil war. But it is the proud distinction of the Emperor, — your honored father, sir, — that he accomplished that great deliverance of his own free and sovereign will and pleasure. By his autocratic word, as was so well said by our lamented Everett in this very hall, at the banquet given to Admiral Lessoffsky and the officers of the Russian fleet, in 1864, — by his autocratic word, he performed the most magnificent act of practical philanthropy ever achieved by man or government. That act of emancipation has clothed him with a glory brighter than his crown, and would almost reconcile us, republicans as we are, to the theory of divine right by which his crown is worn; for earthly power, when exercised for such an end, "doth then show likest God's." The man of whom it shall be recorded, of whom it is already irrevocably recorded, that, by the willing word of his mouth, and by the eager stroke of his pen, he gave freedom to more than twenty millions of his fellow-beings, needs no other record to secure for him the heartfelt homage of all mankind, generaation after generation, to the end of time.

I pause here for a moment, gentlemen, before proceeding to the toast of the occasion, to invite you all to rise with me while I propose to you —

The health of His Imperial Majesty, the Emperor of Russia!

The entire company here rose, and with great enthusiasm answered the toast. Then, as Mr. Winthrop paused, before continuing, His Imperial Highness rose and said: —

"I propose the health of the President, Grant. Hurrah!" and the Duke gave a handsome cheer. The company rose again, and responded, seeming to catch invigoration from the tone of the young Prince's voice. The band then played the "Star Spangled Banner" for one or two minutes.

Mr. Winthrop continued as follows: —

And now, may it please your Imperial Highness, it only remains for me, in the name and behalf of this assembled company of my fellow-citizens, — among whom are so many of the representative men of our community from all the varied walks of labor and of life, official, legal, literary, scientific, commercial, philanthropic, and religious, — in behalf of them all and of all whom they represent, to offer you our warmest wishes for your personal welfare and happiness. Your brief visit to our country is already approaching a close. We know not what future may await you. We know not to what height of influence or authority in your own realm you may be destined to attain; but we would heartily trust that, in whatever circumstances you may be placed, your reception in America, in this early bloom of your manhood, may be among the cherished remembrances of a long and prosperous life. Be assured, sir, that we shall follow you with sincere and earnest hopes that you may return in safety to your native land, and that the best blessings of our common Father and Saviour may never be wanting to you.

I call upon you again, gentlemen, to rise with me and pay all the honors of the occasion in drinking —

The health of His Imperial Highness, the Grand Duke Alexis!

DINNER OF THE ALUMNI OF HARVARD.

REPLY TO A TOAST FROM HON. WILLIAM GRAY, PRESIDENT OF THE ASSOCIATION, JUNE 26, 1872.

I THANK you most heartily, Mr. President, for any part of the compliment just paid, — and I am sensible how small a part it is, — which I am at liberty to appropriate to myself. I am most happy to find myself once more at the table of the Alumni. I find it difficult to credit the idea that fourteen or fifteen years have elapsed since I was present at one of these College festivals. And yet, sir, as I cast my eyes around this board, there is enough, and more than enough, to remind me that it is true. It was my distinguished privilege, when I was last here, in 1857, to occupy the place which you now so acceptably fill, as President of the Association and "Rex Convivii." But I look in vain for those who were on my right hand, or on my left hand, on that occasion. Edward Everett, the orator of that festival, and of every festival which he attended; the elder Quincy, ever honored in the memory of the Sons of Harvard, not only as having written its earlier history, but as having contributed so large a share to the glories of its later history; Lemuel Shaw, the grand old Chief Justice of Massachusetts; the learned and accomplished Sparks; the genial and beloved Felton, — they were all here at my side, and all responded to my call. But their voices have long been hushed to all human hearing, and, I need not say, they have hardly left their peers in the places which now know them no more.

But I have not come back to-day to indulge in sad reminiscences of the past; nor can I pause to hail and welcome the glorious realities of the present. A glorious present, certainly, is ours. Never, in all its long history, were there more gratifying and more inspiring evidences of the prosperity of Harvard than those which greet us on every side at this hour. Never was there a moment when her sons had more cause for gratitude to God and man, for all that has been done, and for all that is in process of being done, for the honor and welfare of our beloved Alma Mater. Why, sir, if we were to keep silent, if we were to lift no glad and grateful voices, the very stones would cry out against us, — the stones of these numerous and noble buildings which are rising so rapidly around us, each one of them bearing the name of some new benefactor! Old things are, indeed, passing away; all things are becoming new. As I entered the College yard an hour or two ago, and looked around on these costly edifices, I could not help feeling that if my good friend, Samuel Atkins Eliot, — the father of our young and vigorous President, — could have been permitted to live long enough to witness the present palmy state of the University which he loved so well, he would not only have been amply repaid for all the cares and labors he underwent in its behalf, as its Treasurer, in the day of its small things, but that he would fully comprehend and realize that his great work for Harvard — his best work after all — was in training up so devoted and excellent a son to her love and service.

The name of ELIOT, Mr. President, in three generations, as Benefactor, as Treasurer, and as President, has now become indissolubly identified with the best interests and highest honor of the University. *Uno avulso, non deficit alter aureus.* Long, long may it be before any other name shall replace that name at the head of our Academic Roll! States and nations may change, or may try to change, their chief magistrates as often as they will, at their own humor or caprice, for good reasons or for bad reasons, or for no reasons at all. But no brief administrations, no shallow system of rotation, no meagre one-term principle, can ever be adapted to the permanent welfare of a great literary republic. The tenure of the presidents of colleges, and more especially of our own College, like that of the judges of our courts, should be a tenure '*Dum bene gesserint,*' — a tenure of good behaviour, which is sure to be all one with a tenure for life.

But I am not here, Mr. President, to indulge in any general remarks. You have called upon me, not so much as one of the Alumni of Harvard, as in my relation to the Peabody Board of Southern Education, which, happening to hold its annual meeting in Boston during the present week, has been favored by an invitation to this festival. In their behalf, as their Chairman, I offer to you, and the Association, the most grateful acknowledgment of the invitation. Sir, we have abundant cause for honoring the memory of George Peabody at this table, for what he did directly and specifically for our own University. Our Museum of American Archæology and Ethnology — the very first of the kind in our whole country — which he founded and endowed, is destined, if I mistake not, under the immediate charge of my eminent and accomplished friend, Professor Jeffries Wyman, — over whose labors I am privileged to watch, and to whose unwearied fidelity I can bear witness, — to make no common or second mark among the scientific institutions of our land. Its pre-historic collections, as I have the best means of knowing, are already surpassed, in interest and value, by those of no American museum, and of but few similar institutions in any part of the world. It was coldly recognized in some quarters, when Mr. Peabody first allowed me to divulge his purpose to establish and endow it. But it has justified itself even to those who held it in the most doubtful esteem, giving a new field for the genius of our modest but admirable Curator, and adding a new fame to the memory of its munificent founder.

But Mr. Peabody did nobler and grander things than this, — not, indeed, for any individual institution, nor for any single section of our country, but for our whole glorious Union, — when he appropriated more than two millions of dollars from his fortune, for the establishment and encouragement of free common schools in those parts of our land which had never before enjoyed them. I do not undervalue museums of science or art. Still less am I insensible to the importance of collegiate education, here and everywhere. But before them all, and above them all, our great Republican system imperatively demands universal education, common-school education, — schools free to all, without money and without price. There is no enduring system of construction or of *reconstruction*, North or South, East or West, for a free country like ours, without a broad, deep, all-sustaining foundation of common schools.

The Board to which Mr. Peabody entrusted his munificent endowment for supplying this great want, this great necessity, at the South, at a moment when the South was in no condition to supply it for itself, — a Board over which I count it the highest honor of my life to have been selected by him to preside, — is represented at this table, not only by the President of the United States, who most kindly gave up the first hours of his vacation to come on and help us to a quorum ; and by my friend, the Secretary of State, Governor Fish, whom we are to hail at no distant day, I trust and believe, as "the Pilot who has weathered the storm," the long, pelting, pitiless storm of "Alabama" contentions and claims, direct and indirect, — but it is represented here, also, by several distinguished gentlemen of the Southern States, whom you all are eager to see and to hear. I need but to name them to elicit the most cordial manifestations of welcome. Here, at my side, are ex-Governor Aiken, of South Carolina ; ex-Governor Graham, of North Carolina ; Alexander H. H. Stuart, of Virginia, a former Secretary of the Interior ; and Richard Taylor, a son of that sturdy and noble-hearted patriot and hero, whom some of us once delighted to call familiarly "Old Zach," but whose premature death, while President of the United States, filled the whole nation with grief, and left us no heart to speak of him except as the lamented Zachary Taylor, of Louisiana. I present them all to you, not merely as cherished associates and friends of my own, but as the chosen Trustees of our great American Philanthropist and Benefactor.

But let me not omit to say, in conclusion, that our Peabody Trust is still more emphatically represented here on this occasion by its accomplished and devoted General Agent, who after five years of faithful service as the Secretary of the Massachusetts Board of Education, and after eleven years of the Presidency of our sister University of Rhode Island, has nobly consented, in the maturity of his experience and wisdom, to remove his residence to Virginia, and devote the remainder of his life — God grant that it may be no brief or contingent remainder! — to the free, common schools of the Southern States. He, above all others, is entitled to the honors of this occasion; and I hasten to make way for his receiving them, by proposing

"THE HEALTH OF DR. BARNAS SEARS!"

THE GREAT BOSTON FIRE.

REMARKS AT A MEETING OF THE MASSACHUSETTS HISTORICAL SOCIETY, NOVEMBER 14, 1872.

GENTLEMEN OF THE MASSACHUSETTS HISTORICAL SOCIETY, — I must beg your attention for a few moments. I have promised our distinguished guest, Mr. Froude, that, after the fatigue of the interesting lecture which he has just delivered at the Tremont Temple, he shall not be involved in any ceremonious utterances again to-night. But as we desire that our meeting shall be a matter of record, and that his name may be entered as among those present, if not as taking part in its proceedings, I am sure he will pardon me, and you will all pardon me, for an informal word or two before we relapse into a mere social party.

Let me say, at the outset, that the arrangements for this occasion were made before the occurrence of the awful calamity which we all so deeply deplore, and from which so many of us are more or less sufferers in common with our fellow-citizens.[1] And our guest was himself the first to suggest that, in presence of such an event, all engagements of this sort might well be cancelled. But on consultation with our worthy host, Mr. Lowell, I found that he saw no reason why a stated meeting of our old Historical Society should not proceed according to the programme under his hospitable roof, — more especially as at this moment we have no sufficient roof of our own for the purpose.[2] Our meeting will at least furnish evidence that, while

[1] The great Boston fire occurred on the 9th and 10th of November, 1872.

[2] The Building of the Massachusetts Historical Society was at this time in process of reconstruction.

we heartily unite with those around us in lamenting the terrible disaster which has befallen our beloved city, we have the fullest faith and confidence that, at no very distant day, it will be ours to witness and to record the reconstruction of all which has been destroyed, the recovery of all which has been lost, the building up again of all these waste places, and of the fortunes of those who have occupied them, and the complete restoration of Boston to its long-accustomed prosperity.

We may well draw consolation and confidence from the records of the past; and I venture to presume so far upon your indulgence, and upon the official relation which I bear to the Society, as to turn back the pages of history for a few moments, and to remind you how often our fathers suffered in the same way before us, and how bravely and triumphantly they met such calamities.

I doubt not that there are many of those present who remember having read a discourse delivered by Cotton Mather, at what was called "The Boston Lecture," on the seventh day of February, 1698, and which is included in the first volume of his "Magnalia." After alluding to the wonderful growth of our town, until it had become known as "The Metropolis of the whole English America," he proceeds to say: "Little was this expected by them that first settled the town, when for a while Boston was proverbially called *Lost-town*, for the mean and sad circumstances of it." And then, after depicting the dangers of famine and the ravages of the small-pox from which it had repeatedly and severely suffered, he goes on as follows: —

"Never was any town under the cope of heaven more liable to be laid in ashes, either through the carelessness or the wickedness of them that sleep in it. That such a combustible heap of contiguous houses yet stands, it may be called a standing miracle. It is not because the watchman keeps the city: perhaps there may be too much cause of reflection in that thing, and of inspection too. No, it is from Thy watchful protection, O Thou Keeper of Boston, who neither slumbers nor sleeps." "TEN TIMES," he continues, "has the fire made notable ruins among us, and our good servant been almost our master; *but the ruins have mostly and quickly been rebuilt.* I suppose that many more than a thousand houses are now to be seen on this little piece of ground, all filled with the undeserved favors of God."

This was in the year 1698, when Boston had but seven thousand inhabitants, and when one thousand houses were as many as Cotton Mather dared positively to count on our whole peninsula. Ten times, it seems, the town had already been devastated by fires. You may find an account of almost all of them in Mr. Drake's elaborate History of Boston.

One of them, in 1654, was long known as "The Great Fire;" but neither its locality nor extent can now be identified. Another of them occurred in November, 1676, which was called "the greatest fire that had ever happened in Boston." It alarmed the whole country, as well as the town, and burned to the ground forty-six dwelling-houses, besides other buildings, together "with a Meeting House of considerable bigness." Only two or three years afterwards, in 1679, another still more terrible fire occurred, when all the warehouses and a great number of dwelling-houses, with the vessels then in the dock, were consumed, — the most woful desolation that Boston had ever seen. "Ah, Boston," exclaimed Mather, in view of this catastrophe, "thou hast seen the vanity of all worldly possessions! One fatal morning, which laid *four-score* of thy dwelling-houses and *seventy* of thy warehouses in a ruinous heap, gave thee to read it in fiery characters."

So fierce were the ravages of this last fire, we are told, that all landmarks were obliterated in several places, and considerable trouble was experienced in fixing the bounds of estates. But, we are also told, "rebuilding the burnt district went on with such rapidity that lumber could not be had fast enough for the purpose;" and, as Dr. Mather said eighteen years afterwards, the ruins were mostly and quickly rebuilt.

We read of another fire in 1702, which was for many years talked of as "the seventh great fire." It broke out near the dock, destroying a great amount of property, and "three warehouses were blown up to hinder its spreading." It thus seems that a hundred and seventy years ago our fathers understood this mode of arresting the flames; perhaps better than we seem to have done in these latter days. But they must have been sadly deficient in other appliances; as, only two days before this fire broke out, a vote had been passed in town-meeting "that the selectmen should procure two water-engines suitable for the extinguishing of fires, either by sending for them to England or otherwise to provide them."

Again, in October, 1711, a still more destructive conflagration took place in Boston. The town-house, the old meeting-house, and about a hundred other houses and buildings, were destroyed, and a hundred and ten families turned out of doors. "But that," it is recorded, "which very much added unto the horror of the dismal night, was the tragical death of many poor men, who were killed by the blowing-up of houses, or by venturing too far into the fire." The bones of seven or eight of these were supposed to be found. "From School Street to Dock Square, including both sides of Cornhill, all the buildings were swept away."

Once more, and finally, we turn over to 1760, when the remembrance of all other Boston fires was almost obliterated by that of the 20th of March of that year, which, it is said, "will be a day memorable for the most terrible fire that has happened in this town, or, perhaps, in any other part of North America, far exceeding that of the 2d of October, 1711, till now termed 'The Great Fire.'" *Three hundred and forty-nine* dwelling-houses, stores, and shops were consumed, and above one thousand people were left without a habitation.

And thus has history repeated itself in the experiences of Boston; and thus we find that our early predecessors in these pleasant places were called to endure calamities by fire almost as great, perhaps quite as great in proportion to the population and wealth and means of relief of their days, as those which have now fallen upon us. We see, too, with what constancy and courage they bore them, and how uniformly the record runs that "the ruins were quickly rebuilt."

I will not come down to later years, though, even within the memory of some now living and present, disastrous and wide-spread conflagrations have occurred, which seemed at first to overshadow the prospect of our prosperity and growth. But we see what Boston has become in spite of all these discouragements and drawbacks, and how the enterprise and bravery of her people, ever mounting with the occasion, have carried us onward and upward to the position and elevation which we have recently enjoyed, — let me say, which we still enjoy. The same enterprise, the same courage, are still ours. With trust in each other, trust in ourselves, and trust in God, we shall go through our furnace of affliction as our fathers went through theirs, — not unscorched certainly, but tried, purified, invigorated; and Boston will resume a leading place in the business of the country and of the world, and rise to greater eminence than she has ever yet attained.

Yes, my friends, I am persuaded that those who succeed us in this Historical Society, — I will not say a century hence, nor even half a century, nor a quarter of a century, but at a much earlier period, — when they recall the incidents of this overwhelming conflagration, and describe the devouring element leaping from roof to roof with such terrible energy, and involving so much of the solidest part of our city in seemingly helpless, hopeless desolation, — will say also, not only that there was no hanging of the head or folding of the arms in despair, but that even while the embers were still casting their glaring light upon the sky, while the wearied firemen were still pouring rivers of water upon the smouldering, treacherous ruins, and before the danger of further destruction was altogether at an end, even then the elastic and irrepressible spirit of our people asserted itself as it had never done before; that even then our noble merchants, with old familiar names at their head, were engaging their architects and making their estimates for reconstruction, while the municipal authorities were running out the lines of new streets and new squares, and projecting the plans of a grander and safer business city than had ever before been witnessed here. And they will add to the record, that these plans were rapidly executed and the reconstruction completely accomplished.

True, we have lost much, and our hearts are in the deepest sympathy with the sufferers. Indeed, we are all sufferers together. There is no exemption from the results of this catastrophe, and I would not underestimate its severity. But how much we have left! Almost all the dwellings of the poor as well as of the rich; Faneuil Hall and the State House and the City Hall; the old State House and the Old South; our Charity Bureau, never more blessed in its ministrations than at this moment; all our court houses and record offices, not one touched; our public library, all our school-houses, and almost all our churches. Still more, the enterprise and liberality of our capitalists; the genius of our engineers and inventors; the public spirit of our citizens; the sympathy of our fellow-men everywhere, — all are left to us; and, above all else, that abiding faith and trust in a wise and merciful Providence, which we inherited from our fathers, and from our mothers also, and which is emblazoned on the very seal of our city, — *Sicut Patribus, sit Deus nobis.* While we are true to that motto, and to the spirit of that motto, Boston will never be called "Lost-town," either proverbially or otherwise, however it may have been so called in the days which Cotton Mather described.

And now let me turn from this painful topic, which could not fail to be uppermost in all our thoughts and hearts to-night, — let me turn to a word of welcome to our distinguished guest. He needs no introduction to any of us. His elaborate and brilliant History has introduced him, long before his arrival, to every reader of the English tongue. Whether or not he has absolutely reversed or even modified our views of some of the great figures of the period which he describes, we all feel that he has gone down deeper into the mines of history than any of his predecessors in the same field, and has brought up things rich and rare for our entertainment and instruction, weaving them with surpassing skill into the most attractive and effective form. He has given a new zest to the reading and the study of that English history, which I well remember that Daniel Webster, when I was a law student in his office, so emphatically enjoined upon me as furnishing the key to all our own free institutions. He has given us, too, the history of the old Mother Country during the very period when the founders of the American colonies, as he has reminded us this evening, were being shaped and moulded for their great wilderness work, under that Maiden Queen, as she was wont to be called, in honor of whom our whole continent, or certainly our whole coast, once bore the name, — which one of our largest and most ancient commonwealths still bears, — the name of Virginia. You all remember that even the Pilgrim Fathers, in the ever memorable compact which they signed in the cabin of the "Mayflower" on the 11th (21st) of November, 1620, designated their voyage as undertaken "to plant the first colony in the northern part of Virginia."

Elizabeth had then been dead for seventeen years, but her imperious refusal of all suitors for her hand had been inscribed where it was never to be forgotten. The great events of the latter part of her reign, at least, were familiar as household words to those by whom our colonies were founded. It was but yesterday that I was showing to Mr. Froude a contemporary account of "the Order and Manner of the execution of Mary, Queen of Scots," which I had found carefully copied into the common-place book of Adam Winthrop, the father of our Governor. And as he thinks that it may never yet have been printed, I propose, with our Secretary's leave, that it shall go into the next serial number of our printed Proceedings.[1]

But I have said more than enough for the introduction of one who, as I have suggested, in writing the history of his own country at a period when it was our country also, or certainly when it was the country of our fathers, has long ago secured for himself the most respectful and cordial welcome to our shores, and who we rejoice has at length come over to receive that welcome. I present to you, gentlemen, our distinguished Honorary Member, Mr. Froude.

[1] This account will be found in the Note on the next page.

NOTE.

[From the MS. Common-place Book of Adam Winthrop.]

The manner & order of ye execution of ye late Queene of Scottes, wth ye wordes wch she spake at her Deathe, truely sett downe by Doctorr ffletcher Deane of Peterborowe.

On Wednesday ye viii of ffebruary ño 1586 there assembled at ye Castle of ffordringham ye Earles of Shrewsbury & Kent, wth divers Knightes & gentlemen Justices of ye peace of ye yeare in those Countries. About viii of ye clocke, ye Earles & Sherifes of ye Shire went upp to ye Scottish Queene, whom they fownde prayinge on hir knees, wth hir gentlewomen & men. And the Sherifes rememberinge hir yt ye time was at hand, she awnswered & sayde she was readie. Then she was ledde by ye armes from hir chamber into the ye chamber of presence, where wth many exhortacions to hir people to feare God, & to live in obedience, kissinge hir women, she gave hir hande to hir men to kisse: prayinge them all not to sorowe, but reioice & pray for hir. She was brought downe ye stayers by two Souldiers: Then beinge belowe she stayed, & lookinge backe she sayed she was evill attended, & desired ye Lordes she might for woman hoodes sake, have two of hir women to wayte uppon hir. Then they sayde, they were onely wthholden for yt it was feared, by their passionate cryinge they would disquiet hir Spirit, & disturbe ye execution. She sayde, I will promise for them yt they shall not doe so. Then two of them whom she willed were brought unto hir. Then she spake muche unto Welbin hir man, & charged him as he woulde answere before God, to deliver hir Speache & message to hir Sonne in suche sorte as she did speake them, all wch tended onely to will him to governe wisely, in ye feare of God, & to take heede to whom he betooke his chiefest trust; & not to geve an occasion to be evill thought of by the Queene of Inglande, hir good sister, to certefie him she dyed a true Skotte, a true ffrenche, & a true Catholique. Aboute X of ye clocke she was brought downe into ye greate hall, where in ye middest of ye howse, & agaynste ye chimnie, (wherein was a greate fire) was a skaffolde sett upp of twoe foote height, & xii foote broade, havinge two steppes to come upp; about ye scaffold went a rayle halfe a yarde highte rownde covered wth black cotten: So was hir stoole, ye Lordes forme, ye blocke, & a pillowe for hir to kneele uppon. There did sitt uppon ye skaffolde ye two Earles, ye Sherife stoode there, & ye two executioners. When they were sett, Mr Beale, Clerke of ye Cowncell did reade hir Maties Commission for hir execution, under ye broade Seale, after wch ye Deane of Peterborowe beinge directed by ye Lordes to speake unto hir, for ye better prparation to dye a penitent Christian, in ye true faythe of Christ, began at ye motion of ye Earle of Shrewsbury his exhortation, wch as sone as he had begoñe, she sayde wth a lowd voice, peace Mr Deane, I will not heare you. I say nothinge sayde he, but yt I will iustifie before ye matie of ye most highest. So proceedinge, she cryed alowde agayne, peace Mr Deane, I will not heare you, you have nothinge to doe wth me, nor I wyth you. Then was he willed to silence, for any further molestinge hir mynde. She sayed, so it is best, for I am fully setled & resolved to dye in ye Catholique Romishe faythe. Wch when ye Lordes hearde; the Earle of Kent sayde, albeit Madam, you refuse ye offered mercies of ye most highest, yet we will offer or prayers to God for you; hopinge he will heare us. And if it might stande wth his good will, he would vouchsafe to open your eies, & to lighten your hearte, wth ye true knowledge of his will, & to dye therin. She sayed, doe, & I will pray. Then ye Deane pronounced a prayer, wch ye standers by folowed; all wch while she havinge a crucifixe betwene hir handes prayed much lowder in latin. The prayer beinge done, she kneeled downe, & prayed to this effect: for Christ his afflicted Churche, & for an ende of their troubles, for hir Sonne yt he might rule uprightly, & be converted to ye Catholique Romishe Churche. She prayed yt ye Queenes Matie might longe reigne peaceably, might prosper, & serve God. She confessed she hoped to be saved onely by ye bloude of Christe, at ye foote of whose picture presented on ye crucifixe she woulde willingly shedd hir bloude. She prayed to all ye Sayntes of heaven to pray for hir, & yt ye God of heaven woulde of his goodnes averte his plauges from this silly Ilande, & yt God would geve hir life, & forgeve hir sinnes, & yt he woulde receave hir Soule into his heavenly handes. And then she rose upp, & was by two of hir women, & ye two executioners disrobed into hir peticoote. Then she sayed, she was not wont to be undressed before such a number, nor by such gromes. Then she kissed hir women, & one of them began to crye, to whom she sayed, peace, cry not, I haue promised ye contrarie: Crye not for me, but reioice, & lifted upp hir handes & blessed them, & likewise hir men not farre of. Then sodenly she kneeled downe most resolutly, & wth ye least token of any feare of deathe y^t^ might be. And after y^t^ one of hir women had knitte a kertcher about hir eies, she spake alowde this psalme in latin — *In te Domine confido, ne confundar in æternū.* Then lay she downe very quietly stretchinge out hir body, & layinge hir necke over ye blocke, cryed, *in manus tuas Domine*, &c. One of ye executioners helde downe hir two handes: & ye other did at two strokes wth an axe cutt of hir heade, wch fallinge out of hir atyre appeared very graye, & neare powlde. So houldinge it upp, ye people sayed, God save ye Queene, & so perishe all hir enemies, & ye enemies of the gospell. All thinges about hir, & belonginge to hir, were taken from ye executioners, & they were not suffered so muche as to haue their aprons before them till they were washed. The bloudy clothes, ye blocke, & whatsoever els bloudy, was brent in ye chymny fire. The body was caryed upp into ye chamber, hir boweles taken out, embawmed, seared, & resteth to the buriall.

[Then follows in a different style of chirography, though by the same hand:]

Shee was first roiallie buried in the Cathedrall Churche of Peterburroughe. But afterwardes shee was brought from thence to Westminster, & buried in Kinge Henry the Seventhes chapple, where a princely tombe was made over her, by the Kinges ma^tie^ her Sonne in the yere of his reigne of Greate Britayne, &c.

The saide Queene of Scottes was the daughter & sole heire of James the 5. Kinge of Scotts, & was borne the 8 daye of December, 1542. beinge but 5. daies olde when her father died. Shee was first maried to Francys the eldest sonne of Henry ye Seconde, Kinge of France, who reigned 2 yeres after his father, by whom shee had no issue. Then shee retourned into Scotlande, & maried Henry the lorde Darly, the eldest sonne unto Mathewe, Erle of Lenox, by whom shee had issue the Kinges ma^tie^ James the 6. who was but a yere olde when his father was slayne, & his mother fled into Englande, where shee remained p^r^soner till she died, wch was the 8 daie of February, 1586, in the 44 yere of her age, & in the 29 yere of the reigne of Queene Elizabethe.[1]

[1] The following letter from Queen Elizabeth to Sir Amias Paulet is also taken from the Common Place Book of Adam Winthrop (b. 1548, d. 1623). William Tytler, in his "Inquiry, Historical and Critical, into the Evidence against Mary, Queen of the Scots" (4th ed. 1790, vol. ii. pp. 320, 403), prints this letter from "a collection of remarkable trials published, London, 1715." In commenting on the letter, he says: "What a picture we have here of the heroine of England! Wooing a faithful servant to commit a clandestine murder, which she herself durst not avow!" Tytler feels that he is justified in giving this interpretation to the letter,

by others which followed from Walsingham and Davison, written by order of the Queen, in which the proposal is made in plain terms. Miss Aikin also prints the letter in her History of Queen Elizabeth; and so does Froude, from "*MSS. Mary Q. of Scots.*" But the text in no two of these copies is alike; and the copy from which we now print varies from all these. Neither copy bears a date, but Froude refers the letter to "August, 1586," which was probably just before Queen Mary left Chartley Manor for Fotheringay Castle, under the conduct of Sir Amias Paulet, one of her keepers. Sir Drue Drury, another of them, was a Suffolk man, not far off from Groton, and Adam Winthrop might have had the letter from him. She was executed on the 8th of February following.

A copie of ye Q. Maties Lrē to Sir Amias Pawlett:

Amias, my most faythfull & carefull servaunt, God rewarde the treble folde for thy most troublesome charge so well discharged, if you knewe, my Amias, howe kindely my gratefull harte accepteth your speedie endevours, faythfull actions, yor. wise orders, & safe regarde, performed in so dangerous & craftie a charge, it would ease your travailes, & reioice your harte: In wch I charge you to carry this most iust thought, y^t^. I cannot ballance in any waight of my iudgment y^e^. value y^t^. I prise you att. And suppose y^t^. no treasure can countervayle so greate a fayth. And I shall condemne myselfe in y^t^. faulte w^h^ I never committed, if I rewarde not such desertes, yea, lett me lacke when I most neede, if I acknowledge not suche a meritt, wth a reward *non omnibus datū*. But lett yor. wicked murtheresse knowe, howe wth hartie sorowe hir vile desertes compell these orders, & bidde hir from me aske God forgevenes, for hir treacherous dealinge towardes y^e^. saver of hir life many yeres: to y^e^. intollerable perill of hir owne: and yet not content wth so many forgevenesses, must fall agayne so horrebly, farre passinge a womans thought, muche more a princes. In steade of excusinge[s] whereof not one can serve, it beinge so playnely confessed by y^e^. actours of my guiltlesse deathe, lett repentance take place, & lett not y^e^. fiende possesse hir so as hir better parte be loste, wch. I pray wth handes lifted upp to him y^t^. may both save & spill, wth my most lovinge adieu, & pray[er] for thy longe life.

Your assured & lovinge Soveraigne
as therto by good desert enduced,
ELIZA: REGINA.

To my faythfull AMIAS.

FOLSOM, SOMERBY, AND SEWARD.

REMARKS AT A MEETING OF THE MASSACHUSETTS HISTORICAL SOCIETY, DECEMBER 12, 1872.

It devolves upon me this morning, gentlemen, to announce to you officially, according to our custom, the recent deaths of one of our Resident Members, one of our Corresponding Members, and one of our Honorary Members.

You will pardon me, I am sure, for speaking of them more cursorily than I might have done, were I not assured that others, far better able than myself to do justice to the characters and services of those whom we have lost, are present and prepared for the purpose. It will be mine only to open the way for their more elaborate tributes.

Mr. Charles Folsom, a Resident Member of our Society, died at Cambridge, on the 8th of November last, in the seventy-seventh year of his age. Graduated at Harvard with the class of 1813, he had served the University faithfully as a tutor from 1821 to 1823, and as Librarian from 1823 to 1826. He was longer known to us all as the Librarian of the Boston Athenæum, to which he rendered most valuable services. He had edited and published several volumes of the Latin Classics, — the Select Orations of Cicero, and the Select Books of Livy, among others, — which were enriched by his learned annotations. During the nine or ten years of his association with our own Society, before illness and infirmities had deprived us of his presence at our meetings, he had made interesting and instructive communications, from time to time, on historical or literary subjects. The conjectural origin of our national motto, *E Pluribus Unum*, in the *Moretum* of Virgil; and an additional verse to the grand old Latin hymn, ***Dies iræ, dies illa,*** which he had somewhere discovered in the course of his diligent researches, — will be remembered by us all.

But no mere enumeration of the offices he had filled, or of the works or words which he had given to the public, can furnish any adequate impression of the man. He was a modest and retiring person; distrustful of himself, almost to a fault; and seemed hardly conscious of his own rich and rare accomplishments. Few more accurate and learned linguists, bibliologists, or classical scholars, have lived in our day and land. And, certainly, there has been no one more ready and eager to devote all the ripe fruit of his careful and critical studies to the service of his friends, in utter disregard of his own fame. If Prescott and Sparks and Palfrey, not to name others of our most noted and valued historians, living or dead, were with us here to-day, they would unite in bearing the fullest testimony to the ever kind, assiduous, and generous aid which he had rendered them in the last corrections, if not in the earlier preparation, of their works. Indeed, the testimony of more than one of them is on record where it cannot be lost. Prescott, in the preface to his "Conquest of Peru," says: "I must not omit to mention my obligations to my friend Charles Folsom, Esq., the learned Librarian of the Athenæum, whose minute acquaintance with the grammatical structure and the true idiom of our English tongue has enabled me to correct many inaccuracies into which I had fallen in the composition both of this and of my former works." And again, in the preface to his History of Philip II., he records his obligations to Mr. Folsom, "who," he says, "has repeated the good offices he had before rendered me in revising my manuscript for the press."

The preface of Dr. Palfrey's admirable History of New England concludes as follows: "It only remains for me to avow my obligations to my almost life-long friend, Mr. Charles Folsom, for the very important favor of a careful revisal of the sheets of this volume as they passed through the press. At every step his critical sagacity and practised judgment have stood me greatly in stead."

Many more names might be added to the three I have mentioned, of those whom he had quietly and disinterestedly helped in winning the reputation they enjoyed. And any one who is in the way of feeling the sore need there is, in our printing establishments at this hour, of faithful, intelligent, accomplished, and learned proof-readers, will be able to appreciate how great was the help which Mr. Folsom afforded, to all who were so fortunate as to secure for their writings his friendly and thorough supervision. I know not where we shall find his like again in this respect.

But I must not omit to lay one wreath on the grave of our worthy friend, which might well excite the envy of any man. It happened to me to be brought into frequent association, during the last years of his life, with the heroic and noble-hearted Farragut. He never met me without the most eager and affectionate inquiries as to his cherished friend Mr. Folsom, and he never hesitated to say that he owed him the deepest debt of gratitude for his early and devoted care and instruction. "He made me almost all that I am," was the substance, if not the exact language, of his emphatic acknowledgment. And when we remember what Farragut was, and what he did and dared for his country, we can appreciate the full value of such a tribute. It might almost recall to us the acknowledged indebtedness of Alexander the Great to Aristotle.

I dare not trust my memory in an attempt to recount the precise circumstances of Mr. Folsom's relations to Farragut. I believe they met in the Mediterranean, when Farragut was a midshipman, and when our friend, soon after leaving college, may have held, as I believe he did, the position of Instructor in the Navy; or it may have been when he was accompanying the late Hon. Luther Bradish, of New York, in his semi-official tour to the East, about the year 1820, with a view of collecting information as to the trade of the Mediterranean, and of facilitating the establishment of commercial relations with the Sublime Porte. Mr. Folsom gave some reminiscences of this tour at our own Society meeting, on the announcement of Mr. Bradish's death in 1863; but with his habitual reserve he prepared no notes of what he had said for our printed Proceedings. And the same modest reserve deterred him from giving any account of his relations to Farragut. But the grand old Admiral's acknowledgments were uttered with all the frankness and simplicity of his noble nature; and if the facts of the case are not within the memory of any one present, as I doubt not they are, and as they ought to be within my own, they will be sure to be forthcoming in the Memoir of our friend, for which it will be our duty to provide.

Meantime it will be for others who may follow me to do ampler justice to his career and character.

In the death of Mr. HORATIO GATES SOMERBY, our Society has lost a most useful and highly valued Corresponding Member. With no previous education or preparation for such pursuits, he was drawn, in mature manhood, by a sort of instinct or elective affinity, to antiquarian and genealogical researches, and soon became devoted to them. He made it his specialty to trace the links between families in New England and those of the same name or blood in Old England; and his occasional, and, of late years, continued residence in London, gave him peculiar facilities for the work. Sometimes for mere love, and sometimes for honorable remuneration, he unravelled the intricacies of not a few Anglo-American pedigrees; and proved that more or less of noble, — or, it may have been, of ignoble, — blood, from a remote ancestry, was running in the veins of some who had hardly pretended to any pedigree at all. His diligent investigations of this sort in the old English counties of Suffolk and Essex, from which so many of our Massachusetts families and founders emigrated, were well known to the antiquaries of that part of England, and Mr. Somerby has long been an Honorary Member of the Suffolk Institute of Archæology. In that relation, he gained the cordial regard and friendship of the late President of that Institute, Lord Arthur Hervey, now Bishop of Bath and Wells, whose name is also on our roll; and not many years ago I had the good fortune to spend a day with him at Ickworth Priory, of which Lord Arthur was then curate.

Mr. Somerby, too, had early won the confidence and regard of our illustrious benefactor, the late George Peabody, and was appointed by him the Secretary and active agent of that distinguished Board of Trustees to which was committed the management of his noble foundation for improving the Lodging Houses of the Poor of London, — a Board of which the Earl of Derby and our own Mr. Adams, as American Minister, were long members. There is the best authority for saying that, in this capacity, Mr. Somerby's services were highly appreciated, not only by the Trustees, but by the London Poor, with whom he was brought into frequent communication and contact. The Annual Reports or Statements of the Board, for the seven years of its existence, have uniformly borne Mr. Somerby's signature; and that signature alone can hardly fail to secure an enviable endurance for his name.

He had been a Corresponding Member of our Society for twelve or thirteen years, and had occasionally made welcome contributions to our Collections. And not a few of us will cherish a grateful memory of the obliging readiness with which he responded to our individual inquiries about names and dates and facts, genealogical and historical, which often cost him long journeys from London, and laborious investigations into ancient wills and time-worn parish registers.

He died in London on the 14th of November last, at sixty-seven years of age, and his remains were interred, only a few days since, at Newburyport, Massachusetts, his native place.

I turn lastly, gentlemen, to a name of wider celebrity. I believe that there have been but two instances, in our history as a Society, where all the prescribed rules relating to the admission of members have been suspended by unanimous consent, and where names have been placed on our Honorary Roll by a sort of acclamation.

The first instance occurred at our November meeting, 1861, when Winfield Scott, after a brilliant military service of nearly fifty years, was obliged by his age and infirmities to resign his place as the Commander-in-chief of the Army of the United States.

The second instance occurred at the Annual Meeting in April, 1865, when tidings of the deepest horror had so recently reached us from Washington. On that occasion, after paying a tribute to the lamented President, who had fallen a victim to assassination, we placed upon our Honorary Roll the name of the Secretary of State who had so narrowly escaped death by the same base and abhorrent conspiracy.

Mr. SEWARD was not without high claims to a compliment of this kind, quite apart from the sympathy which was felt for him at that moment.

As a lawyer who had taken an active part in not a few celebrated cases; as Governor of the great State of New York, at a period when questions of the highest national concern, involving the immediate issues of peace or war with England, were dependent on his acts; as a Senator of the United States, who had been the recognized leader of the political party which finally prevailed throughout what were then called the Free States, and from whose policy, directly or indirectly, resulted the rendering of all States free States, and of all men free men, — in all these relations, he had acquired a name which could not fail to have a prominent place in the history of his times. He had, also, already contributed valuable materials to that history, by arguments in courts, by speeches in Congress, and by various more extended literary publications.

His Life of our own John Quincy Adams, — whom Mr. Seward, I think, early took as his model and exemplar, and whom a little more of early training and fortunate surrounding, and a little more of intellectual and physical vigor, might have enabled him to approach more nearly, — was published in 1849; and a collection of his own writings and speeches, in four volumes, was issued from the press not long afterwards.

Meantime, almost every year of his mature life had furnished its own evidence of his unwearied industry, professional, political, or literary.

It will be, however, as Secretary of State of the United States, during the whole period of the late Civil War, and for nearly four years after that war was closed, and while its results were in daily progress of development, that Mr. Seward will be longest remembered. To him is primarily and principally due the successful administration of our foreign affairs during that eventful and critical period. Volume after volume of official correspondence attests his unceasing labors. And if, in the vast mass of his written or spoken words, in a time of so much anxiety and agitation, there be some which even his best friends would willingly obliterate; or if, amid the many responsibilities he was compelled to assume, there were some acts to be regretted by any of us,—yet all such disparagements of his name and fame will be forgotten hereafter, in the grateful remembrance that through his leading intervention our peace with foreign nations was preserved, and our country left free to fight out the great battle of the Union to its final triumph.

Above all other acts of his, posterity will remember, or certainly ought to remember, with gratitude and admiration, that brave surrender of the two Southern Confederate ambassadors, of which our own Boston Harbor was the witness and the scene. For one, certainly, I have heartily concurred from the first in the judgment so recently and emphatically pronounced by our honored associate and Vice-President, Mr. Adams, whom we welcome here to-day, fresh from his inestimable services at Geneva, and whom we hope presently to hear bearing witness to the abilities and merits of his lamented friend.

In his address before the Historical Society of New York, in December, 1870, after alluding to Mr. Seward, then living, as "a statesman, calm in council, sagacious in action, and fearless of censure when an emergency was to be met," he added these memorable words in regard to the particular transaction to which I have referred; and we all know that they were the words of one who had been in a position to know, more than almost any one else, precisely what he was speaking of: "I do not feel," said he, "that I am exaggerating, when I claim for this courageous resistance to the infatuation of the hour, that it not only was correct in principle, but also that *it saved the Unity of the Nation.*"

I would quote more of Mr. Adams's language, were he not fortunately here in person to renew the expression of the same sentiment.

Since Mr. Seward's release from public service, he had been a wonderful traveller, as we all know; and a posthumous volume is on the point of publication, giving an account of the most remarkable tour — embracing almost the whole circle of the earth's surface — which was ever undertaken and accomplished by one of so many infirmities. But he happily returned to die at home at last in his beloved village of Auburn, New York, in the seventy-second year of his age.

Let me only add, that, though not always agreeing with him in political opinion, I had many pleasant personal associations with Mr. Seward, while I was in Congress with him and afterwards, and that I gladly bear witness to the amiability and kindness which marked his private life.

THE ENVIRONS OF BOSTON.

ADDRESS AT DEDICATION OF THE NEW TOWN HALL OF BROOKLINE, FEBRUARY 22, 1873.

Ladies and Gentlemen of Brookline;
Friends and Fellow-Citizens:

I am deeply conscious how small a claim I have to the distinguished position which has been assigned to me on this occasion. I am, as you all know, but an eleventh-hour Brookline man; while around me are those who have borne the burden and heat of the day, not only in planning and preparing this beautiful Hall, but in building up the Town itself — of which henceforth, so long as it remains a Town, this stately edifice is to be the symbol and the seat of government — to its existing prosperity and importance. In yielding, however, to the kind and complimentary request of your Selectmen and Building Committee, I had the satisfaction of reflecting, that, whatever I might find to say here to-day, in this Inaugural Address, I should at least be free from the temptation, or imputation, of commending any thing to which I had myself contributed, and should be enabled to pass an impartial and dispassionate judgment on the efforts and accomplishments of others. A residence in Brookline for six or seven years, which is all I can claim to have enjoyed, has given me an opportunity for observation and inquiry in regard to the history and growth of the Town, and for acquainting myself somewhat with those who have lived here longer, and who have labored so diligently and devotedly for its improvement and welfare. To them the honors of the occasion belong; and if I shall succeed in doing justice to them and their predecessors, and in illustrating their services and successes, you will feel, I am sure, that all the reasonable expectations of the hour have been fulfilled.

We are here, on this auspicious Anniversary, — which, more than any other day, or all other days, in the calendar of merely human nativities, is associated with whatever is brightest and best in the history of our country and of the world, — to take formal possession of a new and costly Town House, and especially to inaugurate and dedicate this spacious and magnificent Hall. But we do not forget that this is not the first time in our annals that such an occasion has been witnessed here. We do not forget that a similar ceremony has taken place even within the memory of not a few of those who are assembled here to-day. Little more than a quarter of a century has elapsed, since the beloved and venerated Pastor of your first Parish was the chosen and appropriate organ of your Selectmen of that day, in welcoming the people of Brookline to what he then called, and what was then doubtless considered, "a commodious and beautiful," as well as a new, Town Hall. I need not say that it is still standing. You are but just relinquishing its occupation. It has been the scene of not a few interesting deliberations and memorable acts. Wise and weighty counsels have been heard within its walls. Stirring resolutions have been adopted, important measures have been concerted and consummated, by those assembled there. Above all, the sacred right of Freemen — the Elective Franchise — has, year after year, been exercised there. Precious memories of the living, and still more precious memories of the dead, cluster thickly within and around it; and they will continue to be cherished by many of you, as long as it shall survive the changes and chances to which all earthly structures are subject. We shall do well, my friends, if we shall render this far more commodious and costly edifice as worthy of being held in honor by those who may come after us. The past is secure. The future has always its contingencies and uncertainties.

Meantime, there are but few of the occasions which have been witnessed within those old walls, which we should less willingly permit to fall into oblivion, or which some of you, I am sure, still hold in fonder or more vivid remembrance, than that Dedication Service on the 14th of October, 1845, when the excellent Dr. Pierce recounted with so much fulness and fervor, and in so much of minute detail, the earlier and the later history of the Town. He was my father's friend and my own friend. He was the friend of all, young or old, who had the privilege of his acquaintance, or who were in any way brought within the magnetic power of his presence. A man of larger heart, of more genial temper, of kindlier impulses, was hardly to be found here or anywhere. His cheery tone still rings in the ears of all who ever heard it. His erect and stalwart frame was a fit setting for so active, eager, inquisitive a spirit. He made nothing, even to a late day of his life, of walking into Boston from the parsonage on Meeting House Hill, attending Thursday Lecture, or perhaps preaching it himself, at the old Chauncy Place Church, thence proceeding at once to the Monthly Meeting of the Historical Society, then dining with a former President of that Society,[1] where I have so often met him, or with some other friend, and at last completing the circuit of no Sabbath day's journey by walking back to his Brookline home before sunset. And he could always tell you the precise number of minutes, or even of seconds, which the walk either way or both ways had taken. This marvellous appetite for trivial details, however, went along with the keenest relish for historical and local research, or certainly for the results of such research. The history of the town in which he so long resided, and the history of the families and changing fortunes of his parishioners and neighbors and friends, were almost as familiar to him as the Bible from which he took his weekly text, or as that grand old psalm which for so many years he lined and led, to the tune of St. Martin's, at our Annual Commencement dinner. He had passed the full term of threescore years and ten, when he delivered that Inaugural Discourse in 1845. Indeed, I have seen it carefully recorded in his own diary, that on that 14th of October he was "exactly 72 years and three months old." But he was still in complete possession of all his faculties. His memory, and his

[1] The late Hon. Thomas L. Winthrop.

power of employing its ample stores, were alike unimpaired; and he gave free play to them on that occasion. How then can I hope to glean any thing for your entertainment or instruction from a field which he so vigorously and thoroughly reaped? What can I say of the earlier or later history of your beloved town, down certainly to 1845, which he did not abundantly tell you, in an Address which is still extant, still remembered by some of you, and still within the ready reach of you all? There is at least one, however, of his recorded experiences on that occasion, as I have read it in his own account, from which I may take courage. After stating that he occupied an hour and a half in its delivery, he adds: "I contrived to season my facts by many appropriate anecdotes; so that I succeeded in keeping the audience awake throughout the Address." May I not venture to express the hope that, in this respect, if in no other, I may be equally successful?

In that Address, your late venerable Pastor did not fail, of course, to remind his hearers of the fact, which I may be pardoned for recalling with more than common interest to-day, that the very earliest allusion to the place now known as Brookline is found, under date of August 30, 1632, in the Journal or History of Governor John Winthrop; and that the very first authentic record of the place is that, "Notice being given of ten Sagamores and many Indians, assembled at Muddy River, the Governor sent Capt. Underhill with twenty musketeers to discover, &c.; but at Roxbury they heard they were broke up." Let us pause for a few moments, and ponder this brief record, so as to unfold something of its real import and significance.

A little more than two years had now elapsed since the Governor and Company of Massachusetts Bay had taken their birthrights on their backs, and their Bibles and their Charter in their hands, and had come over to found and establish an independent Colony on New England soil; not yet, indeed, independent of the Crown or of the Parliament of Old England, — the time for that consummation was still in the distant future, — but a Colony wholly independent of control by London Committees or Companies or Adventurers; and which, in the bold transfer of its Charter, as was so well intimated by John Adams, foreshadowed, if it did not actually contemplate, the grander Independence, of which he himself was "the Colossus on the floor of Congress," in 1776.

Salem, where the Massachusetts Company landed in June, 1630, had already been planted by the worthy pioneer Governor, John Endicott, whom they had deputed to preside over what was called "London's Plantation," subject to their own regulations and instructions from time to time. But there was now no longer to be any "London's Plantation," or any even nominal subordination to any power, on the other side of the ocean, less exalted than that of Parliament and the Crown. They came in the spirit and for the purpose of Self-government, to be exercised by a Governor and Assistants, and soon by a Legislature, of their own choice and upon their own soil. And so they at once sought out a place for the seat of that government; and after lingering a few months at Charlestown, where about a hundred of the planters who came over successively with Endicott and Higginson had already settled themselves, they decided to cross the river and establish themselves at what the Indians called Shawmut, and what some of the planters designated as Trimontaine, — from the three hills then prominent upon its surface, — but which from the 17th day of September, 1630, was to bear the honored name of Boston.

Less than two years had thus passed, since the birth, or certainly the baptism, of Boston, when the first recognition or mention of the locality in which we are interested to-day was entered in his Journal by Governor Winthrop. That record, I think, is full of implication and suggestion as to the condition of the site on which we are now assembled, as well as in regard to the immediate circumstances and surroundings of the Massachusetts Colony. Swarms of savages were still hovering around them. "Ten Sagamores and many Indians," we are told, were assembled in this very neighborhood.[1] A Sagamore is second only to a Sachem, or King of the tribe; and the titles are sometimes employed indiscriminately. Ten Sagamores would thus imply a large number of warriors under them. They were evi-

[1] The site of one of their old forts is now occupied by the house of my friend William Amory, Esq., at Longwood.

dently understood to be lying in ambush; the Governor's phrase being that our musketeers were despatched "to discover, &c." John Underhill was the most trusted Captain of that day, bearing very much the same relation to the Massachusetts Colony which Miles Standish bore to the earlier but wholly distinct and independent Pilgrim Colony at Plymouth. Twenty musketeers were sent with Capt. Underhill, — more than twice the number which Miles Standish took with him, when he was despatched on a similar expedition ten years before, and when he achieved his grandest victory, or what is called his "capital exploit." Every thing indicated danger, or certainly the strongest apprehension of danger; and before another week had elapsed, although this particular party of Indians had been "broke up" or dispersed, we find Governor Winthrop recording the gravest reasons for suspecting that a conspiracy existed among the Narragansett men and the Neipnett men, under pretence of quarrelling with each other, "to cut us off to get our victuals and other substance." And then the record proceeds: "Upon this there was a Camp pitched at Boston in the night, to exercise the Soldiers against need might be; and Capt. Underhill (to try how they would behave themselves) caused an alarm to be given upon the quarters, which discovered the weakness of our people, who, like men amazed, knew not how to behave themselves, so as the officers could not draw them into any order. All the rest of the plantations took the alarm and answered; but it caused much fear and distraction among the common sort, so as some which knew of it before [that is, which knew that it was a false alarm], yet through fear had forgotten, and believed the Indians had been upon us. We doubled our guards, and kept watch day and night."[1]

Such is the picture which Massachusetts and its principal town present to us, as we unfold the page which contains the earliest record of what is now called Brookline. There was plainly no settlement here at that day, or the Governor would have sent that little army of musketeers to assist and rescue the inhabitants, and not merely to discover and break up an ambush of the natives. And may we not well rejoice that it was so? May we

[1] Winthrop's History of New England, vol. i. p. 89.

not well rejoice that there was no handful of scattered planters here to encounter the wild savagery of those "ten Sagamores and many Indians;" and that Underhill and his twenty musketeers heard at Roxbury that they were already dispersed? Yes, my friends, let us thank God to-day, that the narrative of our beautiful village — I might rather say, of its pre-historic period — does not open with a scene of massacre. Let us thank God, that yonder River — "Muddy" as it was called — was not crimsoned and clotted with the gore of either white men or red men. Let us thank God, that our Brook was not destined to be called "Bloody Brook."

I do not undervalue the gallantry and heroism of those upon whom the dire necessity has been laid, whether in earlier or later days, to wield the sword, and wage war to the death, against an Indian foe. Brookline, as we shall presently see, has exhibited her full share of such heroism. I fully recognize, too, that a real and inexorable necessity has often existed for suppressing and punishing by force of arms the lawless ferocity of the savage tribes. The early Colonists must have abandoned their Plantations altogether, unless they were ready and resolved to defend them at all hazards against the conspiracies and treacheries and mad assaults of the aboriginal race which surrounded them on every side. Even at this hour, there may be Modocs or Appaches uncontrollable except by force. But we may all still sympathize with the sentiment, which was so exquisitely expressed by the pious John Robinson in Holland, when he heard of the first great victory of Miles Standish, in which six Indians had been slain: "It would have been happy, if they had converted some, before they had killed any." We may all rejoice, also, to remember that, within a few months only of the date of this record about the Indians at Muddy River, there arrived at Boston, and was immediately settled at Roxbury, where the first planters of this village so long went for their Sunday worship, a godly minister from England who made it his special mission, in the same spirit which had actuated those brave Jesuit-priests in Canada, to Christianize and civilize the natives; and who, during the next thirty years, had not only preached to many of them, and taught many of them to pray, but had accomplished the more than Herculean labor of translating the whole Bible into their language. No more marvellous monument of literary work, in the service of either God or man, can be found upon earth, than that Indian Bible of the noble John Eliot. Nor can any of us fail to admire and applaud the earnest and seemingly successful efforts for the introduction of a more humane and Christian policy towards the Indian Tribes still left in our land, by the illustrious Soldier who has just been called again to the Executive Chair of the United States. There has been nothing more creditable to our Country since, for a similar exhibition of humanity in the removal of the Cherokees beyond the Mississippi, William Ellery Channing paid that most eloquent and most enviable tribute to Winfield Scott.[1]

Pardon me, my friends, for such a digression. I may seem to have travelled a long way out of our little Brookline record; but it has only been, after all, to explain and amplify the gratification I could not refrain from expressing, and which I am sure you all feel with me, that those ten Sagamores and their followers were fairly dispersed before Underhill and his musketeers arrived here; and that the very first page of your records escaped, as it so narrowly did escape, from the stains of conflict and carnage.

Let me hasten now to resume the more direct story of the Town, and to pursue it with greater rapidity. The venerable Pastor of your first Parish, when he occupied the position which you have done me the honor to assign to me on this occasion, did not omit to inform, or remind, his audience, that under the repulsive name of Muddy River, or sometimes Muddy River Hamlet, the territory which Brookline now covers was for nearly three quarters of a century included within the limits and jurisdiction of Boston. Perhaps, therefore, some of our friends who are so eager to return within the same limits and jurisdiction, may be found hereafter adopting the policy of the friends of Texas many years ago, who, when they had discovered some pretence for the idea that Texas had once been a part of the Louisiana Territory, hastened to prefix the little syllable *re* to *annexation*, and thought to strengthen their case by per-

[1] Channing's Works, vol. v. p. 113.

emptorily demanding the re-annexation of Texas to the United States. I may be pardoned for remembering that a member of Congress at that day from the neighboring City, who shall be nameless on this occasion, ventured to suggest that these zealous and irrepressible advocates of Texas might be wiser, if they would exhibit as much of the *suaviter in modo* as of the *fortiter in re*. But jesting apart, — and I have nothing serious to say in reference to any mooted question of local policy to-day, — we are all well aware, as a matter of history, that for seventy-three years from the time when Boston first had a local habitation and a name on this side of the Atlantic, it embraced the territory now occupied by this town. And its embrace, as we shall see, was a tight one, with a grasp not easily unloosed. It is thus from the old records of Boston, or of the Colony, that we derive almost all which is known of the village hamlet in which Brookline had its origin. I know not exactly at what date the first settler was found here, nor who he was. But as the General Court of the Colony ordered the construction of "a sufficient cart-bridge" over Muddy River as early as August 16, 1633, we may reasonably conjecture that transportation had commenced, and that the lands had then begun to be cultivated and occupied. Yet the order seems to have been very slow of fulfilment; since, on the 4th of March of the following year, we find the General Court passing a more urgent and specific order, "That Mr. Richard Dummer and John Johnson shall build a sufficient cart-bridge over Muddy River before the next General Court, and that Boston, Roxbury, Dorchester, Newtown, and Watertown shall equally contribute to it."

This certainly looked like business; yet it is as late as the 2d of June, 1640, that we find in the records of the Colonial authorities that "The charge of Muddy River Bridge, being 15*l.* 3*s.* 6*d.*, was ordered to be allowed as followeth: By Boston, 6*l.*; by Roxbury, 5*l.*; Dorchester, 1*l.* 7*s.* 8*d.*; Watertown, 1*l.* 7*s.* 11*d.*; Cambridge,[1] 1*l.* 7*s.* 11*d.*" The building of a bridge across Muddy River in those days was probably accounted as great an undertaking as the building of a railroad to the Pacific

[1] Newtown had become Cambridge at this time; the name having been changed in 1638.

in these; and I doubt not that the accounts of Richard Dummer and John Johnson, for fifteen pounds, three shillings and six pence, were analyzed and audited more scrupulously and rigidly than any Erie, Pacific, or even Crédit Mobilier accounts for millions of times as much.

At the General Court, at Newtown, held by adjournment, on the 25th of September, 1634, we find a somewhat singular Order of two parts, in the following terms: "It is Ordered, with the consent of Watertown, that the meadow on this side Watertown weir, containing about 30 acres, be the same more or less, and now used by the inhabitants of Newtown, shall belong to the said inhabitants of Newtown, to enjoy to them and their heirs for ever, &c. Also, it is ordered, that the ground about Muddy River, belonging to Boston, and used by the inhabitants thereof, shall hereafter belong to Newtown, the wood and timber thereof, growing and to be growing, to be reserved to the inhabitants of Boston; provided, and it is the meaning of the Court, that if Mr. Hooker and the congregation now settled here shall remove hence, that then the aforesaid meadow ground shall return to Watertown, and the ground at Muddy River to Boston." Such legislation seems to partake too much of the quality which gave the name to our River to be easily made clear. But as the eminent Thomas Hooker with his congregation did soon afterwards (1636) remove to Springfield, and thence to Connecticut, all orders conditional on his staying in this vicinity may fairly be dismissed as null and void.

Turning now to the Boston Records, we find that in 1635, at a general meeting of the inhabitants, on the 14th of December, "it was agreed, that Mr. William Colbourne, Mr. William Aspinwall, and three others, shall lay out at Muddy River a sufficient allotment for our Teacher, Mr. John Cotton."

This was the celebrated Clergyman who had come over from old Boston to new Boston, and whose historical fame is enough for the glory of both cities. Though I believe he never lived here himself, this allotment was doubtless the origin of the estates which some of his family enjoyed here soon afterwards. At the same meeting of the people of Boston, it was agreed, "that the poorer sort of inhabitants, such as are members, or likely to be [probably meaning members of the Church], and have no cattle, shall have their proportion of allotments for planting ground and other, assigned unto them by the allotters, and laid out at Muddy River by the aforenamed five persons, — those that fall between the foot of the hill and the water to have but four acres upon a head, and those that are farther off to have five acres per head."

Four years later still, in 1639, it was agreed, "that five hundred acres be laid out at Muddy River for perpetual Commonage to the inhabitants there and the Town of Boston, before any other allotments are made."

If this perpetual Commonage, ten times larger than what we now know as Boston Common, had been indeed perpetual, Boston would not now have been in need of seeking land for a public Park. But the small allotment system soon most happily prevailed over any such extensive arrangement for Commonage, and the land was quickly dotted over with those little independent freeholds which have been, and ever will be, the best foundations and the strongest bulwarks of freedom and self-government. No dependent tenantry could have ever made Massachusetts what she is. Nothing but independent freeholds can keep her what she is. Public Parks are grand things for the amusement, recreation, and health of the whole people. Great landed estates are the natural support of an aristocracy. The division of lands is as essential to liberty, as the division of labor to prosperous business and the advancement of industry and the arts.

But something more than independent freeholds was required, and ever will be required, for the security of freedom and for the wise exercise of self-government. I need hardly say that I mean Education; and not until 1686–7 do we find any specific local provision here for that all-important object. It was on the 8th of December, *old style*, of that year, the 18th of December, *new style*, — a little more than one hundred and eighty-five years ago, — that the government of the Colony, then under the temporary Presidency of Joseph Dudley, in answer to a Petition from Muddy River, passed the following memorable Order: "Ordered, that henceforth the said Hamlet of Muddy

River be free from town-rates to the Town of Boston; they maintaining their own highways and poor, and other public charges, amongst themselves; and that within one year they raise a School House, and also maintain an able reading and writing Master; and that the inhabitants annually meet to choose three men to manage their affairs."

The acceptance of that Order, at a full meeting of the inhabitants, precisely a week after it had passed the Colonial Council, with a vote for the maintenance of the School Master, is the first formal entry in the Town Clerk's records of Brookline; and certainly no worthier or more welcome beginning could have been desired or devised for your recorded history. That history, indeed, is still the history of a hamlet appurtenant to Boston. But the freedom from Boston rates, with the liberty "to choose three men to manage their affairs," was a great step towards independence, and made the hamlet a town in almost every thing except the name. The little triumvirate which first administered the powers thus granted to Muddy River, must not fail to be remembered on such an occasion as this. They were Ensign Andrew Gardner, John White, Jr., and Thomas Stedman.

This virtual independence, however, seems to have been of brief duration. No sooner had the tyrannical Andros and his government been overthrown, as they so richly deserved to be, than Boston, in March, 1690, disannulled this arrangement, and voted "that Muddy River inhabitants are not discharged from Boston to be a hamlet by themselves, but stand related to Boston as they did before the year 1686." Ten or eleven years more of quiet submission rolled on, when the inhabitants of this place were emboldened, by the increase of their numbers and of their wealth, to request the consent of Boston to their becoming a separate Town; and curiously enough, in view of the facility of modern locomotion, one of the reasons assigned was the remoteness of their situation! But Boston resisted and resented the petition, and voted that, though the inhabitants of Muddy River "had not for some years been rated in the Town rate, yet, for the time to come, the Selectmen should rate them in the Town tax as the other inhabitants, and as they used to be."

A question of Taxes was thus evidently at the bottom of the controversy with Boston for separation and independence. And questions of taxation seem to have been at the bottom of almost all political controversies, small and great, in our own land and in other lands, from the days of Ship money down at least to the days of the Tea tax. There seems to be in human nature everywhere an inherent aversion for Tax-layers and Tax-gatherers. I recall at this moment only one notable instance of any thing like voluntary submission to taxation. There may be others in Dutch History, or elsewhere. But for this I turn back to the pages of Holy Writ; and even this may have meant something more or less than meets the ear. You all remember the Gospel account of what happened at the time of the first advent of our Saviour, in which it is recorded that "all went to be taxed, every one into his own city." It is a charming narrative, hallowed in all our hearts at once by the sacred volume in which it is contained, and by the exquisite story of which it is the preamble. But I fear that we must wait for the second coming of our blessed Lord before such a record, in its literal interpretation, will be found again anywhere. The tendency of later days, certainly, in some parts of the world not a thousand miles off, has been to flee from one's own City, or one's own Town, to escape taxation! It has been partly the result of extravagant and wanton expenditures by those in authority, and partly of capricious and unjust appraisements of individual estates. But a fair and equal proportion of our property is a debt due to the government, and to a government of our own choice; and debts to the government, whether of the Nation, the State, the City, or the Town, are nothing less or other than debts, and ought to be so recognized and so discharged. Every man knows what he owes, and where he owes it; and it is not only a wrong upon the public treasuries, but a wrong upon our neighbors, throwing upon them the burden of unequal contributions, to run away and leave our part unpaid. I have sometimes thought that in the common case of double residence, if I may so call it, a provision of law might be made that a person should be rated in both places, and one-half of each Tax bill be paid in each place. But the only radical cure must be found in correcting the abuses of our municipal governments, large or small, and in quickening the consciences and the sense of duty of the tax-paying community.

Boston, it seems, desired and determined to hold our little hamlet still amenable to her own assessors; and nothing remained for the inhabitants here except an appeal to the Colonial Legislature. Such an appeal was made without success in 1704, Boston still making strenuous opposition to it. But a new Petition, signed by thirty-two Freeholders, headed by Samuel Sewall, Jr., and which seemed to imply in its terms that the objections of Boston had at length in some way been overcome, was presented during the following year; and on the 13th day of November, 1705, the Act of the 4th year of the reign of Queen Anne, as it carefully sets forth, was passed and signed by Governor Joseph Dudley, creating the inhabitants of Muddy River a Town by the name of Brookline.

The Act was a brief one; but there was at least one remarkable provision in it, by which the inhabitants were "enjoined to build a Meeting House, and obtain an able Orthodox Minister, according to the direction of the Law, to be settled within the space of three years next coming." Religious education was a part of the system by which Massachusetts was built up; and though we have wisely abandoned all attempts at prescribing what is, and what is not, Orthodox, and have adopted the voluntary principle in regard to places for public worship, we shall do well to bear in mind that no mere secular instruction, however complete and thorough, was regarded as sufficient for sustaining free institutions by those who founded them. This condition of the Brookline charter, however, was not fulfilled, it seems, until nearly three times "three years" had expired. It was not until the year 1714 that a Meeting House was erected here. Before that time, the settlers here, we learn, had united in worship with the First Church in Roxbury; and good Dr. Pierce has given us an amusing anecdote of a lady of this place, of the olden time, "rising up early on every Lord's Day morning, adjusting her head-dress over a pail of water, for want of a looking-glass, and then walking five miles to Roxbury meeting"! I know not whether another record of such a mirror can be found since Narcissus admired himself in a fountain, and was metamorphosed into a flower.

No wonder, that in view of the necessity of a walk, or even a drive, to Roxbury, in order to find a place for public worship, the people here made such exhausting efforts to provide a place for themselves, as it would seem from your Records they did. In those days, it will be borne in mind, every Town was called upon not only to send a Representative to the General Court, but to pay his expenses and charges for going, staying, and returning. But on the 14th of May, 1714, — the year the first church here was erected, — we find a vote of the inhabitants deliberately declining to send a Representative "upon account of their building a Meeting House, and the great charges thereof for such *a poor little town*," and desiring and praying the Honorable House of Representatives to excuse them for that year.

It may help us to illustrate the period when Brookline first became a Town, and to fix it in our memory, if we bear in mind that the first newspaper in British North America had been published the very year before, and that a very remarkable child was born in the early part of the very year after. The newspaper was a weekly print, on half a sheet of pot paper, in small pica, and it was called the "Boston News Letter." The child was a strong, vigorous boy, christened on the day of his birth in the Old South Church, and giving the earliest promise of the wonderful career he was to run; and his name was Benjamin Franklin. The great printer followed hard after the first newspaper; and the Boston, of which Brookline was just ceasing to be a part, was the birthplace of them both.

And thus, my friends, seventy-three years after those "Ten Sagamores and many Indians" had been lying in ambush at Muddy River, Brookline at last stands before us, with at least thirty-two freeholders, with all the privileges, and in all the dignity, of a Town.

The Petition itself, singularly enough, asked only to be "a separate village, or peculiar;" and this designation is twice repeated by the Petitioners. "A Peculiar" was an old English ecclesiastical term, which stood for a Parish exempt from the jurisdiction of the Ordinary of the Diocese, and subject only to the Metropolitan. But there was another signification, for which Dr. Worcester has given us the authority of John Milton's glorious prose, — "One's own property." This, doubtless, was the sense in which it was used in the Petition. Brookline was henceforth to be "its own property," and to do its own rating and taxing. We may well be satisfied, however, that the Colonial Council declined to take the Petitioners at their word, and saved them from being laughed at, as they would have been if the inhabitants of Muddy River had been incorporated as "a Peculiar."

But there is another peculiarity about the Petition. Its thirty-two signers had but just half that number of separate surnames among them all. There were five of the name of Gardner, and five of the name of Winchester; three of the name of White, three of Stedman, and three of Ackers; two of the name of Aspinwall, and two of Devotion; and one each of Sewall, Boylston, Sharp, Ellis, Woodward, Holland, Shepard, Chamberlain, and Seaver. These were the old family names of the place. There may have been others, and doubtless were. There may have been differences of opinion about making Brookline a Town or a Peculiar in that day, as there certainly are about unmaking it at this day; or other considerations or circumstances may have prevented some of the inhabitants from signing the Petition. But those sixteen names of those thirty-two Freeholders must ever be associated with your first existence as a Town. Some of them are already inscribed upon your highways, as the names of streets or avenues. Many more of them might well be inscribed there. I know not why we should go out of our own local history to find names for our thoroughfares. I even doubt whether it is worth while to go into the woods and forests for such a purpose, when we have at hand the names of men who cut down the woods and cleared the forests for us. Walnut and Chestnut and Cypress are sonorous and significant titles, more especially if stately rows of shade trees are set out along the roadside in correspondence with the names. But Aspinwall, and Boylston, and Sewall, and Winchester, which you have, and Gardner, and Sharp, and Stedman, which I believe you have not, would sound as well and signify more. It is not enough to write our local history on perishable records. It should be written where he who runs may read it. I have often lamented, with others, that so few of the names of the Founders of my native City were inscribed on its principal streets. The new parts of the City seemed to afford the very opportunity for repairing such an omission. The musical titles of the English Peerage, however, — Arlington, Berkeley, Clarendon, and the rest, — have been allowed to prevail over the honest patronymics of our own settlers and citizens. But henceforth, as long as we are a Peculiar or a Town, I trust that the names of our Brookline streets, and school-houses, too, may be taken from her own earlier or later history.

Not a few of the names signed to that Petition were eminently worthy of such a commemoration, if of no other. Samuel Sewall, Jr., was not only himself the first signer of the Petition, and the Town Clerk who attested the act of incorporation, but his father was one of the largest early landholders of the place; a member of the Colonial Council at the time; one of the Colonial Judges from 1692 to 1728, and Chief Justice for the last ten of those six and thirty years. It is true, and "pity 'tis 'tis true," that, sharing in the delusion which so widely prevailed throughout the Massachusetts Colony during the first year of his long judicial career, he concurred in the condemnation of those convicted of Witchcraft. But so had Sir Matthew Hale, one of the purest and wisest of Old England's Judges, little more than a quarter of a century before. Sewall, too, five years afterwards, made a frank and manly confession of his grievous mistake, imploring publicly "the pardon of man and God for his guilt." Who will not say Amen! to the noble lines of our charming Quaker Poet: —

"Green for ever the memory be
Of the Judge of the old theocracy,
Whom even his errors glorified,
Like a far-seen, sunlit mountain side
By the cloudy shadows which o'er it glide!"

Whittier did not forget, and none of us would be willing to forget, that Sewall's Tract, entitled "The Selling of Joseph,"—

a copy of which, found among my own family papers, was recently reprinted in the Proceedings of the Massachusetts Historical Society, — was among the earliest public protests against Domestic Slavery, then tolerated at the North as well as at the South. He was a man of eminent benevolence and beneficence, of large hospitality and comprehensive charity. His wife was a daughter of John Hull, another of the earliest landholders here, the original Mint-master of the Massachusetts Colony, to whom has been ascribed the device of an Indian with his bow and arrow on our State Shield;[1] and who was the unquestioned coiner of those famous Pine Tree Shillings, bearing the date of 1652, which gave such umbrage to King Charles the Second, — who was only appeased, it is said, by the suggestion of Sir Thomas Temple, or somebody else, that the Tree intended to be designated was the Royal Oak which saved his Royal Majesty! The wife of John Hull was Judith Quincy, daughter of Edmund Quincy,[2] the founder of that distinguished family in New England, whose blood, of course, our first signer inherited. Can any thing more be needed to make the name of Sewall a household memory in Brookline? It has been said that the Judge stood godfather to the Town, and gave it its name from the little brook which ran through his own meadows. If he did, the engrossing clerks of the Colony and the Town failed to adopt his spelling of the name. On turning to his own manuscript Diary, not many days ago, I found the following emphatic entry, under date of November 12, 1705: "Brooklyn is pass'd to be a Township ꝑ the Council;" while more than a year earlier, under date of April 1, 1704, he writes: "Visited my valetudinarious son at Brooklin."[3] The final *e* is needed to bring these discrepancies from the Town name, as it is properly written and pronounced, within the reconciling principle of what the lawyers call the "*idem sonans*."

1 More probably he was only the engraver of it.

2 The marriage ceremony was performed by Governor Winthrop "on the 11th of the 3d month," 1647.

3 The Diary repeats the latter spelling in the following record, dated July 11, 1704: "Son and Daughter Hirst, Joseph and Mary, rode with me in the Coach to Brooklin, and there dined at my son's with the Governour, his lady, Mr. Paul Dudley and wife," and other grand company. "Sung a Psalm."

The name of Gardner stood second on that successful Petition, and five of that name were among its signers, — Thomas, Joseph, Thomas, Jr., Caleb, and one whose Christian name has been worn off in the lapse of years. Perhaps it was Andrew; for Andrew Gardner, you remember, was at the head of the little triumvirate selected to manage the local affairs of the village nine or ten years before. Thomas Gardner was himself the first Deacon of the first Church in Brookline. His grandson, Isaac, a graduate of Harvard in 1747, and afterwards a leading man of the Town, respected and beloved by all, was among those who went out from Brookline on the 19th of April, 1775, and was killed at Cambridge by the British troops on their retreat to Boston; while, on the following 17th of June, Col. Thomas Gardner of the same stock, though then living over the Brighton border, fell nobly at Bunker Hill. Could any worthier name be recalled on this occasion, more especially since it is henceforth to be associated, not only with those heroes of the past, but with a recent munificent donation to your Public Library by one of your living fellow-citizens of the same name? [1]

The name of White stands third on the Petition. It has been found before on the list of those first three Selectmen, and is to be found again in connection with a liberal gift of Woodland for the maintenance of the Brookline minister.

Thomas Stedman, the third of those three Selectmen, is the fourth signer of the Petition; and the fifth is John Winchester, Brookline's first Representative to the General Court, in 1709.

And now we have a name as eminent for its worth, as it is first in alphabetical order. The sixth and seventh signers were Samuel and Eleazer Aspinwall. Capt. Samuel Aspinwall was born here in 1657; and, from that year to this, whether as hamlet, village, peculiar, or town, Brookline has never been without a distinguished bearer of his name and blood. The old house built by his father before 1666 is still standing, or at least trying to stand. Of the venerable elm which overshadowed it

[1] On the 6th of January, 1871, the sum of Ten Thousand dollars was presented to the Public Library of Brookline by John L. Gardner, Esq.

certainly for more than a hundred and fifty years, — if, indeed, it were not coeval with Columbus, — nothing remains but the antique roots, and a few feet of massive but mutilated trunk. They are almost the last relics of the old Muddy River Hamlet, and I wish they could be inclosed and inscribed as a monument of the remote past. What an inspiring stump that would be for an open-air speech on some historical anniversary! If nothing else can be done, I trust that enough of it may be secured as a desk for this very platform. If it were here at this moment, my manuscript would have a most congenial resting-place, — more precious than the most skilful carving or veneering of Oak, or Maple, or Satinwood.

But the old family tree is still fresh and vigorous, and has literally borne leaves for the healing of the people. No name of his period — in Brookline history, certainly — has been more honored, or more worthy of being honored — not always, alas, the same thing — than that of the late Dr. William Aspinwall, so long an eminent physician of the Town; and who, while devoted to the duties of his profession and to the interests of his native place, found time to serve the State with distinction as a member successively of both branches of the Legislature and of the Executive Council. You all know, too, how respected and beloved was his son, the late Augustus Aspinwall. But what may I say of another son still living; who, until a few weeks past, exhibited so little of old age except its experience, its wisdom, and its venerableness, that no one was ready to give credit to the tale which he sometimes told of a birthday in Brookline eighty-six or eighty-seven years ago; with that empty sleeve which he has carried for nearly sixty of those years, as a badge of noble daring while a leader in the Army of the United States, in that war with England which we trust will never lose its designation as "the last war," but who, with the arm which was left him, has done as much of faithful service to his Country and his Country's history, at home and abroad, as any boasted Briareus of ancient or of modern fable? He is not with us here to-day, as he so recently promised to be, but all our hearts are with him in his chamber of sickness; and every one of you will eagerly unite with me in the hope, that he may still be spared to enjoy the respect and affection of all who know him.[1]

The name of Aspinwall is followed by that of William Sharp, the only representative of that name on the Petition; but his father, or it may have been his grandfather, John Sharp, had come here with the earliest Aspinwall, while two of his family, both of them Robert Sharp, father and son, had already fallen in battle while fighting bravely against the Indians. The father fell in King Philip's War, on the 18th of April, 1676; and in the graveyard at Sudbury, not far from the Wayside Inn, which Longfellow and Parsons have both so charmingly illustrated, may be read the following inscription: "Capt. Samuel Wadsworth of Milton, his Lieut. Sharp of Brookline, and twenty-six other souldiers, fighting for the defence of their Country, were slain by the Indian enemy, and lye buried in this place." And if any additional claim could be needed for a grateful remembrance of the name on this occasion, it would be abundantly found in the fact, that from the daughter of John Sharp were descended those admirable and brilliant Buckminsters, the revered pastor of Portsmouth and his eloquent son of Brattle Street, of whose Memoirs it was long ago said by Thomas Carlyle, the Historian, that "it gave a much better account of the higher sort of character in New England than any thing he had seen since Franklin's writings."

I can follow this list of honored names but little farther. Yet I must not omit the very next one; that of Edward Devotion,[2] from whose estate the Town ultimately received no less than seven hundred and thirty-nine pounds and four shillings, lawful money, for the use and maintenance of its schools; as large a sum nominally as John Harvard left to the College at Cambridge in 1638. A century and a quarter had, indeed, made a wide difference in the actual value of the gifts; but, if Harvard's name has been given to a whole University, the name of Devo-

[1] Col. Thomas Aspinwall, for nearly forty years United States Consul at London, who, in 1870, had edited and annotated two volumes of valuable Papers for the Collections of the Massachusetts Historical Society, died on the eleventh day of August, 1876, at ninety years of age.

[2] I learn, from my friend William I. Bowditch, Esq., that the old house of Edward Devotion is still standing.

tion is certainly worthy of being inscribed on one of your Town Schools.

One other name, standing near the foot of the list, but the associations with which are by no means of inferior interest, must close my allusions to these memorable signers of that little declaration, or petition, for independence. I need hardly say that I refer to that of Peter Boylston. A spirit of independence might almost seem to have been transmitted with his blood, for his daughter was the mother of brave old John Adams. Himself the son of the earliest physician of Muddy River, he was, also, the brother of that celebrated physician and surgeon, Dr. Zabdiel Boylston, who during the prevalence, in 1721, of that terrible scourge of which we have recently had so many unwelcome reminders, is recorded, on yonder tombstone, to have "first introduced inoculation into America;" and who persisted heroically in the practice, beginning with his own son, in spite of the menaces and positive assaults of a prejudiced and exasperated populace. He is said to have been "execrated and persecuted as a murderer;" "his house [in Boston] to have been attacked with violence;" he himself to have been shut up at one time for a fortnight in a secret apartment, while "the enraged inhabitants were patrolling the streets with halters, threatening to hang him on the next tree." Yet inoculation was justly regarded, no long time afterwards, as great a discovery and as valuable a preventive as vaccination is at this day. It had been for the first time performed in the English dominions, we are told, only seven or eight weeks before, on a daughter of the celebrated Lady Mary Wortley Montagu, who had witnessed the operation in Turkey, during her residence in Constantinople, where her husband was the British Ambassador. Visiting England a few years afterwards, Boylston was immediately recognized, and was at once the subject of that rare distinction for Americans, an election as a Fellow of the Royal Society. Paul Dudley, a son of Governor Joseph, and John Winthrop, a great-grandson of the first Governor, were Fellows about the same time; and Cotton Mather, who, it is said, co-operated with Boylston, and was, indeed, "the first mover" in introducing inoculation, has also the addendum of

F. R. S., and certainly supposed himself entitled to it, though some shrewd doubts have been rife in later years whether it was ever actually conferred upon him.[1] But Zabdiel Boylston was a man of remarkable qualities; an eminent naturalist for that period, eagerly collecting whatever was rare in the way of plants and animals, and transmitting specimens of them to England; while his skill as a physician and surgeon secured him a distinguished reputation both at home and abroad. No name among the signers of the Petition which resulted in making Brookline a Town, on the 13th of November, 1705, is more worthy of commemoratiou than that of Boylston.

And now, my friends, what was it to be made a Town? What was it in that day? What is it in this? Profound investigations have been made, from time to time, as to the historical origin of these little municipal organizations. I am content to leave this question to-day, certainly, where John Milton left it two centuries ago. "But I say," were the words of that wonderful writer of prose as well as poetry, — "but I say that even Towns and Boroughs are more ancient than Kings; and that the people is the people, though they should live in the open fields." Who can overestimate the importance and dignity of such organizations of the people? The more any one studies the history of New England, and of Massachusetts in particular, the more he will be impressed with the vast and varied influence which has been exerted by our Town System, not only in promoting the moral and social welfare of the inhabitants, but in advancing and sustaining civil freedom, and in preparing the people for meeting those great emergencies and exigencies which have successively marked our political progress. The right and the duty of the citizens to understand and to manage their own local affairs; to establish and superintend their own schools; to organize and enforce their own police; to lay and levy their own taxes, and to regulate and control the expenditure of the moneys raised by taxation, — freely choosing their own agents for all these local purposes, and their own Representatives for the larger concerns and counsels of the Com-

[1] Dr. Allen, in his Biographical Dictionary, says that Mather was made a Fellow in 1713.

monwealth; — the possession and the exercise of these special powers and obligations of Towns, as they were so long known from the earliest period of our Massachusetts history, have done more than all other things combined, to quicken the intelligence, sharpen the faculties, and develop the manhood and self-reliance of the whole people, and to make them capable of achieving and upholding the prosperity and the liberty in which we now rejoice.

We sometimes speak of Education, as if it were confined to the Schoolhouse, the Academy, or the College; and so in great part it must be for the young. But Republican Institutions do not merely demand education for their support, they supply it in their own nature and essence. Free Government is itself an education, which goes on long after Schools and Colleges have done their work. The education of a Free Press; the education of the Jury-box and of open Court-rooms; the education of the Reading-room and the Public Library; the better and more important education of the House of God, where religious freedom and the rights of conscience have been firmly secured; but greater and more vital than either, in every mere worldly view, the education of the Town Hall, — who can exaggerate the results of them all? Yes, my friends, these Town Halls, where men are first trained and exercised in watching and in working the machinery of self-government, and are habituated not merely to observe and inspect, but to take part in setting in motion, and in keeping in motion, the very springs and wheels and levers of all political action, have furnished, and must always furnish, the true Schools of the Citizen. And how much they have done to foster and cherish that spirit of equal rights and individual independence which is at once the source and the safeguard of civil freedom! Tyranny and oppression, at home and abroad, have always dreaded and hated Town meetings. Sir Edmund Andros, when he was playing his fantastic tricks with the New England Colonies, is said to have solemnly prohibited all Town meetings in Massachusetts except once a year on the third Monday in May. When Boston, in 1657, thirty years before Andros, had appointed a Committee to consider the model of a Town House, and to take up a subscription "to propagate such a building," she had taken the first step in a path which could have no doubtful termination. "Propagating Town Houses," as it was quaintly styled, was nothing less than propagating treason and defiance to tyranny and despotism. Had Lord North, a century afterwards, succeeded in shutting up Faneuil Hall, the virtual town house of Boston, a few years earlier than he did, or even in turning the Old South into a Post-Office, — and had silenced Warren and Quincy, and James Otis and Samuel Adams, — the Stamp Act and the Writs of Assistance, the Tea Chests and the British Redcoats, might have encountered a far less stern reception than they did. While, on the other hand, if the centralizing tendencies of modern times, which the wonderful facilities for locomotion and intercommunication have done so much to stimulate, — diminishing so seriously the importance and individuality of the smaller towns, and sometimes swallowing them up bodily in great cities, — if these tendencies had been possible, and had prevailed, a century and a half ago, we should have looked in vain for not a few of the influences which have most effectively moulded the character and developed the capacity of our people, and made them the free, intelligent, self-relying people which they are at this hour. The remission and relegation of all the affairs of a community, and of almost all their rights and duties except the elective franchise, to Boards of Aldermen and Common Councils, is a necessary evil, if not a positive advantage, in great cities; but the nearer power is kept to its original source, in the deliberate consultations and direct acts of the people themselves, the purer and safer will be the administration of local government, and the more will the people be interested, and instructed, and felt, in the working of Republican institutions. An old English Poet, two hundred years ago, spoke of making "one city of the Universe;"[1] and some of our Legislators would seem to have caught the same inspiration. But I may be permitted reverently to doubt, whether the Universe will be quite ready for such a consummation, until the grand prophecy of Holy Writ shall be accomplished, and the New Jerusalem be seen descending from heaven, "into which there shall no wise enter any thing that

[1] Dryden, in his Annus Mirabilis.

defileth, neither whatsoever worketh abomination, or maketh a lie."

Think not, my friends, that I am pleading against any impending danger. If Brookline is indeed ready to relinquish her single-blessedness, and has put on her beautiful garments to-day in preparation for the wedding, it is as little my province to forbid the banns, as it is to give away the bride; though, perhaps, I may be pardoned for hoping, Churchman as I am, that the ceremony may be completed without the employment of a *ring!*

To be made a Town, then, in 1705, was to be admitted to an equal partnership in that great company of Massachusetts municipalities which were gradually but surely building up the Colony into a grand Commonwealth, fit to take its stand and do its whole share in establishing and upholding an Independent and United Nation. The old Colony of Plymouth, with all its cherished Pilgrim associations, after just threescore years and ten of separate existence, had been made a part of Massachusetts, only fifteen years before, under the new Provincial Charter. There were at that time about eighty-two towns in Massachusetts, not including such as have since fallen within the jurisdiction of Maine, or other adjoining States: there are now, I believe, more than three hundred and forty. Brookline was the eighty-third, if my careful friend Mr. W. H. Whitmore has counted correctly; [1] and she was not slow in attesting her title to be included in this goodly fellowship. Her Records, indeed, afford ample evidence of the patriotism and public spirit which have characterized her inhabitants in every memorable period from that day to this. I have taken so much time, however, in recounting the experiences of her earlier days, that I must forbear from following them along in the same detail. I do not regret it, and I hope that you may not regret it. The pioneer planters of our villages and towns, and even the founders and

[1] It is not altogether easy to give these numbers with precision, owing to the changes in the towns, and in the State, since 1705. By the Table, No. VII., in the Massachusetts Census of 1865, Brookline would appear to be the seventy-ninth of the then existing towns, in the order of Incorporation. The annexation of Roxbury and Dorchester to Boston would thus leave her now the seventy-seventh.

fathers of our State, have long been in danger of being overlooked, and almost forgotten, in the larger concerns and louder claims of later generations. The admirations, I had almost said, the idolatries, of the immediate hour absorb us all. The present fills our view. If it is not he that is living and acting to-day, it is he who died yesterday, upon whom all our praises are lavished, and for whom the stateliest monument or the costliest statue is at once prepared. We must go to the humble village churchyards for the crumbling memorials of some of our noblest builders and benefactors: —

> "Their name, their years, spelt by th' unlettered Muse,
> The place of fame and elegy supply."

If I shall only have freshened and deepened the inscriptions on some of those ancient grave-stones, I may safely leave the fame of later generations to others, — more especially as your "Brookline Transcript" is furnishing from week to week, with an affectionate interest which betrays a lady's pen, the materials of a local history, which at no distant day, we trust, may put on the shape of a permanent volume.[1]

Yet I cannot even approach a conclusion of this Address, without a cursory glance at what Brookline has been doing during the more than a century and half since she assumed her majority and asserted her independence; and more particularly during the latter part of that period. I will not attempt to entertain you with figures, either statistical or rhetorical. The gradual growth of the population, until it now counts nearly seven thousand inhabitants and eleven hundred voters, — while in the list of the population of Muddy River, in 1687, there were but just fifty names, and Dr. Pierce told us there were only sixty-five voters when he first came here in 1796; the increase of wealth, real, or certainly appraised, until it has been seriously doubted of late whether it be not the richest town of its size in the whole Union; the diversification of business and industry; the aggregate of crops or of cattle; the improvement of highways; the multiplication of schools and of

[1] A volume, entitled "Historical Sketches of Brookline, by Harriet F. Woods," was published in 1874.

churches; the opening of public Squares and Playgrounds; the establishment of a Public Library, — all such details may well be left for the Census, or the Annual Reports of your Selectmen. Nor will I rob your Town Records of their interest for the future antiquary or annalist, by reproducing too many of the Resolutions and proceedings which have illustrated the patriotism of the Town, at each succeeding epoch of our Colonial or National history. Those records are, indeed, rich in Revolutionary memorials, as I have found by personal examination, and one or two of the most notable of them I must not omit to mention.

On the 15th of December, 1767, it was voted unanimously, "That this Town will take all prudent and legal measures to promote Industry, Economy, and Manufactures in this Province, and in any of the British American Colonies, and will likewise take all legal measures to discourage the use of European superfluities;" and five persons, — William Hyslop, Esq., Capt. Benjamin White, Isaac Gardner, Esq., Mr. John Goddard, and Mr. Samuel Aspinwall, — were thereupon appointed a Committee to prepare a form of subscription against receiving such European superfluities. This was Brookline's first response to the memorable Act of Parliament, which had just imposed a tax of three pence a pound on Tea.

On the 11th of December, 1772, it was voted to choose a Committee to take under consideration the violation and infringements of the Rights of the Colonists, and of this Province in particular; and "said Committee to be a Committee of communication and correspondence with the Town of Boston and any other Towns on the subject of our present difficulties."

On the 26th of November, 1773, Brookline proceeded to initiate further and more decisive action in regard to certain cargoes of Tea, then "hourly expected to arrive." Her Resolutions were strong and uncompromising, as your Records abundantly show. She was, of course, one of the Five Towns — Dorchester, Roxbury, Brookline, Cambridge, and Charlestown — which were forthwith summoned by Samuel Adams to meet Boston, in Mass Meeting, at Faneuil Hall on the 29th. The Committees of those five Towns, with that of Boston, were at Faneuil Hall again, on the 13th of December; and I need not tell anybody that "Boston Harbor was black with unexpected Tea,"—as Carlyle describes it, just three days afterwards.

On the 1st of March, 1775, we find the Boston Committee of Correspondence, in a letter to the Selectmen of this Town, "acknowledging the receipt of £25, 7^{s} $6\frac{1}{2}^{d}$, in cash, by the hands of our worthy friend, Mr. John Heath; also wood, mutton, rice, corn, &c.; it being the very generous donation of the Town of Brookline to this devoted place, now suffering the severity of ministerial vengeance for nobly exerting themselves in the cause of American Liberty."

On the 20th of May, 1776, six weeks before the Declaration of Independence at Philadelphia, it was voted "to advise the person chosen to represent this Town in the next General Court, that if the Honorable Congress should for the safety of the American Colonies declare them Independent of the Kingdom of Great Britain, we the said Inhabitants will solemnly engage with our Lives and Fortunes to support them in the measure." This was Brookline's prompt and categorical response to the question ordered to be propounded to all the towns of Massachusetts, by a vote of the House of Representatives on the 10th of the same month of May, just seven days before. A single week was long enough for notifying and holding the Town meeting, and for deciding on the answer; and my valued friend Richard Frothingham, in his admirable History of "The Rise of the Republic," just published, has cited no response so early within a week as that of Brookline.

You will not have forgotten, my friends, that from July, 1775, to April, 1776, the American Army was encamped around Boston. During a large part, if not the whole, of that period, the Regiment of Colonel Prescott—who had so gallantly thrown up, and so bravely commanded, the redoubt at Bunker Hill—was stationed, together with a Rhode Island Regiment, on yonder Sewall's Farm, a portion of which is now owned and occupied by our worthy fellow-citizen, the Hon. Amos A. Lawrence. The Brookline Fort at Sewall's Point, of which the outlines may still be traced, was a very strong and extensive one, occupying a central position between the right and left wing of our

Army, and commanding the entrance of Charles River. It is a most welcome and inspiring thought, for this Anniversary and this occasion, that Washington himself in those days must often have passed somewhere along these very Brookline roads, such as they then were, on his way from his head-quarters at Cambridge, where Longfellow now lives, to visit the extended lines of the American Camp. He must needs have passed, I think, not far from where we are now assembled, as he crossed from Sewall's Point to Roxbury, and so to South Boston, as it is now called, not many days before he stood in triumph on Dorchester Heights, to witness the British Fleet setting sail in yonder bay, and the British Forces finally driven out from Boston and its vicinity. We may almost venture to picture him to our mind's eye, at this instant, — reining up, perhaps, at the old Aspinwall elm, or galloping on to Corey's Hill, or some lesser height, to catch a clearer glimpse of what the enemy were doing on Boston Common. He is now, at the age of forty-three, in the perfect maturity of his manhood. And what a manhood it is! There is no mistaking him, closely surrounded, though he may be, by a gallant staff and a sturdy body-guard. That form of unsurpassed symmetry! That modest but commanding and majestic presence! The bloom of youth not yet faded from his noble countenance! A shadow of anxiety may, indeed, now and then be seen stealing over that serene brow; for we must confess that our New England Militia, with their short enlistments, and their want of ammunition, and their impatience of discipline, often involved him in the deepest concern and perplexity. But not yet has he been worn and weighed down by the cares and toils of a seven years' war; not yet by the tremendous responsibilities of inaugurating and administering an untried National Government. His great heart, his vigorous frame, are still fresh and buoyant. All that Shakspeare has given us of young Harry the Fifth, " with his beaver on, witching the world with noble horsemanship," — all except, thank God, the profligate early life; all that Virgil has told us of the young Marcellus, — "*pietas, prisca fides, invictaque bello dextera*," — the religious sense of duty, the old-fashioned integrity, the invincible right arm, — all except, thank God, the untimely end, — might help us to picture to ourselves that peerless chief, as he passed this way almost a hundred years ago, — might help us to complete the portrait, of which neither the chisel of Houdon, nor the brush of Stuart, nor the stately bronze of Ball or Crawford, could give more than the cold outlines.

Haply, some Brookline school-boys of that day may have caught the sound of his horse's hoofs, and gazed up idly at him. Haply, some one of their elders may have stared incredulously, if not rudely, at the young Virginian, who had been commissioned by the Continental Congress to supersede and outrank all our veteran Wards and Putnams and Prescotts on their own New England soil. It was too early for any one to take in the full measure and proportions of the destined Father of his Country. But what Brookline school-boy is there at this hour, what man or woman or child is there among us to-day, who would not exchange all other visions of mere humanity which have ever been vouchsafed to any one of them, in a longer or a shorter life, for one distinct and conscious sight of that supreme and incomparable young man! Think over with me, my friends, all whom you have ever seen, or have ever yearned to see, at home or abroad, of American or of foreign distinction and celebrity, — Emperors at the head of triumphant armies; Kings or Queens on some grand festival of coronation; Roman Pontiffs on their Easter throne at St. Peter's; Franklin with his kite, challenging the thunderbolt; Chatham hurling scorn at his own Government for employing Indians against the American Colonies; Burke impeaching Warren Hastings, or pleading the cause of American Conciliation; Napoleon at Austerlitz; Wellington at Waterloo; Webster in the Senate Chamber replying to Hayne, or at once defining and impersonating the noblest eloquence at Faneuil Hall, in his matchless eulogy on Adams and Jefferson; — think over each one of them, and tell me whether, with me, you would not eagerly have exchanged them all, for the single satisfaction of having seen George Washington!

The few remaining eyes which ever enjoyed that satisfaction, even in the closing years of his great career, will soon be sealed to all earthly sights. It is seventy-three years ago to-day, since on Saturday, the 22d of February, 1800, Brookline, in common with all the country, held solemn services on occasion of his death, which had occurred on the 14th of December, 1799. And, from that time to this, nowhere have his character and his principles found warmer admirers or more devoted followers than here; nowhere have his name and his fame been more affectionately and reverently cherished. All honor to his memory, then, on this one hundred and forty-first Anniversary of his birthday, from these scenes and surroundings of his first great triumph in the cause of American Liberty! All honor to the memory of him, to whom one Lord Chancellor of England did not scruple to write: "I have a large acquaintance among the most valuable and exalted classes of men, but you are the only being for whom I ever felt an awful reverence;"[1] and of whom another and later Lord Chancellor of England did not hesitate to say: "Until time shall be no more, will a test of the progress which our race has made in wisdom and virtue be derived from the veneration paid to the immortal name of Washington!"[2]

I am aware, my friends, that, in claims to consideration like those I have thus far suggested, Brookline has for the most part only a joint interest with her sister towns in all quarters of the Commonwealth. But she is not without some peculiar titles to remembrance and regard, which would secure a more than common fragrance for her memory, even should her individuality and her name be merged to-morrow in the renown and grandeur of the neighboring Metropolis.

I think no one will dispute that Brookline was for a long time pre-eminent in the little cordon of towns which have so long constituted the exquisite environs of Boston, embossing it with a rich and varied margin of lawn and lake and meadow and wooded hillside, and encircling its old "plain neck," as William Wood called it, in his "New England Prospect," with an unfading wreath of bloom and verdure. I think no one will

[1] Lord Erskine's letter to Washington, 15 March, 1795.

[2] Lord Brougham, in his Statesmen of the Time of George III.; and repeated, in precisely the same words, in his Installation Address, as Chancellor of the University of Edinburgh, 18 May, 1860.

dispute her claim to have given the earliest celebrity to those environs for rural culture and beauty. Visitors from other countries, or from other States, carried home with them a deeper impression of the charms of this spot and its surroundings than of any other region in New England; and when the well-to-do Bostonian, before there were any railroads or steamers to whirl him off to Scotland or the Alps, or even to Newport or Saratoga or Niagara, for his summer vacation, desired to get a breath of pure air, or a glimpse of green fields, or a scent of fresh flowers, by an afternoon's drive, the horse's head was turned first, and last, and almost all the time, towards Brookline, by the way, perhaps, of Pine Bank [1] and Jamaica Pond. Nature had done much, but cultivation and taste had hardly done less, in producing this result. Nowhere did Horticulture find earlier or more successful votaries than here. Nowhere could there be sought and found more exquisite flowers or more delicious fruits, in season or out of season, in the open air or under glass. Nor was experimental Agriculture without its early and devoted followers here. Meantime there was an elegant and distinguished hospitality to be enjoyed in Brookline homes, then filled by men of large acquaintance and of larger hearts, to say nothing of accomplished and beautiful women, to complete the attraction.

I do not forget that there were individual instances of the same sort of homes in Dorchester or Milton, in Roxbury or Jamaica Plain or Dedham, in Brighton or Watertown or Waltham. Still less do I forget that almost all these places have been catching up with Brookline, — perhaps outstripping her, — in all these particulars; and that both Horticulture and Agriculture may now look elsewhere for more than one of their highest illustrations and their most conspicuous disciples. I speak of half a century sometime closed, during a part of which, certainly, Brookline enjoyed a prestige for culture and beauty, which might almost have entitled her to that appellation of "a Peculiar" for which her old inhabitants petitioned.

[1] Then the beautiful residence of James Perkins, Esq, the eldest of the three liberal and public-spirited brothers, of whom two are named hereafter, as having lived in Brookline.

Let me not be thought too much disposed to narrow the limits either of time or space within which the special graces and attractions of the Town were to be witnessed. But I have sometimes thought that there was a little circle of our territory, from which had emanated, in successive years, as many good influences and examples, in the way of philanthropy and beneficence, of kindness and hospitality, and of every refined culture which pertains to rural enjoyment or improvement, — the culture of the field and of the garden, of the manners and of the human heart, — as from any spot of equal circumference on any part of the globe. Within or around that little circle have lived men of wide distinction in every walk of life, some of whose names are associated with the foremost places of the State or the Nation. From that little circle have come the original foundations of Asylums for the Blind, of State Reform Schools, of a score of the earliest scholarships for Harvard University, of a Free Chapel for the Poor in Boston, to say nothing of countless munificent donations, and of personal services equal to any donation, for Colleges and Athenæums and Schools, for Hospitals for the sick and for monuments of the glorious dead. From that little circle, in days when such things were rarities, went forth, in thoughtful and generous profusion, the choicest flowers and fruits which Nature in her season, or art defying all seasons, could produce, to cheer the hearts of lingering invalids, and moisten the parched lips of the suffering and dying; while within that narrow circle, too, might have been found the highest skill in surgery or medicine for their relief or cure. Need I recall the names of Higginson and Cabot and Mason, of John C. Warren and Richard Sullivan, of William Appleton and John Eliot Thayer, of Benjamin Guild and Theodore Lyman and Nathaniel Ingersoll Bowditch, of Samuel G. Perkins and his noble-hearted brother Thomas Handasyde Perkins, — whose combined services in public or professional life, in the cause of Horticulture or Agriculture, as eminent merchants or bankers or statesmen, united with the plilanthropy and munificence which characterized so many of them, make up an aggregate claim upon the grateful remembrance of their fellow-men, such as can hardly be surpassed or paralleled, for the period in which they lived, by the dwellers upon the same number of rural acres anywhere beneath the sun!

I may be pardoned for not forgetting that within that same little circle, during a later period, not a few of the grandest benefactions of the late George Peabody, during an occasional visit here, were concerted and arranged; and particularly that noble Trust for Southern Schools, in the service of which President Grant came to Brookline in the month of June last. Nor will any of you be likely to forget that a leading spirit in the relief of Chicago and of Boston,[1] after the terrible conflagrations which have so recently visited them, has been found, for many summers past, under the shadows of the trees which surrounded the home, and which were planted by the hands, — as he has often told me, — of the grand old Colonel Perkins. But I am speaking of the past and of the dead, and must not be betrayed into compliments to the living.

Who can estimate the blessings which have radiated in time past from this charmed and charming little circle in Brookline! Who can enter within its limits without catching something of the contagion of philanthropy and charity which so long pervaded it! May it not well be an object of ambition, for any one whose lot has of later years been cast within it, that he may not be counted unworthy of the traditions and associations with which it is crowded; that, as he enters one of those cherished mansions, the Genius of the place may confront him with no handwriting on the wall, "*O tecta ipsa misera — quam dispari domino!*"

True, the men to whom I have referred were mostly but summer residents here, and Boston as well as Brookline may claim them for her own roll of honor. But some of them, certainly, were not only men of hearts large enough for two cities, but wore worthy to be claimed, like Homer of old, by seven cities.

But can I forget that another and a sadder radiance rests upon that little circle? Shall it ever be forgotten that from the same narrow precincts went forth those noble brothers, whose remains, brought home from the battle-fields of the Union, are among the

[1] Hon. William Gray.

precious dust of yonder beautiful Cemetery?[1] When the tidings from Antietam, ten years ago, informed us that the elder of those heroic young men had fallen in the lap of one of the grandest and most momentous victories of the War, I could not but recall the touching lines of an old English Poet,[2] whose every phrase and epithet, though written a century and a half ago, seemed chosen and prepared for his elegy: —

"Ah, why, dear youth, in all the blooming prime
Of vernal genius, where disclosing fast
Each active worth, each manly virtue lay,
Why wert thou ravish'd from our hope so soon?
What now avails that noble thirst of fame,
Which stung thy fervent breast? that treasur'd store
Of knowledge early gain'd? that eager zeal
To serve thy country, glowing in the band
Of youthful patriots, who sustain her name?
What now, alas! that life-diffusing charm
Of sprightly wit? that rapture for the Muse,
That heart of friendship, and that soul of joy,
Which bade with softest light thy virtues smile?
Ah! only show'd, to check our fond pursuits,
And teach our humbled hopes that life is vain!"

But no, no, my friends, it was for something more and better than to teach our humbled hopes that life is vain! It taught us the very reverse of all this. Such a life was not vain. Such a death was not vain. They have lighted the way of patriotic resolve and noble self-sacrifice in a thousand young hearts; and the names of Wilder Dwight and his gallant brother will be the watchwords and countersigns of heroic daring, as often as any cause of our country shall call for the efforts of its best and bravest, to the last syllable of its recorded history.

But the services of Brookline, and of Brookline men, and women, too, must not be dismissed with this brief allusion to the deaths of any two of her sons. In the excellent "History of Massachusetts during the Civil War," by the late lamented General Schouler, this Town is recorded as having furnished thirty-four commissioned officers, with the gallant General Wild at their head, and seven hundred and twenty men, — "a surplus

[1] Forest Hills. [2] Thomson.

of one hundred and thirty-five over and above all demands." That History, — one volume of which, as I cannot but remember in passing, was so appropriately dedicated to the late Mrs. Otis, whose memory will long be associated with the observance of Washington's Birthday as a holiday, — that History contains the record, too, of not less than twenty thousand dollars raised by the ladies of the Town and expended for the comfort of the soldiers; of more than thirty thousand dollars subscribed for the organization and equipment of the Second Regiment of Volunteers; and of nearly a hundred and thirty-five thousand dollars appropriated and expended by the Town from its own treasury on account of the War. Your worthy Town Clerk, Mr. Baker, does not regard even these figures as doing full justice to all that was done here; but they are more than enough, as they stand, to show that the sons and daughters of Brookline were in no degree behind any of their neighbors in responding to the demands of that momentous struggle. The names of those whom Brookline lost in that struggle are to be recorded, I understand, on commemorative tablets in the spacious vestibule of this Building, so that they may never fail to be remembered and honored by all who enter it.

I would gladly feel that a moment were left to me for doing justice to others who have lived here, in earlier or later days, and who have been distinguished in their various professions or pursuits, — devoted clergymen, following in the footsteps of James Allen, the first of them; faithful school-teachers, with John Searle as their forerunner; worthy citizens and residents, Clarks and Goddards, Heaths and Davises, Hyslops and Harrises, Childs and Seavers, Griggses and Tappans and Lees, and other Perkinses and other Warrens than those I have named, and other Amorys than those I might name, were they not still happily among the living. I cannot attempt to include one half of those worthy to be included; but I must by no means omit at least one most eminent lawyer, Jeremy Gridley, for whom it was glory enough that James Otis was his pupil in the law, and treated him with the greatest deference, respect, and affection, even while he totally demolished his arguments in the memorable cause concerning Writs of Assistance, in 1761.

Nor would I fail to recall such as have made their mark in the field of letters. If we are compelled to go a few feet over our boundary line to find the home of Parkman, with his "Pontiac," his "France in America," and his "Book of Roses," we cannot forget that the authoress of those Buckminster Memoirs which Carlyle admired, and of "Naomi" and other charming stories of the Olden Time, was long a resident here; that the author of "The German Prose Writers" and of so many excellent versions of Schiller and Goethe, to say nothing of later Works, has but just left the old Parsonage which almost belonged to him as a family inheritance; that "Suffolk Surnames" found here their genial and humorous collector and commentator; that one of the earliest and most careful writers of the Diplomatic History of our Country,[1] as well as one of the latest and best writers on Private International Law,[2] long had a home here; that here, in a mansion then owned or occupied, it may be, by his eminent father, was passed at least one of the summers of Prescott, when, under so many clouds, he was first seriously pondering his way of life and ripening for that rich harvest which is among the glories of American Literature; that perchance the last edition of the best History of Spanish Literature may have received some final touches from the accomplished Ticknor during his recent and repeated residences here; that not only have more than one of the Daily Journals of Boston had leading Editors and Proprietors here, but that the "Living Age" — that pure and perpetual reservoir and fountain of entertainment and instruction, so welcome at all our firesides — has almost from the first been edited here; and, finally, that if there have been any Diarists or Annalists in New England, since the days of Bradford and Winthrop and Prince, worthy to be named with Pepys and Evelyn and Sir Henry Holland and Crabb Robinson of Old England, they are the elder Sewall and the late Reverend Drs. Holmes and Pierce, two of whom we have found so intimately associated with our local history.

Our Public Library should not be without a special alcove,

1 The Diplomacy of The United States, by Theodore Lyman.

2 A Treatise on the Conflict of Laws, or Private International Law, by Francis Wharton, LL.D.

or certainly a special shelf, for every thing which has emanated, in whole or in part, from Brookline, as well as for every thing which may illustrate its own rise and progress and the history of the Town. And, one of these days, this very Town Hall, in some one of its numerous apartments, should not be without portraits — not full lengths, for they would soon fill up the spaces and leave no room for the men of the future, but Heads, at least — of those who have been prominent in your earlier or later annals. There is no worthier patronage of American art than that which may be afforded in procuring such memorials of the honored dead. The living may well be postponed for the verdict of those who come after them.

And now, fellow citizens and friends, with these historical reminiscences, and these sacred memories, in full and fresh contemplation, we are here to-day to inaugurate this noble Hall, and to dedicate it to all the manifold and varied uses to which such an edifice may be legitimately appropriated. We can hardly imagine that any increase of population, or any multiplication of offices or affairs, or any caprice of taste or fancy, will ever call for a more spacious or commodious edifice of the kind. Should it escape, as we all pray God that it may escape, the one great casualty which the flames of yonder City have so recently and so sadly impressed upon our minds, we can hardly look forward to its standing less than a full century, as a place for the exercise of whatever rights and powers may be possessed by the people who dwell here. So long as Brookline shall remain a Town by itself, or shall in any way preserve the separate existence which it has enjoyed for more than a hundred and sixty-seven years, no other place, certainly, can be contemplated for the discharge of that great duty of choosing your own rulers which belongs to you as freemen. And even should it be your destiny, or your will, to relapse into the condition from which your fathers in 1705, and thirty years before, struggled so hard to release themselves; and, following the example of some of your neighbors, to become a District or a Ward of Boston, — still I know not that any more central or commodious locality could be assigned for the exercise of such privileges and prerogatives as may be left to you. We shall none of us, I think, be sorry, even in that case, that the good old Town went down with its flag still flying; and flying on so worthy a symbol of its long-cherished individuality and independence.

But your political rights and duties, whatever they may be, are by no means all for which this costly Building has been erected. We dedicate it to-day to other and larger uses. Here, from time to time, the popular assembly may be held, to give utterance to opinions or resolutions on matters of local or of general concern. Here, thrilling appeals of patriotism may be heard, in some exigency of public danger or alarm. Here, eloquent and instructive Lectures may be listened to, on Literature or History, on Art or Science, on Horticulture or Agriculture, or on some of those great moral and social reforms which the welfare of the Community may demand. Here, some profound and exhaustless Agassiz may unveil the mysteries of the earth, and of the sea, and of all that they contain. Here, some admirable and accomplished Tyndall may illustrate the marvels of polarized light and of the circumambient ether, reversing all our old-fashioned notions, and showing us precisely how the dark rays of the Sun, instead of the bright ones, do the main work of melting the glaciers, evaporating the rivers, distilling the ocean, and heating the Universe. Here, some learned and adventurous Froude may charm us with stories of English Elizabeths and Scottish Marys, — certain to be followed by some eloquent and indignant Father Burke, if he ever so unwittingly lend color to an idea that Irishmen are not as brave and as true and as trustworthy as their neighbors. Here, some Holmes or Hillard or veteran Emerson, some Cooke or Hayes or Lovering, some John B. Gough or Wendell Phillips or Henry Ward Beecher, may at least serve to remind you that popular and brilliant Lecturers are by no means altogether exotic. Here, some Charlotte Cushman may delight us with a life-like rendering of Shakspeare's Queen Katharine, or overwhelm us with the power and pathos of Walter Scott's Meg Merrilies. Here, Music may pour forth her inspiring and ennobling strains, — the grand Symphony, the majestic Choral, the sublime Oratorio; or, it may be, the lighter harmonies of Glees and Madrigals and Part-songs from your own Brookline Club. Here, galleries of ancient or modern Art may sometimes be arranged, borrowed from the abounding treasures of not a few of the neighboring mansions. Here, Charity may spread her alluring tables, with the choicest contributions of the garden and the conservatory, and with the tasteful products of hands ever ready and eager for any work of love. And here, gay and happy children, of all classes and sects and nationalities, may be seen mingling in the frolic dance, on some holiday of the Schools, or on some Anniversary festival of the Town, the State, or the Nation.

I may not venture to depict, or attempt to anticipate, all the various scenes which this Hall may exhibit, in the long vista of time and change and chance through which we look forward to-day, as through the ever-changing, still-combining colors of a kaleidoscope. To every use which may become a free, intelligent, and moral People, we devote and dedicate it; to rational Amusement, to enlightened Culture, to freedom of Speech and of Conscience, to Virtue, to Philanthropy, to Patriotism, to Liberty and Law; — to every use which may be for the welfare of the community, or, in the good old phrase of the great Father of Modern Science, "for the relief of man's estate."

But, oh, let us not forget those other words which were coupled by Lord Bacon with that good old phrase! Let us not forget that it was to "the glory of the Creator," as well as to the welfare of man's estate, that our fathers dedicated every thing, even themselves! We have opened our exercises with prayer, and we shall presently close them with praise. Let it never be imagined that these are mere empty, conventional forms! The walls which have grown cold and hard without catching some impress of supplication and thanksgiving, breathing from sincere and believing hearts, and vibrating from glad and grateful lips, have lost more than could be supplied by the frescoes of a Raphael. We can do without every thing else in this world better — immeasurably better — than without the blessing of God; and that blessing is to be invoked, here and everywhere, in every hour, in all conditions, under all circumstances. The winds and the storms may paralyze the machinery, and sweep down the stoutest props of all earthly intercommunication; but the humblest aspirations Heavenward of a devout and loving soul have an ever-fixed support, "that looks on tempests and is never shaken," — the Same yesterday, and to-day, and for ever!

Clinical calendars and therapeutic tests may well be relied on for every thing conceivable or even inconceivable, within their own domain. They cannot be too highly prized for all that they have done, and all that they are doing, for the physical welfare of mankind. Nor can I think it altogether fair or wise to take up too seriously a somewhat sudden and sensational suggestion for enlarging the sphere of Hospital statistics. The subject of that suggestion, if not beyond the range of human argument, is certainly far beyond the reach of medical or material experiment. It is enough, perhaps more than enough for me, to express the conviction, that no fears or doubts or faintest misgivings, — that nothing, nothing but the profoundest compassion and sorrow, in every Christian breast, — will await or follow an attempt, should it ever unhappily be made, to prove that prayer to God for the sick, the suffering, and the dying is not the rational and natural, as well as the revealed, resort and refuge of the anxious and agonized heart. Every such heart will utterly disown the jurisdiction, and pour out its petitions with renewed faith and fervor.

The sense of an all-seeing Eye, of an all-hearing Ear, of an all-pervading and all-controlling Providence, is the strongest safe-guard of Society, as well as of the individual man. It must be cherished by the sons, as it was by the fathers, if our liberty is not to degenerate into licentiousness, and our boasted Self-government into anarchy or despotism. Massachusetts was founded, and has been built up, as a Christian Commonwealth, and as a Christian Commonwealth it must stand or fall. Conscience must be free as the air. Sects and denominations must range themselves, according to their own convictions, under banners of their own choice. The State can never again support or favor any particular creed or form of religion. But Religion, in all its forms, must still support the State; must still supply the corner-stone and the capstone, the strong foundations and the sustaining buttresses and bulwarks, both of State and Nation, if free government, or any government, is to endure and prosper.

"Of all the dispositions and habits which lead to political prosperity," said he whose birthday we commemorate, in that Farewell Address, which ought to be read in our schools on every anniversary of its date, — "Of all the dispositions and habits which lead to political prosperity, religion and morality are indispensable supports. In vain would that man claim the tribute of patriotism, who should labor to subvert these great pillars of human happiness, these firmest props of the duties of men and of citizens. The mere politician, equally with the pious man, ought to respect and cherish them. A volume could not trace all their connections with private and public felicity. Let it simply be asked, Where is the security for property, for reputation, for life, if the sense of religious obligation desert the oaths which are the instruments of investigation in courts of Justice? And let us with caution indulge the supposition that morality can be maintained without religion. Whatever may be conceded to the influence of refined education on minds of peculiar structure, reason and experience both forbid us to expect that National Morality can prevail in exclusion of religious principles."

All other words of Washington may become obsolete. His great appeals for Peace, domestic and foreign, for Union and the Constitution, may be shorn of their application and significance. The Constitution may be discarded, and the Union itself perish. His own example may cease to be reverenced, and his memory lose its hold upon our hearts. But even should such deplorable and unimaginable results ever be witnessed in our land, these noble words will be as just and true as when they first issued from his lips or from his pen. And at this moment, above all other moments in our history, when National Morality is in danger of becoming a jest and a by-word, they should sink deeper than ever before into the soul of every American Patriot.

To the glory of God, then, as well as to the relief of man's estate, let us dedicate our Hall this day! And may the blessing of God ever overshadow it, and ever rest upon all who, in successive generations, shall be gathered within it; until, with the lapse of years, these glowing colors shall have faded, these massive walls shall have fallen, and all the high hopes and joyous associations of this occasion, with the remembrance of all who have participated in it, shall be buried in oblivion!

JAMES SAVAGE, LL.D.

REMARKS AT A MEETING OF THE MASSACHUSETTS HISTORICAL SOCIETY, ON THE EVENING OF MARCH 13, 1873.

GENTLEMEN OF THE MASSACHUSETTS HISTORICAL SOCIETY,—We have so recently been called to attend the funeral of our late venerable Senior Member and former President, the Hon. JAMES SAVAGE, that it is only as a matter for record that his death, on Saturday, the 8th inst., requires any formal announcement to the Society this evening. I need hardly say that we cannot consider it a subject for the expression of sorrow. Even those nearest and dearest to him, who have so tenderly watched over him in his infirmities, during the last eight or nine years, must have abundant consolation for their bereavement. We may all, indeed, have found cause for satisfaction and gratitude as we learned that, in the good providence of God, our aged friend was at length happily released from the burdens of the flesh and of the spirit, which have weighed upon him so heavily since he had come to fourscore years.

Yet none of us, I am sure, can see his name disappearing at last from the very top of our living roll, altogether without emotion; and, certainly, not without pausing to pay a more than common tribute of respect and affection to his memory. Quite apart from all the personal qualities and associations which had endeared him to us so warmly, we cannot forget that the removal of his name from that roll has sundered the last link between our Society of this generation and the little company of historical students and lovers of antiquity in which it originated more than eighty years ago. We have, it is true, still in our ranks, — and we rejoice to remember that it is so, — more than one of those who have seen as many years of human life as our departed friend. But there is no one now left, among our existing members, whose relation to our Society commenced within a quarter of a century of the date of his election; no one, who witnessed the small beginnings of our work, or who was associated, as he was, with any of those by whom that work was originally organized.

Mr. Savage was chosen a member of this Society on the 28th of January, 1813. He had thus been a member for a little more than sixty years, — a longer term than any on our records, as I believe, except that of the late venerable Josiah Quincy, who had completed his sixty-eighth year of continuous membership, when he died, in 1864, at ninety-two years of age.

When Mr. Savage was elected, Dr. Jeremy Belknap, our honored founder; Governor Sullivan, our first President; the Rev. Dr. Thacher, and the Hon. George Richards Minot, — were, indeed, no more. But the Rev. Dr. Eliot, the Rev. Dr. Freeman, the Hon. William Tudor, Thomas Wallcut, Esq., the Hon. James Winthrop, and the Hon. William Baylies, — six of our Decemvirs, — six of the ten whose election dates back to the 24th of January, 1791, and who met on that day and organized the Society, — were still living and active members. With them, when Mr. Savage was elected, were associated, among others, Governor Gore, then the President of the Society; Judge Davis, and Lieutenant-Governor Winthrop, who succeeded him in that office; Dr. Manasseh Cutler, who, twenty years before, had led the way of the pioneer emigrants to the Ohio River; Dr. Thaddeus Mason Harris; Dr. Prince and Dr. Bentley, of Salem; Dr. Homer, of Newton; Dr. Morse, the geographer; Dr. Abiel Holmes, the annalist; John Adams, Caleb Strong, Alden Bradford, Professors Peck and McKean, President Kirkland, and Dr. Pierce, — besides Josiah Quincy and John Quincy Adams, whose membership, to a few of us, at least, is something more than a tradition.

Mr. Savage was but twenty-nine years of age when he became associated with these men in our ranks; and as no professional or public duties ever took him far away from his native place, for any considerable length of time, his services to our Society, and his attendance at its meetings, were in the way of being, and unquestionably were, more prolonged, continuous, and constant, than those of any other member, from its foundation.

Accordingly, we find him Librarian, from 1814 to 1818; a member of the Publishing Committee of five several volumes of our Collections, in 1815, 1816, 1819, 1823, and 1825; Treasurer from 1820 to 1839; a member of the Standing Committee from 1818 to 1820, and from 1835 to 1841; and the President of the Society from 1841 to 1855. Having then passed the term of threescore years and ten, he claimed, as he certainly had a right to claim, an honorable dismission from the routine of official duty.

It seems but yesterday that I succeeded him in this chair, at the close of our Annual Meeting, on the 12th of April, 1855, when, on motion of our late accomplished associate, Mr. Ticknor, it was unanimously resolved, "That the members of this Society, — mindful of the excellent services which, for fourteen years, the Hon. James Savage has rendered as its President, and of his peculiar fitness for that place, not only on all other grounds, but from his extraordinarily accurate knowledge of whatever relates to the early history of New England, — do now express their great regret at his resignation, and offer him their thanks for his long-tried and uniform fidelity to their interests." It seems but yesterday that, in taking the seat which he had so held and honored, I was speaking of that fulness of information, that richness of reminiscence, that raciness of remark and repartee, which had so often given the highest relish to our monthly meetings, which was then to be lost to the chair, — and which is now lost to us for ever. Eighteen years have since passed away, during the first half of which he continued to be one of our most punctual and assiduous members, ever entering our rooms with that eager, animated, joyous look, which betokened that he felt as much pleasure as he imparted. Since then, for us, all has been silence.

Was I not right, gentlemen, in suggesting that, while his name remained at the head of our roll, even though it were only a name, or even but the shadow of a name, we seemed to have a living tie to the old traditions, the old worthies, and the old workers and organizers of our Society, which is now finally sundered? Certainly, his death at this moment, — just as we are about entering on the occupation of our reconstructed Halls, — seems to conspire most impressively with that event, in marking still a new departure for our Society, still another era in its history, when the responsibilities for its future usefulness and honor are to be unshared with even one of those who had been witnesses, or partakers in any way, of its earlier experiences and its narrower fortunes. Certainly, it seems to call upon us, — as we enter on that era, with nothing left of the Founders and their immediate associates and followers except their inspiring memory and example, — for a warmer interest in the welfare of the Institution which they so loved and honored, and for a deeper devotion to the work for which they established it.

The most interesting and valuable contributions which were made by Mr. Savage to our own published volumes, were undoubtedly his "Gleanings for New England History," prepared by him immediately on his return from a summer visit to England in 1842, and which were followed by "More," and "More Gleanings," not long afterwards.

But the great historical labors of his life, his two Editions and Annotations of "Winthrop's History of New England from 1630 to 1649," and his wonderful Genealogical Dictionary of New England, were hardly less in our service than if they had formed a part of our own Collections. If a new edition of the Winthrop, certainly, should ever be demanded, it might well be placed side by side with the Bradford, and under the care of the same hand, among the publications of this Society; and it would be a fit monument to the memory of our departed friend.

I am aware, however, gentlemen, that we are all thinking at this moment much more of the man we have lost, than of his services to our Society, or of his work in the cause of New England history, which can never be lost. He comes back to many of us, to-night, as he was twenty years ago, in the old Pilgrim Chair, before the old Provincial Desk, in the old dusty rooms of our Society, — before the name of Thomas Dowse had been breathed among us; or, certainly, before his benefactions, by the marvellous alchemy of good George Livermore, had transmuted all that belonged to us into something more precious than gold.

He was at that day, — and with those surroundings, — the perfect impersonation of an Antiquary, in form and feature, in speech and in spirit. He had few or none of the smoothnesses and roundnesses of conventional life; and though he did not affect or cultivate singularity, he by no means scorned that part of his nature which rendered him singular. He would be called, in common parlance, — and he has often been called, — a man of strong and even intense prejudices. Yet I think he never prejudged any thing or anybody. It was only when he had known any person in society, or had studied any person or any passage in history, that he conceived opinions which nothing could change, and which clung to him, and he to them, ever afterwards. His impulsive and even explosive utterances of such opinions were never to be forgotten by those who witnessed them. Still less could any one ever forget his exuberant exultation, when his searches and researches were rewarded, by verifying some disputed date, or discovering some historical fact, or by lighting upon some lost historical manuscript. He rejoiced, as the Psalmist describes it, "as one that findeth great spoil." His "Eureka" had all the elation and ecstasy of that of the old philosopher of Syracuse.

He was eminently a character, even for a tale or a drama. His marked peculiarities would have given a vivid interest to any story, and his racy utterances would have enlivened any dialogue. If he had chanced to be one of the neighbors of Sir Walter Scott, he could never have escaped the fate, let me rather say the felicity, which befell so many of those neighbors, of figuring in one of the Waverley Novels.

I remember that Thackeray once passed an evening with him at my own house, at a meeting of the old Wednesday Night Club of 1777, of which he was so long a member. When I met Thackeray afterwards, his immediate remark was, "I want to see that quaint, charming, old Mr. Savage again."

In a conversation with Walter Savage Landor, then eighty years old, at his own villa in Florence, in 1860, he greeted me by saying, "I know all about your family and the old Founder of New England;" and then he forthwith went on to speak of the Savage family, whose name he bore, including the old Earl of Rivers and our James Savage, of Boston, whose edition of Winthrop he had evidently seen. There were occasional scintillations and coruscations exhibited in common by Landor himself and by our departed friend, which might have indicated an affinity or consanguinity, even after the genealogists had failed to trace them.

If there was anybody whom the late Lord Braybrooke, the editor of Pepys; or Dr. Bliss, the editor of Wood's Athenæ Oxonienses; or Joseph Romilly, the late Registrar of Old Cambridge; or Joseph Hunter, the Antiquary *par excellence* of Her Majesty's Record Office, — remembered and valued in America, it was Mr. Savage. He had corresponded with them all, and had known them all personally, while he was visiting England.

To come nearer home, I may not forget that I rarely if ever met, after a longer or a shorter absence, my late lamented friend, John P. Kennedy, of Baltimore, who had as keen a relish and as quick an appreciation of wit and of wisdom as Thackeray or even Sydney Smith, that it was not his second exclamation, if not his first, "How is our old friend Savage? Is he as earnest, and humorous, and funny as ever?"

I may be pardoned for remembering, too, that it was from a member of this Society, elected eight years after him, but who died, in early manhood, forty years before him, who sympathized with him in all his pursuits, and aided him in many of his researches and labors, and was unto him for many years almost as a brother, as he was to myself an own brother, — the late James Bowdoin,[1] — that I first learned to appreciate the sterling qualities of our friend's mind and character; his minute exactness; his untiring perseverance; his inexhaustible patience of

[1] The second son of the late Lieutenant-Governor Winthrop, who died in his thirty-ninth year, on the 6th of March, 1833, and of whom a brief Memoir is contained in Vol. IX., 3d Series, of the Collections of the Massachusetts Historical Society.

research; his mingled impetuosity and tenderness; his sympathy with the sufferings of others, and his brave endurance of his own sufferings.

But I must not forget how many there are around me who have known him longer and better than myself, and who will more than supply any deficiencies of my own tribute. I omit, therefore, all notice of the public trusts in the City and in the State, and as a member of the Constitutional Convention of 1820, which he discharged so well; all notice of the grand work he did for the community in organizing and presiding over that Provident Institution for Savings, where, for a few years, I was monthly at his side; all notice, too, of the Christian resignation and bravery with which he bore domestic trials, which might have crushed a feebler spirit. Let me but say, in conclusion, that the death of his only son in the late Civil War, — a son of the same name with himself, and who had given every promise of transmitting it with increased distinction to future generations, — has doubled the obligation which rests upon us, to guard that name from being lost to the records either of patient and successful historic research, or of patriotic and heroic self-sacrifice.[1]

[1] Lieutenant-Colonel James Savage, Jr., died at Charlottesville, Virginia, Oct. 22, 1862, of wounds received at the battle of Cedar Mountain. He was born April 21, 1832, and graduated at Harvard University with the class of 1854. An interesting Memoir of him may be found in the first volume of "Harvard Memorial Biographies."

CHIEF-JUSTICE TANEY.

REMARKS AT A MEETING OF THE MASSACHUSETTS HISTORICAL SOCIETY, MARCH 13, 1873.

I HOLD in my hand a long and very interesting letter from the late Chief-Justice Taney, addressed, in 1857, to the late Rev. Samuel Nott, then a clergyman in Wareham, Massachusetts. Mr. Nott was a nephew of the late Dr. Eliphalet Nott, so long the honored President of Union College, Schenectady, New York. He had himself been graduated at that college in 1808; and, entering at once upon the missionary cause, he lived to be the last survivor of the first band of missionaries sent out to India by the American Board in 1812. He published several volumes of sermons, and was always a laborious Christian scholar and writer. In his later years, he was the author of a pamphlet which went through five editions, and received many supplements, until it almost reached the dimensions of a volume, entitled "Slavery, and the Remedy; or, Principles and Suggestions for a Remedial Code." The last edition, published in 1857, contained "A Review of the Decision of the Supreme Court in the Case of Dred Scott."

It was a very able and carefully considered production, and attracted a good deal of notice at the South, as well as at the North, while Slavery was a living question. Mr. Nott had sent a copy of it to the late Chief-Justice, and this letter was written in acknowledgment. It happened that Mr. Nott called upon me not long after its receipt, and read it to me confidentially. While reading lately the Memoir of Chief-Justice Taney, by a distinguished lawyer of Maryland, Samuel Tyler, Esq., LL.D.,[1] — a work of great interest, though containing some passages in which many of us might not concur, — I was reminded of this letter, and, with the obliging aid of our associate, Mr. Ellis Ames, took measures for procuring it. It has now been kindly sent to me by the son of the late Rev. Mr. Nott, to be placed in the archives of this Society. It will be seen that it contains some items of autobiography, and also a request that it may not be published. But both parties to the correspondence being now dead, — the Chief-Justice having died in 1864, and the Rev. Mr. Nott in 1869, — I have found, on consultation with Mr. Tyler, to whom all the private papers of the Chief-Justice were intrusted by himself and his family, that there is no objection to its being printed; and it will probably be included hereafter in an Appendix to the Memoir. It is, certainly, a most interesting and characteristic letter from a most distinguished man, whose long service on the Supreme Bench of the United States, as the successor of Chief-Justice Marshall, was marked by the highest ability, and to whose memory the warmest tributes were paid by not a few of those who had not concurred in some of his decisions.

LETTER OF CHIEF-JUSTICE TANEY.

FAUQUIER, WHITE SULPHUR SPRINGS, VIRGINIA,
August 19, 1857.

SIR, — I received some time ago your letter, and pamphlet on "Slavery, and the Remedy," which you have been kind enough to send me. They were received when I was much out of health, and about to leave home for the summer. And it was not in my power to give the pamphlet an attentive perusal until within a few days past. I have read it with great pleasure. The just, impartial, and fraternal spirit in which it is written entitles it to a respectful consideration, in the South as well as the North. And if any thing can allay the unhappy excitement which is daily pro-

[1] The death of this gentleman is announced while this volume is in the press.

ducing so much evil to the African as well as the white race, it is the discussion of the subject in the temper in which you have treated it. For you have looked into it and considered it in all its bearings, in the spirit of a statesman as well as a philanthropist. I am glad to find that it has been so well received as to reach the fifth edition.

Every intelligent person whose life has been passed in a slaveholding State, and who has carefully observed the character and capacity of the African race, will see that a general and sudden emancipation would be absolute ruin to the negroes, as well as to the white population. In Maryland and Virginia every facility has been given to emancipation where the freed person was of an age and condition of health that would enable him to provide for himself by his own labor. And before the present excitement was gotten up, the freed negro was permitted to remain in the State, and to follow any occupation of honest labor and industry that he might himself prefer. And in this state of the law manumissions were frequent and numerous. They sprang from the kindness and sympathy of the master for the negro, or from scruples of conscience; and were often made without sufficiently considering his capacity and fitness for freedom. And in the greater number of cases that have come under my observation, freedom has been a serious misfortune to the manumitted slave; and he has most commonly brought upon himself privations and sufferings which he would not have been called on to endure in a state of slavery. In many cases, however, it has undoubtedly promoted his happiness. But all experience proves that the relative position of the two races, when placed in contact with each other, must necessarily become such as you describe. Nor is it felt as a painful degradation by the black race. On the contrary, upon referring to the last census, you will find that more free negroes remain in Maryland than in any one of the Northern States, notwithstanding the disabilities and stricter police to which they are subjected. And there is a still greater number in Virginia. I speak from memory, without having the census before me. But I think I am not mistaken in the fact.

It is difficult for any one who has not lived in a slaveholding State to comprehend the relations which practically exist between the slaves and their masters. They are in general kind on both sides, unless the slave is tampered with by ill-disposed persons; and his life is usually cheerful and contented, and free from any distressing wants or anxieties. He is well taken care of in infancy, in sickness, and in old age. There are, indeed, exceptions, — painful exceptions. But this will always be the case, where power combined with bad passions or a mercenary spirit is on one side, and weakness on the other. It frequently happens when both parties are of the same race, although the weaker and dependent one may not be legally a slave.

Unquestionably it is the duty of every master to watch over the religious and moral culture of his slaves, and to give them every comfort and privilege that is not incompatible with the continued existence of the relations between them. And so far as my knowledge extends, this duty is faithfully performed by the great body of hereditary slaveholders in Maryland and Virginia. I speak of these States only, because with respect to them I have personal knowledge of the subject. But I have no reason to suppose it is otherwise in States farther south. And I know it has been the desire of the statesmen of Maryland to secure to the slave by law every protection from maltreatment by the master that can with safety be given, and without impairing that degree of authority which is essential to the interest and well-being of both. But this question is a very delicate one, and must at all times be approached with the utmost caution. The safe and true line must always depend upon existing circumstances, and they must be thoroughly inquired into and understood before there can be any safe or useful legislation in a State.

The pains which have unhappily been taken for some years past to produce discontent and ill-feeling in the subject race, has rendered any movement in that direction still more difficult. For it has naturally made the master more sensitive and jealous of any new restriction upon the power he has heretofore exercised, and which he has been accustomed to think essential to the maintenance of his authority as master. And he also feels that any step in that direction at the present time might injuriously affect the minds of the slaves. They are, for the most part, weak, credulous, and easily misled by stronger minds. And if in the present state of things additional restrictions were placed on the authority of the master, or new privileges granted to them, they would probably be told that they were wrung from the master by their Northern friends; and be taught to regard them as the first step to a speedy and universal emancipation, placing them on a perfect equality with the white race. It is easy to foresee what would be the sad result of such an impression upon the minds of this weak and credulous race.

Your review of the decision in the case of Dred Scott is a fair one, and states truly the opinion of the court. It will, I hope, correct some of the misrepresentations which have so industriously been made; and made, too, I fear, by many who must have known better. But I do not mean to publish any vindication of the opinion; or of my own consistency, or the consistency of the court. For it would not become the Supreme Court, or any member of it, to go outside of the appropriate sphere of judicial proceedings, and engage in a controversy with any one who may choose from any motive to misrepresent its opinion. The opinion must be left to speak for itself. And it is for that reason that I hope you will pardon me for requesting that you will not permit this letter to be published in the newspapers or otherwise. Not that I am not perfectly ready on all proper occasions to say publicly every thing I have said in this letter. But in the judicial position I have the honor to occupy, I ought not to appear as a volunteer in any political discussion; and still less would it become me out of court and off the bench to discuss a question which has been there determined. And I have written to you (although a stranger) thus freely from the personal respect with which the perusal of your pamphlet has inspired me. I am not a slaveholder. More than thirty years ago I manumitted every slave I ever owned, except two, who were too old, when they became my property, to provide for themselves. These two I supported in comfort as long as they lived. And I am glad to say that none of those whom I manumitted disappointed my expectations, but have shown by their conduct that they were worthy of freedom, and knew how to use it.

With great respect, I am, sir,

Your obedient servant,

R. B. Taney.

The Rev. Samuel Nott,
Wareham, Mass.

RE-OPENING OF THE DOWSE LIBRARY.

ADDRESS AT THE ANNUAL MEETING OF THE MASSACHUSETTS HISTORICAL SOCIETY, APRIL 10, 1873.

I AM sure, gentlemen, you will all agree with me that this is an occasion for brief mutual felicitations rather than for formal addresses. You would hardly pardon me, however, if I were to take the chair this morning in silence.

I congratulate you cordially that we are once more in possession of our own Building; once more assembled in the Dowse Library; once more surrounded by the beautiful books and memorials of our greatest benefactor; with all the associations which have endeared these apartments to us during the last sixteen years.

A full year has elapsed since we relinquished the occupation of this Building, and gave it up to the purposes of reconstruction. We then undoubtedly looked forward to a somewhat earlier return, and some impatience may have occasionally been felt that the work was not more rapidly advanced and sooner completed. But we have no regrets to-day. We are all satisfied that the committee of our Society, who have superintended the changes, have done their whole duty faithfully and thoroughly, and that they have no share of the responsibility of the delay, if delay there has been, in bringing the work to a successful completion. Our best thanks are due to them all; and I can do no injustice to any one else, by naming Mr. Mason, Mr. E. B. Bigelow, and Mr. Brooks, not forgetting our Treasurer and Librarian, who were associated with them, as those to whom our special acknowledgments are due. They will present their own report in the course of the morning, and I will not anticipate the statements which that report will abundantly contain.

It does not become us to speak too boastfully of what has been accomplished. We may well use the word "fire-proof" with something more of reserve than we might have done before the great conflagration of the 9th and 10th of November last. There may be casualties and catastrophes in a crowded city like ours, against which no precautions can entirely protect us. But it is an unspeakable satisfaction to those who are called officially to watch over these historical treasures, and to myself, certainly, as one of them, to know that they are at last secure from all common dangers, and that we have done every thing in our power, even to the extent of subjecting ourselves to the inconvenience of ascending an additional stairway, in order to place the precious books and papers which have been intrusted to our care beyond the reach of ordinary accidents.

It is no small enhancement of our satisfaction that the changes have been made in co-operation with our City Government, whose prompt acceptance of the apartments provided for such important places of deposit as the Probate Office and the Registery of Deeds, is the best guaranty that no considerations of safety have been neglected in what has been done here.

It is, certainly, not less a matter of congratulation that, costly as the reconstruction has been, the Society has incurred no debt which it may not confidently hope to see liquidated by a persistent application of a part of our income to a sinking-fund for the next fifteen or twenty years. To such a course the good faith of the Society is pledged.

If the result of the whole operation shall be to leave us, for some time to come, with more restricted resources than we could wish, we shall still have a larger income than we have ever heretofore enjoyed; while the very fact of our having made so considerable an outlay for the security of treasures in which the whole community are interested, as well as ourselves, may, it is hoped, commend us to the favor of those whose generous benefactions are the pride of our City and State, and who are never long wanting to a really worthy cause. Some other Thomas Dowse, some other Samuel Appleton, some other George Peabody, may hereafter appear, to complete the endowments which we so much need. Some other James Savage may remember us, living or dying, and secure a grateful memory for himself, while aiding us to illustrate and perpetuate the history of our Commonwealth and Country.

Well, then, may we enter on the occupation of our renewed apartments, to-day, with hopeful as well as grateful hearts, and look forward confidently to a new term of prosperity and usefulness and honor for the Society which is so dear to us all.

It was just sixteen years yesterday, since we first entered on the possession of the noble library of Thomas Dowse, which is arranged around us again precisely as it was on that day. None of those who were then present as members of the Society can fail to recall the scenes and circumstances of that Annual Meeting. The late venerable Josiah Quincy and James Savage, you all remember, marshalled us into our beautiful room; and they were followed by Edward Everett and Jared Sparks and George Ticknor, by Chief-Justice Shaw and Judge White, by the Rev. Drs. Jenks and Frothingham and Francis, by Nathan Appleton and David Sears, and William Appleton and William Sturgis, by Dr. Joseph E. Worcester and President Felton and Nathaniel Ingersoll Bowditch, and by not a few other eminent and excellent men, whom we may look to see no more in the old accustomed seats. We recall them all at this hour with respectful and affectionate remembrance, and feel deeply how hard it has been, how hard it will ever be, to fill the places which they left vacant.

But there is one form which rises before me at this moment, out of the associations of that occasion, which cannot be grouped with any of those whom we have since lost. It stands alone. Eager, ardent, impulsive, full of hope, never tired of labor in any good service, — and least of all in our service, — good, kind George Livermore presents himself before the eyes of many of us at this hour as he did then, with the key of our new room in his hand, from which it was my privilege to receive it, beckoning us forward, and bidding us enter and take formal possession of the Library which we had owed in so great a degree to his effective intervention; and adding, in behalf of the late lamented Eben Dale and himself, the executors of Mr. Dowse, a gift of $10,000 as a fund for its preservation.

To no one of its members has our Society been more indebted than to George Livermore. No one was more valuable to us in every way while he lived. No one has been more missed by us since his death. I should feel that I had omitted one of the first obligations of this occasion, if I had not given some expression to the grateful and tender regard with which we all cherish his memory. His portrait upon these walls must never be displaced.

I must not conclude, gentlemen, without a special word of congratulation, that we return to the same old site which has been so long associated with the labors and the laborers of our Society, and that our windows still look out on so many memorials of the earliest Ministers and Magistrates of our State and City. The first meeting of our Society, in 1791, when there were but ten members, was held at Judge Tudor's house. Before the year of the organization was completed, a room had been obtained in what was known as "The Manufactory House," in Hamilton Place; and subsequent meetings were held in one of the attics of Faneuil Hall. But since the incorporation of the Society, in 1794, it has had, I believe, but two places of meeting. Simultaneously with the Act of Incorporation, "a spacious and convenient apartment for the Library and Cabinet, in Franklin Place," was given to the Society "by the gentlemen who first improved that spot in the town for useful and elegant building." So says the printed circular letter which I hold in my hand. It forms a part of my own original certificate of membership, dated October 31, 1839. It is the only certificate, let me add, which I ever received. I trust my membership will not be disputed, because I cannot produce one of the parchment diplomas, which were introduced at a later day. This certificate, and the circular letter subjoined to it, signed by Thaddeus Mason Harris, were prepared and printed while the Society was still occupying the apartment given to it, in 1794, by Charles Bulfinch, William Scollay, and Charles

Vaughan, the projectors of the improvements of which it formed a part, and which is described in the circular as "over the arched way, in the Crescent, Franklin Place, Boston." These words, however, in my own certificate, were, of course, erased, and the words "over the Savings Bank, Tremont Street," written with a pen; the Society having relinquished that room just six years before my election, and having established itself here.

That old "arched way in the Crescent" has long since disappeared, and the magnificent warehouses which replaced it have recently perished in the flames of the great Boston fire. We may well be grateful that we were no longer within the range or reach of that disastrous conflagration. The Society had occupied that site, — if site it could be called, being a suspended arch in whose foundations we had no fee, — for thirty-nine years. We have had possession of this site for just forty years.

Let us hope that, in the good providence of God, another term, of at least forty years, may be enjoyed here, by us and our successors, in security. At this hour, certainly, we will contemplate no other removals or changes. Sufficient unto this day is the good thereof. As I look back on the perplexities and discouragements which surrounded us during the whole year which preceded our final decision to do what we have now done, and as I remember the impatience and almost despair of which I was myself at some hours conscious, I cannot but feel that light has indeed sprung up out of darkness, and joyful gladness for such as have the true interests of our Society at heart. It only remains for us to resolve that our future work shall not be unworthy of the opportunities and advantages which have now been so auspiciously opened to us.

BISHOP McILVAINE.

ADDRESS AT THE ANNUAL MEETING OF THE TRUSTEES OF THE PEABODY EDUCATION FUND, JULY 16, 1873.

GENTLEMEN OF THE BOARD OF TRUSTEES OF THE PEABODY EDUCATION FUND:

YOU will not have forgotten that, at our last meeting, it was voted, after much deliberation and discussion, that the Annual Meeting of the Board should hereafter be held in the city of New York, in the month of July, — the precise day to be fixed by the Chairman and General Agent, after due consultation with the members individually.

We are here, accordingly, on the day agreed upon by Dr. Sears and myself, after such correspondence with others as gave us the best hope that we might rely on the attendance of at least a majority of the Board. In that hope I am glad to perceive that we are not disappointed, — a quorum of the Trustees being now present, and ready for business.

But before proceeding to the formal duties for which we are assembled, it is fit that I should call your attention to the sad vacancy which has been created in our little circle since we last met.

Our venerable and beloved associate, Bishop McIlvaine, died at Florence, Italy, on the thirteenth day of March last. He had been one of the Trustees from our first organization at Washington, on the 8th of February, 1867, and was named by Mr. Peabody, in his original letter of endowment, as the second Vice-Chairman of the Board. He was at the head of our Executive Committee from that time until his death, and our records bear constant testimony to the diligence and efficiency with which he discharged the duties of that position. He had, from the outset, a deep sense of the importance of the work committed to us, and of his own share of the responsibility for its faithful execution. No personal inconvenience or discomfort, in long journeys from Cincinnati to Washington, or Richmond, or Philadelphia, or New York, ever prevented his punctual attendance at our Annual or Special Meetings; and, even in the depth of the winter of 1870, while already suffering from symptoms which foreshadowed the end, he could not be deterred from coming on to unite with us, at Danvers, in paying the last tribute to our illustrious Founder.

We missed his wonted presence, for the first time, at our Annual Meeting in Boston last year; but he had then already been ordered by his physicians to seek rest and recreation once more in foreign lands, and had sailed for Europe, on the previous 18th of May, never to return.

This is not the occasion for speaking of our venerated and lamented friend in his relations to the Church of which he was so eminent a minister. As pastor of more than one conspicuous parish; as Chaplain, and Professor of Ethics, at the United States Military Academy at West Point; as the author of a little work on the Evidences of Christianity, of which hardly less than fifty thousand copies have been printed, in our own and other languages, and which is still among the class-books of our theological schools; and, more than all, as the devoted Bishop of the Diocese of Ohio for more than forty years, — he has left a record which might well be envied by any prelate of his country or his age, and which will not fail to secure an enduring reverence for his name and memory.

Nor will his services in connection with the Christian Commission during the late civil war, and his *quasi* diplomatic employment abroad, by our department of State, during the most critical period of that war, be suffered to pass into oblivion, by those whose province it may be to make up the recent history of our country.

It is only for us, however, to remember, to-day, his unwearied devotion to the work in which we are engaged, and the wise, kind, genial spirit in which he entered into all our deliberations and doings. No presence at our Board was ever more welcome than that of "the good Bishop," as we involuntarily found ourselves calling him. No counsel was more judicious, no speech more conciliatory, no social intercourse more winning and inspiring than his. Of a form and countenance which often suggested the image of Washington; of a life and conversation ever in keeping with the dignity and sacredness of his calling, — there was yet a cheeriness intermingled with his gravity, a vivacity and gayety "within the limits of becoming mirth," which made him one of the most charming of companions. Meantime, the grand spirit of Christian courtesy and charity and love, which so conspicuously distinguished his whole career, in every sacred as well as in every secular relation, made us all feel, as I am sure we all do feel at this moment, that it was a privilege to be associated with him in our work, and that his loss is one which, for ourselves, we cannot too deeply deplore. For him, at so advanced an age, with such a life to look back upon, and such a life to look forward to by faith in the future, there can be no regret. Writing to me in 1869, he said in reference to Mr. Peabody: "There is a difference of four years between his age and mine. There may be much less between the times of our going hence. I have no desire to remain here. To be with our blessed Lord is far better."

Bishop McIlvaine had the good fortune many years ago to win the confidence and affection of our ever-honored Founder. Nor is it only with this one of Mr. Peabody's great benefactions that his memory is entitled to be associated. It was to him, then in England, that Mr. Peabody, in 1859, communicated, among the very first, his purpose of making a great gift for the benefit of the poor of London. At Mr. Peabody's request, the Bishop entered at once into confidential correspondence with the eminent philanthropist, Lord Shaftesbury, in regard to the particular form which this gift should assume, and the special purpose to which it should be applied. I have been privileged to see that correspondence, and have thus been enabled to appreciate the important part taken by our lamented friend in the original arrangement of that munificent London endowment. And when, two years afterwards, the scheme was finally consummated and divulged, Bishop McIlvaine, being again in England, was one of the few friends of whom Mr. Peabody took counsel in preparing his memorable letter to the Lord Mayor of London, announcing the donation of one hundred and fifty thousand pounds sterling for improving the dwellings of the poor. At the close of the last year, that noble Trust represented a total sum of £228,000, and another sum of £150,000 is to be added to the principal during the present year, if it has not already been done, in accordance with the will of Mr. Peabody; while no less than eight hundred and forty-seven families, consisting of 3,407 persons, as appears from special inquiry in May, 1872, were then occupying apartments which had been provided from this Fund.

There was thus a peculiar appropriateness, — greater than was perhaps understood at the time, and quite apart from his eminence as a churchman and a Bishop, —that the remains of one who had been so leading an adviser of this great English benefaction, should have found, as they did find, a temporary repose, — on their way to their final resting-place, near his own American home, — in the same renowned and consecrated Abbey, within whose walls, under similar circumstances, the remains of George Peabody himself, a few years before, had been the subject of funeral honors.

Our good Bishop rejoiced, as indeed we all do, in the signal success of that endowment for the London Poor, hardly less than in the prosperous progress of our own work. Differing in their design and character as widely as they do in their locality, but prompted by the same benevolent heart and established by the same munificent hand, these two great Trusts have had a common blessing upon them thus far; and no one has been more constant or more fervent, than our lamented associate, in invoking that blessing from Him, from whom alone it could come.

I will not anticipate the Report of our excellent General Agent by entering into any account of what has been accomplished in our own peculiar field of labor during the past year.

That Report will tell its own story, and will show, if I mistake not, that more than a hundred and thirty-five thousand dollars from our own Fund have been expended, in co-operation with six or seven times that sum contributed by the people of the Southern States, in the cause of education since our last meeting; — thus making hardly less than a full million of dollars, expended in a single year, under the direction of our General Agent, and as the result of the Peabody Trust, for free common schools in the South.

But I will not detain you longer from the satisfaction of listening to the details of that Report. I have only desired to bring before you, for your formal notice, the great loss we have sustained in the death of Bishop McIlvaine, and to open the way for entering on our records some expression of the deep sense, entertained by us all, of his noble character and faithful services.

BISHOP WILBERFORCE.

REMARKS AT A MEETING OF THE MASSACHUSETTS HISTORICAL SOCIETY, AUGUST 15, 1873.

THE Right Reverend SAMUEL WILBERFORCE, D.D., whose name has been on our foreign Honorary Roll since August, 1855, met with a fatal accident on the 19th of July last, near London. A more sudden removal from the highest associations of earth has rarely been deplored. The stumbling of a horse, on which he was riding in company with Her Majesty's Secretary of State for Foreign Affairs, on their way to meet the Prime Minister of England, brought his busy and brilliant career to a close. Unlike the late Sir Robert Peel, who was the victim of a similar accident in 1850, he was spared from any lingering agonies, expiring without a struggle on the spot, and at the instant, of his fall.

Born on the 7th of September, 1805, he had hardly completed his sixty-eighth year, while his health and strength seemed to promise many more years of usefulness and honor. He was a younger son of that renowned philanthropist and Christian statesman, William Wilberforce, whose deserved celebrity was wide enough and enduring enough to distinguish a whole family for a dozen generations. But he early extricated himself from the often oppressive shadow of a great paternal or ancestral name, and asserted his individual title to a place both in the ecclesiastical and the civil history of his country. Indeed, few prelates of the English Church, in our own day or in any day, have taken a more conspicuous stand, or enjoyed a wider distinction.

Nominated by Sir Robert Peel to the Bishopric of Oxford when hardly forty years of age, he became at once a notable figure in the House of Lords, as well as in the Convocations of the Church. Industrious, devoted, accomplished, with a rare facility and felicity of diction, he turned himself with marvellous versatility to every sphere of public service, and was recognized at home and abroad as one of the leading orators both of the Pulpit and of Parliament. I owed to his own kind intervention, many years ago, an opportunity of hearing him deliver one of his memorable charity sermons. Nothing but his own note to the verger or the warden could have enabled me to secure a place in the crowd which always thronged the churches in which he was advertised to preach. No one could have listened to him on that day without emotion, nor without the warmest appreciation of the mingled grace and power with which he set forth the claims of the poor and the responsibilities of the rich. More recently, I stood, with Longfellow, on the floor of the House of Lords, and heard the Bishop reply to an admirable speech of the Duke of Argyll on the Bill for Disestablishing the Irish Church. If I found him less impressive as a debater than as a preacher, it may have been because the adroitness and dexterity of the rhetorician seemed, to one not quite accustomed to the blending of the temporal with the spiritual authority, less in keeping with the lawn sleeves which he wore, and with the sacred office which they designated.

Translated to the See of Winchester only within a few years past, his name and fame will be most prominently associated with the field of his earlier and longer labors, and with his now familiar signature, which, I remember, perplexed me for a moment when I first received it, more than a quarter of a century ago, — *S. Oxon.* I have it before me here, at the close of a note thanking me for a copy of the admirable pamphlet of the late Hon. Francis C. Gray on Prison Discipline, and concluding: "May I ask you to convey to our common friend, Mr. Everett, the expression of my cordial regard, and of the great pleasure which the sight of his handwriting would give me, had he time to write?"

It was through his little "History of the American Church,"

of which the first edition was published in 1844, and the second in 1846, that Dr. Wilberforce became known to our Society. It was not a very elaborate or exhaustive work, but it contained the fruit of some most fortunate researches among old manuscripts not within our reach, and it led directly to the discovery and identification of that precious History of the Pilgrims, by Governor Bradford, which had so long been missing.

To Samuel Wilberforce, then Bishop of Oxford, and to Charles James Blomfield, then Bishop of London, through the intervention of the late Dr. Joseph Hunter, we owe the possession of the exact copy of the Bradford Manuscript, which Mr. Deane has so admirably edited and annotated.[1] That association would alone be sufficient to secure a grateful remembrance for the subject of this brief notice.

[1] We were afterwards indebted to Dr. Tait, now Archbishop of Canterbury, for the opportunity of examining the manuscript at Fulham, while he was Bishop of London.

SIR WALTER RALEIGH.

COMMUNICATION AT A MEETING OF THE MASSACHUSETTS HISTORICAL SOCIETY, SEPTEMBER 10, 1873.

It may be remembered that at our Stated Meeting in November last, when we had the pleasure of welcoming Mr. Froude to Boston, I alluded to a contemporaneous account of the Execution of Mary, Queen of Scots, which I had found in the Common-Place Book of Adam Winthrop, the father of the first Governor of Massachusetts. I did not suppose that it contained any thing new in regard to that event, and I had many misgivings about offering it for publication. But no one was able to point to the same precise version of that sad story in print; and our Committee of Publication thought proper to include it in our last volume of Proceedings, where it has been read with interest, as I have reason to know, both at home and abroad.

In the same old manuscript Note-book, I have found several other accounts of historical events of a somewhat similar character, carefully copied from seemingly authentic sources; and, among them, "The Confession and Execution of Sir Walter Raleigh." Sir Walter was executed in October, 1618, when Adam Winthrop was living at Groton, England, at seventy years of age, — a magistrate of the old county of Suffolk, who, a few years before, had resigned the Auditorship of Trinity College, Cambridge, which he had held for sixteen or seventeen years. His son, who twelve years afterwards came over to New England as Governor of Massachusetts, was then about thirty years old. Both of them were thus in the way of taking an intelligent interest in the public affairs of their country, and both might have personally witnessed the execution of Raleigh, had they chanced to be in London at the time. I find no evidence, however, that either of them was there. Meantime, no newspaper had as yet been published in England. The first regular English newspaper, entitled "The Weekly News," dates from 1622. It may thus not be without interest to inquire from what original, in manuscript or in print, this account of what is called "The Confession and Execution of Sir Walter Raleigh" was copied, or from what source it was procured.

A new and elaborate Life of Sir Walter, together with his Letters, "now first collected," has been published in England within the last five years, by Mr. Edward Edwards, the author of "Memoirs of Libraries," and other works, which gives a detailed report of Raleigh's speech on the scaffold, in regard to which the author says, in a note, as follows: "In this speech I have very much followed Archbishop Sancroft's transcript, preserved amongst the Tanner MSS., but have collated it with other reports. *No known report can, I think, be trusted exclusively.*" This work was published in 1868. In the following year (1869), Mr. James Augustus St. John, who had previously published a Life of Raleigh, gave a new edition of it to the public, in the preface to which he says, with plain allusion to the Life by Mr. Edwards, as follows: "Since the first publication of this biography, another Life of Sir Walter Raleigh has been laid before the public. This performance must have been produced some years ago, since the author is unacquainted with the discoveries recently made at Simancas and Madrid, which have thrown an entirely new light on the latter portions of Raleigh's Life." Mr. St. John, accordingly, in the last chapter of his volume, in describing the death of Raleigh, says: "He made a short speech, the meaning of which has scarcely been preserved. What we possess under that name it is impossible he should have uttered, unless we assume the letter to James of the 5th of October, together with his examinations, and those of La Chêne, and all his communications with the French authorities, to be forgeries.

Had he denied, as he is said to have done, that he ever saw any commission, letter, or seal, from the French King, his admission to the contrary in his own handwriting would doubtless have been produced on the scaffold, to confound and silence him. We must consequently believe, either that the documents referred to were mere fabrications, or that several gentlemen who were present at his death, and heard him deliver his farewell address to the world, either misunderstood his language, or purposely misrepresented it." Upon this ground, Mr. St. John omits any detailed report of the Speech, consigning the received versions of it to entire discredit. At the same time he candidly states that the original of Raleigh's letter to the King, of the 5th October, has not been discovered, and that it is only produced in the form of a "retranslation from the Spanish version, to be found in the General Archives of Simancas." From the same source have recently come the conflicting and contradictory replies of La Chêne, the French Secretary, at his successive examinations before the English Council of State, in the first two of which he positively denies almost every thing which he confesses in the third.

Now, as to the letter of October 5, nothing can perfectly convince one that Raleigh wrote that letter within twenty-four days of his death, except the production of the original in his own handwriting, or certainly with his own unmistakable signature. Mr. St. John himself, in the paragraph with which he precedes it, gives us no small ground for suspecting the genuineness of all such copies. "Sir Thomas Wilson," he says, "it cannot be doubted, received both from the King and his Secretary [Sir Robert Naunton] orders to extract from Raleigh, by solemn promises of pardon, such admissions and confessions as, in the opinion of those who were to judge of them, would compromise his life. In doing this, he was to insinuate, though not positively to assert, that he had high authority for the language he employed; if the bait took, his masters were to disavow his proceedings, and overwhelm him with censure, but to base nevertheless upon his artifices the destruction of their victim. Naunton acknowledges frankly that such was the practice; and the number of heads which were thus brought under the axe was doubtless considerable." The admissions and confessions of this letter might thus seem to have been extracted or extorted from Raleigh by a base agent of the King and his Secretary, "by solemn promises of pardon," which were to be disavowed as soon as "the bait had taken," and the letter used to justify his execution. The men capable of contriving such a trap would be entirely capable of forging the letter. But it is not necessary to suppose forgery in its full meaning. What more natural than that a man, charged with the execution of such a villany, should have prepared a draft of the letter containing "such admissions and confessions as, in the opinion of those who were to judge of them, would compromise his life," and should have offered it to the destined victim for adoption? How else could it be made sure that enough for the purpose would be admitted and confessed? If such a draft were made, — even though it were indignantly rejected, — there might well be a "retranslation from the Spanish version, to be found in the General Archives of Simancas," and yet no original letter written and signed by Sir Walter Raleigh. The letter may indeed have been written and signed by Sir Walter; but the style is quite unlike that of others of his letters to the King, and it has too much the character of a made-up letter, which Wilson, under the instigation of Naunton and his master, had arranged to meet the exact exigencies of the case.

A most striking illustration of the manner in which Sir Thomas Wilson, well called "Raleigh's gaoler and the King's spy," arranged the examinations, and concocted the correspondence of his victim, may be seen in the second volume of Edwards's Life and Letters, at pages 364–5, and so to page 373. On page 370, there is given a letter from Raleigh to his wife, "from a copy in the hand of a clerk of Sir Thomas Wilson, made, as it seems, *before the delivery of the letter* to Lady Raleigh;" and on the same page is found Lady Raleigh's reply, "from a copy, made as above, and upon the same sheet." On page 372, will be seen another letter of Raleigh to his wife, "from a copy made by Sir Thomas Wilson, *before, as it seems, the original was delivered* to Lady Raleigh." The Prefatory Note to this last, on the previous page (371), is most instructive. It is as follows: "The letter to which this is an answer appears to have been written by Lady Raleigh, at the instigation either of Secretary Naunton, or of some other person about the King. Neither the letter nor any copy of it is now to be found among the State Papers. But it is plain from the correspondence between Naunton and Wilson that, whilst the writer must have fondly hoped that some benefit would result to her husband from his answering the questions she was instigated to put to him, the ingenious contrivers had a purpose directly the opposite of this." (See the whole note.) What faith is to be put in the accuracy of copies which have passed through such unclean hands! Mr. St. John describes this course of proceeding as follows: "If he [Raleigh] requested permission to write a few lines to his wife, Naunton and James had to be consulted before so poor a favor could be granted, and when written — though this he did not know — his letters were subjected to the scrutiny of both Secretary and Monarch before they reached their destination. In fact, his seal was broken, and the letters having been read were resealed and returned to Wilson, who then sent them to Lady Raleigh, whose answers were subjected to the same examination"!

An interesting account of Raleigh's death may be found in a late "Chapter of English History," entitled "Prince Charles and the Spanish Marriage," by Samuel Rawson Gardiner, Esq., who speaks thus of the letter to the King, which Mr. St. John regards as discrediting the reports of the speech on the scaffold: "And so the wretched game of falsehood on both sides went on; till at last, on the 25th of September,[1] Raleigh, weary of the struggle, wrote to the King, acknowledging that he had sailed with a commission from the Admiral of France, and that La Chesnée had, by Le Clerc's directions, offered to assist him in his escape." But, while thus admitting the letter, Mr. Gardiner admits also the genuineness of the Speech. "As soon [says he] as he had mounted the scaffold, he asked leave to address the people. His Speech had been carefully prepared. Every

[1] We presume that the letter here styled of September 25th is the same with that of October 5th, the difference of ten days being that between old and new style.

word he spoke was, as far as we can judge, literally true; but it was not the whole truth, and it was calculated in many points to produce a false impression on his hearers." "On the commission which he had received from the French Admiral he was altogether silent, but he was emphatic in repudiating the notion that he had ever received a commission from the French King." Mr. Gardiner adds, in a foot note, "The part which relates to the French commission is a marvel of ingenuity. Not a word of it is untrue, but the general impression is completely false."

We have thus three accomplished English writers, within a few years past, adopting widely variant views of the same facts: one, accepting and indorsing the Speech; the second, discrediting it altogether; and the third, accepting it in its literal sense, but pronouncing its general impression, on one point at least, "completely false." The Speech itself by no means loses its interest in the face of such conflicting judgments, and every contemporaneous version of it may haply aid in solving the problem of its authenticity and of its truth.

Let us turn then to the Speech and the contemporary accounts of it. The earliest notice of it which we have been able to find is in a Letter of Rev. Thomas Lorkin to Sir Thomas Puckering, Bart., printed in Birch's "Court and Times of James the First" (vol. ii. p. 99). It is dated November 3, 1618, just a week after the execution of Raleigh, in which the scene and the Speech are described minutely, and in substantial conformity to the detailed report given by Mr. Edwards. Next, in order of date, is a letter, found at page 104 of the same volume, from John Chamberlain, Esq., to Sir Dudley Carleton, then Minister at the Hague, which, after acknowledging some papers he had received from Sir Dudley, proceeds as follows: "For some part of amends, I return you two papers in exchange: the one a letter from Sir Walter Raleigh to the King, before he came to Salisbury; and withal half a dozen verses he made the night before his death, to take farewell of poetry, wherein he had been a pidler, even from his youth. The other is a remembrancer left with his lady, written likewise that night, to acquaint the world withal, if perhaps he should not have been suffered to speak at his death, as he was cut off from speaking somewhat he would have said at the King's Bench; and they had no thanks that suffered him to talk *so long* on the scaffold;[1] but the fault was laid on the sheriff, and there it rests. His lady had been to visit him that night, and told him she had obtained the disposing of his body. To which he answered smiling, 'It is well, Besse, that thou mayest dispose of that dead, that had'st not always the disposing of it when it was alive;' and so dismissed her anon, after midnight, when he settled himself to sleep for three or four hours." A third notice of the scene and Speech is in a letter from Dr. Robert Tounson, Dean of Westminster, afterward Bishop of Sarum, who attended Sir Water Raleigh on the scaffold, and wrote a letter to Sir John Isham, dated November 9, 1618, only a fortnight after the event of which he had been an eye-witness, in which he says: "I hope you had the relation of Sir Walter Raleigh's death: for so I gave order, that it should be brought unto you. I was commaunded by the lords of the counsayle to be with him, both in prison and att his death as nere as I could: there be other reports of itt, but that which you have from me is treu: one Craford, who was sometimes Mr. Rodeknight's pupil, hath penned it pretily, and meaneth to putt itt to the presse, and came to me about it, but I heare not that it is come forth. The summe of that which he spake att his death, you have, I suppose, already." (See p. 780 of "Sir W. Raleigh's Works," vol. viii. Oxford, 1829.)

Lastly, in Walter Scott's Edition of "The Somers Tracts" (vol. ii. p. 438), there is a detailed report of the scene and Speech, which is ascribed to "Crawford, or Craford."

We might allude to other reports or descriptions of the Speech and the scene. But that which is thus traced to "Crawford, or Craford," — who, it seems, had consulted with the Dean of Westminster, who was with Raleigh on the scaffold "as nere as he could," and who must have heard every word he said, — would seem to be the most authentic. The Dean's expression that "Craford hath penned it pretily, and meaneth to putt itt to the presse," may, perhaps, be construed to imply that the ac-

[1] It is thus clear that the Speech was not a short one.

count was skilfully arranged, or even adorned, but it certainly casts no discredit upon its accuracy.

We are not in the way of ascertaining exactly where Archbishop Sancroft's account in the Tanner MSS. came from. The Archbishop himself was born in Suffolk County, England, in January, 1617, which, according to old style, would be less than one year before Raleigh's death. Of course, he could have had no personal knowledge on the subject.

The account contained in Adam Winthrop's Common-Place Book was undoubtedly written soon after the event,[1] and it is substantially Craford's account. Now and then there is something transposed or omitted; and now and then there is a difference of phraseology. But after a careful comparison it can hardly be doubted that it was taken from the "pretily penned" report which the Dean of Westminster described, and of which he said that Craford "meaneth to putt itt to the presse." It may have been printed on a broadside at the time, but we believe that not even the countless treasures of the British Museum, as thus far searched, contain a contemporaneous printed copy. The earliest printed report of "the Speech on the Scaffold," to which any allusion has been found, bears date 1648;[2] but of that no copy is at command for comparison. We should hardly know where to look for one on this side of the ocean. The earliest within reach is that appended to the Life of Sir Walter, printed in 1677, of which our Recording Secretary (Mr. Deane) has a copy in his valuable library, which he has kindly placed at our disposal, with other rare volumes on the subject. That version of the Speech conforms, also, to the one ascribed to "Crawford or Craford" in the Somers Tracts, but with some omissions and variations of phraseology. Under such circumstances Adam Winthrop's copy may have an interest and even a value. It may, at least, contribute something to "the various readings" out of which the true version is to be made up, if it has not been made up already.

Few greater men have ever lived in England, or anywhere

[1] Adam Winthrop died in April, 1623. The latest date in his MS. book is Nov. 24, 1621.

[2] See Watt's Bib. Brit., II. 788°.

else, than Raleigh. No man contributed more, if so much, towards the earliest American Colonization. "It was Raleigh," says Mr. Edwards, "who, in the teeth of Spain, when at her prime, laid the first foundations of the British Colonies in North America. . . . The future destinies of America, as well as the profits of a new trade, were with him themes of thought, of conversation, and of active effort, from the age of thirty-two when he first joined in the enterprise of his half-brother (Sir Humphrey Gilbert) to his latest hour of life." No man has left grander monuments of enterprise, courage, and genius. That, after a long and dreary imprisonment in the Tower, he should at last have been beheaded, at a day's notice, under a sentence passed fourteen or fifteen years before, which Bacon himself has been stated to have said was virtually superseded by his commission for Guiana, was an unspeakable atrocity. Well does John Forster, in his admirable Life of Sir John Eliot, pronounce it "the climax and consummation of the baseness of James's reign; — a shameless sacrifice of one of the greatest men of the English race to the rage and mortification of the power most hated by Englishmen." Sir John Eliot, an eye-witness, as is believed, of the tragedy, — himself afterwards a martyr to Free Speech, — has included a description of Raleigh's bearing on the occasion among his illustrations of the "Monarchy of Man." "Matchless, indeed," says he, "was his fortitude! All preparations that were terrible were presented to his eye. Guards and officers were about him, the scaffold and the executioner, the axe, and the more cruel expectation of his enemies. And what did all this work on the resolution of our Raleigh? Made it an impression of weak fear, or a distraction of his reason? Nothing so little did that great soul suffer. He gathered only the more strength and advantage; his mind became the clearer, as if already it had been freed from the cloud and oppression of the body; and such was his unmoved courage and placid temper, that, while it changed the affection of the enemies who had come to witness it and turned their joy to sorrow, it filled all men else with admiration and emotion, leaving with them only this doubt, whether death were more acceptable to him or he more welcome unto death."

All this does not look like the bearing of a man who had a lie, or even a prevarication, in his mouth. It is true, however, that the standard of morality, public and private, was any thing but exalted at that day. Bacon, who meanly consented to Raleigh's death, and vindicated his master for the act, was himself, at last, deposed for corruption. We would not suppress or extenuate any faults or follies of Raleigh, of which there is historical evidence. Faults, infirmities, and follies he certainly exhibited. The editor of Birch's Papers, in relation to Raleigh's feigned sickness, says in a foot-note: "The mind of the gallant Raleigh had given way beneath an accumulation of troubles. He had lost his son in a contest with the Spaniards, one of his captains had committed suicide, and the object of his voyage had been defeated by the treachery of the King, — proof of which exists in a letter of Buckingham to Secretary Winwood, to be found in Hardwicke's State Papers, vol. i. p. 398." [1]

Indeed, if the account of Manourie, the French apothecary, as given by Lord Bacon, is to be taken for true, Raleigh must have been goaded to absolute madness during these last few weeks, and a jury in our time would have justly returned a verdict of insanity. But Manourie, the principal accuser of Sir Walter (according to a letter of Rev. Thomas Lorkin to Sir Thomas Puckering, of Feb. 16, 1618–19), was not only convicted soon afterwards as a clipper of gold, but "confessed that his accusation against Raleigh was false, and that he was moved thereto by the practice and importunity of Stukely, and now acknowledged this, his present miserable condition, to be a judgment of God upon him for that!"

Was there ever such "confusion worse confounded"? No wonder that Gibbon himself, even before Simancas unfolded her treasures, shrunk in despair from disentangling the truth from the falsehood of Raleigh's life. But make the worst of him, and still his execution, under such circumstances, will stand out for ever, as one of the most abhorrent and abominable acts in English History. Occurring, as it did, a year or two only before the Pilgrims came over to Plymouth, and little more than ten years before the settlement of Massachusetts, it

[1] Court and Times of James I., p. 85.

must have been one of the events by which the minds of the New England Colonists were impressed and agitated while they were meditating a departure from their native land. And the mere fact that the account now submitted comes from an ancient manuscript which was undoubtedly brought over by Governor Winthrop in 1630, and which has but recently been discovered among the old papers of his father, greatly enhances its interest. Even should it not add a single new reading, or one better phrase, for Sir Walter's last words, as we think it does, it may serve to revive the remembrance of his marvellous career and of his heroic death on our side of the Atlantic, where it would most have gratified him to know that he should not be forgotten.

To a Society like ours, devoted to historical pursuits, his career has a peculiar interest, in view of the well-remembered fact that so large a part of his long imprisonment in the Tower was employed in writing that "History of the World," which is one of the most remarkable works in English literature, and of which the closing passage is doubly impressive in connection with the fate which was so soon to befall him: "It is therefore Death alone," he says, "that can suddenly make man to know himself. He tells the proud and insolent that they are but abjects, and humbles them at the instant, makes them complain and repent, yea, even to hate their forepast happiness. He takes the account of the rich and proves him a beggar, a naked beggar, which hath interest in nothing but the gravel that fills his mouth. He holds a glass before the eyes of the beautiful, and makes them see therein their deformity and rottenness, and they acknowledge it. Oh, eloquent, just, and mighty Death! Whom none could advise, thou hast persuaded; what none hath dared, thou hast done; and whom all the world hath flattered, thou only hast cast out of the world and despised; thou hast drawn together all the far-stretched greatness, all the pride, cruelty, and ambition of man, and covered it all over with these two narrow words, — *Hic jacet!*"

In conclusion, we can hardly doubt that this Speech was made substantially as it has been reported. A strong reason for questioning the authenticity of the Simancas copy of the alleged letter of October 5, or, as Mr. Gardiner gives the date, of September 25, is found in the fact that it is not mentioned, or in any way referred to, in Lord Bacon's Vindication of his Master, printed within a few months of the execution. If the King had such an answer to Raleigh's dying words as they were reported, how could it have failed to be used by Bacon to mitigate the popular indignation at the time? How could it have been unheard of for two centuries and a half, if it had been received by the King and known to all his counsellors? But the letter, if written, confessed only a commission from the Duke de Montmorenci, as Mr. Gardiner says, while the Speech denies only a commission from the King of France; and if Raleigh had already confessed the former, it may explain his confining his denials to the latter. That he did persistently and unequivocally deny the latter, is proved not only by the Speech, but by the little "Answer to some things at his death," which, we presume, is the "remembrancer left with his lady, written likewise that night [the night before his death], to acquaint the world withal, if perhaps he should not have been suffered to speak at his death," as described in the letter of Chamberlain to Sir Dudley Carleton, heretofore quoted.[1] We are not aware that this brief "Answer" has ever been called in question, and it seems to be entirely consistent with the Speech. It declares as explicitly as the reported Speech, "I never had commission from the French King; I never saw the French King's hand or seale in my life." Sir Lewis Stukely wrote a long letter to the King in his own defence, and in reply to this dying declaration of Raleigh; but, though it refers distinctly to what it calls Raleigh's "perjury in swearing he had no design for Fraunce," it contains no allusion to the alleged letter of October 5.[2] Once more, it may be urged, if the King had possessed a letter which might have counteracted the impression produced both by the brief "Answer" and the long Speech, or which could have been used in any way to Raleigh's discredit, could Bacon and Stukely both have failed to use it in

[1] This brief "Answer" will be found appended to The Essays of Raleigh, printed "by T. W.," for Humphrey Moseley, London, 1655.

[2] See "Somers Tracts" (Scott's ed.), vol. ii. p. 444.

their labored vindications of themselves and their master? Ah, what a glory it would have been for Bacon's fame, if he had saved the life of Raleigh, instead of consenting to his death, and apologizing for the act after it was perpetrated! Some discrepancy of dates, as given by different writers, might leave room for a doubt whether Bacon was not rewarded for this Apology by a promotion from the office of Lord Keeper to that of Lord Chancellor. A more careful inquiry, however, clears away any such imputation. But it is enough to have exhibited some of the intricate problems in this great Tragedy of English, — we had almost said, of American, — History; and so to leave them for the solution of others. The manuscript account of the Execution is as follows: —

The Confession and Execution of Sir Walter Raleighe.

Uppon Wedensdaie beinge the 28th of October, 1618, the Lieuttenant of the Tower, accordinge to a warrant to him directed, brought Sr Wa: Raleigh from the tower to the Kinges benche barre at Westminster, where the records of his arraignment at Winchester were opened, and he was demanded why execution shoulde not be done uppon him; accordinge to Judgement therein pronounced against him: To wh he began by waie of answere to iustifie himselfe in his proceedinges in the last voiage. But the L. chiefe justice silenced him, sainge there was no other matter in question, but concerninge the Judgement of Death wh had formallye beene given against him. And it was the Kinges pleasure (uppon some occasion beste knowen to himselfe) nowe to have the same executed, unles he coulde shewe good cause to the contrary. Unto wh Sr Wa: R. saide, that he was tolde by his Counsell, that in regarde his Matie, since the saide Judgement, had bin pleased to imploie him in his service (as by Commission he had done) it made voide the saide Judgement, and was vivification unto him. But the Lorde chiefe Justice toulde him, he was therin deceived; and that the opinion of the Courte was to the contrary. Wherewth he rested satisfied, and desired that some reasonable time might be allowed him, to prepare himselfe for deathe. But it was answered him, that the time of deathe appointed to him was to-morrowe: and that it was not to be doubted, but yt he had prepared himselfe for deathe longe since. And I am glad, saide the L. chiefe Justice, that [you have] given the worlde so good satisfaction of your Religion: as by some bookes published by you, you have done. And so Mr Attorneye generall required in the Kinges behalfe, that execution might be done uppon the prisoner, accordinge to the saide Judgement. Then the Shrifes of Middlesex were commanded to take him into their custodie, who p^r^sently caried [him] to the gate house in Westm^r^ from whence the next morninge he shoulde goe betweene the saide Shrives to the olde pallace of Westminster; where a large scaffolde was erected for his execution. Whereuppon when he came wth a cheerefull countenance he saluted the Lordes, knightes and gentlemen there present. After wth a proclamation beinge made for silence, he addressed himselfe to speake in this maner: I desire to be borne wth all, for this is the thirde daye of my fevere, and if I shall shewe my weakenes, I beseeche you to attribute it to my maladie, for this is the houre it was wonte to come. Then pausinge awile, he sett and directed himselfe to a windowe, where satt the Earles of Arundel, Northampton and Doncaster, wth some other Lordes and knightes, and spake as followeth: I thanke God of his infinite goodnes that he hathe sent mee to die in the light, and not in the darkenes; but because the place where the Lordes satte was farre distant from the scaffolde, that he perceived they coulde not heare him well, therfore he saide, I will straine my voice, for I woulde willinglie have yor honors heare mee. But the L. of Arundel said nay, but wee will rather come downe to the scaffolde to heare thee, w^h^ he and some other did. Wither beinge come, he saluted theme generallie, and so began to speake as followeth: As I said before, so nowe I saie againe, I thancke God, &c., but not in the darke prison of the Tower, where I have suffered a great deale of adversitie and cruell sickenes. And I thancke God that the fevere hathe not taken me at this time, and I pray God it may not. There are so many pointes of suspition that his Matie hath conceived against mee, and wherein he cannot be satisfied, w^h^ I desire to cleere and to resolve yor L^ps^ of. One is that his Matie hathe bin informed that I have ofte had plotts wth France, and his Matie had good reason to induce him thereunto: The first was, that when I came backe from Guyana, beinge come to Plymmouth, I indevored to have gone in a Barke to Rochel, w^h^ was because I woulde have made my peace before I came to Englande. The 2 was that uppon my flight, I did intende to flye into France for the savinge of my life, that had some terro^r^ from above.

A thirde was that the French agent came to mee; besides it was reported, that I had a Comission from the Frenche Kinge at my goinge forthe. These are the reasons that caused the Kinge to suspecte mee. Nowe for man to call God to witnesse a falsehoode, were a grevous synne: for what comfort can we then hope for at the daie of Judgement, before God's tribunal seate: But to call Godde to witnesse a false thinge at the houre of deathe, is a facte more grevous and fearefull, seeinge suche a one havinge no tyme of repentance, cannot hope to be saved at all. Then what can I expecte, that at this instant am goinge to render my accompte. I doe therfore call the Lorde to witnes (as I hope to bee saved, and to see him in his kingdome, wch I trust I shall, wth in this quarter of an houre) that I never had any Comission from the Frenche Kinge: neither did I ever see the Frenche Kinges handewritinge, nor his seale, in all my life. Nor yet did I knowe that there was an Agent heere, nor what he was, till I mette him in the galery in my lodgine, unlooked for. If I speake not true, then O Lorde let me not come into thy kingedome. The 2 suspicion was that his Matie had bin informed, that I shoulde speake dishonorably, and disloiallie of him my sovereigne: But my accuser was a base frenchman, a runnagate, and one that had no dwellinge, and a kinde of chimicall fellowe. One that I knewe to bee pfidious. For being drawne in the accion of scarringe [myself] at Winchester, (into wch I confesse [my shame that] my hande was at all) beinge sworne to secrecie one night, he revealed it the next morninge. But (let me speake) what have I nowe to doe wth rogues? I have nothinge to doe wth them, neither doe I feare them; for I have onlie to doe wth my God, in whose presence I stande: therfore for me to tell a lie, therby to gaine the Kiuges favoure, were in vaine. But as I hope in the Lorde to be saved at the last daie, I denye that I ever spake dishonourably, disloiallie or dishonestlie of the Kinge, neither to that frencheman, nor to any other. No I protest I never had a thought of ill, of his Matie, in all my life. And therfore I cannot but thincke it strange, that the slaunde^r beinge so base and meane a fellowe, shoulde bee so farre credited as he hathe beene. And so muche of my double resolution to the Kinges double suspicion. I confesse I did attempte to escape; yea I cannot excuse that, but it was onlie to save my life. And I likewise confesse, I did faine myselfe to bee ill disposed at Salisbury; but I hope it was no syn; for the prophet David did make himselfe a foole and suffer spittle to fall on his bearde, to escape ye hands of his enymies, and it was not imputed to him. So in what I did, I intended no ill, but to gaine and prolonge time till his Matie came, hopinge of some comiseration from him. But I forgive this frencheman and Sr Lewes Stukeley also wth all my harte. I have received the Sacrament this morninge of Mr. Deane, and I have forgiven all the worlde. But that they are pfidious, I am bounde in charitie to speake, that all men may take heede of them. Sr Lewes Stukeley my keeper and kinsman hathe affirmed, that I shoulde tell him, that my L. Carewe and my lorde of Doncaster there, did advize me to escape; but I protest before God I never tolde him any suche thinge, neither did the Lordes advise me any suche thinge, neither is it likelie that I shoulde tell him any suche matter of the two privie counsellers. Neither I had any reason to tell him; for tis well knowne, that hee lefte me IX or X times alone to goe whether I woulde, whilst he ridde aboute the country. He farther accuseth mee, that I shoulde tell him that these two lordes woulde meete me in France, wch I never spake nor thought. Thirdlie, that I shoulde proferre him a letter, wherby I did signifie unto him, that I woulde give him a thousand pound for my escape. But Lord cast my soule into everlastinge fire, if I ever made any suche proferre of a 1000li or a 100li. But indeed I shewed him a letter, that if he woulde goe wth me, there shoulde bee order taken for the payem^t^ of his detts, when he was gone: neither had I 1000li, and if I had, I coulde have made my peace wth it other wise. Lastlie, when I came to Sr Edw. Pelhams, who had bin a follower of myne, and given me good intertainement, he gave out speaches that I had received some Drame [of poison], when I assured him that I feared no suche thinge, for I was well assured of them in the house; and therfore wished him to have no suche thought. Nowe God forgive him, for I doe. And I desire God to forgive him, even as I desire to bee forgiven. Then lookinge on his note of remembrance, well, saide hee, thus farre I am gone nowe; a little more, and I shall have done. It was toulde the Kinge, that I was brought into Englande ꝑ force; and that I did not intende to come againe; but Sr Charles Parks, Mr Tatsham, and Mr Leete knowe howe I was delte w^th^all by the comon soldiours, wch were 150 in number; who sent for mee to come into the guard roome unto them, for they woulde not come to mee; and there was I inforced to take an oathe, that I woulde not goe into Englande till they woulde have mee. I heare likewise that there was a reporte, that I went not purposelye to goe into Guiana at all, and that I knewe not of any myne, nor intended any suche matter; but only to gette my libertie (wch I had not the witte to keepe), but I protest it was my full intent, to seeke the mine of goulde for the benifite of myselfe and his Matie and those that adventured wth mee and the rest of my countrymen that went wth mee. But he that knewe the head of the mine woulde not discover it, when he sawe my sonne was slaine, but made himselfe awaie. And then turninge to the Earle of Arundell, he saide as followeth: Beinge in the gallerie of my shippe at my departure, I remember yor honor tooke me by the hande, and said you woulde request one thinge of mee, that whether I made a good voiage or a bad, I would not faile to returne againe into Englande: wch I promised you, and gave you my faith that I woulde, and so I did. To wch my Lorde then present answered, it is true, I well remember it, they were the last woordes I spake then unto you. Another opinion was helde of mee, that I carried to sea 1600 peeces, and that I was desirous (for all the voiage y^{t} I intended) only to get mony into my handes, and that I had made my voiage before; whereas I protest at my goinge to sea, I had but a C peeces in all, whereof I gave 25 to my wife, and the rest I tooke wth mee, and the remaind^{r} I brought backe wth me into Englande. Another scandall was charged on me that I woulde have gone awaie from my companie, and lefte them at Guiana; but there are a great many woorthy men, wch accompanied me alwaies and knowe my intent was nothinge so. All these are the material pointes wch I thought good to speake of.

I am at this instant, (beinge the subiecte of deathe), to render accounte to God, and I proteste (as I shall appeare before him) this that I have here delivered and spoken is true: yet I will speake a worde or two more, and but a word or two, because I will not bee over troublesome to Mr Shr. There was a reporte spred, that I should reioice at the death of my L. of Essex: and that I shoulde, at that instant, take Tobacco in his presence; when (I proteste) I shed teares at his deathe, thoughe I was (I confesse) one of the faction. At the very time of his deathe, and all the while of his preparation, I was in the Armorie, and at the further ende, where I coulde but see him. He sente for mee, but I did not goe to him: for I hearde he desired to see mee.[1] Therefore I lamented his deathe, as I had good cause, for it was the woorse for mee, as it proved: for after he was gone, I was little beloved. Nowe I intreate you all to ioigne wth me in prayer, that the great God of heaven, whom I have grevously offended, woulde forgive mee. For I have beene a man full of all vanities, and have lived a synfull and wicked life in a synfull callinge; havinge bin a Soldio^{r}, a Captaine bothe by lande and sea, and also a Courtier, wch are only helpes and waies to make a man wicked in all these places. Wherfore I desire you all to praye wth mee that God woulde pardon and forgive me my synnes, and cast them all out of his sight and remembrance; and that for his Sonne, my only Savio^{r} Jesus Christ his sake, he woulde receive me into his everlastinge kingdome, where is life eternal. And so I take my leave of you all, and will nowe make my peace wth God.

And after a proclamation made, that all shoulde departe from of the scaffolde, he prepared himselfe to die, givinge awaie his bever hatte, and wrought night cap, wth some mony to some of his acquaintance that stoode neere him: and then tooke his leave of the Lordes, knightes, and gentlemen. Hee desired the Erle of Arundell, y^{t} he woulde informe his Matie

1 There is some confusion here, probably arising from the omission of a line or two in copying.

of that wch he spoke; and to intreat him, that there might bee no scandalous pamphletts or wrightings published to defame him after his deathe. And so puttinge of his gowne and dublet, he made a longe prayer upon his knees, the Deane of Westm^{r} knelinge by him, and prayinge wth him all the while; wch beinge ended, he called to the Executioner to fetche the fatall instrument (as he called it) wch beinge denied him, he saide, I pray you let mee see it; thincke you, I am afraide of it? Whereupon it was shewed him; and he felte the edge wth his thumbe, and wth a smilinge countenance he saide [to] the Shr. — This is a sharpe medicine, but a phisitian that will cure all diseases. Then goinge to eche side of the scaffolde, he intreated the people to praye for him, that God woulde assist him, and give him strengthe. Then being asked wch waie he woulde lie, towardes the windowe, where the Lordes stoode, or no, he went aboute the blocke, and laide his hed from the Lordes, and said, So bee it the harte bee stronge, it is no matter where the hed lieth; and then prayinge, havinge forgiven the Executioner, and givinge him a signe when he shoulde doe his office (as he laye prayinge and callinge upon God) at twoe strookes he tooke of his head.

I may observe, in conclusion, that the same old MS. volume contains also a copy of the familiar lines said to have been found in Sir Walter's Bible after his death, but with some variations from the commonly received version, as follows: —

Even so dooth tyme take up withe truste,
Our youthe, and ioies and al wee have;
And paies us but wth age and duste,
In darkenes, scilence and the grave:
So havinge wandred all our waies,
Shuttes up the story of our daies. —
From darkenes, silence, age and duste,
The Lorde shal raise me up I truste.

QTH Wa: RALEYGH.

THE BOSTON LIGHT INFANTRY.

SPEECH AT THE DINNER ON THEIR SEVENTY-FIFTH ANNIVERSARY, OCTOBER 18, 1873.

I THANK you, Gentlemen, most heartily for this kind reception. I thank you, in behalf of your past Commanders, for the compliment you have paid them, and more particularly for any part of that compliment which I may appropriate to myself. I did not fail to recognize amidst your cheers some sounds which, though strange and unaccustomed of late years, were once familiar and welcome music to my ears.

I am here to make no formal or elaborate speech. I have come merely to answer once more to the roll-call of the old Corps with which I was so actively and proudly associated in years long past. I could not resist the summons to join you, though at some personal inconvenience, in celebrating this seventy-fifth anniversary of a Company which was originally organized under the excellent Daniel Sargent, at a critical period of our history, to support John Adams as President of the United States, and George Washington as Lieutenant-general of the American Provisional Army. Had I failed of an appearance, I should have been afraid to meet our worthy associate, Sheriff Clark, lest he should have a *Capias* in his pocket, and should serve it upon me without ceremony.

It is nearly forty years since I resigned the command of the Corps, and about forty-five years since I first joined it as Ensign. I may be pardoned for remembering that I was offered at the same moment, in 1829, the ensigncy of the Boston Light Infantry and the captaincy of one of the other volunteer companies of Boston. I chose the humbler station in your service, and have never regretted the decision. I may remember, too, that I was then fresh from the command of the Harvard Washington Corps, — a company of the undergraduates of the University at Cambridge, which had no little celebrity in its day, and which I have often regretted was ever suffered to die out. I know of no more manly and useful exercise for young men, not even cricket matches or boat races. John Milton, I think, included military discipline in his scheme of a perfect education. And at the very time that essay was written in Old England, the earliest legislators of New England were giving unequivocal evidence that they understood the value of training the youth, and even the children of their day, to the service of defence. It is a striking historical fact, which I have never seen alluded to elsewhere, and which recently met my eye in looking over our old colonial records, that the Great and General Court of Massachusetts, as early as 1645, provided by law for children, as young as ten years of age, being exercised with small arms, and even with bows and arrows. Here is the record, with all its queer spelling and quaint abbreviations: —

"Whereas it is conceived y^t ye training up of youth to ye art & practice of armes wilbe of great use in y^s country in divers respects, and amonge ye rest y^t ye use of bowes and arrowes may be of good concernment in defect of powder, upon any occasion, It is therefore Ordered, y^t all youth wthin this jurisdiction, from ten yeares ould to ye age of sixteen yeares, shalbe instructed by some one of ye Officers of ye band, or some other experienced Souldier whom ye chiefe Officer shall appoint, upon ye usual training dayes, in ye exercise of armes, as small guns, halfe pikes, bowes & arrowes, &c., according to ye discretion of ye said Officer or Souldier, provided y^t no child shalbe taken to y^s exercise against y^{eir} parents minds; — Y^s order to be of force wthin one month after ye publication hereof."

This was in May, 1645. It must have been an amusing sight, — those little companies of boys, in their primitive costumes, with their little guns and bows and arrows, solemnly drilling on the Common, — then, and for a century afterward, in the joint occupancy of the cows. It was no exercise of sport or play, but a matter of legal regulation and enforcement, a part of the discipline by which our State was built up.

And thus it is in strict accordance with old Puritan precedents that we now find our Latin schools and High schools and Chauncy schools furnishing some of the best examples of military drill, and sometimes supplying the chosen escorts of our civic processions. Our fathers, it is true, in their day, had wild beasts and wilder men to contend against. But the extermination or extinction of such dangerous and ferocious creatures — all except the Tigers,[1] which this occasion seems to show have not been extinguished, — has by no means put an end to the necessity of being prepared for self-defence. We have too recently been involved in the stern realities of war, for the preservation of the Union, to require any reminder on that point. I, certainly, cannot forget that one of the very last services I performed in connection with this Corps was to present a standard, in their name, to the Forty-third Regiment of Massachusetts Volunteers, in November, 1862, on Boston Common, just as it was going forth to the battle-fields of the Constitution.

My friends, I am a member of the Peace Society, and one of its honored vice-presidents. I sympathize most heartily in the general aims and principles of that Society, and especially in that great principle of Arbitration which has been so grandly signalized and vindicated, during the last year or two, under the leading influence of the father of one of your recent lieutenants, Mr. Adams. I pray God that neither foreign war nor civil war may ever call again for the intervention of force, at home or abroad, on land or on sea. As deeply as any one I feel, and have always felt, that war of any sort is a reproach and a stain upon Christian civilization. But I am by no means sanguine that preparations for defence can ever be safely abandoned. More especially do I see little chance of an entire cessation of those emergencies and exigencies in our great cities, which, like the terrible Boston Fire last November, may call imperatively for the employment of bayonets to aid the civil police in repressing robbery and violence. And hence I am here to offer my best

[1] The familiar title of the Company.

wishes to our Corps on its revival and reorganization, and to express my ardent hope that it may be numbered again, as it was in times past, among the cherished ornaments and defences of our beloved city.

You have called me out first as the oldest Commander, living and present, of the old Boston Light Infantry. But I must not forget that there are those around me who, though never Commanders, were associated with the Corps, either as officers or members, long before I was. Here is Josiah Quincy, known to us all as one of the most vigorous and popular Mayors of Boston, as his father had been before him; the son of an honored father and the father of a gallant son, whose service in the late war will not soon be forgotten. He was many years before me. And here, too, is my valued friend William Amory, of whom it may be said that, if he never rose above an ensigncy, it was our loss and his own fault, as he ran away, not from his enemies, but from his friends, for a long sojourn in Europe, and hardly left his peer in our ranks. My own immediate predecessor in command, the late Edward Blake, a faithful and excellent officer, whose memory is cherished by many friends as a devoted lawyer and a worthy citizen, has but recently gone to his rest; and I gladly pay this passing tribute to his virtues.

But his predecessor, the Captain under whom I first enlisted, under whose lead I have marched, and at whose side I have slept on more than one tented field, is still living, I rejoice to say, — a prosperous gentleman, the head of that great banking house in London, of which Joshua Bates, the benefactor of our Boston Public Library, was so long one of the honored members, — a house not founded on irredeemable paper, and which has stood, as it now stands, unshaken by any financial panic, however sudden or severe. This Company never had a more popular Commander than Russell Sturgis; and the only fault we have to find with him is that he will not break away occasionally from "No. 8 Bishopsgate within," and come over to receive the cordial welcome of his countless American friends.

But I hasten to remark, in conclusion, that there is one at this table who never, I believe, aspired to be more than a private soldier, but who was an active member of the Corps in the year 1802, before almost any of the rest of us were born, — seventy-one years ago, four years only after the Company was organized, — and who, at the close of a long and useful and honorable life, at the age of ninety-three, has come to exhibit his interest in this occasion. It is to him, pre-eminently, that the earliest personal honors are due from us all, and I call upon you to rise with me while I propose the health of the venerable TIMOTHY DODD.

THE BOSTON TEA-PARTY.

I.

SPEECH AT THE CENTENNIAL CELEBRATION OF THE "BOSTON TEA-PARTY," IN FANEUIL HALL, DECEMBER 16, 1873, IN REPLY TO A COMPLIMENTARY CALL FROM HON. JOSIAH QUINCY, THE PRESIDENT OF THE OCCASION.

I THANK you, Mr. President, for the kindness of your allusions both to the living and to the dead. There is certainly no blood in my veins which I prize more highly to-day than the old Huguenot blood of James Bowdoin, — the friend of Washington and Franklin, of Samuel Adams and John Adams and Josiah Quincy, Jr., — and who co-operated with them all in the great work of American independence. Nor would I willingly forget my somewhat more remote relationship to that John Winthrop, the eminent Professor of Natural Philosophy at Harvard College for forty years, who, while he so eagerly observed a comet, or an earthquake, or a transit of Mercury, did not fail to keep a sharp look-out upon the political sky also, and counted no eclipse of sun, or moon, or stars, so important to be watched and noted as the faintest approach to an eclipse of liberty. I thank you again, sir, for calling on me in connection with such names and such men, — both of whom had the honor to be dismissed from the council board of Massachusetts in 1775, by an arbitrary provincial governor, as unsuited to his purposes, and uncompromisingly hostile to his policy.

But I may be pardoned, I trust, to-day, for saying what little more I have to say here, in no representative capacity, and by no mere right of inheritance, but simply as one who claims the birthright of a Bostonian. And let me assure you at the outset, ladies and gentlemen, that I rejoice to understand that only brief speeches are to be expected here from any one. That was, indeed, distinctly impressed on the complimentary card of admission with which I was favored; for while your ingenious artist has portrayed a very large and capacious tea-pot, — big enough to hold ship and cargo, tea-chests, Mohawks and all, — he has plainly indicated a very short *spout*.

Seriously, my friends, I was most highly honored in being selected by the ladies as one of the minute-men, or five-minutes-men, of this occasion; and I am only afraid that I have used so much of my time in the preamble that there will be none left for the peroration, to say nothing of the staple thread of my discourse. But indeed you desire no discourse. You have not come here this afternoon to listen to elaborate details of what was said or done in Boston just a hundred years ago to-day. Those details are all familiar to you. That rainy, winter morning; those countless multitudes from all parts of the town, and of the neighboring towns, thronging to the Old South; the consultations with the consignees; the message to Governor Hutchinson, at Milton; the wise and eloquent words of Quincy; the unanimous vote, at half-past four, that the tea should not be landed; the stern and repulsive answer of the Governor — reported and listened to by dimly-burning candles — at six; the final word of Samuel Adams, "This meeting can do nothing more to save the country;" the war-whoop at the door; the response from the galleries; the rush of the Mohawks to Griffin's Wharf; the boarding of the vessels; the drowning of the tea; the dispersion of the crowd, and the quiet night which followed, — who can add a fact or a figure, a light or a shade, to a picture already so indelibly engraved on the pages of history, and even more deeply imprinted in all our memories and in all our hearts? You have not assembled here to be told what you know so well, and remember so vividly.

Nor are we here to-day, I am sure, to renew our accusations or revive our resentments against provincial governors, or British parliaments or ministries. The presence and participation of the ladies would alone be a sufficient pledge that we are here in no spirit of animosity or bitterness toward anybody. We delight to remember Old England this day and every day as our mother-country; and we thank God that she, of all the nations of the earth, was our mother-country. No other mother could have produced such children. It was from her history and her example that we imbibed those great lessons of freedom which led to independence. From the days when the Barons at Runnymede extorted the great charter from King John, her history was the history of advancing freedom. When John Hampden so heroically resisted the forced loans and the ship-money of Charles I., he pointed the way for James Otis and Joseph Warren and Samuel Adams to resist the stamp act and the tea tax of George III.

No, no, my friends; we have not come to Faneuil Hall to-day to arraign or reproach any one — whether tyrants abroad or tories at home — for measures which, as we look back upon them now, in the calm, clear light of history, and in the reverent recognition and grateful acknowledgment of an overruling God, seem almost to have been providentially arranged and designed to rouse up the American colonies to assert and maintain their rights as freemen and their independence as a nation. How slowly the evolution of our great Republic might have gone on, how the grand development of constitutional liberty and union might have lagged and dragged, but for the persistent madness of Hillsborough and Dartmouth and Lord North, to say nothing of their Royal Master, on the other side of the ocean, and of Bernard and Hutchinson and Gage, on this side! I think we may well afford to recall all their memories without infusing a particle of bitterness in our cup of tea this evening.

Once more, my friends, — and I will detain you but little longer, — we are not here to-day, I think, to glory over a mere act of violence, or a merely successful destruction of property, however obnoxious that property may have been. "Liberty and law" is, now and ever, the fundamental principle of our American institutions. And there can be no secure liberty without law. Irresponsible and irrepressible resistances to authority must always be, I suppose, — as they always have been, — the beginning of revolutionary movements. But now that a free, constitutional government has existed and prospered in our land for more than three-quarters of a century, the very last lesson we would even run the risk of teaching our children, or of teaching anybody, at home or abroad, is that any thing but evil and mischief and wrong is to be accomplished by a resort to lawless violence.

But let it never be forgotten that the destruction of the tea was no part of the original purpose of the Boston patriots. They endeavored in every way to avoid the possibility of such a necessity, or even of such a temptation. They besought the consignees, they implored the governor, that it should not be landed; that it should be sent safely back where it came from. But when the British Parliament had resolved that taxation "in all cases whatsoever," and taxation without a shadow of representation, should be enforced and submitted to, and had sent over these particular tea-chests to test that issue, it became a simple question, which should go under, British tea or American liberty. We all know which did go under, and which remains uppermost, erect and triumphant; and we are here to-day to thank God that it was so, and to honor our fathers for standing fast and firm, at every hazard, in defence of the great right of representation.

We know not exactly who prompted the precise mode of proceeding, or whether any of the patriot leaders of the day, disguised or undisguised, had a hand in the act. It seemed to have been performed by a spontaneous rising of the young blood of the town, from the workshops and the printing-offices of men like Benjamin Edes and Paul Revere, to whom we owed so much in the later stages of the Revolution. They knew how to do what they undertook to do without boasting or blustering, or even revealing their names, and to go quietly home after it was over, with the all-sufficient satisfaction of feeling that the tea was at least beyond the reach of the tax-gatherer, and that the question of paying duties in all cases whatsoever, or in any case whatsoever, was settled, finally and for ever. They did the deed, and let the glory go.

But there was hardly an act ever performed by human hands which produced more immediate or more permanent results; and from it may fairly be dated the practical beginning of the struggle for independence. From that moment might have been seen written on every patriot brow the maxim of John

Hampden, "No steps backward." An angry and avenging spirit was not unnaturally aroused in the British Parliament; and blow after blow — port bills and military bills, and I know not what all — came pouring down upon our devoted town. But every blow struck out a new spark, and every spark kindled a fresh flame, not merely in Massachusetts, but in every colony on the continent. New York and Pennsylvania, Virginia and the Carolinas, and all the rest, were heard declaring at once and together that "the cause of Boston was the cause of all;" and all eagerly united in supporting and vindicating that cause.

Yes, my friends, from those scattered tea-leaves — not on the bottom of cup or saucer, after the fashion of the old itinerant fortune-tellers, whom some of us remember, but strewed along the sands of yonder shore — might have been foreseen and foretold the rising fortunes of our country, as they have since been so gloriously unfolded. That illustrious philosopher, — Agassiz, — who has done so much more than all other men to give an impulse to scientific study and research in our day and land, and whose death — I hardly dare trust myself to speak of him as dead — whose unspeakable loss is, at this very hour, casting so profound a gloom over the whole scientific world, as well as over the wide social sphere of which he has so long been the joy and the pride, has taught us by precept and by example the importance of dredging the bottom of the ocean for ascertaining the structure of the earth, as well as for discovering the deposits and contents of the mighty deep. The historical inquirer may confine himself to a narrower field. He needs only to dredge our little Boston Bay to ascertain the primary elements of our great struggle for freedom. A single tea-leaf, if it could be plucked up from the huge mass which furnished strange food for the fishes, at Griffin's wharf, a hundred years ago, — one fossilized tea-leaf, if it could be found, would furnish him an ample clue to the whole story.

"Who knows how tea will mingle with salt water?" is said to have been the exclamation of one of the Liberty Boys, at some stage of the discussions at the Old South. I am not aware that the experiment of such a mixture was ever tried before, or ever has been since; and the result in this particular case may have been somewhat exceptional. I should hardly venture to recommend another such trial to the British East India Company, or even to the Boston Oriental Company. But certain it is that those three hundred and forty-two chests of Bohea, or Hyson, or Souchong, or Imperial Gunpowder, or whatever they were, thoroughly soaked and saturated with iced salt water, have produced a wider, a more wholesome, and a more enduring inspiration in men and in women, wherever there was a head or a heart to be inspired for any cause of human rights, than the whole crop of the Celestial Empire from that day to this, — even though it were steeped in urns of silver or gold, and poured into porcelain of Sévres or Dresden, and every cup served out by hands as fair as those which are so kindly and gracefully ministering it to us at this moment!

Mr. President, my time is more than up. Pardon me for a word, and but a word more. You, Sir, have been doing a good service of late for our city and State, if I mistake not, as the head of our harbor commissioners. There has been much to be done in the way of improving and preserving the channels, and in preventing nature and art from conspiring successfully together to bring about what the British Parliament once tried so vainly to effect, — the shutting-up of the port of Boston. You will accomplish, I hope and trust, all which you may attempt, and the good wishes of us all will go with you in your work. But there is one thing which you will never attempt, and never accomplish, if you should attempt it. You can never obliterate the tracks and traditions of the 16th of December, 1773. You can never alter the current or divert the channel of history. Your sea-walls and breakwaters may do any thing and every thing but that. "You may break, you may shatter," — no; let me never admit that idea, but let me paraphrase the well-remembered lines of the charming Irish songster: —

"You may narrow or widen the port, if you will,
But the scent of the *tea-leaves* will hang round it still!"

II.

INTRODUCTORY REMARKS AT A SPECIAL MEETING OF THE MASSACHUSETTS HISTORICAL SOCIETY, HELD IN THE EVENING OF THE SAME DAY, AT THE HOUSE OF REV. ROBERT C. WATERSTON.

WE are here, Gentlemen, at the invitation of our valued associate, Mr. Waterston, to spend a social evening in recalling the events which have rendered this anniversary so conspicuous in our Colonial history. Some of us have been at Faneuil Hall this afternoon, to take a commemorative cup of tea with the ladies of Boston, and to give brief expression to the feelings which the place and the day could not fail to excite in the hearts of all who were assembled there. Under this quiet domestic roof, we are privileged to indulge in calmer reflections on what occurred just a hundred years ago, and to contribute, as any of us may be able, in the most informal and colloquial manner, such historical statements or facts as may befit the sober records of our Society, and such contemporaneous accounts and traditions as may serve to illustrate the spirit or the conduct of those who took part in the memorable transactions of the 16th of December, 1773.

At the meeting at Faneuil Hall, this afternoon, the chair, as you all know, was assigned to a grandson of the "Josiah Quincy, Junior," of our early Revolutionary period. We meet to-night under the roof of a grand-daughter of the same distinguished patriot. And I cannot refrain from giving expression, at the outset, to what seems to me the eminent appropriateness that the family name of the young Quincy of 1773 should be thus distinctly associated with these observances. We cannot look back upon the history of that period without remembering how soon and how sadly his name was to disappear from the rolls of the living, and to be lost to every thing except the grateful and affectionate memories of his fellow-countrymen.

Of the leading men of the Revolution whom Massachusetts is privileged and proud to claim as her children, the larger number lived to reap the rewards of their labors and sacrifices, in greater or less measure, after the struggle was ended and the victory won. I will say nothing of Franklin, in this connection, as the glories of his mature life belong to Pennsylvania. And James Otis, it is true, the great orator of the earlier days of the Stamp Act, — that "flame of fire," as John Adams called him, against "Writs of Assistance," — had been the subject of a base assault some years before the event we commemorate; and had been compelled by disability to retire from the public service, and to await, in a condition worse than death, that merciful stroke of fire from Heaven which at last released him to his rest. There is said to have been a glimpse of him at Bunker Hill. His presence there, however, was only the shadow of a name, whose place in American history, and in American hearts, had been already and unchangeably fixed.

But, for the others, great opportunities and great achievements were still in the future. John Hancock lived to write his name where all the world should read it to the end of time, as President of the Congress of Independence, and the first signer of the Declaration; and afterwards to be the first Governor of our Commonwealth under its established constitution. John Adams lived not only to be the Colossus of Independence on the floor of Congress, but to be the first American Minister to England, and afterwards Vice-President and President of the United States. Samuel Adams, the foremost man of all, perhaps, at the period of which we are speaking, lived to be a leader in the Congress of the Declaration, and did not die without the highest honors of his native State; while if he failed to receive all the consideration to which he was entitled in his lifetime, it has been more than made up, for his posthumous and permanent fame, by the statue of him which Massachusetts has so recently ordered to be sent to Washington, as one of her two representative characters in the gallery of the Capitol. James Bowdoin, older than almost any of them, many years older than any except Samuel Adams, and upon whose feeble constitution the infirmities of age came early and heavily, lived to preside over the convention which framed our State Constitution, as well as to take a prominent part in the convention which adopted the Federal Constitution; and, as Governor of Massachusetts, to conduct the State with distinguished wisdom and safety through the perilous period of Shays's Rebellion. Even Warren, who played no second part in 1773, was spared for two years longer, to die a death more glorious, as far as historical fame is concerned, than any life, and to be associated for ever with the great events at Lexington, and Concord, and Bunker Hill. When the Centennial Anniversary of those events arrives, his name, we all know, — with that of the gallant Colonel Prescott, — will have its rightful pre-eminence.

But when Josiah Quincy, Jr., at the early age of twenty-nine, made that brilliant speech in the Old South Meeting-house, one hundred years ago to-day, — the last formal speech made by any one before the destruction of the tea was consummated, — his career was rapidly approaching its close. The fever flush was already on his cheek. An admirable and masterly pamphlet remained to be written by him, and many other powerful contributions to the newspaper press. But a voyage to England was soon rendered necessary by his failing health, and from that voyage he only returned to die within sight of his native shores on the 26th of April, 1775, — seven days only after the fight at Lexington, of which he could never have heard; twenty days only before the battle of Bunker Hill, when Warren, the friend whom he so much yearned to see, was to follow him to the skies.

Am I not right, then, in speaking of the peculiar fitness, that the name of one who was thus so soon to be cut off from all part or lot in the other great days of that struggle for liberty, for which, young as he was, he had done so much to prepare the way, should be recalled with special distinctness, and with special distinction, on this first commemoration of our grand centennial era?

I have here the original draft of a letter from James Bowdoin, in his own hand, to Benjamin Franklin, then in London, which may be interesting on this occasion. It is dated Boston, Sept. 6, 1774, after the destruction of the tea had brought upon us the vengeance of the British Parliament in the shape of Port Bills and Army Bills, and contains the following language: "The several Acts of Parliament relative to this town and province will instamp eternal infamy on the present administration, and 'tis probable that they themselves will soon see the beginning of it. The spirit those Acts have raised throughout the colonies is surprising. It was not propagated from colony to colony, but burst forth in all of them spontaneously, as soon as the Acts were known; and there is reason to hope it will be productive of an Union that will work out the salvation of the whole. The Congress now holding at Philadelphia, which was intended to effect such an Union, it is earnestly wished may be the means of establishing, on a just and constitutional basis, a lasting harmony between Britain and the colonies." "'*Pro aris et focis*, our all is at stake,' is the general cry,." he continues, "throughout the country. Of this I have been in some measure a witness, having these two months past been journeying about the province with Mrs. Bowdoin on account of her health, the bad state of which has prevented my attending the Congress, for which the General Assembly thought proper to appoint me one of their Committee."

The main interest of this letter, however, in connection with what I have been saying, is in the fact, that it was a letter introducing Josiah Quincy, Jr., to Benjamin Franklin, and borne by him across the Atlantic in that voyage from which he was not to return alive.

"It is needless," says Bowdoin, "to enlarge on the subject of American affairs, as the worthy and ingenious gentleman, Mr. Josiah Quincy, Junior, of distinguished abilities in the profession of law, who does me the favor to take charge of this letter, can give you the fullest information concerning them, and his information may be depended on. To him I beg leave to refer you, and at the same time take the liberty to recommend him to your friendship and acquaintance."

The "acquaintance and friendship" of Franklin! Who does not envy those who were privileged to enjoy them, as the young Quincy so eminently did? But hardly less might one envy the appreciation which Quincy soon won from Franklin. "His coming over," says the Great Bostonian, in a letter to Quincy's father, "has been of great service to our cause, and would have been much greater if his constitution would have borne the fatigues of being more frequently in company;" while in a later letter, after the death of the young patriot, he says: "The notes of the speeches taken by your son, whose loss I shall ever deplore with you, are exceedingly valuable, as being by much the best account preserved of that day's debate."

And may I not say that if Josiah Quincy, Jr., had left no other fruit of his visit to England than his grand report of the noble speech of Lord Chatham on American Affairs, on the 20th of January, 1775, he would have entitled himself to the endless gratitude of every admirer of eloquence, and of every friend of freedom?

But I cannot conclude these introductory remarks without a more distinct reference to the speech of Quincy himself, at the Old South, a hundred years ago to-day. Only a short paragraph of that speech has ever been found in print, and I know not that any thing more of it is to be found anywhere. That paragraph contains an eloquent and noble plea for moderation. He was evidently, I think, inclined to hold back his native town from plunging precipitately into a struggle which he knew must come, but for which the country at large might not yet be ready. He loved liberty so well and so wisely, that he was reluctant, I think, to have the sacredness and the lustre of its cause in the slightest degree dimmed or tarnished by any outbreak of irresponsible or lawless violence. Accordingly, in his masterly "Observations on the Boston Port Bill," a few months afterwards, he vindicates the town from the charges of riot and disorder. He maintains that "Boston had, as a town, cautiously and wisely conducted itself; not only without tumult, but with studied regard to established law." He alludes to the very last town-meeting before the proceeding which we commemorate, and to what he calls "the mere temporary events which took place in Boston in the matter of the tea," as having occurred "without any illegal procedure of the town;" and he challenges "the greatest enemy of the country" to "point out any one step of the town of Boston, in the progress of this matter, that was tumultuous, disorderly, and against law."

It is thus, I think, rather with the great principles of freedom which led to the destruction of the tea, than with the act itself, that his name is ever to be associated; and, in the clear, calm light of history, it will never be less honored on that account. That volunteer band of Liberty-Boys, in the disguise of Mohawks, performed their work "better than they knew," — averting contingencies which must have caused immediate bloodshed, and accomplishing results of the greatest importance to the American cause. But Quincy was right in claiming that it was not the act of Boston, as a town; that the people, or a part of the people, took matters into their own hands on that occasion; and that, while the act was exactly what might have been expected under the circumstances, and had actually been predicted, it was one which the truest and most ardent friends of freedom, as our associate, Mr. Frothingham, has justly said, "would have gladly avoided," if they could have done so without sacrificing the best hopes of their country.

But, Gentlemen, Mr. Frothingham, the Historian of all this period, is with us to-night; and I will not detain you a moment longer from the statement which, at our request, he has kindly prepared for this occasion. For, indeed, all the rest of the acts of the Tea Party, all that they did, and all the great results to which their proceedings directly and indirectly led, — are they not written in the Chronicles of the "Siege of Boston," and the "Life of Warren," and the "History of the Rise of the Republic"? Let me, then, call upon the author of these works without further delay.

OUR HOME MUSIC.

SPEECH AT THE DINNER OF THE HARVARD MUSICAL ASSOCIATION, JANUARY 26, 1874.

I AM greatly honored, Gentlemen, in being numbered among your invited guests this evening, and I am sure that the best way of showing my gratitude will be to make my acknowledgments brief. I came here, indeed, only to manifest my interest in the objects of your Association, and to express publicly, as I have often done privately, my obligations, as a lover of music, to your excellent President, Mr. Dwight, for all that he has done, and for all that he has written, for so many years past, in the cause of musical culture in Boston.

It was with real regret and concern that I learned, a few days ago, that your Symphony Concerts had not thus far, during the present season, received an adequate public support. How far this may have resulted from the change which has been made in the manner of disposing of the tickets, and how far from the financial embarrassments of the community, I may not venture to pronounce. But I cannot help feeling that the poorest economy which could be resorted to, by any friend of musical entertainments, or of moral and æsthetic culture, is to withhold his patronage from a class of concerts so moderate in their cost, and so popular in their character.

It is now nine years since this Symphony Series was regularly organized. It has thus stood the old classical test, — *Nonum prematur in annum.* And I do not hesitate to express the opinion that during this period, apart from all the pleasure these concerts have afforded, they have done more than all other things combined to educate and elevate the musical taste of our community. They have now fairly become one of the recognized institutions of Boston. To some of us they have become, not merely one of the luxuries, but, I had almost said, one of the necessaries, of life. For myself, certainly, I would not have exchanged the satisfaction and recreation and inspiration I have so often derived from them, for any other public secular enjoyments which have been within my reach.

It has happened to me, Mr. President, in the course of my life, — if I may be pardoned for the egotism of saying so, — to have met with not a few fortunate opportunities of hearing the best music. I heard the "Elijah," in London, on the second night of its original performance, with Mendelssohn himself wielding the baton. I saw Verdi conducting the first representation of one of his own operas, on a Queen's night, at Covent Garden, nearly thirty years ago. I have heard the "Israel in Egypt," under Costa's lead, with an orchestra of five hundred, and with a perfectly trained chorus of four thousand voices, and with Mr. Simms Reeves for the solos. I have heard Beethoven's Ninth Symphony, by a hundred picked performers in Vienna, — and we all know what picked performers in Vienna are, — with the "Song of Joy," sung by the artists and chorus of the Vienna Opera, in presence of the Emperor and Empress of Austria, on the One Hundredth Anniversary of Schiller's birthday. I might recall other occasions of the same sort, and hardly less memorable.

All these, however, were accidental ecstasies, — momentary raptures, — to be remembered for ever, but to be enjoyed only once in a life-time; and I should no more think of comparing them with the sober certainty and assured satisfaction of good music, at stated intervals, at home, than I should of comparing a passing glance at Niagara, or Mont Blanc, with the quiet daily enjoyment of the rural beauties of Brookline, or of the bolder scenery of Beverly Shore or the Berkshire Hills.

What we need, and what we have a right to demand, and what we ought steadfastly to support, is good stated music at home. We owe it to ourselves and to our children, and we owe it not less to the accomplished musicians who reside among us, whether native or foreign, to have regular concerts of our own; and it ought to be accounted a matter of loyalty to Boston to sustain them with a liberal and generous hand, for the good of the community, even if not for our immediate personal gratification.

We have as fine a Hall for the purpose as almost any in the world, with its charming Statue of Beethoven, and its magnificent Organ. It requires only a little better ventilation, and a little more elbow-room — for some of us "whose shadows *broaden* as our Sun declines" — to render it quite perfect. We have the old Handel and Haydn Society for the grand Oratorios, and the new Apollo Club for the charming Glees and Part Songs. Long life and prosperity to them both! But this Association has furnished the crowning complement to the whole. It would be a reproach to our civilization, and to our liberal culture, if any of these organizations were to fail for want of patronage. But no one of them is more entitled to support than that of the Symphony Concerts.

Without them, we should have been almost strangers to the splendid instrumental compositions of Beethoven and Mendelssohn, of Mozart and Haydn and Schumann. We might have had scraps and snatches of them, — an Adagio from one, an Andante from another, a Scherzo from a third, a Finale from a fourth, — elegant extracts, served up in exquisite style by some itinerant orchestra, to catch the popular ear. But we could never have had them, as this Association has given them to us, in all their grand unity and entirety, with all their parts following each other in dramatic sequence, like the successive Acts of some great play of Shakspeare.

I trust, Mr. President, that the time is past when we are to be dependent for our musical entertainments on the occasional and capricious visits of artists from other countries or other cities. We will welcome them when they come. But we have a right to stated music of our own; and the experience of the last nine years has proved abundantly that we can have it. Doubtless there are grander orchestras than you have been able to supply us; or than you could have supplied, perhaps, even if your treasury had been more adequately replenished from year to year. I would certainly speak with nothing but admiration of the attractions and perfections of Mr. Thomas's Band, which is just coming to pay us another of its "angel visits, few and far between." We shall all go to hear them; and we shall all be rewarded for doing so. But I cannot help recalling in this connection, — with the change of a word or two, — the lines of an old poet: —

> "What tho' some charming caterer Thomas
> Hangs a new Angel two doors from us; —
> I hold it both a shame and sin
> To quit the true old Angel Inn."

Now, my friends, our Music Hall next Thursday afternoon, if never before, with Carl Zerrahn as the Conductor, and Mr. Lang at the Piano; with a charming Overture of Mozart at the beginning, and a glorious Symphony of Beethoven at the end; with the Prelude to a new Cantata by an accomplished American composer; and with Longfellow's touching Ode on the Fiftieth Birthday of the lamented Agassiz, set to music which, to assure us in advance that it will be as full of soul as of science, needs only the name of Otto Dresel; — the Music Hall, I repeat, next Thursday afternoon, with all this feast of good things, and with the genial countenance of your President, ever welcome in its accustomed sphere in the gallery, will surely be the "true old Angel Inn" for us, and for all the music lovers of Boston; and there ought not to be an unoccupied seat in the Hall.

Let me only, in conclusion, express the earnest hope that this, and the few other opportunities which remain to us this season, may not be neglected by our fellow-citizens, to make amends for any meagre attendance during the past months; and to show that the Stated Concerts of this Association are still held in the high estimation which they so richly deserve, and that they will never be suffered to die out.

HON. WILLIAM MINOT.

MEMOIR READ AT A MEETING OF THE MASSACHUSETTS HISTORICAL SOCIETY, MARCH 12, 1874.

On the 28th of May, 1802, our late illustrious associate, John Quincy Adams, in a public Address, spoke of his friend the Honorable George Richards Minot, then recently dead, as follows: "The community to which such a man as this belongs, confer honor upon themselves by every token of distinction they bestow upon him. Mr. Minot was successively employed in various offices of trust and of honor. To vice, a merciful but inflexible judge; to misfortune, a compassionate friend; to the widow, a protector of her rights; to the orphan, one in place of a father; in every station which the voice of his country called him alternately to fill, he displayed that individual endowment of the mind, and that peculiar virtue of the heart, which was most essential to the useful exercise of its functions."

On the 12th of June, 1873, our honored Vice-President, Charles Francis Adams, at a meeting of our Society, said of the Honorable William Minot, then recently dead, as follows: "It becomes my duty to note the decease, since the last meeting, of one of our most venerable and respected members. Though never taking any prominent part in the public action of life, no person passed his days in the performance of duties more useful to society or honorable to himself. Confidence in the fulfilment of obligations of pecuniary trusts is only merited by a life of the purest integrity. The many who reposed it in him, during the long course of his active career, had cause to congratulate themselves, when reflecting how much shifting sand was visible always around them, that they had built their house on a rock."

It is a rare thing for a father and son to be the subjects successively of such enviable tributes, from sources so distinguished. It is not less rare for another father and son, at an interval of more than seventy years, to be the privileged authors of such tributes. The double coincidence may well be noted.

Of George Richards Minot, one of the original members of our Society, and who made such early and substantial contributions to the work in which we are engaged, — by his History of Shays's Rebellion, and his continuation of Hutchinson's History of Massachusetts, — a Memoir will be found in the Eighth Volume of our Collections. It was undoubtedly prepared by his pastor, the Rev. James Freeman, D.D., then the Recording Secretary of the Society; who, however, marked the Memoir as his own only by affixing "R. S.," in small type, to the last printed page. To that Memoir, made up in large part from a Eulogy previously delivered by himself in King's Chapel, nothing needs be added; as it sets forth fully the life, character, and services of its subject, at a moment when they were fresh in the affectionate memory of the writer and of the community.

William Minot was born in the homestead of his father and grandfather, in what is now known as Devonshire Street, Boston, opposite the New Post Office, on the 17th of September, 1783; and he took his Bachelor's Degree at Harvard University, with the distinguished Class of 1802, a few months after his father's death. He was admitted to the Bar of Suffolk County in 1805, and entered at once on the professional pursuits in which his father had been so eminent. To those pursuits he perseveringly adhered; only abandoning them when compelled to do so by the infirmities of old age. He was particularly devoted to the Law of Wills and Trusts. A man of the purest life, of the highest principles, of the most scrupulous and transparent integrity, — his counsel was eagerly sought, during a long term of years, by those who had estates to bequeath, or trusts to be arranged and executed; and no one enjoyed a greater share than he did, in these and in all other relations, of the esteem and confidence of the community in which he lived.

Among other Funds committed to his care, was that bequeathed to the town of his birth by Benjamin Franklin, with a primary view of encouraging young and meritorious mechanics. This Fund was placed in Mr. Minot's hands by the authorities of Boston in 1804, and was gratuitously administered by him for the long period of sixty-four years, when it had increased from four thousand to one hundred and twenty-five thousand dollars. The City Government did not fail to enter upon its records a grateful acknowledgment of the eminent prudence and probity with which the Fund had been managed.

Naturally of a retiring disposition, Mr. Minot never sought public office, and very rarely yielded to the solicitation of friends by accepting it. He served his native place for a year or two, when it was first incorporated as a City, as the presiding officer of one of its wards; and he served the Commonwealth, for another year or two, with fidelity and honor, as a member of the Executive Council, during the administration of Governor Everett. He rendered valuable services, also, to the community, for a considerable time, as an Inspector of Prisons. But his tastes were for professional and domestic life, and he resolutely declined all further public employment.

No one could be more charming in the family or social circle, which often included Sedgwicks and Saltonstalls, the Lees and the Deweys, with Mrs. Fanny Kemble, and others of similar gifts. His noble countenance and genial manner attracted the regard and admiration of all who were admitted to his friendship, while his Christian faith and principle gave the crowning grace to his life and character.

He was of an ancient family, which has been traced back to Thomas Minot, the Secretary to the Abbot of Saffron Walden, in Essex County, England, in the reign of Henry VIII., whose coat-of-arms was surmounted by a Cross, with the motto "Ad astra per aspera." The family name, indeed, finds a distinguished wearer, still further back, — in the reign of Edward III., — in the person of Laurence Minot, whose Poems, written about 1352, — earlier even than those of Chaucer, — were printed in London in 1795. A copy of the little volume has recently been added to our library.

Mr. Minot was elected a member of this Society in 1843, and had thus been associated with us for thirty years, — his name standing, at the time of his death, sixth in the order of seniority of membership, on our Resident Roll. He took a warm interest in our prosperity, and delighted to remember that his father had been one of our founders. To his thoughtful consideration for our welfare, — as I have the best reason to know, — we have owed more than one of the substantial contributions to our funds, which have helped to relieve our treasury within the past few years.

He was a great reader during the later period of his long life. Few men were more familiar with the sterling productions of English literature, and he was always eager to converse, with the friends who visited him in his old age, on the books of history or philosophy, of romance or poetry, which were seldom out of his hands. Rarely, however, could he be induced to prepare any thing for the Press. He communicated, indeed, to the "Polyanthos," — a periodical now forgotten, — in 1806, a graceful sketch of his father's life and character, which has lately been privately reprinted in a separate form, and a copy of it added to our collection of pamphlets. But a single other production completes the list of his published writings. At the request of our own Society, he prepared, in January, 1862, a Memoir of his distinguished classmate and life-long friend, the Hon. Samuel Hoar, which is among our printed papers. It is brief, simple, just to its subject, and eminently characteristic of its author. He was impatient of the long, and often extravagant, posthumous tributes which have become customary of late years; and it would be an offence to his own memory to extend this notice by further details of his excellent, but quiet and uneventful life.

He died, — in the house in Beacon Street, which he had occupied for sixty years, — in the ninetieth year of his age, on the 2d of June, 1873. His old family tomb, in the "Granary Burying Ground," — in which the remains of General Joseph Warren had reposed for many years after they were identified at Bunker Hill, — having been vacated and surrendered by him to the City, he was buried in "Forest-Hills Cemetery," where the dust of those dear to him had already been gathered, and not far from his pleasant summer residence at Jamaica Plain.

Mr. Minot was married, in 1809, to a daughter of a former well-remembered Solicitor-General of Massachusetts, — Daniel Davis, — the father, also, of the present Admiral Charles H. Davis. She was a lady of rare accomplishments, whose death in 1858 was felt as a bereavement far beyond the large domestic circle of which she was an ornament. Two daughters and three sons survived him; and to one of the latter, bearing his name and engaged in the same professional pursuits, we are already indebted for an excellent account of his father's life and character, privately and anonymously printed, which has left little to be added by any one else, and which has given a warmth and a truth of delineation and color to the portrait it presents, which could only be supplied by a loving, filial hand.

It is enough for others to bear witness to its fidelity.

FILLMORE AND SUMNER.

REMARKS AT A MEETING OF THE MASSACHUSETTS HISTORICAL SOCIETY, MARCH 12, 1874.

THE grave closes to-day, Gentlemen, over one of our most distinguished honorary members, who, having held the office of President of the United States, has been recognized at the capital and throughout the country as the fit subject of national funeral honors. It is, however, by no means only to the exalted position which Mr. FILLMORE was privileged to occupy, more than twenty years ago, that his name will owe the respectful remembrance and grateful regard of his fellow-citizens. His political career was, indeed, an elevated and a proud one. As a member of the Legislature of New York, and for a time the Comptroller of its finances; as a member of the House of Representatives of the United States, and for a time its chairman of the Committee of Ways and Means; as the elected Vice-President, and, for more than two years, owing to the lamented death of General Taylor, the President of our Republic, and this during a period of great sectional agitation and disturbance, — in all these relations he has made a mark in the history of the country which cannot easily be erased or overlooked.

It certainly will not be forgotten by us of Massachusetts, that Daniel Webster and Edward Everett were successively his Secretaries of State, and that he enjoyed the confidence, the respect, and the warm regard and friendship of them both. Indeed, his whole Cabinet Council, during the period of his Presidency, including as it did the names of Webster and Everett, of Crittenden and Corwin, of Graham and Kennedy, of Stuart and Conrad and Nathan K. Hall, — but few of whom are now left among the living, and the last of whom, so long the law partner of the ex-President, by a striking coincidence has preceded him to the grave by only two or three days, — that whole Cabinet, I repeat, presents a group, which will be recognized even by those who differed most widely from its policy, as reflecting lustre on him who had so surrounded himself. I may be allowed to remember that I was myself, for several years, associated with him in Congress, and was thus a daily witness to his devoted labors, his scrupulous integrity, and his great practical ability as a debater and a statesman.

But the official career of Mr. Fillmore, long and distinguished as it was, served only to give public exhibition of the sterling qualities of a just and true man. He may have made mistakes like other men; he may have disappointed hopes like other men; he may have subjected himself to suspicion or reproach from partisan opponents, or even from partisan friends. But no one who was ever brought into any degree of personal intimacy with him could fail to recognize and appreciate the strong elements of his character, — his amiability, his moderation, his modesty, his firmness, his sturdy common sense, his inflexible principle, the purity of his life, and his many Christian virtues.

"That worthy Mr. Fillmore" — as I well remember — was the habitual expression of Irving, after a casual residence at the capital, in the prosecution of researches for his Life of Washington, had brought our charming author into familiar acquaintance with the then occupant of the executive mansion. "That worthy Mr. Fillmore" has fallen from a thousand lips before and since, and might well be taken as the brief, but just and comprehensive, inscription for his tombstone.

Without the advantages of earlier or later education, a stranger to colleges, and almost a stranger to schools in his youth, he fulfilled, as few other men so remarkably have done, the true idea of a self-made, self-educated man, and became a sound lawyer and an eminent statesman by the mere force of his own native energy and manly perseverance. No vain ambition, no miserable office-seeking, no reckless resolve to lift himself by any and all means into popular notice and notoriety, no degrading design to live and fatten upon the perquisites of public station, ever entered into the processes of his preferment. Always ready to serve his State or his Country, when he was clearly called to do so, he knew how to retire with dignity and self-respect when the voice of the people was no longer in his favor. He knew, too, how to employ his retirement in ways worthy of a good citizen and a Christian gentleman, and worthy of the distinction and influence which attached to him as an ex-President of the United States. He was particularly interested in the local history of Western New York, and was one of the founders and the first president of the Historical Society of Buffalo.

Mr. Fillmore was born on the 7th of January, 1800, and died on the 8th of March, 1874, having thus entered on the seventy-fourth year of his age.

Gentlemen, the ink with which I had penned the brief tribute which I have just paid to my friend, President Fillmore, was hardly dry, when the telegraph wires from Washington were trembling with the tidings of a death which makes a breach in our own immediate little circle of a hundred; but a far wider breach in the larger sphere of the national councils. The death of the HON. CHARLES SUMNER, which occurred yesterday afternoon, but of which I only heard the certainty this morning, is an event too sudden and too impressive to be the subject of any off-hand utterances. Yet, assembled here as we are to-day, with so striking an event uppermost in all our thoughts, it cannot be passed over in silence, — certainly not by me. To us, as a Society, Mr. Sumner was, indeed, but little; his name having been added to our resident roll only within a few months past, and it never having been convenient to him to be present at even one of our meetings. We had all sincerely hoped, however, that in some future interval between the sessions of Congress, in some breathing-time from his arduous and assiduous public labors, we might have enjoyed the benefit of his large acquaintance with historical subjects, and of the rich accomplishments by which he was distinguished. That hope is now suddenly brought to an end, and we have only the satisfaction of knowing that his election, as one of our restricted number, afforded him a moment's gratification, in what have so unexpectedly proved to be the last few months of his life.

In the Senate of the United States, of which for more than three terms he has been so prominent and conspicuous a member, the gap created by his death cannot easily be measured. There, for so many years, he has been one of the observed of all observers. There, for so many years, scarce a word or an act of his has failed to be the subject of wide-spread attention and comment. No name has been oftener in the columns of the daily press, or on the lips of the people in all parts of the country, — sometimes for criticism, and even for censure, but far more generally for commendation and applause. Such a name, certainly, cannot pass from the rolls of living men, without leaving a large void to many eyes and to many hearts.

One of the pioneers in the cause of anti-slavery, while yet in private life, he breasted the billows of that raging controversy with unsparing energy, until the struggle ceased with the institution which had given rise to it. The same untiring energy was then transferred to what he regarded as the rights of the race which had been emancipated. Indeed, every thing which could be associated with the idea of human rights was made the subject of his ardent advocacy, according to his own judgment and convictions. Devoting himself early, also, to the cause of Peace, and making the relations of the United States with other nations a matter for special study, — his unwearied labors as Chairman of the Committee of Foreign Affairs for several years, and his acknowledged familiarity with international law, can never be undervalued or forgotten.

As a writer, a lecturer, a debater, and an orator, he had acquired the strongest hold on public attention everywhere, both at home and abroad; and few scholars have brought to the illustration of their topics, whether political or literary, the fruits of greater research. His orations and speeches, of which a new edition, revised by his own hand, is understood to be approaching a completion, cannot fail to be a rich store-house of classical and historical lore, and will certainly furnish a most valuable series of pictures, from his own point of view, of the stirring scenes to which they relate.

I dare not attempt, Gentlemen, to dwell at greater length on the crowded and eventful public career of Mr. Sumner. The tidings of his death have come upon us all with too painful a surprise to allow of our dealing with the subject as we might desire to do. And for myself, I need hardly say here that any detailed discussion of his course might involve peculiar elements of delicacy and difficulty; as it has been my fortune, or, as others may think, my misfortune, to differ from him so often and so widely, — sometimes as to conclusions and ends, but far more frequently as to the means of reaching those conclusions, and of advancing those ends.

I am glad to remember, however, that every thing of personal alienation and estrangement had long ago ceased between us, and that no one has been more ready than myself, for many years past, to welcome him into this Association. His praises will be abundantly, and far more fitly, spoken elsewhere, if not here, by the countless friends to whom he was so dear; and you will all pardon me, I know, if the suddenness of the announcement has prevented me from paying a more adequate tribute to his culture, his accomplishments, his virtues, and to those commanding qualities by which he impressed himself on the period in which he lived.

Born in Boston on the 6th of January, 1811, he had more than completed his 63d year.

AGASSIZ.

REMARKS AT A MEETING OF THE MASSACHUSETTS HISTORICAL SOCIETY, APRIL 16, 1874.

I HAVE thought, Gentlemen, that I might occupy a few moments this evening, not altogether inappropriately, by presenting to the Society, with a few words of explanation, a letter from the late Professor Agassiz, on a subject of public interest, addressed to me nearly nine years ago, under somewhat peculiar circumstances.

It happened that Mr. George Peabody, on his arrival in this country, in the summer of 1866, did me the honor to take me into his confidence and counsel, in regard to the great benefactions which he was proposing for his native land. He came out to my residence at Brookline, and spent two or three days with me in consultation. On one of these days I sent for Professor Agassiz to meet him at dinner. Agassiz accepted the invitation and came. But, before coming, he addressed this letter to me, understanding that Mr. Peabody might possibly be influenced, in some degree, by my advice.

In this letter, without asking any thing for himself, or for the particular work in which he was engaged, he unfolded, in the most unselfish way, his own views as to one of the great needs for the successful prosecution of scientific, and indeed of philosophical and literary, studies in our country.

The letter is too interesting and too important to be lost or left unpublished; and as Mr. Peabody, not long afterwards, became one of our greatest benefactors, and was placed on our

Honorary Roll, and as he made the President of our Society (*ex officio*) one of the Trustees and Guardians of his Museum of Archæology and Ethnology at Cambridge, it has seemed to me not unfit that this letter of Agassiz should find a place in our archives, and be printed in our Proceedings.

The letter is as follows : —

NAHANT, Oct. 1, 1866.

DEAR SIR, — I accept with great pleasure your invitation for next Wednesday at 5 o'clock, and shall be most happy to see you and Mrs. Winthrop at home. You say it is to meet Mr. G. Peabody, of London, and this induces me to write a few lines more. I have met Mr. P. before, but never made an allusion to his liberality that could look like begging, as I hate to bore rich men in that way; but I am told Mr. P. intends to benefit our public institutions, and that he has consulted with you upon this subject. Permit me, therefore, to lay before you a few thoughts which have lately occupied my mind, and indeed excited me much; and, if you see fit, communicate this letter to him.

The great boast of Monarchies is that they patronize letters, arts, and science as Republics never did and never can. Is there no way to remedy this difficulty? Can Republics, and ours in particular, not be made to do as much, if not more, in that direction, than ever was done anywhere and at any time? And can it not be done in a truly republican spirit, relieving those that are benefited from the feeling of dependence, without depriving the patrons of any credit due to them? This is the theme which I have been discussing and which I think susceptible of solution. The man or men who carry out an efficient plan to solve this difficulty will have done more for the United States than the founders of some empires did for humanity.

To show the full extent of the difficulty, I will suppose a case. How could a work like Lepsius' Egypt be published in this country? The Government would not and should not undertake it, in accordance with the spirit of our institutions. No bookseller could do it without ruining himself. There remains the resort to a subscription by which rich men are expected to give money for what they do not care. This is an objectionable method, and one which may at any time be stopped after it has been carried too far. We want permanent arrangements to supply at all times the means for carrying out any great artistic, literary, or scientific undertaking, without boring anybody.

It might be thought that an immense fund — millions of dollars — would be insufficient to establish a machinery that would do such work.

I think not. I am even satisfied that one single organization which would assume such responsibilities would fail, even if it had money enough; as it would of necessity be under the supervision and guidance of a few men, who would foster what *they* like and leave what they do not like to take care of itself. It would, moreover, be local in its character and influence. I want something that shall work with equal intensity North and South, East and West; and that should go into operation at the rate of the advancing civilization of the whole country.

Suppose, now, we had all over the States two or three thousand associations akin in organization to those which the instincts of the people are so quick in establishing when politics are concerned, but intended to foster letters, arts, and science. Suppose that each of these associations could spend fifty or a hundred dollars a year for these noble purposes, — there is not a literary, or artistic, or scientific undertaking of any magnitude that need be given up from want of means, if these associations would co-operate, and in their disagreements they would support what single men or single institutions would allow to perish. The question is simply how to organize such associations and give them vitality. Time and proper stimulants may do it. And now I come to my special point. If what I propose is not a panacea, — which I do not believe it to be, any more than any other Utopian plan, — I am sure it would be a potent stimulus in the right direction.

Our people are greedy for knowledge; and if science does not make more rapid progress in this country, it is simply owing to the fact that knowledge is extensively circulated only *in its cheap elementary forms.* Our academies, and even the Smithsonian Institution, publish only a few hundred copies of their transactions: the Smithsonian, about one thousand, most of which are distributed ABROAD. Great scientific works are never seen in our schools, hardly in our public libraries; and where they are on hand, it is difficult to secure access to them. I want to see such publications reach the whole population. And, as I understand scientific matters better than literary or artistic ones, I will limit my remarks to what I consider practicable for science in that direction. A series of handsomely illustrated original works on Natural History, *printed in large editions,* and distributed gratuitously to every association that would itself undertake to spend annually a small sum of money for the purchase of other costly books, would go far towards stimulating the organization of associations like those to which I have alluded above. But, even considered in itself, the plan of publishing a large series of costly original works, to be distributed gratuitously, is worth considering as a national benefit. In the first place, I know of the existence of numerous such works, which neither the Smithsonian Institution, nor any other learned society, have the means of publishing, and therefore remain in the authors' desks, as no bookseller will touch such works. The country and the world are the losers for this. I know that the authors of such investigations would gladly give them away, if they only could be published. I am certain that such works could be published in a manner to serve as models for other original researches, and to stimulate such researches where the methods of scientific investigations are not even dreamed of. Such publications could not fail to raise the character of the studies in every other department throughout the country. There are only two difficulties in the way of giving publicity to such intellectual labors: (1) There is no learned society so organized as to undertake the superintendence of such publications; (2) There are no means to carry out the publications, if anybody would undertake to superintend the work.

It is to this I would request you to call Mr. Peabody's attention. You need not mention my name in connection with the subject, unless he should wish to inquire in what manner the first of the above-named difficulties, that of superintending such publications, might be obviated, as I believe I could suggest a practicable plan; and there would be no use in broaching the subject unless some gentleman looked with sufficient favor upon such a plan as to furnish the means of carrying it out.

Hoping you may have the patience to read through this long epistle,

I remain,

With high regard,

Yours very truly,

L^s^. Agassiz.

Hon. Robert C. Winthrop.

P.S. — Perhaps a few hints as to how and where may be of practical use. Suppose Mr. Peabody should feel inclined to give the necessary money to carry out such a plan, I would propose that all the works or papers so publishing should appear in the form of quarto volumes, or parts of volumes, with numerous, most finished, and, if necessary, colored plates, of uniform size, under the title of "*Peabody's Contributions to the Natural Sciences.*" An edition of 2500 or more copies to be printed, and the successive volumes to be distributed gratuitously: First, to the first 2000 associations which would furnish the evidence that they spend a certain sum annually in the purchase of serious books, and are prepared to spend another smaller sum in the support of the publication of costly works, which could not be published by the ordinary means of the book trade; Second, 500 copies to be reserved for future use, or to be in part given to the authors for private circulation, or as a compensation to the institution or men who would superintend the publication and distribution of the volumes as they can be brought out. With sufficient means, I am certain that *one large quarto volume* could easily be published *annually*, of such high value as to be not only an equivalent for the co-operation of scientific associations in this great work, but even to stimulate the organization of other similar associations where none exist thus far, gradually calling into existence a sufficient number of such associations as would relieve science from all necessity of future government or individual patronage.

As soon as the Museum of Comparative Zoölogy at Cambridge is fully organized, according to the plans which I have laid before the Faculty, that Institution could easily undertake the superintendence and publication of such a series of Works and Papers without any expense to the founder of the future " Contributions to the Natural Sciences." It should be amply compensated for its co-operatfon by appearing upon the title as "published under the supervision of the Museum of Comp. Z. in Cambridge ; " nobody's name there except that of the founder of the contributions.

The great idea of this letter, as you will have perceived, is the importance and necessity, for Science, Literature, and the Arts, and we may well add for History also, of *Publication Funds*, through which Works which have no element of popularity in them, and which could not command a publisher or a remunerating sale, may not be allowed to perish in the manuscript, or be suffered to die unwritten in the brains of discouraged students, but may be printed and circulated for the benefit of mankind.

I did not fail to communicate the letter to Mr. Peabody, and, possibly, we may have in some degree owed to its suggestions the Publication Fund of $20,000, with which he not long afterwards endowed our own Society. But his plans were already too nearly matured for him to adopt the idea of Agassiz in its full comprehensive scope. That idea, however, I have always considered as of great interest and value ; and I cannot help hoping that the very Memorial Fund, for which his lamented death has given occasion, may be so far extended as to include what was so near his own heart, as a Publication Fund for the purposes of his great Museum, if not of Science in general.

Meantime, I present the original letter as a precious autograph for our Collections. He once reclaimed it for the purpose of making a copy for his own keeping, thus showing the importance he attached to it; but he soon returned the original, and left it at my disposal.

I cannot part from the subject of Agassiz, Gentlemen, without giving you an anecdote which has been recalled to my mind during my preparations for another ocean voyage. In 1859, I was a fellow-passenger of his across the Atlantic, and, of course, I enjoyed not a little of his charming society and conversation. We sailed from Boston on the 15th of June, and for several days we were enveloped in a dense fog. On the sixth day out, June 20th, the fog continued till nearly 7 o'clock in the evening, when it suddenly vanished, and we had the full glory of a setting sun at sea. Meanwhile, however, the lifting mist had unveiled two enormous icebergs, one on our larboard and the other on our starboard, ten or twelve miles distant from the ship, — near enough to be exquisitely beautiful, but, happily, not near enough to be immediately dangerous. Yet we might easily have run on one of them, had not the cloudy curtain been seasonably withdrawn, as it was, by an unseen Hand. Agassiz had never before encountered an iceberg, and I shall not soon forget his exclamations of delight. "O Captain," he cried out, "if I could only have a boat to go and examine one of those icy masses! I could find out all about it, and tell you exactly where it came from." "But one of these days," he added, "I will go out in a Coast Survey steamer, and make a special examination of an iceberg for myself." We passed safely through the crystal gateway, leaving both its columns astern, before bedtime; but hardly had I reached my state-room when Agassiz was calling out to me to come up again and see the wonderful phosphoresence of our wake. We were passing through a field of Medusæ, and they seemed to have put on an unwonted sparkle and splendor, as their great observer and investigator stood watching them over the taffrail.

It was during this voyage, too, that, knowing I was about to visit Switzerland for the first time, he was eager to tell me exactly how to get a first view of the Alps to the best advantage.

"Enter Switzerland," said he, "by Dijon, Besançon, and Pontarlier, taking a private carriage through the pass of the Jura to a height called La Tourne, and so by Val Travers to Neufchâtel." "The view which bursts upon you at La Tourne," said he, "is the finest view in all Switzerland."

I have carefully preserved a little map of the route, which he made with his own pencil at the moment, — for fear I should forget his instructions, — and which I followed implicitly at the time.

But there was one other brief conversation of his, which was worth all the rest. Humboldt had recently died, and I had called his attention to the fact that some European Naturalist, whose name I will not attempt to recall, had said of Humboldt, by way of distinction and eulogy, that he had fairly ruled God out of the universe. "Yes," said Agassiz, with all his characteristic energy and emphasis, "and I have just written to a friend, to tell that man that he has uttered an infamous slander on Humboldt."

Humboldt, you may all remember, was one of our early Honorary Members, elected when our Society embraced Natural, as well as Civil, History in its designs. Had we not abandoned that field of research to other Associations more expressly adapted for its culture, I need not say how proudly we should have included Agassiz on our roll. And I am sure that it will give us all pleasure to have found an occasion, this evening, for remembering, as a Society, one whom so many of us will never forget as the most charming and cherished of friends; whom Massachusetts and our whole country will ever count among the grandest and noblest of our adopted sons; and whom Science throughout the world has long ago enrolled among its most illustrious votaries.

CAMBRIDGE IN OLD ENGLAND, AND CAMBRIDGE IN NEW ENGLAND.

SPEECH AT THE VICE-CHANCELLOR'S BANQUET, IN THE HALL OF ST. PETER'S COLLEGE, ON THE EVENING BEFORE COMMENCEMENT, JUNE 15, 1874.

I AM most deeply sensible, Mr. Vice-Chancellor,[1] to the honor of being numbered among the distinguished guests at your table this evening, and still more of being specially named in the toast to the visitors which you have just given. I thank you too, sir, for joining my name with that of the eminent astronomer, M. Leverrier. He is by no means a stranger to me, though I may be one to him. I had the pleasure of shaking hands with him twenty-seven years ago, at the little palace of Neuilly, — not long before it was so sadly destroyed, — in presence of a Sovereign who is always remembered with respect on both sides of the Channel and on both sides of the Atlantic. M. Leverrier had then just won his earliest celebrity. I am most glad to renew my acquaintance with him in the full maturity of his scientific fame.

But I have still other favors to acknowledge, as unexpected as they are agreeable. Few things, certainly, could have taken me more by surprise than the telegram which reached me at Dublin not many days ago, — soon after I had landed from America at Queenstown, — inviting me to be present at this Commencement, and proposing for me an honor which, although I had received it twenty years ago from the Cambridge of my own country, I had not dreamed of receiving in England. I may hardly be at liberty, sir, to offer my thanks to the Univer-

[1] The Rev. Dr. Cookson.

sity for a Degree which still waits to be conferred by the hand of your noble Chancellor,[1] — a hand which, I may not forget, will in the meantime have won new "golden opinions" for itself, from the friends of Science throughout the world, by the munificent foundation of his Cavendish Laboratory. Nowhere will that foundation be hailed with greater delight than at Cambridge in New England, where Science, in all its departments, is holding no second place in the hearts both of students and of professors.

But, indeed, Mr. Vice-Chancellor, the privileges and pleasures of this evening are enough, and more than enough, for me to acknowledge most gratefully, without anticipating the promise of the morrow. To sit down at this sumptuous board, in this splendid Hall of the very oldest College of your venerable University, in company with so many of the most distinguished scholars and eminent living men of Old England, and amid so many memorials and so many memories of the illustrious dead, who, generation after generation, century after century, have been associated with these classic walls, — this alone is a privilege which no stranger — no American, certainly — can enjoy without emotion.

It would be but the barest and baldest commonplace, were I to allude to the measureless indebtedness of the world at large to the time-honored Universities of England — not forgetting those of Scotland and of Ireland, also — for all they have done for so many ages in the cause of Education and Learning. But to us of New England there are peculiar associations, of the most interesting character, with this particular University of Cambridge, of which I must not fail to speak. For indeed, sir, if it were vouchsafed to me at this moment, by some reversal of the mental telescope, to catch even the faintest vision of your ancient Halls and Colleges, as they stood here two centuries and a half or three centuries ago, — not far from the time when Sir Walter Mildmay was founding Emmanuel, and so along to the day when John Milton was planting his mulberry, and meditating his odes on the Nativity or on the Passion, at Christ's, — if, by some magic wand, I could summon back to view the young men

[1] The Duke of Devonshire.

and the old men who were then occupying these chambers and attending these chapels, and passing and repassing along these hallowed walks and grounds, — I could not fail to recognize, among the hosts of Cambridge scholars who have left imperishable memories in Old England, not a few, also, of those who soon afterwards became most prominent in the earliest history of New England, — not a few, especially, who were most instrumental in founding and fostering our own American University of Cambridge.

From some quiet chamber of Emmanuel itself, I should be sure to see, modestly coming out to his examinations or his prayers, no less distinguished a person than John Harvard, whose destiny it was, by a noble bequest, as early as 1638, to give his name, not to a single College only, but to our whole University. And if your kind allusion, Mr. Vice-Chancellor, to my own ancestry, may be an apology for any thing so personal, — it might be, nay, it certainly would be, that among the students, among the officers, and even among the benefactors of your Colleges at that day, I should descry more than one of my own name and blood, and more than one of more or less affinity to those who then wore that name and were veined with that blood, — Mildmays and Stills, and Downings and Barnardistons, as well as Winthrops, — whose titles are not yet wholly obliterated from your old rolls and registers. Two centuries and a half or three centuries, I know, make up a long period to look back upon in our American history, and indeed comprise almost the whole of it. But they include a far briefer period in the history of Old England, and only an infinitesimal moment in that Antiquity of Man, which, whether we entirely credit it or not, has been so ably asserted and illustrated by my venerable friend, Sir Charles Lyell, with whom I take a peculiar pleasure in being associated in the honors of this occasion.

There is hardly any thing, sir, more remarkable in the history of American Colonization, — I might rather call it English Colonization, — than the fact, that within six years only after the Fathers of Massachusetts had taken their charter into their own hands, and had established themselves permanently on the soil of New England, they laid the foundations, not of a school or an academy only, but of a College, — as an institution of the first necessity even there in the wilderness, amid physical trials and deprivations, and dangers from wild beasts and wilder men, which might well have diverted their attention from all intellectual wants. And it is most interesting to remember, here and on this occasion, that the name of the place where it was established, having previously been Newtown, was forthwith changed to Cambridge; and that there, from the year 1636, a University has been gradually rising up, and going on from strength to strength, I will not say in vain emulation of this University, but under the undoubted influence and inspiration of your example, and by the direct lead and original aid of more than one of your ancient Alumni.

It is not less pleasant for us, certainly, on our side, to remember that the ample fortune which had been hoarded up by one of the nine first year's graduates of our Cambridge, — one who, with all his weaknesses and failings of character and of conduct, was yet nothing less than a great English statesman and diplomatist,[1] and whose name still designates the street and office in London from which all British diplomacy emanates, and from which my friend Lord Derby is at this moment dating his daily despatches, — was ultimately employed in the establishment and endowment of your own Downing College.

I may not dwell longer on these historical details. I have recalled enough of them to show how immediate and how intimate was the relationship between Old Cambridge and New Cambridge, and how important was the influence of this ancient University upon the settlement of Massachusetts. Let me only confirm the idea by reminding you of the striking fact, that when the Fathers of New England were at last coming to the solemn decision to abandon their old homes and firesides and native land, and to go over to the New World with their wives and children, to plant what has proved to be a great and glorious Nation, they assembled here, within the precincts of this very University, for their final deliberations; and that the Solemn Agreement or Compact, upon which the whole fortunes and

[1] Sir George Downing, a graduate of Harvard University in 1642.

future of the Massachusetts Colony at that moment hinged and pivoted, if I may so speak, was signed by the twelve leading members of the Company, on the 26th of August, 1629, here at Cambridge.

Would that some Cambridge antiquary could discover beneath what ancient roof, in what Hall or Chamber, under what oak or elm in yonder groves, — or in what concealed covert, it may be, — that conference was held and that agreement signed! It would be a sacred spot, for every American visitor, certainly, and one which might well be marked by some simple Memorial Tablet, containing, perhaps, a copy of that brief but ever memorable compact. We should approach it in something of the same reverential spirit in which Runnymede is visited by all who inherit a share in the great legacy of Magna Charta.

I pray the pardon of His Grace the Chancellor, and of yourself, sir, and of the whole table, for trespassing so long on your indulgence. It was the more unpardonable after the signal example of brevity given us by the Lord Chief Justice. Perhaps he will kindly credit me with a little of the time which he might so much better have occupied himself. Let me only conclude, as an Alumnus of the Cambridge of New England and a Son of Massachusetts, by expressing the most earnest wishes for the continued prosperity and welfare of this venerable University; and in hailing her, not merely as the mother of scholars and patriots and heroes — of Bacon and Newton and Dryden and Milton, and a host of later worthies — *magna parens, magna virûm*, — but as, in a peculiar sense, the parent of a University on the other side of the broad Atlantic, which was first in point of time on our whole American Continent, and which has never been second, and I trust never will be second, in any thing which pertains to sound learning, to thorough scholarship, and to a comprehensive Christian education.

Prosperity and perpetuity to both Cambridges!

WILLIAM A. GRAHAM.

ADDRESS AT THE ANNUAL MEETING OF THE TRUSTEES OF THE PEABODY EDUCATION FUND, NEW YORK, OCTOBER 6, 1875.

GENTLEMEN OF THE BOARD OF TRUSTEES OF THE PEABODY EDUCATION FUND:

I AM sincerely glad to be with you once more, and to find a quorum assembled for business. It was with great regret that I found myself detained in Europe much longer than I anticipated when I left home, and that I was thus prevented from attending the last Annual Meeting of this Board. I may add without affectation that I willingly encountered the chances of a stormy passage across the Atlantic, during the recent equinoctial period, rather than arrive too late for the present meeting.

I trust that I need not assure you that absence from the country by no means diminished my interest in your proceedings; and that, as one who had been intrusted by Mr. Peabody with something of peculiar responsibility in the organization of the Board and the management of the Trust, I watched the course of your action at a distance, as eagerly and anxiously as if I had been at home. My good friend, our indefatigable and invaluable General Agent, Dr. Sears, will bear witness to the earnest interest, indicated in my correspondence with him, in all that was said or done here last year, and to the cordial concurrence which I expressed in the important declaration of purposes and policy which was so seasonably and unanimously adopted.

It was a special satisfaction to me that, with Dr. Sears's aid, I had completed, before my departure, the preparation of the permanent record of our Proceedings, for the first seven years of our existence, in the noble volume which was laid on your table during my absence. A considerable number of copies of this volume were transmitted to me at my request, under the authority given to the General Agent and myself; and I took occasion to present them to not a few of the Public Libraries abroad, and to such individuals as seemed to me peculiarly entitled to receive them. Copies were deposited in the British Museum, in the Bodleian Library at Oxford, in the library of the University at Cambridge, in the libraries of the Royal Society and of the London Society of Antiquaries, in the library of the City of London at Guildhall, in the Bibliothèque Nationale in Paris, and in the library of The Institute of France. Copies were also presented to the Earl of Derby, and others of the Trustees of Mr. Peabody's munificent and most successful Endowment for improving the Dwellings of the Poor in London, and to Dean Stanley, under whose authority the remains of our illustrious Founder were the subject of such signal honors in Westminster Abbey. I may add that, through the hands of Dean Stanley, a copy was placed in the library of the Queen, from whom Mr. Peabody, living and dying, had received such kind and marked attention.

Nor did I fail to remember, while I was in Rome, the deep interest in all Mr. Peabody's great benefactions expressed by His Holiness the Pope, at an audience to which I had accompanied Mr. Peabody seven years before; and, through the hands of the venerable Baron Visconti, a copy of the volume found its way to the Vatican.

I shall file with our General Agent or Secretary a complete list of the libraries in which this first volume of our Proceedings has been deposited, and of the individuals to whom it has been presented, in order that any succeeding volume or volumes may follow the first in future years. It is due to the memory of our Founder, as well as to ourselves and those who have been or may be associated with us, that the formal record of our administration of so large and noble a Trust should be placed within reach of all, on either side of the Atlantic, who may be interested in examining it. In London, especially, where Mr. Peabody's memory is so warmly cherished, and where Story's noble statue keeps him ever in the eyes of all who congregate on the Royal Exchange, the practical workings of the great benefactions which justify his fame are watched with interest, and the record of their progressive success should be always at hand. In no other way can the great example of his munificence be commended so effectively to the admiration and imitation of others; and, however much he may have coveted celebrity, it would have been worthless, even in his own estimation, unless that example should be productive of fruit and following.

I am reminded afresh, Gentlemen, on resuming the chair to-day, of the losses which the Board had sustained, previously to your last meeting, by the deaths of our esteemed associates, Mr. Macalester, and Mr. Eaton, — to whose memories I paid a passing tribute in a letter to Dr. Sears, which was included in the last record of our Proceedings. But it gives me peculiar pleasure to recall at this moment the names of the distinguished persons who were elected to fill the vacancies thus created. In the venerable Bishop of Minnesota and the Chief Justice of the United States, — both of whom we all welcome to our meeting to-day, — you have selected associates who would add dignity and strength to any organization, and whose participation in our proceedings will afford renewed assurance that they will be conducted with a scrupulous regard to the terms and tenor of the Trust under which we act.

I cannot forget, however, that still another breach has more recently been made in our little circle, and that we miss from our meeting to-day — for almost the first time since we received our commission from Mr. Peabody — the ever-welcome presence of one whom we all held in the warmest personal regard. A few weeks only before I embarked for America I heard, with great sorrow, of the death of the Hon. William A. Graham, of North Carolina. The event occurred somewhat suddenly, I learn, on the 11th of August, at Saratoga Springs, where he had been passing a few days for the benefit of his health. He had held, as you all know, many distinguished offices in the service of his State and country. As Governor of North Carolina, as a Senator in Congress for several years, and as Secretary of the Navy of the United States in the cabinet of President Fillmore, from which post he retired on being nominated by the Whig party as a candidate for the Vice-Presidency, — in all these relations he had won for himself a wide-spread reputation and regard, which any man, North or South, might have envied. I knew him intimately during this period of his public career, and have always cherished his friendship as one of the privileges of my Washington life. During the seven or eight years of his association with us in this Trust, we have all learned to appreciate his sterling qualities as a friend and a gentleman. One of the original members of the Board, receiving his appointment from Mr. Peabody on my own recommendation, he has fulfilled every promise I had made for him. No one of us has been more punctual in his attendance at our meetings, or has exhibited a more earnest and intelligent interest in all our proceedings, while his dignified and genial presence has given him a warm hold on all our hearts.

I am sure, Gentlemen, that you will unite with me in desiring that a committee may be appointed to prepare an appropriate resolution expressive of our deep sense of the loss we have sustained by his death; so that our permanent records may bear testimony to his faithful and valuable services.

Before this is done, however, I shall be pardoned for reading to you a portion of a letter, received just as I was leaving England a few weeks ago, from our friend and associate Governor Clifford, whom we all miss on this occasion, and who begged me to express to you his sincere regret at being unable to return from Europe in season for our meeting. Writing to me from Florence on the 1st of September, he speaks of having just seen an announcement of Governor Graham's death, and then proceeds as follows: "Alas and alas! He was not one of those who, when we last met, I had any forebodings might be starred on our fast-diminishing roll of Mr. Peabody's original appointments before the Board assembled again. But it will not be long before that roll will bear more of these sad and impressive signs of our common mortality. Already the little band of sixteen counts but one more among the living than it does of those who have joined the venerated founder of the Trust in that spirit-land to which we are all rapidly hastening; and it is the simple truth to say of this last departed of our associates, Governor Graham, that there was no one of us all, either of the living or the dead, who more faithfully fulfilled the duties he had assumed in accepting the trust with which Mr. Peabody had honored him, or who more fully realized the value and importance of that Trust to that portion of the country with whose interests his own were identified, and to whose honor and prosperity he devoted himself with such conscientious zeal. As in the earlier discussions and debates of the Board I was, perhaps, more frequently brought into opposition to Governor Graham, upon certain points of policy, than any other of his associates, — an opposition, however, always maintained on both sides with entire courtesy and good feeling, and invariably terminating in perfect concord, — I hope, when you announce his death at the next meeting, you will do me the favor to say, that, if I could be present, I should not fail to bear my testimony to his thorough fidelity, his manly frankness, and his amiable temper, which had made him one of the most agreeable, as he was one of the most useful, members of the Board; and that I shall unite most cordially with the members who may be present in any expression which they may adopt of affectionate and sincere respect to his memory."

RETURN TO THE DOWSE LIBRARY.

REMARKS AT A MEETING OF THE MASSACHUSETTS HISTORICAL SOCIETY, OCTOBER 14, 1875.

It gives me, Gentlemen, more pleasure than I know how to express, to find myself once more in the Dowse Library, with so many, around and before me, of those whom I have been long accustomed to meet here. I went abroad with reluctance; I stayed abroad with greater reluctance; and I eagerly returned home as soon as the condition of others, whose health and welfare I was bound to consult, before any wishes of my own, allowed me to return. I had many "compunctious visitings" about permitting my relation to this Society, as its President, to continue during so considerable an absence; and there are those present who would bear witness, I am sure, if any witness were needed, how more than willing I was to make way for others better entitled to such a distinction. But, by the blessing of God, here I am; and, by your favor, I resume the chair which I have occupied for so many years; and I can only assure you that I have returned with a deep sense of obligation to make up, as far as I can, for lost time, and to spare no efforts for promoting the continued prosperity and welfare of a Society, which has ever been indulgent alike to my short comings and to my long stayings.

My first impulse this morning, Gentlemen, is to offer, as I here do, my grateful acknowledgments to Mr. Adams, who has so kindly and punctually supplied, and more than supplied, my place; and to whom the thanks of the Society will, I doubt not, be offered, as they should be, in a formal vote. Let me myself propose, without further delay or preamble, that the thanks of this Society be presented to our first Vice-President, the Hon. Charles Francis Adams, for his faithful and obliging discharge of the duties of the chair during the absence of the President for nearly eighteen months past.

I am really appalled, Gentlemen, as I frame the resolution, at the length of absence of which I am compelled to make confession. But I will at least couple the confession with the promise never to do the like again.

And next, Gentlemen, let me thank you all most heartily for the "welcome home" which I cannot fail to read, in the unwontedly large attendance which greets my return to the chair to-day. I can never be insensible to such a manifestation of regard, and I am only sorry to be so inadequately prepared to meet the expectation which such a gathering may seem to imply.

But, alas! I miss from your number not a few of those whom I have been accustomed to meet on such occasions; not a few of those whom I might have confidently counted on taking by the hand, once more, to-day. I had, indeed, been gone from you but a few months, before I heard of the death of my good friend, Judge Warren, who once told us, at a Special Meeting at his own house, on one of the anniversaries of the Pilgrims' Landing, that he had in his own veins the blood of at least five of the passengers in the "Mayflower," and the solace of whose declining age was to spend it within sight of Plymouth Rock. The death of Judge Warren was soon followed by that of the excellent Jeffries Wyman, to whom I had been bound, for seven or eight years past, by peculiar ties of association and of affection, and whose name I cannot mention without a fresh and deep sense of the loss to Science, to the University, and to us all, which his early and lamented departure has involved. Then came successively the deaths of the eminent jurist, Judge Curtis; of the zealous antiquary, Dr. Shurtleff; of the venerated pastor, president, moralist, Dr. Walker; and of the veteran Boston banker-poet, Charles Sprague.

Our "last enemy," as he is persistently called, — though he so often comes to the suffering and the infirm as their best friend,

— could hardly have found, in our own ranks, or in those of any other association, six men of more striking characters, of more distinguished careers, of more varied and attractive gifts, to be grouped together as the shining marks of his unerring shafts, during a single year.

To all these deceased associates and friends, however, I have already paid some humble tribute in letters to our invaluable Secretary, Mr. Deane, which have received more attention than they deserve.

But still other breaches had been made in our little band of one hundred before my return. While on the eve of embarking, I heard, with great regret, of the deaths of the Hon. Charles Wentworth Upham, whom I have always remembered affectionately as the oldest boy of good Deacon Greele's school, when I was the youngest; and of Professor Joel Parker, whose sturdy and vigorous old age had given promise of many more years of usefulness and honor. Both of them had done excellent work for history and for our own Society; but I am conscious that I can say nothing of either of them which has not been better said, and very recently said, by others.

Meantime, I cannot forget that our Honorary and Corresponding roll has been robbed in its turn of the names of Almack and Twisleton; of Cyrus Eaton and John Carter Brown; of D'Avezac, whom I visited twice in Paris while he was rapidly approaching his end; and of Guizot, whom I had the privilege of knowing personally in former years, but whom I was now too late to see again.

I may be pardoned for mentioning, in passing, that I was fortunate enough to be in Paris during the sale of Guizot's library, and to obtain a valuable volume from it, with an autograph note on the fly-leaf. And though I am not much of a collector of autographs, I could not resist the temptation of securing half a dozen of his collection, which will serve to illustrate the characters and careers in which he had taken special interest. They included Bossuet and Mirabeau, two men of the most widely contrasted lives and periods, but in their several spheres, perhaps, the most brilliant orators France has ever produced. They included William of Orange, whose name speaks, and will ever speak, for itself. They included Wilberforce, the great English philanthropist; and Chalmers, the grand Scotch thinker and preacher. And they included Walter Scott.

But I cannot pass from the losses which our Honorary roll has sustained without alluding to the latest, and to us the most memorable of all.

The venerable Horace Binney, of Philadelphia, had already passed safely through the first half of his ninety-sixth year, with his eyes hardly dimmed, his natural strength scarcely abated, and his intellectual faculties all unclouded; and we had fondly hoped that he might have been held back still longer from the skies, not only to witness the completion of his country's Century, and to be the most interesting and illustrious living figure in the great celebration in his own city next year, but to complete his own century of life, not long afterwards, and to impersonate for us, as indeed he so long had done, that grand description of the old prophet, "the ancient and the honorable man, the prudent, the counsellor, and the eloquent orator."

But this hope of us all was not to be fulfilled. I had just been reading a letter from him, a copy of which had been kindly enclosed to me by Mr. Grigsby, to whom it was addressed as late as the 7th of July last, in which he alluded to the prospect of attaining to "the higher life," when a telegram in a London paper, which had outrun the mail, apprised me that the *higher life* was indeed already his.

I have always counted it among my special privileges to have heard Horace Binney in the greatest effort of his life, — his magnificent argument before the Supreme Court at Washington, in the Girard College Case, — when, though so much of my sympathy was with his illustrious antagonist, Mr. Webster, and with the peculiar views of which Mr. Webster was the advocate, I received such an impression of the power, the research, and the eloquence of Mr. Binney, and of the weight of character — like that of our own old Samuel Hoar — which he threw into the case, that I have always regarded that effort as among the very grandest forensic displays and triumphs which the courts of law in our own land, or in any other land, have ever witnessed.

I paid Mr. Binney a visit, only a few years ago, in his own office at Philadelphia, built for him, as he told me, more than sixty years before; and certainly a more interesting and beautiful exhibition of a serene, philosophic, and Christian old age could have been seen nowhere else. But my friend and his friend, Mr. Grigsby, has furnished us with a full account of his career and of its close; and I forbear from adding further to tributes which have been abundantly paid.

Let me turn, then, for an instant from the dead to the living, to mention a few of our Honorary and Corresponding Members in foreign lands, whom it was my good fortune to meet, and from whom I received so many kind attentions. I could hardly forgive myself, indeed, were I to omit all acknowledgment of my obligations to the distinguished historian, Earl Stanhope, whose name is now the only one left on our roll of those elected from Old England, prior to the amendment of our charter in 1857; to Mignet, the eminent and eloquent Academician whose name is at the head of our later roll, and who has just published two new historical volumes on "The Rivalry between Francis I. and Charles V.;" to Count Adolphe de Circourt, who is engaged in publishing a work on the Alliance between France and the United States in 1778; to Thiers, the great writer, orator, and statesman of France; to Dean Stanley and Lord Arthur Hervey; to John Forster and Edward A. Freeman; and lastly, to our American Minister at Rome, George P. Marsh, who intrusted me with a photographic copy of a rare and perhaps unique old print of our revolutionary period, as a contribution to our Cabinet. The print purports to have been designed, "after nature," in Boston, and to have been engraved in Philadelphia, and Mr. Marsh gives the following account of its strange discovery: —

ROME, May 31, 1875.

DEAR MR. WINTHROP, — The engraving emblematical of the relief of Philadelphia, by the "Ange de la France," was found by Colonel H. Yule, the editor of the new edition of Marco Polo, bound into a folio, entitled: Wahrhaftige ausführliche Beschreibung der Berühmten Ost-

Indischen Küsten Malabar und Coromandel durch Philippum Baldaeun weiland Diener des Göttlich. Worts ans Zeylon. Amsterdam, 1672.

It was bound into the middle of the section: Abgötterey der Ost. Indischen Heyden, by some old person, who probably took the dancing party for *heathen*, performing some licentious rite.

I presume the *dessiné d'après nature* refers rather to the landscape than to the saltatory group, though I do not know but the *vertueux Insurgens* may have sometimes indulged in such frisky expressions of exultation. I suppose the design is good authority for the form of the *Bonnet de la Liberté* used at that period; but how is it with the flag? And is the town in the background Philadelphia, as it was in 1778? If the design was made at Boston, probably the artist found the *nature* after which he drew nearer at hand. Is there any thing in it that suggests Boston as the original?

Very truly yours,

GEO. P. MARSH.

HON. R. C. WINTHROP.

Once more, Gentlemen, let me offer you my grateful acknowledgments of your indulgence, and renew the assurances of my devoted interest in the prosperity and welfare of this Society.

PORTRAITS OF WASHINGTON AND FRANKLIN.

REMARKS AT A MEETING OF THE MASSACHUSETTS HISTORICAL SOCIETY, NOVEMBER 11, 1875.

It will not have been forgotten, I am sure, that, soon after I went to Europe last year, I was instrumental in procuring for our Historical Gallery, through the liberality of Mr. Alexander Duncan, an exact copy of the portrait of Washington which was captured, in 1780, on its way to the Stadtholder, by Captain Keppel, of the British Navy.

It seems to have been satisfactorily shown, by our Cabinet-keeper, Mr. Appleton, in his communication to the Society, at the November meeting of last year, that this portrait, now at Quidenham Park, the seat of the Earl of Albemarle, was one of five or six copies made by Mr. Charles Wilson Peale, of an original painted by himself by the order of the Council of Pennsylvania in 1779, the copies differing from each other only in some variations of scenery or background. Four of these copies or repetitions have been traced as belonging respectively to the United States Government, France, Princeton College, and the Earl of Albemarle.

All this, however, would hardly have been brought to light without the investigations to which our copy gave occasion. And there is, moreover, I need hardly say, something of special interest attaching to the precise picture, with its varying details, which was the subject of capture in connection with Laurens; which had been so long preserved by the family of the captor, remote from the common eye; and which had been the subject of so much discussion heretofore among ourselves.

But the investigations by Mr. Appleton, and by others, to which our copy gave rise, have had further results. Mr. Appleton, in his communication, alluded to an original portrait of Washington, painted by Le Paon, and which had belonged to Lafayette, and he exhibited an engraving of this portrait by Le Mire. It happened that I, also, had previously obtained a copy of this engraving, through my cousin, Mr. Frederic Temple Palmer, who resides at Versailles, and had laid it aside to bring home as a contribution to our Cabinet. Here it is, and I present it to the Society without further delay. Le Paon, who is styled the painter of battles of the Prince de Condé, was probably never in this country, and had no opportunity of painting Washington from the life; and I think no one can doubt, on examining the engraving, that he must have taken the head substantially from the portrait of Peale. Lafayette, if it were really painted for him, may possibly have suggested some changes, from his own familiarity with Washington's features. But he would certainly seem to have accepted it as a likeness of Washington, at that period of his life.

Meantime I have come upon the track of two other portraits of Washington, during my absence abroad, which may be worth a moment's allusion. In the National Portrait Gallery of England, — a most interesting and noble collection, — near Kensington Gardens, there is a fine colored crayon of Washington, by Sharpless. The catalogue says by "Mrs. Sharples," but I can hardly doubt that it was by the same person, so many of whose crayons have recently been discovered in Philadelphia, and who is well known to have had Washington among his subjects.

Then there is another original crayon of Washington in the possession of the Rector of Wymington, Bedfordshire. It is said to have been taken by a French artist, who persevered in his resolution to obtain a sitting from Washington, while he was in camp, until at last Washington gave him permission to sketch him as he was writing his despatches. The crayon is said to have come to its present possessor through Mrs. Grant of Laggan, whose "Letters from the Mountains," and "Memoirs of an American Lady," were well known to our fathers and mothers, and whose intimacy with the Schuylers of Albany, and her early residence for four years in America, may have given her the opportunity of securing such a portrait.

Passing, for a moment, from Washington, I may proceed to say, what is hardly of less interest, that another of the Rectors of Bedfordshire, the Rev. C. C. Beaty-Pownall, Rector of All Saints, Milton-Ernest, has an original portrait of Franklin. It was given to him by his mother, who received it from her cousin, Sir George Pownall, to whom it was given by Governor Pownall of New England. An autograph letter of Franklin was formerly, I learn, "stuck in the back of the frame, within the memory of the present owner, but a servant, thinking it looked untidy, is said to have destroyed it." The portrait is thought to be by Copley, and is understood to have been given to Governor Pownall by Franklin himself.

It was certainly striking to hear of original portraits of Washington and Franklin, not far from each other, in different rectories in Bedfordshire; and I was sorry that I was unable to accompany my friend, the Rev. Mr. Horwood, of Turvey, — whose wife was one of the Church family of Western New York, and from whom I obtained the account of them, — to see them.

In the Milton-Ernest Rectory, too, I should have seen an engraving inscribed as follows: —

"Cotes. pinxit: Earlow fecit. Thomas Pownall, Esq., Member of Parliament, late Governor, Captain General, and Commander in Chief and Vice Admiral of His Majesty's Provinces, Massachusetts Bay and South Carolina, and Lieut. Governor of New Jersey. 5 June, 1777."

The original portrait is at Earl Orford's in Norfolk. How far it corresponds with the portrait of Pownall in our own gallery, presented to us by the late Lucius Manlius Sargent, Esq., I do not know. Mr. Sargent's portrait is believed to have been copied from an engraving, — perhaps a duplicate of the very one now in possession of the Rev. C. C. Beaty-Pownall, of which I have just given the inscription.

Several other portraits of Franklin came to my knowledge in England, one of them on the walls of the Royal Society at Burlington House, and another in the National Portrait Gallery, not far from the Sharpless crayon of Washington. A third, said to be an original Greuze, and to have been given by Franklin to the famous traveller Denon, was understood to await a purchaser, and I took an opportunity to go and see it. But the attractions of the portrait were not sufficient to reconcile me to the large price which was put upon it.

Still another original portrait of Franklin came to my knowledge, as I was crossing the ocean,—a duplicate by Chamberlin, of the well-remembered picture with the large spectacles and the hand at the chin. This was in Scotland, in possession of one of the relatives of the William Penn family.

Surely, if a man's fame is to be measured by the number of his portraits at home and abroad, Franklin was by far the most famous American of his period, as, indeed, there can be no doubt he was. His likeness is to be found in oils and crayons, on canvas, on paper, on ivory, on porcelain, and in pottery, and not only on pitchers and tea-cups, like Washington's, but it is said to have been complimented, as it was called, by being presented on some of the least dignified utensils of household crockery.

I cannot conclude without recalling a somewhat ludicrous arrangement of Washington and Franklin which I observed more than once, in one of the shop windows, in the Rue de la Paix, in Paris. A handsome frame was conspicuously suspended to attract the passers-by, in which were four miniatures arranged as a *partie carrée*. At the top was Franklin, in the fur cap and big goggles, *vis-à-vis* with Pope Pius IX.; and below was Washington, as a pendant to Rachel, the great actress! I presume that the collocation was accidental, and the miniatures might probably have been sold separately, but the exhibition was not the less amusing to an American eye. I may add that one of the attendants of the shop, to whom I applied for information, and who knew the likenesses of all the other three, could not tell me who was the lady with whom Washington had been so strangely mated. He may probably have regarded it as the head of the Goddess of Liberty.

During my absence in Europe, and while I still cherished the hope of returning in season to take some part in the Centennial celebrations of the present year, I requested our Corresponding Member, Mr. Sainsbury, to send me an abstract of any papers in Her Majesty's Public Record Office, which might be interesting and instructive in connection with the events of 1775. He accordingly examined the old files, and prepared a paper of nearly forty pages, which I received in Paris in May last. I had been obliged, long before that time, to abandon the hope of returning until the autumn, and I found no leisure for examining the paper with any care. I have gone through it since my return, and do not perceive much that is altogether new or very important.

But others, more familiar with these old records, may be more fortunate, and I leave them, without recourse, for their examination.[1]

[1] These papers, including the letter of Lord Percy to Governor Gage, April 20, 1775, are printed in the Proceedings of the Massachusetts Historical Society, 1875-1876, pp. 340 to 358.

HENRY WILSON AND JUDGE METCALF.

REMARKS AT A MEETING OF THE MASSACHUSETTS HISTORICAL SOCIETY, DECEMBER 9, 1875.

SINCE we last met here, Gentlemen, our city and State have been overshadowed by a succession of bereavements of no common significance and sadness.

In the death of the Rev. JAMES B. MILES, the cause of philanthropy and peace has lost one of its most earnest and devoted apostles and advocates.

In the death of the Hon. JOHN WELLS, the Supreme Court of our Commonwealth has lost one of its ablest and most valuable judges.

In the death of the Hon. HENRY WILSON, the Vice-President of the United States, and so long a senator of Massachusetts, the whole country has lost a public servant of large experience and great practical ability, whose career does not require to be contrasted with the humble circumstances of its origin to be counted among the most striking in our annals.

His ardent nature, his untiring energy, his devoted advocacy of every cause which he espoused and of every opinion which he entertained, and the many amiable personal qualities which he displayed, — more especially under the influence of the deep religious impressions of his later years, — had given him a strong hold on the hearts of his fellow-citizens, and had quite overcome any antipathies or prejudices which may have been engendered by political differences in the earlier stages of his life.

His name, too, is honorably associated with more than one

volume,[1] which, though not accepted on all sides as containing altogether dispassionate or accurate representations of individuals or of parties, will furnish a valuable contribution to the history of the period which they cover.

Neither of the lamented gentlemen whom I have named was a member of our Society, but this brief reference to their deaths, in such close and sad succession, will not, I am sure, be regarded as otherwise than appropriate to our proceedings and our records.

Meantime we are called to-day to notice a more direct loss to our own little number in the death of the Hon. THERON METCALF, the eminent lawyer, and formerly a distinguished judge of the Supreme Court of our State. Had Judge Metcalf passed away like those to whom I have just referred, while still in official life, and still in the unimpaired enjoyment of his remarkable faculties, his death like theirs would have been the subject of profound public sorrow. His labors as a reporter, as an annotator, as an advocate, and as a judge, could not have been arrested, while he still had strength to pursue them, without occasioning the impression of an almost irreparable loss. We can measure what would have been left undone by what has been done. But he long ago finished his work and retired from public view, and he has died at last, after completing his ninetieth year, with hardly one of his contemporaries left to bear witness to the vigor of his mind and the value of his labors.

The younger members of his profession, however, both at the bar and on the bench, have not been wanting to his memory, and I should in vain attempt to add any thing to the tributes which they have so recently paid him. During the fourteen or fifteen years of his association with us here, we have all witnessed with interest the eagerness he exhibited in historical and antiquarian pursuits, and his perseverance in coming to our rooms and attending our meetings until within a few months of his death. We may well cherish the remembrance of such an example of punctuality and fidelity, and commend it to the imitation of others.

[1] "Rise and Fall of the Slave Power in America," by Henry Wilson.

EX-GOVERNOR CLIFFORD.

REMARKS AT A MEETING OF THE MASSACHUSETTS HISTORICAL SOCIETY, JANUARY 13, 1876.

It is not, Gentlemen, without a deep sense of personal loss, that I announce the death of the Hon. John H. Clifford, who has been one of the Resident Members of this Society for more than twenty years.

It may not be forgotten that I mentioned, at our last monthly meeting, that he had promised to be with us on that occasion, to pay a tribute to his venerable friend, Judge Metcalf. He had gone, however, a fortnight before, — soon after his arrival from Europe, — to pass Thanksgiving Day at his old home in New Bedford; and, while there, he was struck with sudden and serious illness. Under the care of skilful physicians, and of a devoted family, his alarming symptoms were alleviated; and there was the best reason for hoping that he would soon be able to resume his winter residence in Boston, and to enter anew upon his chosen pursuits. But New Year's Day was destined to be the last day of his earthly life; and, before another morning dawned, the mysterious call had come, and his spirit returned, without a struggle, to God who gave it.

In company with several of our associates, I attended his funeral at New Bedford on Thursday last, where the presence of a great throng of his friends and fellow-citizens attested the respect and affection in which he was held by all who knew him.

It is more than forty years since we entered the Legislature of Massachusetts, as young men, together, and took an early fancy for each other, which ripened into a life-long friendship. During that protracted period, there have been but few months, — I might almost say but few weeks, — in which we have not held more or less of communication, either personally or by correspondence. I can recall no friend with whom I have ever been on the same footing of intimacy for so long a time, except the late excellent John Pendleton Kennedy of Baltimore. We were long associated in the friendship and confidence of Edward Everett. We were more recently associated in the friendship and confidence of George Peabody; and in the administration of one of his most interesting and important trusts. In view of these intimate relations, I have willingly acceded to the request of the Council, that I would take it upon myself to prepare hereafter a brief Memoir of him, according to usage, for the next volume of our Proceedings. I forbear, therefore, at present, from any attempt to delineate his character or career.

There are those with us here, this morning, who have known him in youth and in manhood; at his own University in Providence, and in his associations with our University at Cambridge; at the Bar, in the Legislative Halls, as Attorney-General, and as Governor of Massachusetts, as well as in his relations to the other public institutions with which he was connected. I leave it to them to bear their testimony to his abilities, his usefulness, and his virtues. It is enough for me to say on this occasion, as I sincerely can say,

"Multis ille bonis flebilis occidit,
Nulli flebilior quam mihi."

MEMOIR.

In the beautiful town of New Bedford, long since incorporated as a city, there might have been found, some thirty or forty years ago, as charming a group of choice spirits as could be gathered anywhere within the limits of Massachusetts. Among them was Ephraim Peabody, the pastor of the Unitarian parish of the town, afterwards the rector of King's Chapel in Boston; wise, accomplished, amiable, eloquent, beloved by all who knew him. Among them was Charles Henry Warren, widely known afterwards as Judge Warren, whose sparkling wit, and racy anecdote, and keen irony were the delight of every circle in which he moved. Among them was William W. Swain, whose jurisdiction over "Naushon" had won for him the familiar sobriquet of "Governor," and whose great heart and genial hospitality had made willing subjects for him far beyond the narrow domain of the Elizabeth Islands. These and others of that little group have passed away. At least one of them, however, is still living, — the venerable Joseph Grinnell, — born before any of them, and now surviving them all; who, after many years of valuable public service in the Congress of the United States, is to-day, in his eighty-ninth year, conducting successfully and vigorously a great manufacturing establishment, and who, by his firmness and discretion, has just succeeded in putting down a formidable strike of its workmen.

But of this little circle of choice spirits in New Bedford, into which I was so often admitted as a guest on occasional visits from Boston or Washington, the subject of this Memoir was the central figure. Younger than any of his associates; with less accomplishment, perhaps, than one; with less wit, perhaps, than another; with not more of heart or head than a third or fourth of them, — he had yet a combination of qualities, intellectual, moral, and social, which gave him an easy lead, and secured for him a ready following. No one, I think, could have spent a day in New Bedford, at that period, without feeling that the active, moving spirit of its social and intellectual life was John Henry Clifford.

Thus early — for he was then hardly more than thirty years of age — did he exhibit that practical tact, that genial disposition, that magnetic temper, which always gave him one of the foremost places among those with whom he was associated, whether in public or in private life. Of great executive ability, and with a peculiar faculty of organization, he was at least the prompter and the manager of scenes in which he may not have assumed or aspired to play the first part. He would, indeed, have counted himself at that time the humblest of that little group; but not the less did his earnest nature impart animation and inspiration to them all.

Governor Clifford, however, — for by that title he will be most readily remembered, — was not a native of New Bedford, nor of Massachusetts. He was born in Providence, Rhode Island, on the 16th of January, 1809, and continued to reside there with his parents until he had completed his school and college education. It was only after he had gone through his four years' course and taken his degree, as Bachelor of Arts, in 1827, at Brown University, that he left his parental home and native State. He then entered on the study of law with Timothy G. Coffin, Esq., of New Bedford, and subsequently studied with the late Judge Theron Metcalf at Dedham, Massachusetts. In 1830 he was admitted to the Bar of the county of Bristol, having in the same year received his degree of Master of Arts at Brown, when he delivered an oration on "the Perils of Professional Life." Thenceforth he was to confront those perils himself, in the daily practice of his chosen profession. He established himself as a lawyer in New Bedford, and two years afterwards gave "a hostage to fortune," and left no further doubt where his permanent home was to be fixed. On the 16th of January, 1832, his twenty-third birthday, he married Sarah Parker Allen, daughter of William Howland Allen, Esq., and granddaughter of the Hon. John Avery Parker, of New Bedford; and from that day to his death he resided nowhere else.

Three years afterward, in 1835, he took his seat in the Legislature of Massachusetts, as a representative from New Bedford. There I met him for the first time; and from that association resulted a friendship and an intimacy which ended only with his life. It was the year of the Revision of the Statutes of the Commonwealth, and he did good and faithful service on the large committee which had that subject in charge. In 1836 he became one of the aides-de-camp of Governor Everett, and retained that position until, by a single vote out of a hundred thousand votes, Mr. Everett's chief magistracy was brought to a close in 1840.

Before Mr. Everett went out of office, however, — in 1839, — he had conferred upon Colonel Clifford, in whom he had the highest confidence, the appointment of District Attorney for the Southern District of Massachusetts; an office in which he served the Commonwealth assiduously and successfully for nearly ten years.

Meantime, in 1845, the county of Bristol had elected him a member of the Senate of Massachusetts, where he gave renewed evidence of his ability and accomplishments as a debater and a legislator. But his taste for legal practice predominated over all others, and in 1849 he entered upon the duties of an office which was to be the field of his longest and most distinguished public service. In that year he received from Governor Briggs the appointment of Attorney-General of the State.

Early in the following year it fell to his lot to conduct a memorable trial, with which his name will be always most prominently and honorably associated. No trial in the history of our country for many generations, if ever, has excited a deeper interest, or challenged a more anxious and critical attention, than that of Professor John W. Webster for the murder of Dr. George Parkman. Even to this day, the circumstances of the crime and the proceedings to which it gave occasion, as contained in the detailed report prepared and published by our associate member, Mr. George Bemis, the junior counsel for the Commonwealth, have the attraction and fascination of some tragic drama. The responsibility and the labor which it threw upon the Attorney-General were of the most arduous character; and it is enough to say of the manner in which they were met, that when the verdict was obtained, and the full details of evidence and argument were published to the world, he had earned a reputation for ability and force, as well as for discretion and fairness, as a prosecuting officer, which was recognized far beyond the limits of New England.

Few things, if any thing, could have gratified him more than the following passage from an article in "Blackwood's Magazine" for June of that year, on "Modern State Trials,"—being one of a series of articles from the pen of the eminent barrister, Samuel Warren,[1] the author of the "Diary of a Physician," and of "Ten Thousand a Year":—

[1] The death of Samuel Warren, Q. C., on the 29th of July, 1877, was announced from England, while these pages were first going through the press.

"It was our intention to have included in this paper a sketch of a great American trial for murder, — that of the late Professor Webster for the murder of Dr. Parkman; a fearful occurrence; a black and dismal tragedy from beginning to end; exhibiting most remarkable indications, as it appears to us, of the overruling Providence, which sometimes sees fit to allow its agency in human affairs to become visible to us. We have, however, now concluded the present series; but it is not impossible that we may take an early opportunity of giving some account of this extraordinary case, of which, even while we are writing, a report has been courteously transmitted to us from America. All we shall at present say on the subject is, that the reply of Mr. Clifford for the prosecution cannot be excelled in close and conclusive reasoning, conveyed in language equally elegant and forcible. Its effect, as a demonstration of the guilt of the accused, is fearful."

The following letter, dated the day after the sentence had been pronounced, affords a striking view of his own impressions at the result: —

"New Bedford, April 2, 1850.

"My dear Winthrop, — The long agony is over, and I am once more by my own hearthstone, trying to restore the equilibrium which two weeks' straining of my entire being had deranged and disturbed. I have never been before, and can never be again, kept up to such an extreme tension; but in looking back, and sternly scrutinizing my whole course from the commencement of my connection with the case to its close, I cannot find any cause of self-reproach. God knows I have compassionated the poor criminal; and my heart has bled for his family almost as if they were my own.

"Personally, I cannot help feeling this trial to have been a great crisis in my life. A failure in it would have been fatal; a moderate degree of success would have been scarcely less unfortunate: and I fervently thank the Good Being who has guided and strengthened and sustained me, for the eminent success which the assurances that I have received from all quarters leave me not at liberty to doubt my having achieved. . . . I am going to New York this week with my wife, and it is not impossible that I may run on and pass a day with you in Washington.

"Yours ever,

"J. H. Clifford."

In the autumn of 1852, the convention of the Whig Party of Massachusetts nominated Attorney-General Clifford for

Governor of the State. He accepted the nomination with reluctance; and, though he received nearly twenty-five thousand more votes than either of the opposing candidates, he was not elected by the people. The plurality system had not yet been adopted, and the Constitution of the State at that time required for an election an absolute majority of all the votes cast by the people. On the meeting of the Legislature, however, he was chosen by the votes of the two branches; and was inaugurated as Governor of Massachusetts on the 14th of January, 1853.

In his Inaugural Address he dwelt strongly on "the tendency to an excess of legislation," and gave evidence of his adherence to the principles of the old Whig Party, of which he had been the candidate, by saying: "It seems to me, therefore, that the wise moderation which avoids both the extremes, — of a blind conservatism which clings to every thing that is established, because it is old, and the reckless and impatient radicalism which is ready to adopt every new project or theory, merely because it is new, — a moderation which consults that vital element in every well-governed community, the adaptation of an established system of laws to the usages and habits of the people, — is one of the safest guides in practical and beneficent legislation." "In all matters of civil government," he added, "the Law is our only sovereign. The loyalty, which in other countries is rendered to the mere accident of birth, is here due to that invisible but omnipresent power which we have voluntarily enthroned and established, for our protection and guidance, under the majestic name of Law."

Governor Clifford discharged the duties of the chief magistracy with great fidelity and dignity, and it was only for him to say whether he should remain in the office for a second year. But his interest in his profession determined him to decline a renomination, and on the election of Governor Emory Washburn, as his successor, he was at once called on by him to resume his place as Attorney-General of the Commonwealth. He continued to hold that office, — by executive appointment for one year, by legislative election for another, and again, for a third, by the choice of the people of the State, — until 1858.

He had thus served the Commonwealth as its highest law-officer for a full term of seven years in all; and in that capacity had certainly rendered his best public service, and acquired his greatest public distinction.

In retiring finally from this position he did not abandon his professional labors, but was frequently to be found in the highest courts of the Commonwealth and of the Nation, in the argument of important cases. During the terrible Civil War, which soon afterwards afflicted the country, he omitted no efforts in his power to sustain the cause of the Union according to the convictions of his own conscience. More than once he was summoned to Washington to hold council with Cabinet officers, in regard to measures in contemplation. At home, too, he spared neither time nor money in encouraging the soldiers who went out from his own city or county. In 1862 he accepted an election to the State Senate, and was at once chosen President of that body, — in that capacity rendering conspicuous service to the Commonwealth at the most critical period of the War. In 1868 he was one of the electors at large, and united in giving the vote of Massachusetts to President Grant.

In the previous year, however, — 1867, — he had entered upon a line of life which was finally to separate him from further professional or political service, and to confine him to the routine of practical business. Assuming the charge of the Boston and Providence Railroad Corporation, as its President, he devoted himself to its affairs with all his accustomed earnestness and energy. Under his auspices the new and spacious Station of that Railroad was erected in Boston, which will always be a monument of his administration; and in which, within a few months of his death, he gave, as we shall presently see, so memorable a manifestation of the spirit in which that administration had been conducted.

Meantime he had not allowed the engrossments of practical business to cut him off wholly from other interests and associations. He was a member of the American Academy of Arts and Sciences. He was a member of our own Society, and occasionally took part in our proceedings. His tribute to his old commander-in-chief, Edward Everett, was among the most felicitous utterances of our Special Meeting on the occasion of his death. But he rendered larger services to Harvard University at Cambridge, of which he was for many years one of the Overseers, and repeatedly the President of that Board. He had been called on, while Governor, to perform a prominent part at the inauguration of the late Rev. Dr. Walker, as President of the University, on the 24th of May, 1853; and a sufficient testimony to the impressive character of his Address on that occasion may be found in the following sentence of President Walker's reply: "I have listened — we all have listened — to what your Excellency has said, with such just and fervid eloquence, of the dignity and responsibilities of the teacher; of the need there is that education should be improved and extended in order to meet the advancing wants of the age; and, above all, that the whole should be touched by Christian influences: — but this only makes me feel my incompetency the more."

Governor Clifford was called on again, as the head of the Board of Overseers, to officiate at the induction of President Eliot, on the 19th of October, 1869; and from his Address on that occasion the following passages will furnish a good illustration of the earnest spirit in which he spoke: —

"When its venerated founders, the Fathers of New England, inscribed the simple motto 'Veritas' upon the college seal, and when their immediate successors enlarged its legend by the adoption of that which it now bears, 'Christo et Ecclesiæ,' as the watchword and token of its allegiance to the highest truth, they surely never dreamed — may the day never dawn when their descendants shall declare — that there is an 'irrepressible conflict' between the truths of ethical and of physical science. Truth is one: — 'vital in every part, it cannot, but by annihilation, die;' and he is but poorly armed in its panoply of proof, who fears that any speculation, study, or research can establish a want of harmony between the revelations of God through the spirit he has breathed into his noblest creation, and those he has imparted through his imprints upon the insensate rocks.

"Idle, too, is the boast, or the dread, that, if such a conflict is to come, its predestined and ignoble issue will be, that the highest and most precious truth man can comprehend, and which ennobles human life and all its acquisitions and accomplishments with their chief dignity and value, shall surrender to the hasty generalizations and unwarranted and unchastened speculations of the presumptuous sciolist, whose 'mind has been subdued to what it works in, like the dyer's hand.' Were such to be the result of what is called the progress of science, as taught within these walls, that He is to be ignored to whose glory they were reared, — of what significance are these idle ceremonials, from which we might as well turn away, 'one to his farm, and another to his merchandise,' contenting ourselves only with the reflection, that, like the beasts that perish, we can 'eat and drink, for to-morrow we die'?

"In the progress of what is complacently called the 'advanced thought of New England,' and it may be at no distant day, there doubtless will be waged a conflict of opinion of the highest import to the cause of truth and the welfare of the race. Whenever it comes, Harvard College can hold no subordinate place among the institutions of the country, in whose armories must be forged the weapons with which it will be fought. Her friends can have no misgivings as to the position she will occupy on such a field. Her great influence can never be arrayed on the side of those whose arrogant self-conceit can find no higher object of worship than the pretentious intellect of man, — to-day, asserting its own omnipotence; to-morrow, 'babbling of green fields,' as its possessor sinks beneath the turf that covers them, to mingle with his kindred clod; — of those whose misty speculations shut out the life-giving rays of the 'Star of Bethlehem,' and who, with puny but presumptuous hand, would —

'hang a curtain on the East,
The daylight from the world to keep.'"

Governor Clifford was, also, one of the original Board of Trustees of the great Education Fund, established by the munificence of George Peabody, for the impoverished and desolated States of the South; and I can bear witness to the zeal and assiduity with which he attended their meetings, and entered into all their discussions. No one was more faithful to that noble Trust, and no one will be more affectionately and gratefully remembered by all who were associated with him in its labors and responsibilities.

But the health of our lamented friend had more than once during these latter years given warning that he needed relaxation. Indeed, there is the best authority for saying, that nothing but the earnest admonitions of his physician, and his own consciousness of waning strength, had originally induced him to renounce the professional career in which he had won so distinguished a reputation, and to which he was so ardently attached. The efforts and excitements of the court-room had more than once been followed by serious prostration, and he had reluctantly yielded to the necessity of exchanging them for the quieter, though hardly less arduous and responsible, duties of presiding over a great business corporation. But in the spring of 1873 he was compelled to abandon all occupation, and fly to the salubrious airs of Florida. In the spring of 1875, a visit to Europe was recommended to him, and he sailed for Liverpool on the 24th of April of that year. It was his first visit to the Old World; and, though he prudently denied himself to the attentions and hospitalities which were abundantly offered to him in London, he went through the laborious round of sight-seeing, there and everywhere, with all the enthusiasm of his nature. I was in Europe myself at that time, and saw him more than once, and had frequent letters for him along his route. England and Scotland, France, Switzerland, and Northern Italy were traversed in the half-year's absence from home which he allowed himself. His family were with him, and he enjoyed every moment. As he approached the limit which he had assigned to his absence, he was compelled to abandon all thought of Rome and Naples. A letter from him, dated Florence, Sept. 1, 1875, speaks of the struggle it has cost him to give up seeing the Eternal City; but adds that "he looks towards *home* with infinitely more desire than towards Rome, Pompeii, or even the Holy Land."

"You were quite right," he proceeds, "in your judgment of Switzerland as the true Paradise of the American traveller. There is nothing to be compared with it; and, if I were to be restricted to one view in Europe, it would be that magnificent combination of the grandeur of the Creator's works with the marvellous skill and genius of man, which is exhibited in the audacious conception and wonderful execution of the road built by Napoleon over the Pass of the 'Simplon.' Waldo Emerson once told me if he were to have but one day in Europe, it should be spent in the Square of St. Marc, in Venice. To me, interesting as Venice is, making one feel all the while as if he were in a dream, the great realities of the Alps are a thousand-fold more impressive; and indeed the whole effect of my journeyings amongst those sublime exhibitions of Nature, and the myriad treasures of ancient and modern art which I have had opened to me on every hand, has been to satisfy me that my tastes are better suited to the enjoyment of the works of Him, the great Artist and Architect of the universe, than to those of the most gifted of His children, wonderful and beautiful as they are."

In less than six weeks from this date he had embarked at Liverpool, and he reached his native shore safely about the middle of November following. He felt, as he said, like a new man, and resumed his work without the interval of a day. On the 17th of November he presided at the Annual Meeting of the Boston and Providence Railroad Corporation, and made a felicitous address to the assembled stockholders, who had come together under the discouragement of a reduced dividend. Among other things, he spoke of the new Station-house, in which they were assembled, as having been pronounced by a German architect, — who, after visiting the Centennial Exposition at Philadelphia, had come from Philadelphia to Boston expressly for the purpose of inspecting it, — "the model Railway Station of the world." But his remarks were rendered especially memorable by his declaration, that he was not only entirely satisfied that the dividend had been rightly reduced, but that he desired, if any reduction of the pay-roll of the road was to be made, that his own salary should be reduced first, and the wages of the workmen last, or not at all. He struck a true chord, and kindled a responsive note all along the line. Had such an example been followed in other parts of the country, it is not impossible that some of the deplorable outbreaks of later days might happily have been averted. No wonder that, when his funeral took place a few weeks afterwards, not a few of the flowers heaped upon his coffin were the offerings of the employés of the Road, and that one of them was heard exclaiming, "I would give every dollar I have in the world for the Governor."

Before Governor Clifford embarked for Europe, he had declined appointments as United States Minister both to Russia and to Turkey, which had been successively offered to him by the Administration at Washington. He had, however, previously accepted an appointment as United States Commissioner on the Fisheries under the Arbitration Treaty with Great Britain, — now at last in session at Halifax, — and had always contemplated fulfilling that appointment.

But his work was ended, public and private. Indeed, he had hardly reached his home in New Bedford, after a brief stay in Boston where he arrived, and was but just beginning to receive from his old friends and neighbors the tokens of welcome which had awaited him, when a disease of the heart, which had given mysterious indications in former years, was now unmistakably manifested. A very few weeks sufficed to bring it to a crisis; and on the morning of the 2d of January, 1876, his death was announced.

Happily for him, and for all to whom he was so dear, he was permitted to die in his native land, under his own roof, surrounded by life-long friends and a devoted family. Not without hopes of recovery to the last, he was yet ready for the summons when it came; and no murmur ever escaped his lips at the dispensations of the kind Providence in which he had always lovingly trusted.

Cordial tributes to his career and character were paid by the Legislature of Massachusetts, then in session; by the Bar of the Southern District; by the various Associations with which he was connected; by the Overseers of the University; by the Railroad corporation over which he had presided; and by the public journals throughout the country. His funeral was attended by a great concourse of his friends and fellow-citizens at New Bedford, on the following Thursday.

Thus truly did he fulfil the idea contained in a letter written by him, just as I was embarking to return from Europe, in September, 1868: "But all our journeyings, whether on one side or both sides of the ocean, are only carrying us all to that home, which at the farthest is not distant from any one of us."

Governor Clifford's life had not been altogether unclouded. In his earlier years he had many sorrows. Any one who shall visit the stately granite Monument which has just been placed over his remains in the New Bedford cemetery, will observe at its side the humbler stones which tell of the death of four children, — two daughters and two sons, — all cut off at a very early age. On the stones which mark the graves of the little boys, are inscribed, "Edward Everett Clifford," and "Robert Winthrop Clifford."

I should hardly be pardoned, were I to omit from this cursory record of his life an extract from his touching letter of 29 August, 1843, informing me of the death of this latter child: —

"MY DEAR FRIEND, — Your heart I know will bleed for me when I announce to you that your sweet little namesake has left us for a better world. We have added another to the angel throng; and although that world is as real to me as the earth upon which I tread, and the blessed existence of my precious flock is as certain as my own, it has been an inexpressibly bitter trial to part with my only boy. I had indulged in high hopes for him, and he gave all the promise that infancy could give that his future career would justify them all. He was the sweetest tempered, the most equable and placid, of all my children; and in his beautiful expression of countenance and his finely-formed head we could not but discover the germ of a rich maturity. With his name, too, I need not say, were associations which increased and strengthened the interest and hopes with which I looked forward to his future years. It has not infrequently occurred to me that, if I should be called away from him before his education for this life's duties had been completed, your interest in him would have given him the advantage of your counsel and direction; and that, for his father's sake and his own, you would have so watched his progress as that he should bear that name through the trials and temptations of youth with honor. But alas, for my desolate hearthstone, — not alas for *him*, — he has exchanged our guidance for His who will 'lead him by the still waters' of Paradise, and 'make him to lie down in its green pastures' by the side of those dear ones who have already welcomed him to their eternal *home*."

These early sorrows, however, were abundantly compensated by the blessings of his later life; and, at his death, he left three sons, — all of them graduates of Harvard, — and two daughters, to comfort their mother, and to do honor to his own memory.

I can close this brief Memoir with nothing more appropriate

than the following passage from the tribute paid to Governor Clifford by a distinguished statesman of Virginia (the Hon. Alexander H. H. Stuart), when his death was announced at the Annual Meeting of the Peabody Trustees, at the White Sulphur Springs, in Virginia, last August: —

"It requires no effort of memory, on our part, to recall his manly figure and noble face. They are indelibly imprinted on our minds and hearts. Nature had so moulded his form and features as to give the world assurance of his admirable character. There was a quiet dignity and grace in every movement, and his countenance beamed with intelligence and benignity. To a mind of great power he united a heart which throbbed with generous impulses, and a happy facility of expression which gave a peculiar charm to his conversation. There was a frankness in his bearing and a genial urbanity about him, which at once commanded confidence and inspired good-will. Every one who approached him felt attracted by a species of personal magnetism, which was irresistible.

"When last autumn, in New York, I was urging that the present session of our Board should be held here, in the mountains of Virginia, one of the great pleasures which I anticipated was the opportunity which it would present of introducing Governor Clifford to my Virginia friends. I felt sure that they would share my favorable regard for him, and thus a new link of fraternity would be added to the chain of memories which unite Massachusetts and Virginia. But it has pleased an All-wise Providence to ordain that it should be otherwise; and all that I can now do is, on behalf of the people of Virginia and of the South, to tender to Massachusetts the assurance of their profound sympathy in the loss which she has sustained in the untimely death of her distinguished son!"

October, 1877.

LORD STANHOPE.

REMARKS AT A MEETING OF THE MASSACHUSETTS HISTORICAL SOCIETY, JANUARY 13, 1876.

In some introductory remarks, on resuming the chair at our October meeting, I alluded to Earl Stanhope, as the only survivor of our Honorary and Corresponding Members, elected from Old England, prior to the amendment of our Charter in 1857; and as one, also, from whom I had received many kind attentions during my late visit to Europe. I have learned, with sincere sorrow, that he died on the 24th of December last.

Few men have filled a larger space than he has done, for thirty years past, in the literary circles of England. As President of the old London Society of Antiquaries during that whole period; as an active Trustee, for many years, of the British Museum; as Chairman of the Trustees of the Historical Portrait Gallery, of which he was the original proposer; as President of the Literary Fund Society, over one of whose annual festivals, as he told me, he once invited Longfellow to preside; as one of the earliest suggesters and supporters of that Historical-Papers Commission, which is bringing to light, from year to year, so many precious memorials of the olden time, and which has lately added some new pages to the records of the old Council for New England; — in all these, and in still other relations, he has identified himself with the best interests of history, literature, and art.

Meantime, his own contributions to historical literature have been numerous and important. Many of them were published before his succession to the Earldom in 1855, and the original editions are found in our libraries under the title of Lord Mahon. His whole works can hardly be contained in less than twenty volumes. His largest and most elaborate production, in seven or eight volumes, is a History of England, from the Peace of Utrecht, in 1713, to the Peace of Versailles, in 1783; and it includes, of course, a somewhat detailed account of our own Revolutionary struggle, and of the stirring controversies which preceded it. There are, doubtless, many things in that account which would hardly be accepted on our side as entirely accurate or just; but no one can read it, I think, without being impressed with the sincerity and general fairness of the writer, nor certainly without recognizing the diligence and depth of his researches. His tribute to Washington may be recalled, as an illustration of the spirit in which it is written: —

"It has been justly remarked," says he, "that of General Washington there are fewer anecdotes to tell than perhaps of any other great man on record. So equally framed were the features of his mind, so harmonious all its proportions, that no one quality rose salient above the rest. There were none of those chequered hues, none of those warring emotions, in which biography delights. There was no contrast of lights and shades, no flickering of the flame; it was a mild light that seldom dazzled, but that ever cheered and warmed. His contemporaries or his close observers — as Mr. Jefferson and Mr. Gallatin — assert that he had naturally strong passions, but had attained complete mastery over them. In self-control, indeed, he has never been surpassed. If sometimes, on rare occasions, and on strong provocation, there was wrung from him a burst of anger, it was almost instantly quelled by the dominion of his will. He decided surely, though he deliberated slowly; nor could any urgency or peril move him from his serene composure, his calm, clear-headed, good sense. Integrity and truth were also ever present in his mind. Not a single instance, as I believe, can be found in his whole career where he was impelled by any but an upright motive, or endeavored to attain an object by any but worthy means. Such are some of the high qualities which have justly earned for General Washington the admiration even of the country he opposed, and not merely the admiration, but the gratitude and affection of his own. Such was the pure and upright spirit, to which, when its toils were over and its earthly course had been run, was offered the unanimous homage of the assembled Congress, all clad in deep mourning for their common loss, as to 'the man first in war, first in peace, and first in the hearts of his fellow-citizens.' At this day in the United States the reverence for his character is, as it should be, deep and universal, and not confined, as with nearly all our English statesmen, to one party, one province, or one creed."

Before publishing this History of England, in successive volumes, between 1837 and 1852, Lord Stanhope had written a Life of Belisarius, a Life of the Great Condé, a History of the War of the Succession in Spain, an account of the Court of Spain in the time of Charles II., and a volume of Historical Essays; besides editing the Letters of his distant kinsman, the celebrated Earl of Chesterfield, whose admirable portrait by Gainsborough was among the treasures of Chevening, his seat in Kent, — where, too, I saw the splendid Sir Joshua of Lord Chatham.

Since the History of England was published, he has written a Life of his illustrious relative, the younger William Pitt, in four volumes, and a History of the Reign of Queen Anne, in one volume.[1] This last work was undertaken in order to bridge over the gap between the unfinished History of England, by his friend Lord Macaulay, and his own History from the Peace of Utrecht. Amid all this labor, he was, also, a frequent contributor to the "Quarterly Review" and other periodicals, and published at least two little volumes of Miscellanies, in one of which there is an interesting correspondence between him and our late associate, Mr. Ticknor.

Lord Stanhope was a statesman as well as an historian. He was for twenty years or more a member of the House of Commons, during the life of his father. He was Under-Secretary of State for Foreign Affairs, while the great Duke of Wellington was Secretary; and, during a part of the ministry of Sir Robert Peel, he was Secretary of the Board of Control.

It was a striking tribute to the confidence which Lord Stanhope's character had inspired, that both the Duke of Wellington and Sir Robert Peel made him one of their literary executors. He was one of the editors of Peel's Papers, and it seems to be

[1] Two volumes, 12mo.

understood that a posthumous publication of his will furnish new illustration of the Duke's career.

From the time of his succession to the Earldom, Lord Stanhope has been a diligent attendant on the House of Peers, and from time to time has participated in important debates. He made no pretensions, however, to the fame of an orator; nor had his style, either as a speaker or writer, any thing of the brilliant flow and glow of Macaulay, or of the rugged strength and raciness of Carlyle. But his language is precise and clear; his narrative lively and entertaining; and his works will always be consulted and read for their substantial merits, and as valuable authorities on the subjects to which they relate. He was a laborious student, a classical scholar, a devoted historian and antiquary, careful to sift as well as to search, indulging in few speculations, and never perverting the materials he had gathered to the support of any previously conceived theories. He earnestly sought truth, and independently maintained the views to which his researches and convictions led him.

In 1872, Earl Stanhope was elected one of the six foreign associates of the French Academy of Moral and Political Sciences, in the place of the late Mr. Grote, — a distinction which no American, except Edward Livingston, has ever yet enjoyed.[1]

It is interesting to-day, as we make mention of his labors and announce their close, to recall the circumstances under which Lord Stanhope's name was placed on our own roll. There had been a painful controversy between him and the late excellent Jared Sparks. Explanations had abundantly intervened; and if all misunderstandings were not cleared up, and all differences reconciled, there was at least that respectful recognition of each other's claims and character, which left no room for personal asperity or animosity. President Sparks soon afterwards came to one of our meetings, and, with many kind and complimentary remarks, presented the name of Lord Stanhope for the highest honor we could pay him. It was a charming exhibition of the

[1] This distinction was subsequently enjoyed by our lamented associate, Mr. Motley; and, since his death, has been awarded to Mr. R. W. Emerson, another of the resident members of our Society.

spirit in which "the quarrels of authors" should end. The name of Dr. Sparks, not long before, had been added to the honorary roll of the Society of Antiquaries, under the auspices of Lord Stanhope.

The last two years of Earl Stanhope's life had been darkened by the death of his wife, a lady of great attractions, endeared to him and to all around her by the most amiable and brilliant qualities, the ornament of the circle in which she moved. It was my privilege to be present, last summer, on the first occasion when he received any formal company after his afflicting bereavement. It was a dinner for the Council and Directors of the Antiquaries, over whom he still presided; and it was not difficult to perceive how great an effort it cost him to seem resigned and cheerful. But from this time he systematically resumed the discharge of his duties both to Parliament and to the literary associations with which he was connected; and was even beginning, as he told me, to contemplate some new publications. But his work was ended. An attack of pneumonia proved fatal after a few days. Born at Walmer Castle on the 30th of January, 1805, he died on the 24th of December, 1875.

WILLIAM LAMBARDE.

REMARKS AT A MEETING OF THE MASSACHUSETTS HISTORICAL SOCIETY, JANUARY 13, 1876.

ONE of my last visits in England was to Seven Oaks, one of the most beautiful little towns in the lovely County of Kent. Being there on a Sunday, I attended service at the old church, and there — as almost everywhere else, indeed, in England — I found something of historical, and even of American, interest. In the chancel was a large tablet to the memory of Jeffrey, Lord Amherst, with a reference to the conquest of Canada under his lead in 1760. His country-seat, still occupied by his descendants, is quite near to the town, and is named Montreal.

But in the same church I found the original monument to William Lambarde, the old perambulator of Kent, and "the father of County Historians." This monument was the more interesting to me from the fact that we have in our library a copy of the second edition of the "Perambulation of Kent," which belonged to Adam Winthrop, the father of the first Governor, and which has many notes and comments in Adam's handwriting; some of them in prose, and some of them in verse, and all proving abundantly that Adam was thoroughly acquainted with the contents of the book, and was a personal friend of its author.

On the reverse of the title-page Adam has inscribed a Latin ode, — Carmen Sapphicum, as he calls it, — in honor of Lambarde. This I will not read, or vouch for the Latinity or the metrical accuracy of it. But on the fly-leaf I find a brief biography of Lambarde, which is not uninteresting; and it is due to the memory of this old "father of County Historians" that it should not be lost. It is as follows: —

Mr. Wm. Lambarde was ye soonne and heire of John Lambarde an Alderman, and Shryve of London, año. D. 1551. & (E. 6. 3d,) who was free of the company of the Drapers. He was first brought up in Oxforde, and afterwards a student of the cōmmon Lawes in Linconnes Inne, and there was made ā utterbarrester, & a Bencher of ye same house, and by Sr. Tho. Bromley then L. Chancelor he was put into the Cōmission of ye peace in Kent, and by the Lorde Cobham, lately L. Chamberlayne, he was much used bothe in publike, and also in his private affaires, for he was wise, learned, and religious, as appereth by this booke, and divers others wch he compiled: He builded certaine almes houses in Greenewyche, (where he died) and gave landes of a good yerely value for ever, to maintaine them. He departed out of this lyfe in the threescore and third yere of his age, the 21th day of August, año. 1601, and in the three and fortith yere of the blessed reigne of Queene Elizabeth, and lyeth buryed in Sainte Alphegs Churche, in Greenwyche. In memoriâ erit justus. Mr. Lambarde's firste wife was the daughter of Mr. Moulton; by whom he had issue three sonnes & one daughter. Their youngest sonnes were twynnes, and died after their father, in the 17 yere of their ages, whose names were Gore and Vane. Their elder brother's name is Moulton, who was knighted by Kinge James.

It seems from this account that Lambarde died and was buried in Greenwich. But I learned at Seven Oaks, and I believe it is so stated on the monument itself, that this was the very monument which had been originally placed over his remains in the church at Greenwich, but which had been removed to the church at Seven Oaks, where the family now reside, when the Greenwich church was rebuilt.

THE EVACUATION OF BOSTON.

REMARKS AT A MEETING OF THE MASSACHUSETTS HISTORICAL SOCIETY, MARCH 16, 1876.

I NEED not assure you, Gentlemen, how glad I am to welcome you all once more under my own roof. Our old Society, as every one knows, has not been unobservant of any of those great historical events which succeeded each other so closely and so marvellously a century ago. As the dates of those events have come round, we have felt bound to put into shape, upon our records, such materials as our archives might contain, or as the researches of our members might supply, for a just and worthy illustration of the great deeds of our fathers.

We meet for this purpose to-night, on the eve of a most interesting and most memorable anniversary. It is not too much to say, that, from the day when our City had "a local habitation and a name" to the present hour, there has been no event in its history of greater magnitude and moment than that which is to be publicly celebrated — for the very first time, I believe — to-morrow.

The 17th of March, 1776, might well stand second only to the 17th of September, 1630, in the illuminated calendar of Boston. Indeed, in the annals of our whole country, there is hardly a date more significant and signal. We can never do too much honor to the men of Lexington and Concord and Bunker Hill. The events, however, which made those men immortal, were, after all, but glorious defeats, on a larger or smaller scale. But here, a hundred years ago to-morrow, was a glorious success; all the more glorious that it was effected, as Washington said in his letter to the selectmen of our town, "with so little effusion of human blood." It was the first victory of the Revolution. It was the first triumph of Washington. It gave assurance to all the world, not only that Independence must soon be declared, but that the declaration, whenever made, would be maintained and vindicated. It gave, too, the desired prestige of a grand success to him, who, in the good providence of God, was destined to lead our armies so nobly in the long and trying struggle which awaited them.

In all its relations, local, national, and personal, — to Boston, to our Country, and to the Father of our Country, — the influence and importance of the event, of which to-morrow is the hundredth anniversary, cannot be over-estimated.

To Boston itself it was a day of unspeakable deliverance, — never to be forgotten, nor ever to be remembered without the most grateful acknowledgments to God and man. Dr. Ellis, in his Oration, will tell us all to-morrow how great that deliverance was; and Mr. Frothingham will, I trust, renew our remembrance this evening of some of those striking scenes of which his "Siege of Boston" is so full. But in vain would any one attempt, at this day, to give an adequate idea of the emotions which must have filled every patriot heart to overflowing when that Sabbath morning dawned, — for the 17th of March, 1776, was Sunday, — and when the great result was revealed and gradually realized, that the enemy had at last embarked, that the British fleet was under sail, and that our town and harbor were once more to be freed from military occupation and oppression.

It was the grand *finale* of the first act — a long and eventful act — of the great drama of Independence; and the scene was not slow in changing. Boston, so long the source and centre of the most stirring words and deeds of that stirring period, now passed into comparative peace and quiet, never again for a century, thank God, — never again, as we hope and believe, till time shall be no more, — to be trodden by a hostile soldiery. Her crown of martyrdom, which had so attracted the sympathy and the succor of all America, was now exchanged for a crown of triumph; and she wore it becomingly and worthily.

We do not forget to whom, under God, Boston owed that great deliverance, and to whom the Continental Congress awarded the grand Medal which commemorated it; and if it shall prove to-morrow — as it is now more than whispered — that this very Medal, after remaining in the family of the Father of his Country for a hundred years, is to find a place henceforth in our Boston Public Library, as the property of the City, it will add an interest to our Centennial Day which hardly any thing else could equal.[1]

No ingot of gold which ever came from the land of Havilah or from the mines of Ophir, or which was ever wrought into exquisite form by the most renowned artificers of Greece or Rome, could be so precious to us and our children, for a thousand generations, as the identical Medal, which was designed under the direction of John Adams and John Jay and Stephen Hopkins, under the order of Congress, and which was won and worn by George Washington for driving a foreign army out of the oppressed and suffering Boston of a hundred years ago.

But I will not anticipate what the Mayor may say publicly to-morrow, or what he may feel willing to communicate to us privately this evening. Inheriting as he does the blood of him who said "he would sit as a judge, or die as a general," I am sure he will say and do the right thing now and always.

Meantime, before calling on the Mayor, I am unwilling to conclude these few introductory remarks without reading to you a brief letter from the noble John Adams to his son the late John Quincy Adams, not then nine years old, which is full of the true feeling for to-morrow, and which ought to be read in all our schools on every returning seventeenth day of March:

PHILADELPHIA, 18 April, 1776.

I thank you for your agreeable letter of the 24th March. I rejoice with you that our friends are once more in possession of the town of Boston; am glad to hear that so little damage is done to our house.

I hope you and your sister and brothers will take proper notice of these great events, and remember under whose wise and kind Providence

[1] See Note on next page.

they are all conducted. Not a sparrow falls, nor a hair is lost, but by the direction of Infinite Wisdom. Much less are cities conquered and evacuated. I hope that you will all remember how many losses, dangers, and inconveniences have been borne by your parents, and the inhabitants of Boston in general, for the sake of preserving freedom for you and yours; and I hope you will all follow the virtuous example, if, in any future time, your country's liberties shall be in danger, and suffer any human evil rather than give them up.

NOTE.

City of Boston.

Resolved, That the thanks of the City Council be presented to the Hon. Robert C. Winthrop and his associates for their active interest and successful effort in procuring and presenting to the City of Boston the valuable Medal which was given to General Washington, in commemoration of his distinguished services in compelling the evacuation of the town of Boston by the British army in 1776.

Resolved, That the Members of the City Council are especially gratified that this precious memorial of Washington is henceforth to abide in this City, whose relief from peril was the occasion of its emission one hundred years ago.

Approved, March 28, 1876. Saml. C. Cobb, *Mayor*.

THE SANDERS THEATRE.

SPEECH AT THE DINNER OF THE ALUMNI OF HARVARD UNIVERSITY, JUNE 28, 1876.

I AM greatly obliged and honored, Mr. President, by the kind words with which you have introduced me once more to the Association of the Alumni. I have so rarely been in the way of attending their festivals of late years, that I feel myself quite in need of a fresh introduction of some sort, whenever I come here. Indeed, my relations to my Alma Mater have become in more than one sense quite pre-historic, — my only official tie being as Chairman of the Trustees of that Archæological and Ethnological Museum, which, under the direction of the late lamented Jeffries Wyman, has grown to be so interesting an addition to the scientific department of the University, and so worthy a memorial of its beneficent founder, Mr. Peabody. Before another year shall have passed away, I trust that, with the assistance of Colonel Lyman and Professor Alexander Agassiz, we shall have completed the Museum Building, which we are just commencing, and be in a condition to display the treasures we have collected in a manner more commensurate with their interest and their importance.

I thank you, sir, for associating my name so pleasantly with that venerable ancestor, under whose auspices, as Governor of the Massachusetts Colony, the very first appropriation was made for the establishment of this College, two years before the legacy of John Harvard. It has sometimes been doubted, I am aware, whether the infant Colony ever paid that appropriation. If not, it is certainly quite time that it was paid, and paid with compound interest; and I venture to commend the subject to the special attention and favor of my friend, Governor Rice, upon whom the honors of the University have just been so worthily bestowed. Meantime, however, it may well be questioned whether John Harvard would have been likely to bequeath the whole of his little fortune to the institution, if he himself had not understood it to have been previously established and endowed by the State.

But let me turn at once, and abruptly, to another topic, — the only topic which would have brought me here to-day. It was not my good fortune to be on this side of the Atlantic when this noble Memorial Hall was dedicated. It was about the time, Mr. President, when you and I were witnesses to each other's honors, so well merited on your part,[1] from the venerable mother of our Alma Mater — perhaps I might call her our venerable grandmother — Cambridge University, in Old England.

This, then, is my very first view of the interior of this Hall, and I may be pardoned for expressing something of enthusiastic admiration for its stately proportions and arrangements. Old Cambridge herself would hardly be ashamed of it, — nay, she might well be proud of it. But to-day we have entered on the occupation of a new portion of the massive edifice, and it is in relation to that Theatre, or rather to him whose name it so deservedly bears, that I feel a peculiar obligation to say a few words without delay.

It is now nineteen years since it was my privilege, as President of this Alumni Association, to occupy at one of our annual festivals the chair which you now so worthily fill. The Appleton Chapel was then just completed, and about to be opened for its sacred uses. The Plummer Professor, or Preacher to the University, of that day — the predecessor of my esteemed friend, Dr. Peabody — was the Rev. Dr. Huntington, now the Bishop of Central New York. A few weeks only before our festival, he had written to me to express a strong wish that steps might be taken by this Alumni Association for securing a hall for the secular festivals of the College, so that the new Chapel might be reserved

[1] Prof. James Russell Lowell was in the chair.

exclusively for religious services. This communication from Dr. Huntington, by something more than a happy chance, concurred precisely with a previous purpose of my own; and in my opening remarks at the dinner-table on the 16th of July, 1857, I ventured to urge upon this Association to undertake the work of erecting a commodious and spacious hall, — like the Senate House at Old Cambridge, or the Theatre at Oxford, — where, to use my own words from the speech printed at the time, "the exhibitions and class days and commencements of the University might find worthy accommodations; where the living Alumni might hold their anniversary festivals; and where, perhaps, the memorials of the distinguished dead might find a fit gallery for their display."[1]

These remarks were in the newspapers of the following morning; and, within forty-eight hours after they were printed, I received a confidential letter from the late venerable Charles Sanders, expressing his warm interest in the proposal, and offering an immediate subscription of $5000, on certain conditions, for the prosecution of the enterprise. I did what I could, by articles in the public journals, by personal applications, and by subsequent appeals to the Association, to obtain seconders and followers of this generous lead; but without success. In the meantime, however, in replying to Mr. Sanders, and in repeated letters to him, I ventured to express the earnest hope that he would not abandon the design, but that he would make such provisions for carrying it out as would not be dependent on his own life.

I hold in my hand a letter from him, dated Sept. 18, 1857, in which he says, "In regard to the Alumni Theatre I do not despair, although I have not met with much success in my applications to two old friends." He adds, "I will, however, venture a prediction that it will be accomplished within a few years." We all know what has followed. We all know how noble a provision he made in his life-time and by his will, and to-day we are rejoicing that his prediction has at length been verified, and verified by his own means. There is no prophecy so safe and sure as that of a man who is able and willing and

[1] Winthrop's Addresses and Speeches, Vol. II. p. 359.

resolved to fulfil his own prediction. And though the Sanders Theatre has been the last portion of this grand edifice to be finished, it may safely be said — and in justice to his memory it ought to be said, and all the early reports and consultations of the Committee of Fifty, of which I had the honor to be a member, will bear me out in saying — that the provision of Mr. Sanders gave the direction and encouragement to the whole work of that committee; that the noble Memorial Hall in which we are assembled would hardly have been undertaken without it, but that some other and less costly mode of commemorating the gallant sons of Harvard who had fallen in the war would have taken its place.

It is thus to Charles Sanders, more than to any other man or men, that the University and its Alumni are indebted for these noble Halls. And as it was to myself that Mr. Sanders first communicated his purpose, — in response to a fortunate suggestion of Bishop Huntington and my own, — I have felt it incumbent on me not to let this occasion pass without publicly recalling these facts, and manifesting my own grateful remembrance of his noble endowment.

He was a member of that old Class of 1802, which included on its rolls the admirable Governor Levi Lincoln, the genial and noble-hearted Leverett Saltonstall, the late venerable William Minot, and good Samuel Hoar, whose name was the synonyme of personal, professional, and political integrity, — a Class whose meetings, when I was a young man, were almost as famous as those of the Class of 1829 now are. There is not one of them left. But that Class of 1802 will have no more enduring distinction than in the large public and permanent charities established by Charles Sanders, and in this University Theatre which now bears his name.

As I turned to his name in the triennial catalogue not long ago, I saw that it had no designation but that of simple *Mr.*; and I could not help thinking how fit it would be to introduce into our triennial, after his name — and after many other names, also — a new addendum, — some Latin phrase, which Professor Lane or Professor Everett would easily improvise, — to designate a great benefactor of the College. We are careful in noting the professional and literary and political dignities and degrees which our graduates have acquired. But if to the name of Edward Bromfield Phillips were added, "Principal Contributor to the Astronomical Observatory," and to Christopher Gore's name, "Builder of the Library," and to Charles Sanders's name, "Founder of the University Theatre," and so on with other names which will readily occur to us all, — we should not only render an act of justice to our benefactors, but we should do something to create a not unworthy ambition and emulation in that line of beneficence upon which we so much depend. I leave all this, however, to our excellent President and our venerable Librarian, Mr. Sibley, and will only trespass longer on your time by asking you all to rise with me while I propose

"The Memory of Charles Sanders."

CENTENNIAL ORATION.

DELIVERED BEFORE THE CITY COUNCIL AND CITIZENS OF BOSTON, JULY 4, 1876.

Again and again, Mr. Mayor and Fellow Citizens, in years gone by, considerations or circumstances of some sort, public or private, — I know not what, — have prevented my acceptance of most kind and flattering invitations to deliver the Oration in this my native city on the Fourth of July. On one of those occasions, long, long ago, I am said to have playfully replied to the Mayor of that period, that, if I lived to witness this Centennial Anniversary, I would not refuse any service which might be required of me. That pledge has been recalled by others, if not remembered by myself, and by the grace of God I am here to-day to fulfil it. I have come at last, in obedience to your call, to add my name to the distinguished roll of those who have discharged this service in unbroken succession since the year 1783, when the date of a glorious act of patriots was substituted for that of a dastardly deed of hirelings, — the 4th of July for the 5th of March, — as a day of annual celebration by the people of Boston.

In rising to redeem the promise thus inconsiderately given, I may be pardoned for not forgetting, at the outset, who presided over the Executive Council of Massachusetts when the Declaration, which has just been read, was first formally and solemnly proclaimed to the people, from the balcony of yonder Old State House, on the 18th of July, 1776;[1] and whose privilege it was,

[1] James Bowdoin.

amid the shoutings of the assembled multitude, the ringing of the bells, the salutes of the surrounding forts, and the firing of thirteen volleys from thirteen successive divisions of the Continental regiments, drawn up "in correspondence with the number of the American States United," to invoke "Stability and Perpetuity to American Independence! God save our American States!"

That invocation was not in vain. That wish, that prayer, has been graciously granted. We are here this day to thank God for it. We do thank God for it with all our hearts, and ascribe to Him all the glory. And it would be unnatural if I did not feel a more than common satisfaction, that the privilege of giving expression to your emotions of joy and gratitude, at this hour, should have been assigned to the oldest living descendant of him by whom that invocation was uttered, and that prayer breathed up to Heaven.

And if, indeed, in addition to this, — as you, Mr. Mayor, so kindly urged in originally inviting me, — the name I bear may serve in any sort as a link between the earliest settlement of New England, two centuries and a half ago, and the grand culmination of that settlement in this Centennial Epoch of American Independence, all the less may I be at liberty to express any thing of the compunction or regret, which I cannot but sincerely feel, that so responsible and difficult a task had not been imposed upon some more sufficient, or certainly upon some younger, man.

Yet what can I say? What can any one say, here or elsewhere, to-day, which shall either satisfy the expectations of others, or meet his own sense of the demands of such an occasion? For myself, certainly, the longer I have contemplated it, — the more deeply I have reflected on it, — so much the more hopeless I have become of finding myself able to give any adequate expression to its full significance, its real sublimity and grandeur. A hundred-fold more than when John Adams wrote to his wife it would be so for ever, it is an occasion for "shows, games, sports, guns, bells, bonfires, and illuminations, from one end of the continent to the other." Ovations, rather than orations, are the order of such a day as this. Emotions like those which ought to fill, and which do fill, all our hearts, call for the swelling tones of a multitude, the cheers of a mighty crowd, and refuse to be uttered by any single human voice. The strongest phrases seem feeble and powerless; the best results of historical research have the dryness of chaff and husks, and the richest flowers of rhetoric the drowsiness of "poppy or mandragora," in presence of the simplest statement of the grand consummation we are here to celebrate: — A Century of Self-Government Completed! A hundred years of Free Republican Institutions realized and rounded out! An era of Popular Liberty, continued and prolonged from generation to generation, until to-day it assumes its full proportions, and asserts its rightful place, among the Ages!

It is a theme from which an Everett, a Choate, or even a Webster, might have shrunk. But those voices, alas! were long ago hushed. It is a theme on which any one, living or dead, might have been glad to follow the precedent of those few incomparable sentences at Gettysburg, on the 19th of November, 1863, and forbear from all attempt at extended discourse. It is not for me, however, to copy that unique original, — nor yet to shelter myself under an example, which I should in vain aspire to equal.

And, indeed, Fellow Citizens, some formal words must be spoken here to-day, — trite, familiar, commonplace words, though they may be; — some words of commemoration; some words of congratulation; some words of glory to God, and of acknowledgment to man; some grateful lookings back; some hopeful, trustful, lookings forward, — these, I am sensible, cannot be spared from our great assembly on this Centennial Day. You would not pardon me for omitting them.

But where shall I begin? To what specific subject shall I turn for refuge from the thousand thoughts which come crowding to one's mind and rushing to one's lips, all jealous of postponement, all clamoring for utterance before our Festival shall close, and before this Centennial sun shall set?

The single, simple Act which has made the Fourth of July memorable for ever, — the mere scene of the Declaration, — would of itself and alone supply an ample subject for far more than the little hour which I may dare to occupy; and, though it has been described a hundred times before, in histories and addresses, and in countless magazines and journals, it imperatively demands something more than a cursory allusion here to-day, and challenges our attention as it never did before, and hardly ever can challenge it again.

Go back with me, then, for a few moments at least, to that great year of our Lord, and that great day of American Liberty. Transport yourselves with me, in imagination, to Philadelphia. It will require but little effort for any of us to do so, for all our hearts are there already. Yes, we are all there,—from the Atlantic to the Pacific, from the Lakes to the Gulf,—we are all there, at this high noon of our Nation's birthday, in that beautiful City of Brotherly Love, rejoicing in all her brilliant displays, and partaking in the full enjoyment of all her pageantry and pride. Certainly, the birthplace and the burial-place of Franklin are in cordial sympathy at this hour; and a common sentiment of congratulation and joy, leaping and vibrating from heart to heart, outstrips even the magic swiftness of magnetic wires. There are no chords of such elastic reach and such electric power as the heartstrings of a mighty Nation, touched and tuned, as all our heartstrings are to-day, to the sense of a common glory,—throbbing and thrilling with a common exultation.

Go with me, then, I say, to Philadelphia;—not to Philadelphia, indeed, as she is at this moment, with all her bravery on, with all her beautiful garments around her, with all the graceful and generous contributions which so many other Cities and other States and other Nations have sent for her adornment,—not forgetting those most graceful, most welcome, most touching contributions, in view of the precise character of the occasion, from Old England herself;—but go with me to Philadelphia, as she was just a hundred years ago. Enter with me her noble Independence Hall, so happily restored and consecrated afresh as the Runnymede of our Nation; and, as we enter it, let us not forget to be grateful that no demands of public convenience or expediency have called for the demolition of that old State House of Pennsylvania. Observe and watch the movements, listen attentively to the words, look steadfastly at the countenances, of the men who compose the little Congress assembled there. Braver, wiser, nobler men have never been gathered and grouped under a single roof, before or since, in any age, on any soil beneath the sun. What are they doing? What are they daring? Who are they, thus to do, and thus to dare?

Single out with me, as you easily will at the first glance, by a presence and a stature not easily overlooked or mistaken, the young, ardent, accomplished Jefferson. He is only just thirty-three years of age. Charming in conversation, ready and full in counsel, he is "slow of tongue," like the great Lawgiver of the Israelites, for any public discussion or formal discourse. But he has brought with him the reputation of wielding what John Adams well called "a masterly pen." And grandly has he justified that reputation. Grandly has he employed that pen already, in drafting a Paper which is at this moment lying on the table, and awaiting its final signature and sanction.

Three weeks before, indeed, — on the previous 7th of June, — his own noble colleague, Richard Henry Lee, had moved the Resolution, whose adoption, on the 2d of July, had virtually settled the whole question. Nothing, certainly, more explicit or emphatic could have been wanted for that Congress itself than that Resolution, setting forth as it did, in language of striking simplicity and brevity and dignity, "That these United Colonies are, and, of right, ought to be, Free and Independent States; that they are absolved from all allegiance to the British crown, and that all political connection between them and the State of Great Britain is, and ought to be, totally dissolved."

That Resolution was, indeed, not only comprehensive and conclusive enough for the Congress which adopted it, but, I need not say, it is comprehensive and conclusive enough for us; and I heartily wish, that, in the century to come, its reading might be substituted for that of the longer Declaration which has put the patience of our audiences to so severe a test for so many years past, — though, happily, not to-day.

But the form in which that Resolution was to be announced and proclaimed to the people of the Colonies, and the reasons by which it was to be justified before the world, were at that time of intense interest and of momentous importance. No graver responsibility was ever devolved upon a young man of thirty-three, if, indeed, upon any man of any age, than that of preparing such a Paper. As often as I have examined the original draft of that Paper, still extant in the Archives of the State Department at Washington, and have observed how very few changes were made, or even suggested, by the illustrious men associated with its author on the committee for its preparation, it has seemed to me to be as marvellous a composition, of its kind and for its purpose, as the annals of mankind can show. The earliest honors of this day, certainly, may well be paid, here and throughout the country, to the young Virginian of "the masterly pen."

And here, by the favor of a highly valued friend and fellow-citizen, to whom it was given by Jefferson himself a few months only before his death, I am privileged to hold in my hands, and to lift up to the eager gaze of you all, a most compact and convenient little mahogany case, which bears this autograph inscription on its face, dated "Monticello, November 18, 1825:" —

"Thomas Jefferson gives this Writing Desk to Joseph Coolidge, Junr. as a memorial of his affection. It was made from a drawing of his own, by Ben Randall, Cabinet-maker of Philadelphia, with whom he first lodged on his arrival in that City in May, 1776, and is the identical one on which he wrote the Declaration of Independence."

"Politics, as well as Religion," the inscription proceeds to say, "has its superstitions. These, gaining strength with time, may, one day, give imaginary value to this relic, for its association with the birth of the Great Charter of our Independence."

Superstitions! Imaginary value! Not for an instant can we admit such ideas. The modesty of the writer has betrayed even "the masterly pen." There is no imaginary value to this relic, and no superstition is required to render it as precious and priceless a piece of wood, as the secular cabinets of the world have ever possessed, or ever claimed to possess. No cabinet-maker on earth will have a more enduring name than this inscription has secured to "Ben Randall, of Philadelphia." No pen will have a wider or more lasting fame than his who wrote the inscription. The very table at Runnymede, which some of us have seen, on which the Magna Charta of England is said to have been signed or sealed five centuries and a half before, — even were it authenticated by the genuine autographs of every one of those brave old Barons, with Stephen Langton at their head, — who extorted its grand pledges and promises from King John, — so soon to be violated, — could hardly exceed, could hardly equal, in interest and value, this little mahogany desk. What momentous issues for our country, and for mankind, were locked up in this narrow drawer, as night after night the rough notes of preparation for the Great Paper were laid aside for the revision of the morning! To what anxious thoughts, to what careful study of words and phrases, to what cautious weighing of statements and arguments, to what deep and almost overwhelming impressions of responsibility, it must have been a witness! Long may it find its appropriate and appreciating ownership in the successive generations of a family, in which the blood of Virginia and Massachusetts is so auspiciously commingled! Should it, in the lapse of years, ever pass from the hands of those to whom it will be so precious an heirloom, it could only have its fit and final place among the choicest and most cherished treasures of the Nation, with whose Title Deeds of Independence it is so proudly associated!

But the young Jefferson is not alone from Virginia, on the day we are celebrating, in the Hall which we have entered as imaginary spectators of the scene. His venerated friend and old legal preceptor, — George Wythe, — is, indeed, temporarily absent from his side; and even Richard Henry Lee, the original mover of the measure, and upon whom it might have devolved to draw up the Declaration, has been called home by dangerous illness in his family, and is not there to help him. But "the gay, good-humored" Francis Lightfoot Lee, a younger brother, is there. Benjamin Harrison, the father of our late President Harrison, is there, and has just reported the Declaration from the Committee of the Whole, of which he was Chairman. The "mild and philanthropic" Carter Braxton is there, in the place of the lamented Peyton Randolph, the first President of the Continental Congress, who had died, to the sorrow of the whole country, six or seven months before. And the noble-hearted Thomas Nelson is there, — the largest subscriber to the generous relief sent from Virginia to Boston during the sore distress occasioned by the shutting up of our Port, and who was the mover of those Instructions in the Convention of Virginia, passed on the 15th of May, under which Richard Henry Lee offered the original Resolution of Independence, on the 7th of June.

I am particular, Fellow Citizens, in giving to the Old Dominion the foremost place in this rapid survey of the Fourth of July, 1776, and in naming every one of her delegates who participated in that day's doings; for it is hardly too much to say, that the destinies of our country, at that period, hung and hinged upon her action, and upon the action of her great and glorious sons. Without Virginia, as we must all acknowledge, — without her Patrick Henry among the people, her Lees and Jefferson in the forum, and her Washington in the field, — I will not say, that the cause of American Liberty and American Independence must have been ultimately defeated, — no, no; there was no ultimate defeat for that cause in the decrees of the Most High! — but it must have been delayed, postponed, perplexed, and to many eyes and many hearts rendered seemingly hopeless. It was Union which assured our Independence, and there could have been no Union without the influence and coöperation of that great leading Southern Colony. To-day, then, as we look back over the wide gulf of a century, we are ready and glad to forget every thing of alienation, every thing of contention and estrangement which has intervened, and to hail her once more, as our Fathers in Faneuil Hall hailed her, in 1775, as "our noble, patriotic sister Colony, Virginia."

I may not attempt, on this occasion, to speak with equal particularity of all the other delegates whom we see assembled in that immortal Congress. Their names are all inscribed where they can never be obliterated, never be forgotten. Yet some others of them so challenge our attention and rivet our gaze, as we look in upon that old time-honored Hall, that I cannot pass to other topics without a brief allusion to them.

Who can overlook or mistake the sturdy front of Roger Sherman, whom we are proud to recall as a native of Massachusetts, though now a delegate from Connecticut, — that "Old Puritan," as John Adams well said, "as honest as an angel, and as firm in the cause of American Independence as Mount Atlas," — represented most worthily to-day by the distinguished Orator of the Centennial at Philadelphia, as well as by more than one distinguished grandson in our own State?

Who can overlook or mistake the stalwart figure of Samuel Chase, of Maryland, "of ardent passions, of strong mind, of domineering temper, of a turbulent and boisterous life," who had helped to burn in effigy the Maryland Stamp Distributor eleven years before, and who, we are told by one who knew what he was saying, "must ever be conspicuous in the catalogue of that Congress"?

His milder and more amiable colleague, Charles Carroll, was engaged at that moment in pressing the cause of Independence on the hesitating Convention of Maryland, at Annapolis; and though, as we shall see, he signed the Declaration on the 2d of August, and outlived all his compeers on that roll of glory, he is missing from the illustrious band as we look in upon them this morning. I cannot but remember that it was my privilege to see and know that venerable person in my early manhood. Entering his drawing-room, nearly five-and-forty years ago, I found him reposing on a sofa and covered with a shawl, and was not even aware of his presence, so shrunk and shrivelled by the lapse of years was his originally feeble frame. *Quot libras in duce summo!* But the little heap on the sofa was soon seen stirring, and, rousing himself from his midday nap, he rose and greeted me with a courtesy and a grace which I can never forget. In the ninety-fifth year of his age, as he was, and within a few months of his death, it is not surprising that there should be little for me to recall of that interview, save his eager inquiries about James Madison, whom I had just visited at Montpelier, and his affectionate allusions to John Adams, who had gone before him; and save, too, the exceeding satisfaction for myself of having seen and pressed the hand of the last surviving signer of the Declaration.

But Cæsar Rodney, who had gone home on the same patriotic errand which had called Carroll to Maryland, had happily returned in season, and had come in, two days before, "in his boots and spurs," to give the casting vote for Delaware in favor of Independence.

And there is Arthur Middleton, of South Carolina, the bosom friend of our own Hancock, and who is associated with him under the same roof in those elegant hospitalities which helped to make men know and understand and trust each other. And with him you may see and almost hear the eloquent Edward Rutledge, who not long before had united with John Adams and Richard Henry Lee in urging on the several Colonies the great measure of establishing permanent governments at once for themselves, — a decisive step which we may not forget that South Carolina was among the very earliest in taking. She took it, however, with a reservation, and her delegates were not quite ready to vote for Independence, when it was first proposed.

But Richard Stockton, of New Jersey, must not be unmarked or unmentioned in our rapid survey, more especially as it is matter of record that his original doubts about the measure, which he is now bravely supporting, had been dissipated and dispelled "by the irresistible and conclusive arguments of John Adams."

And who requires to be reminded that our "Great Bostonian," Benjamin Franklin, is at his post to-day, representing his adopted Colony with less support than he could wish, — for Pennsylvania, as well as New York, was sadly divided, and at times almost paralyzed by her divisions, — but with patriotism and firmness and prudence and sagacity and philosophy and wit and common-sense and courage enough to constitute a whole delegation, and to represent a whole Colony, by himself! He is the last man of that whole glorious group of Fifty, — or it may have been one or two more, or one or two less, than fifty, — who requires to be pointed out, in order to be the observed of all observers.

But I must not stop here. It is fit, above all other things, that, while we do justice to the great actors in this scene from other Colonies, we should not overlook the delegates from our own Colony. It is fit, above all things, that we should recall something more than the names of the men who represented

Massachusetts in that great Assembly, and who boldly affixed their signatures, in her behalf, to that immortal Instrument.

Was there ever a more signal distinction vouchsafed to mortal man, than that which was won and worn by John Hancock a hundred years ago to-day? Not altogether a great man; not without some grave defects of character; — we remember nothing at this hour save his Presidency of the Congress of the Declaration, and his bold and noble signature to our Magna Charta. Behold him in the chair which is still standing in its old place, — the very same chair in which Washington was to sit, eleven years later, as President of the Convention which framed the Constitution of the United States; the very same chair, emblazoned on the back of which Franklin was to descry "a rising, and not a setting sun," when that Constitution had been finally adopted, — behold him, the young Boston merchant, not yet quite forty years of age, not only with a princely fortune at stake, but with a price at that moment on his own head, sitting there to-day in all the calm composure and dignity which so peculiarly characterized him, and which nothing seemed able to relax or ruffle. He had chanced to come on to the Congress during the previous year, just as Peyton Randolph had been compelled to relinquish his seat and go home, — returning only to die; and, having been unexpectedly elected as his successor, he hesitated about taking the seat. But grand old Benjamin Harrison, of Virginia, we are told, was standing beside him, and with the ready good humor that loved a joke even in the Senate House, he seized the modest candidate in his athletic arms, and placed him in the presidential chair; then, turning to some of the members around, he exclaimed: "We will show Mother Britain how little we care for her, by making a Massachusetts man our President, whom she has excluded from pardon by a public proclamation."

Behold him! He has risen for a moment. He has put the question. The Declaration is adopted. It is already late in the evening, and all formal promulgation of the day's doings must be postponed. After a grace of three days, the air will be vibrating with the joyous tones of the Old Bell in the cupola over his head, proclaiming Liberty to all mankind, and with the responding acclamations of assembled multitudes. Meantime, for him, however, a simple but solemn duty remains to be discharged. The Paper is before him. You may see the very table on which it was laid, and the very inkstand which awaits his use. No hesitation now. He dips his pen, and with an untrembling hand proceeds to execute a signature, which would seem to have been studied in the schools, and practised in the counting-room, and shaped and modelled day by day in the correspondence of mercantile and political manhood, until it should be meet for the authentication of some immortal act; and which, as Webster grandly said, has made his name as imperishable, "as if it were written between Orion and the Pleiades."

Under that signature, with only the attestation of a secretary, the Declaration goes forth to the American people, to be printed in their journals, to be proclaimed in their streets, to be published from their pulpits, to be read at the head of their armies, to be incorporated for ever into their history. The British forces, driven away from Boston, are now landing on Staten Island, and the reverses of Long Island are just awaiting us. They were met by the promulgation of this act of offence and defiance to all royal authority. But there was no individual responsibility for that act, save in the signature of John Hancock, President, and Charles Thomson, Secretary. Not until the 2d of August was our young Boston merchant relieved from the perilous, the appalling grandeur of standing sole sponsor for the revolt of Thirteen Colonies and Three Millions of people. Sixteen or seventeen years before, as a very young man, he had made a visit to London, and was present at the burial of George II., and at the coronation of George III. He is now not only the witness but the instrument, and in some sort the impersonation, of a far more substantial change of dynasty on his own soil, the burial of royalty under any and every title, and the coronation of a Sovereign, whose sceptre has already endured for a century, and whose sway has already embraced three times thirteen States, and more than thirteen times three millions of people!

Ah, if his quaint, picturesque, charming old mansion-house, so long the gem of Beacon Street, could have stood till this day, our Centennial decorations and illuminations might haply have so marked, and sanctified, and glorified it, that the rage of reconstruction would have passed over it still longer, and spared it for the reverent gaze of other generations. But his own name and fame are secure; and, whatever may have been the foibles or faults of his later years, to-day we will remember that momentous and matchless signature, and him who made it, with nothing but respect, admiration, and gratitude.

But Hancock, as I need not remind you, was not the only proscribed patriot who represented Massachusetts at Philadelphia on the day we are commemorating. His associate in General Gage's memorable exception from pardon is close at his side. He who, as a Harvard College student, in 1743, had maintained the affirmative of the Thesis, "Whether it be lawful to resist the Supreme Magistrate, if the Commonwealth cannot otherwise be preserved," and who during those whole three-and-thirty years since had been training up himself and training up his fellow countrymen in the nurture and admonition of the Lord and of Liberty; — he who had replied to Gage's recommendation to him to make his peace with the King, "I trust I have long since made my peace with the King of kings, and no personal considerations shall induce me to abandon the righteous cause of my country;" — he who had drawn up the Boston Instructions to her Representatives in the General Court, adopted at Faneuil Hall, on the 24th of May, 1764, — the earliest protest against the Stamp Act, and one of the grandest papers of our whole Revolutionary period; — he who had instituted and organized those Committees of Correspondence, without which we could have had no united counsels, no concerted action, no union, no success; — he who, after the massacre of March 5, 1770, had demanded so heroically the removal from Boston of the British regiments, ever afterwards known as "Sam. Adams's regiments," — telling the Governor to his face, with an emphasis and an eloquence which were hardly ever exceeded since Demosthenes stood on the Bema, or Paul on Mars Hill, "If the Lieutenant-governor, or Colonel Dalrymple, or both together, have authority to remove one regiment, they have authority to remove two; and nothing short of the total evacuation of the Town, by all the regular troops, will satisfy the public mind or preserve the peace of the Province;" — he, "the Palinurus of the American Revolution," as Jefferson once called him, but — thank Heaven! — a Palinurus who was never put to sleep at the helm, never thrown into the sea, but who is still watching the compass and the stars, and steering the ship as she enters at last the haven he has so long yearned for: — the veteran Samuel Adams, — the disinterested, inflexible, incorruptible statesman, — is second to no one in that whole Congress, hardly second to any one in the whole thirteen Colonies, in his claim to the honors and grateful acknowledgments of this hour. We have just gladly hailed his statue on its way to the capitol.

Nor must the name of Robert Treat Paine be forgotten among the five delegates of Massachusetts in that Hall of Independence, a hundred years ago to-day; — an able lawyer, a learned judge, a just man; connected by marriage, if I mistake not, Mr. Mayor, with your own gallant grandfather, General Cobb, and who himself inherited the blood and illustrated the virtues of the hero and statesman whose name he bore, — Robert Treat, a most distinguished officer in King Philip's War, and afterwards a worthy Governor of Connecticut.

And with him, too, is Elbridge Gerry, the very youngest member of the whole Continental Congress, just thirty-two years of age, — who had been one of the chosen friends of our proto-martyr, General Joseph Warren; who was with Warren, at Watertown, the very last night before he fell at Bunker Hill, and into whose ear that heroic volunteer had whispered those memorable words of presentiment, "Dulce et decorum est pro patriâ mori;" who lived himself to serve his Commonwealth and the Nation, ardently and efficiently, at home and abroad, ever in accordance with his own patriotic injunction, — "It is the duty of every citizen, though he may have but one day to live, to devote that day to the service of his country," — and died on his way to his post as Vice-president of the United States.

One more name is still to be pronounced. One more star of that little Massachusetts cluster is still to be observed and noted.

And it is one, which, on the precise occasion we commemorate, — one, which during those great days of June and July, 1776, on which the question of Independence was immediately discussed and decided, — had hardly "a fellow in the firmament," and which was certainly "the bright, particular star" of our own constellation. You will all have anticipated me in naming John Adams. Beyond all doubt, his is the Massachusetts name most prominently associated with the immediate Day we celebrate.

Others may have been earlier or more active than he in preparing the way. Others may have labored longer and more zealously to instruct the popular mind and inflame the popular heart for the great step which was now to be taken. Others may have been more ardent, as they unquestionably were more prominent, in the various stages of the struggle against Writs of Assistance, and Stamp Acts, and Tea Taxes. But from the date of that marvellous letter of his to Nathan Webb, in 1755, when he was less than twenty years old, he seems to have forecast the destinies of this continent as few other men of any age, at that day, had done; while from the moment at which the Continental Congress took the question of Independence fairly in hand, as a question to be decided and acted on, until they had brought it to its final issue in the Declaration, his was the voice, above and before all other voices, which commanded the ears, convinced the minds, and inspired the hearts of his colleagues, and triumphantly secured the result.

I need not speak of him in other relations or in after years. His long life of varied and noble service to his country, in almost every sphere of public duty, domestic and foreign, belongs to history; and history has long ago taken it in charge. But the testimony which was borne to his grand efforts and utterances, by the author of the Declaration himself, can never be gainsaid, never be weakened, never be forgotten. That testimony, old as it is, familiar as it is, belongs to this day. John Adams will be remembered and honored for ever, in every true American heart, as the acknowledged Champion of Independence in the Continental Congress, — "coming out with a power which moved us from our seats," — "our Colossus on the floor."

And when we recall the circumstances of his death, — the year, the day, the hour, — and the last words upon his dying lips, "Independence for ever," — who can help feeling that there was some mysterious tie holding back his heroic spirit from the skies, until it should be set free amid the exulting shouts of his country's first National Jubilee!

But not his heroic spirit alone!

In this rapid survey of the men assembled at Philadelphia a hundred years ago to-day, I began with Thomas Jefferson, of Virginia, and I end with John Adams, of Massachusetts; and no one can hesitate to admit that, under God, they were the very alpha and omega of that day's doings, — the pen and the tongue, — the masterly author, and the no less masterly advocate, of the Declaration.

And now, my friends, what legend of ancient Rome or Greece or Egypt, what myth of prehistoric mythology, what story of Herodotus, or fable of Æsop, or metamorphosis of Ovid, would have seemed more fabulous and mythical, — did it rest on any remote or doubtful tradition, and had not so many of us lived to be startled and thrilled and awed by it, — than the fact, that these two men, under so many different circumstances and surroundings, of age and constitution and climate, widely distant from each other, living alike in quiet neighborhoods, remote from the smoke and stir of cities, and long before railroads or telegraphs had made any advances towards the annihilation or abridgment of space, should have been released to their rest and summoned to the skies, not only on the same day, but that day the Fourth of July, and that Fourth of July the Fiftieth Anniversary of that great Declaration which they had contended for and carried through so triumphantly side by side!

What an added emphasis Jefferson would have given to his inscription on this little desk, — "Politics, as well as Religion, has its superstitions," — could he have foreseen the close even of his own life, much more the simultaneous close of these two lives, on that Day of days! Oh, let me not admit the idea of superstition! Let me rather reverently say, as Webster said at the time, in that magnificent Eulogy which left so little for any one else to say as to the lives or deaths of Adams and Jefferson:

"As their lives themselves were the gifts of Providence, who is not willing to recognize in their happy termination, as well as in their long continuance, proofs that our country and its benefactors are objects of His care?"

And now another Fifty Years have passed away, and we are holding our high Centennial Festival; and still that most striking, most impressive, most memorable coincidence in all American history, or even in the authentic records of mankind, is without a visible monument anywhere!

In the interesting little city of Weimar, renowned as the resort and residence of more than one of the greatest philosophers and poets of Germany, many a traveller must have seen and admired the charming statues of Goethe and Schiller, standing side by side and hand in hand, on a single pedestal, and offering, as it were, the laurel wreath of literary priority or preëminence to each other. Few nobler works of art, in conception or execution, can be found on the Continent of Europe. And what could be a worthier or juster commemoration of the marvellous coincidence of which I have just spoken, and of the men who were the subjects of it, and of the Declaration with which, alike in their lives and in their deaths, they are so peculiarly and so signally associated, than just such a Monument, with the statues of Adams and Jefferson, side by side and hand in hand, upon the same base, pressing upon each other, in mutual acknowledgment and deference, the victor palm of a triumph for which they must ever be held in common and equal honor! It would be a new tie between Massachusetts and Virginia. It would be a new bond of that Union which is the safety and the glory of both. It would be a new pledge of that restored good-will between the North and South, which is the herald and harbinger of a Second Century of National Independence. It would be a fit recognition of the great Hand of God in our history!

At all events, it is one of the crying omissions and neglects which reproach us all this day, that "glorious old John Adams" is without any proportionate public monument in the State of which he was one of the very grandest citizens and sons, and in whose behalf he rendered such inestimable services to his country. It is almost ludicrous to look around and see who has been commemorated, and he neglected! He might be seen standing alone, as he knew so well how to stand alone in life. He might be seen grouped with his illustrious son, only second to himself in his claims on the omitted posthumous honors of his native State. Or, if the claim of noble women to such commemorations were ever to be recognized on our soil, he might be lovingly grouped with that incomparable wife, from whom he was so often separated by public duties and personal dangers, and whose familiar correspondence with him, and his with her, furnishes a picture of fidelity and affection, and of patriotic zeal and courage and self-sacrifice, almost without a parallel in our Revolutionary Annals.

But before all other statues, let us have those of Adams and Jefferson on a single block, as they stood together just a hundred years ago to-day, — as they were translated together just fifty years ago to-day: — foremost for Independence in their lives, and in their deaths not divided! Next, certainly, to the completion of the National Monument to Washington, at the Capital, this double statue of this "double star" of the Declaration calls for the contributions of a patriotic people. It would have something of special appropriateness as the first gift to that Boston Park, which is to date from this Centennial Period.

I have felt, Mr. Mayor and Fellow Citizens, as I am sure you all must feel, that the men who were gathered at Philadelphia a hundred years ago to-day, familiar as their names and their story may be, to ourselves and to all the world, had an imperative claim to the first and highest honors of this Centennial Anniversary. But, having paid these passing tributes to their memory, I hasten to turn to considerations less purely personal.

The Declaration has been adopted, and has been sent forth in a hundred journals, and on a thousand broadsides, to every camp and council chamber, to every town and village and hamlet and fireside, throughout the Colonies. What was it? What did it declare? What was its rightful interpretation and intention? Under what circumstances was it adopted? What did it accomplish for ourselves and for mankind?

A recent and powerful writer on "The Growth of the English

Constitution," whom I had the pleasure of meeting at the Commencement of Old Cambridge University two years ago, says most strikingly and most justly: "There are certain great political documents, each of which forms a landmark in our political history. There is the Great Charter, The Petition of Rights, the Bill of Rights." "But not one of them," he adds, "gave itself out as the enactment of any thing new. All claimed to set forth, with new strength, it might be, and with new clearness, those rights of Englishmen, which were already old." The same remark has more recently been incorporated into "A Short History of the English People." "In itself," says the writer of that admirable little volume, "the Charter was no novelty, nor did it claim to establish any new Constitutional principles. The Charter of Henry I. formed the basis of the whole; and the additions to it are, for the most part, formal recognitions of the judicial and administrative changes introduced by Henry II."

So substantially, — so, almost precisely, — it may be said of the Great American Charter, which was drawn up by Thomas Jefferson on the precious little desk which lies before me. It made no pretensions to novelty. The men of 1776 were not in any sense, certainly not in any seditious sense, greedy of novelties, — "*avidi novarum rerum.*" They had claimed nothing new. They desired nothing new. Their old original rights as Englishmen were all that they sought to enjoy, and those they resolved to vindicate. It was the invasion and denial of those old rights of Englishmen, which they resisted and revolted from.

As our excellent fellow-citizen, Mr. Dana, so well said publicly at Lexington, last year, — and as we should all have been glad to have him in the way of repeating quietly in London, this year, — "We were not the Revolutionists. The King and Parliament were the Revolutionists. They were the radical innovators. We were the conservators of existing institutions."

No one has forgotten, or can ever forget, how early and how emphatically all this was admitted by some of the grandest statesmen and orators of England herself. It was the attempt to subvert our rights as Englishmen, which roused Chatham to some of his most majestic efforts. It was the attempt to subvert our rights as Englishmen, which kindled Burke to not a few of his most brilliant utterances. It was the attempt to subvert our rights as Englishmen, which inspired Barré and Conway and Camden with appeals and arguments and phrases which will keep their memories fresh when all else associated with them is forgotten. The names of all three of them, as you well know, have long been the cherished designations of American Towns.

They all perceived and understood that we were contending for English rights, and against the violation of the great principles of English liberty. Nay, not a few of them perceived and understood that we were fighting their battles as well as our own, and that the liberties of Englishmen upon their own soil were virtually involved in our cause and in our contest.

There is a most notable letter of Josiah Quincy, Jr.'s, written from London at the end of 1774, — a few months only before that young patriot returned to die so sadly within sight of his native shores, — in which he tells his wife, to whom he was not likely to write for any mere sensational effect, that "some of the first characters for understanding, integrity, and spirit," whom he had met in London, had used language of this sort: "This Nation is lost. Corruption and the influence of the Crown have led us into bondage, and a Standing Army has riveted our chains. To America only can we look for salvation. 'Tis America only can save England. Unite and persevere. You must prevail — you must triumph." Quincy was careful not to betray names, in a letter which might be intercepted before it reached its destination. But we know the men with whom he had been brought into association by Franklin and other friends, — men like Shelburne and Hartley and Pownall and Priestley and Brand Hollis and Sir George Saville, to say nothing of Burke and Chatham. The language was not lost upon us. We did unite and persevere. We did prevail and triumph. And it is hardly too much to say that we did "save England." We saved her from herself; — saved her from being the successful instrument of overthrowing the rights of Englishmen; — saved her "from the poisoned chalice which would have been commended to her own lips;" — saved her from "the bloody instructions which would have returned to plague the inventor."

Not only was it true, as Lord Macaulay said in one of his brilliant Essays, that "England was never so rich, so great, so formidable to foreign princes, so absolutely mistress of the seas, as since the alienation of her American Colonies," but it is not less true that England came out of that contest with new and larger views of Liberty; with a broader and deeper sense of what was due to human rights; and with an experience of incalculable value to her in the management of the vast Colonial System which remained, or was in store, for her.

A vast and gigantic Colonial System, beyond doubt, it has proved to be! She was just entering, a hundred years ago, on that wonderful career of conquest in the East, which was to compensate her, — if it were a compensation, — for her impending losses in the West. Her gallant Cornwallis was soon to receive the jewelled sword of Tippoo Saib at Bangalore, in exchange for that which he was now destined to surrender to Washington at Yorktown. It is certainly not among the least striking coincidences of our Centennial Year, that at the very moment when we are celebrating the event which stripped Great Britain of thirteen Colonies and three millions of subjects, — now grown into thirty-eight States and more than forty millions of people, — she is welcoming the return of her amiable and genial Prince from a royal progress through the wide-spread regions of "Ormus and of Ind," bringing back, to lay at the foot of the British throne, the homage of nine principal Provinces and a hundred and forty-eight feudatory States, and of not less than two hundred and forty millions of people, from Ceylon to the Himalayas, and affording ample justification for the Queen's new title of Empress of India! Among all the parallelisms of modern history, there are few more striking and impressive than this.

The American Colonies never quarrelled or cavilled about the titles of their Sovereign. If, as has been said, "they went to war about a preamble," it was not about the preamble of the royal name. It was the Imperial power, the more than Imperial pretensions and usurpations, which drove them to rebellion. The Declaration was, in its own terms, a personal and most stringent arraignment of the King. It could have been nothing else. George III. was to us the sole responsible instrument of oppression. Parliament had, indeed, sustained him ; but the Colonies had never admitted the authority of a Parliament in which they had no representation. There is no passage in Mr. Jefferson's paper more carefully or more felicitously worded, than that in which he says of the Sovereign, that "he has combined *with others* to subject us to a jurisdiction foreign to our constitutions and unacknowledged by our laws, — giving his assent to *their acts of pretended legislation.*" A slip of "the masterly pen" on this point might have cost us our consistency; but that pen was on its guard, and this is the only allusion to Lords or Commons. We could recognize no one but the Monarch. We could contend with nothing less than Royalty. We could separate ourselves only from the Crown. English precedents had abundantly taught us that kings were not beyond the reach of arraignment and indictment; and arraignment and indictment were then our only means of justifying our cause to ourselves and to the world. Yes; harsh, severe, stinging, scolding, — I had almost said, — as that long series of allegations and accusations may sound, and certainly does sound, as we read it or listen to it, in cold blood, a century after the issues are all happily settled, it was a temperate and a dignified utterance under the circumstances of the case, and breathed quite enough of moderation to be relished or accepted by those who were bearing the brunt of so terrible a struggle for life and liberty and all that was dear to them, as that which those issues involved. Nor in all that bitter indictment is there a single count which does not refer to, and rest upon, some violation of the rights of Englishmen, or some violation of the rights of humanity. We stand by the Declaration to-day, and always, and disavow nothing of its reasoning or its rhetoric.

And, after all, Jefferson was not a whit more severe on the King than Chatham had been on the King's Ministers six months before, when he told them to their faces: "The whole of your political conduct has been one continued series of weakness, temerity, despotism, ignorance, futility, negligence, blundering, and the most notorious servility, incapacity, and corruption." Nor was William Pitt, the younger, much more measured in his language, at a later period of our struggle, when he declared: "These Ministers will destroy the empire they were called upon to save, before the indignation of a great and suffering people can fall upon their heads in the punishment which they deserve. I affirm the war to have been a most accursed, wicked, barbarous, cruel, unnatural, unjust, and diabolical war."

I need not say, Fellow Citizens, that we are here to indulge in no reproaches upon Old England to-day, as we look back from the lofty height of a Century of Independence on the course of events which severed us from her dominions. We are by no means in the mood to re-open the adjudications of Ghent or of Geneva; nor can we allow the ties of old traditions to be seriously jarred, on such an occasion as this, by any recent failures of *extraditions*, however vexatious or provoking. But, certainly, resentments on either side, for any thing said or done during our Revolutionary period, — after such a lapse of time, — would dishonor the hearts which cherished them, and the tongues which uttered them. Who wonders that George the Third would not let such Colonies as ours go without a struggle? They were the brightest jewels of his crown. Who wonders that he shrunk from the responsibility of such a dismemberment of his empire, and that his brain reeled at the very thought of it? It would have been a poor compliment to us, had he not considered us worth holding at any and every cost. We should hardly have forgiven him, had he not desired to retain us. Nor can we altogether wonder, that with the views of kingly prerogative which belonged to that period, and in which he was educated, he should have preferred the policy of coercion to that of conciliation, and should have insisted on sending over troops to subdue us.

Our old Mother Country has had, indeed, a peculiar destiny, and in many respects a glorious one. Not alone with her drum-beat, as Webster so grandly said, has she encircled the earth. Not alone with her martial airs has she kept company with the hours. She has carried civilization and Christianity wherever she has carried her flag. She has carried her noble tongue, with all its incomparable treasures of literature and science and religion, around the globe; and, with our aid, — for she will confess that we are doing our full part in this line of extension, — it is fast becoming the most pervading speech of civilized man. We thank God at this hour, and at every hour, that "Chatham's language is our mother tongue," and that we have an inherited and an indisputable share in the glory of so many of the great names by which that language has been illustrated and adorned.

But she has done more than all this. She has planted the great institutions and principles of civil freedom in every latitude where she could find a foot-hold. From her, our Revolutionary Fathers learned to understand and value them, and from her they inherited the spirit to defend them. Not in vain had her brave barons extorted Magna Charta from King John. Not in vain had her Simon de Montfort summoned the knights and burgesses, and laid the foundations of a Parliament and a House of Commons. Not in vain had her noble Sir John Eliot died, as the martyr of free speech, in the Tower. Not in vain had her heroic Hampden resisted ship-money, and died on the battle-field. Not in vain for us, certainly, the great examples and the great warnings of Cromwell and the Commonwealth, or those sadder ones of Sidney and Russell, or that later and more glorious one still of William of Orange.

The grand lessons of her own history, forgotten, overlooked, or resolutely disregarded, it may be, on her own side of the Atlantic, in the days we are commemorating, were the very inspiration of her Colonies on this side; and under that inspiration they contended and conquered. And though she may sometimes be almost tempted to take sadly upon her lips the words of the old prophet, — "I have nourished and brought up children, and they have rebelled against me," — she has long ago learned that such a rebellion as ours was really in her own interest, and for her own ultimate welfare; begun, continued, and ended, as it was, in vindication of the liberties of Englishmen.

I cannot forget how justly and eloquently my friend, Dr. Ellis, a few months ago, in this same hall, gave expression to the respect which is so widely entertained on this side of the Atlantic for the Sovereign Lady who has now graced the British throne for nearly forty years. No passage of his admirable Oration elicited a warmer response from the multitudes who listened to him. How much of the growth and grandeur of Great Britain is associated with the names of illustrious women! Even those of us who have no fancy for female suffrage might often be well nigh tempted to take refuge, from the incompetencies and intrigues and corruptions of men, under the presidency of the purer and gentler sex. What would English history be without the names of Elizabeth and Anne! What would it be without the name of Victoria, — of whom it has recently been written, "that, by a long course of loyal acquiescence in the declared wishes of her people, she has brought about what is nothing less than a great Revolution, — all the more beneficent because it has been gradual and silent!" Ever honored be her name, and that of her lamented consort!

> "Ever beloved and loving may her rule be;
> And when old Time shall lead her to her end,
> Goodness and she fill up one monument!"

The Declaration is adopted and promulgated; but we may not forget how long and how serious a reluctance there had been to take the irrevocable step. As late as September, 1774, Washington had publicly declared his belief that Independence "was wished by no thinking man." As late as the 6th of March, 1775, in his memorable Oration in the Old South, with all the associations of "the Boston Massacre" fresh in his heart, Warren had declared that "Independence was not our aim." As late as July, 1775, the letter of the Continental Congress to the Lord Mayor and Corporation of London had said: "North America, my Lord, wishes most ardently for a lasting connection with Great Britain, on terms of just and equal liberty;" and a simultaneous humble petition to the King, signed by every member of the Congress, reiterated the same assurance. And as late as the 25th of August, 1775, Jefferson himself, in a letter to the John Randolph of that day, speaking of those who "still wish for reunion with their parent country," says most emphatically, "I am one of those; and would rather be in dependence on Great Britain, properly limited, than on any nation on earth, or than on no nation." Not all the blood of Lexington, and Concord, and Bunker Hill, crying from the ground long before these words were written, had extinguished the wish for reconciliation and reunion even in the heart of the very author of the Declaration.

Tell me not, tell me not, that there was any thing of equivocation, any thing of hypocrisy, in these and a hundred other similar expressions which might be cited. The truest human hearts are full of such inconsistency and hypocrisy as that. The dearest friends, the tenderest relatives, are never more overflowing and outpouring, nor ever more sincere, in feelings and expressions of devotion and love, than when called to contemplate some terrible impending necessity of final separation and divorce. The ties between us and Old England could not be sundered without sadness, and sadness on both sides of the ocean. Franklin, albeit his eyes were "unused to the melting mood," is recorded to have wept as he left England, in view of the inevitable result of which he was coming home to be a witness and an instrument; and I have heard from the poet Rogers's own lips, what many of you may have read in his Table-Talk, how deeply he was impressed, as a boy, by his father's putting on a mourning suit, when he heard of the first shedding of American blood.

Nor could it, in the nature of things, have been only their warm and undoubted attachment to England, which made so many of the men of 1776 reluctant to the last to cross the Rubicon. They saw clearly before them, they could not help seeing, the full proportions, the tremendous odds, of the contest into which the Colonies must be plunged by such a step. Think you, that no apprehensions and anxieties weighed heavily on the minds and hearts of those far-seeing men? Think you, that as their names were called on the day we commemorate, beginning with Josiah Bartlett, of New Hampshire, — or as, one by one, they approached the Secretary's desk on the following 2d of August, to write their names on that now hallowed parchment, — they did not realize the full responsibility, and the full risk to their country and to themselves, which such a vote and such a signature involved? They sat, indeed, with closed doors; and it is only from traditions or eaves-droppings, or from the casual expressions of diaries or letters, that we catch glimpses of what was done, or gleanings of what was said. But how full of import are some of those glimpses and gleanings!

"Will you sign?" said Hancock to Charles Carroll, who, as we have seen, had not been present on the 4th of July. "Most willingly," was the reply. "There goes two millions with a dash of the pen," says one of those standing by; while another remarks, "Oh, Carroll, you will get off, there are so many Charles Carrolls." And then we may see him stepping back to the desk, and putting that addition — "of Carrollton" — to his name, which will designate him for ever, and be a prouder title of nobility than those in the peerage of Great Britain, which were afterwards adorned by his accomplished and fascinating granddaughters.

"We must stand by each other — we must hang together," — is presently heard from some one of the signers; with the instant reply, "Yes, we must hang together, or we shall assuredly hang separately." And, on this suggestion, the portly and humorous Benj. Harrison, whom we have seen forcing Hancock into the Chair, may be heard bantering our spare and slender Elbridge Gerry, — levity provoking levity, — and telling him with grim merriment that, when that hanging scene arrives, he shall have the advantage: — "It will be all over with me in a moment, but you will be kicking in the air half an hour after I am gone!" These are among the "asides" of the drama, but, I need not say, they more than make up in significance, for all they may seem to lack in dignity.

The excellent William Ellery of Rhode Island, whose name was afterwards borne by his grandson, our revered Channing, often spoke, we are told, of the scene of the signing, and spoke of it as an event which many regarded with awe, perhaps with uncertainty, but none with fear. "I was determined," he used to say, "to see how all looked, as they signed what might be their death warrant. I placed myself beside the Secretary, Charles Thompson, and eyed each closely as he affixed his name to the document. Undaunted resolution was displayed in every countenance."

"You inquire," wrote John Adams to William Plumer,

"whether every member of Congress did, on the 4th of July, 1776, in fact, cordially approve of the Declaration of Independence. They who were then members all signed it, and, as I could not see their hearts, it would be hard for me to say that they did not approve it; but, as far as I could penetrate the intricate internal foldings of their souls, I then believed, and have not since altered my opinion, that there were several who signed with regret, and several others with many doubts and much lukewarmness. The measure had been on the carpet for months, and obstinately opposed from day to day. Majorities were constantly against it. For many days the majority depended upon Mr. Hewes of North Carolina. While a member one day was speaking, and reading documents from all the Colonies to prove that the public opinion, the general sense of all, was in favor of the measure, when he came to North Carolina, and produced letters and public proceedings which demonstrated that the majority of that Colony were in favor of it, Mr. Hewes, who had hitherto constantly voted against it, started suddenly upright, and lifting up both his hands to Heaven, as if he had been in a trance, cried out, 'It is done, and I will abide by it.' I would give more for a perfect painting of the terror and horror upon the faces of the old majority, at that critical moment, than for the best piece of Raphael."

There is quite enough in these traditions and hearsays, in these glimpses and gleanings, to show us that the supporters and signers of the Declaration were not blind to the responsibilities and hazards in which they were involving themselves and the country. There is quite enough, certainly, in these and other indications, to give color and credit to what I so well remember hearing the late Mr. Justice Story say, half a century ago, that, as the result of all his conversations with the great men of the Revolutionary Period, — and especially with his illustrious and venerated chief on the bench of the Supreme Court of the United States, John Marshall, — he was convinced that a majority of the Continental Congress was opposed to the Declaration, and that it was carried through by the patient, persistent, and overwhelming efforts and arguments of the minority.

Two of those arguments, as Mr. Jefferson has left them on

record, were enough for that occasion, or certainly are enough for this.

One of the two was, "That the people wait for us to lead the way; that *they* are in favor of the measure, though the instructions given by some of their representatives are not." And most true, indeed, it was, my friends, at that day, as it often has been since that day, that the people were ahead of their so-called leaders. The minds of the masses were made up. They had no doubts or misgivings. They demanded that Independence should be recognized and proclaimed. John Adams knew how to keep up with them. Sam. Adams had kept his finger on their pulse from the beginning, and had "marked time" for every one of their advancing steps. Patrick Henry and Richard Henry Lee and Thomas Jefferson, and some other ardent and noble spirits, were by no means behind them. But not a few of the leaders were, in fact, only followers. "The people waited for them to lead the way." Independence was the resolve and the act of the American people, and the American people gladly received, and enthusiastically ratified, and heroically sustained the Declaration, until Independence was no longer a question either at home or abroad. Yes, our Great Charter, as we fondly call it, though with something, it must be confessed, of poetic or patriotic license, was no temporizing concession, wrung by menaces from reluctant Monarchs; but was the spontaneous and imperative dictate of a Nation resolved to be free!

The other of those two arguments was even more conclusive and more clinching. It was, "That the question was not whether by a Declaration of Independence we should make ourselves what we are not, but whether we should declare a fact which already exists."

"A fact which already exists!" Mr. Mayor and Fellow Citizens, there is no more interesting historical truth to us of Boston than this. Our hearts are all at Philadelphia to-day, as I have already said, rejoicing in all that is there said and done in honor of the men who made this day immortal, and hailing it, with our fellow-countrymen, from ocean to ocean, and from the lakes to the gulf, as our National Birthday. And nobly has Philadelphia met the requisitions, and more than fulfilled the expectations, of the occasion; furnishing a fête and a pageant of which the whole Nation is proud. Yet we are not called on to forget, — we could not be pardoned, indeed, for not remembering, — that, while the Declaration was boldly and grandly made in that hallowed Pennsylvania Hall, Independence had already been won, — and won here in Massachusetts. It was said by some one of the old patriots, — John Adams, I believe, — that "the Revolution was effected before the war commenced;" and Jefferson is now our authority for the assertion that "Independence existed before it was declared." They both well knew what they were talking about. Congresses in Carpenters' Hall, and Congresses in the old Pennsylvania State House, did grand things and were composed of grand men, and we render to their memories all the homage and all the glory which they so richly earned. But here in Boston, the capital of Massachusetts, and the principal town of British North America at that day, the question had already been brought to an issue, and already been irrevocably decided. Here the manifest destiny of the Colonies had been recognized and accepted. It was upon us, as all the world knows, that the blows of British oppression fell first and fell heaviest, — fell like a storm of hail-stones and coals of fire; and where they fell, and as soon as they fell, they were resisted, and successfully resisted.

Why, away back in 1761, when George the Third had been but a year on his throne, and when the printer's ink on the pages of our Harvard "Pietas et Gratulatio" was hardly dry; when the Seven Years' War was still unfinished, in which New England had done her full share of the fighting, and reaped her full share of the glory, and when the British flag, by the help of her men and money, was just floating in triumph over the whole American continent, — a mad resolution had been adopted to reconstruct — Oh, word of ill-omen! — the whole Colonial system, and to bring America into closer conformity and subjection to the laws of the Mother Country. A Revenue is to be collected here. A Standing Army is to be established here. The Navigation Act and Acts of Trade are to be enforced and executed here. And all without any representation on our part. — The first practical step in this direction is taken.

A custom-house officer, named Cockle, applies to the Superior Court at Salem for a writ of assistance. That cockle-shell exploded like dynamite! The Court postpones the case, and orders its argument in Boston. And then and there, — in 1761, in our Old Town House, afterwards known as the Old State House, — alas, alas, that it is thought necessary to talk about removing or even reconstructing it! — James Otis, as John Adams himself tells us, "breathed into this nation the breath of life." "Then and there," he adds, and he spoke of what he witnessed and heard, "then and there the child Independence was born. In fifteen years, *i.e.*, in 1776, he grew up to manhood, and declared himself free."

The next year finds the same great scholar and orator exposing himself to the cry of "treason" in denouncing the idea of taxation without representation, and forthwith vindicating himself in a masterly pamphlet which excited the admiration and sympathy of the whole people.

Another year brings the first instalment of the scheme for raising a revenue in the Colonies, — in the shape of declaratory resolves; and Otis meets it plumply and boldly, in Faneuil Hall, — at that moment freshly rebuilt and reopened, — with the counter declaration that "every British subject in America is, of common right, by act of Parliament, and by the laws of God and Nature, entitled to all the essential privileges of Britons."

And now George Grenville has devised and proposed the Stamp Act. And, before it is even known that the Bill had passed, Samuel Adams is heard reading, in that same Faneuil Hall, at the May meeting of 1764, those memorable instructions from Boston to her representatives: "There is no room for delay. If taxes are laid upon us in any shape without our having a legal representation where they are laid, are we not reduced from the character of free subjects to the miserable state of tributary slaves? . . . We claim British rights, not by charter only: we are born to them. Use your endeavors that the weight of the other North American Colonies may be added to that of this Province, that by united application all may happily obtain redress." Redress and Union — and union as the means, and the only means of redress — had thus early become the doctrine of our Boston leaders; and James Otis follows out that doctrine, without a moment's delay, in another brilliant plea for the rights of the Colonies.

The next year finds the pen of John Adams in motion, in a powerful communication to the public journals, setting forth distinctly, that "there seems to be a direct and formal design on foot in Great Britain to enslave all America;" and adding most ominously those emphatic words: "Be it remembered, Liberty must be defended at all hazards!"

And, I need not say, it was remembered; and Liberty was defended, at all hazards, here, upon our own soil.

Ten long years, however, are still to elapse before the wager of battle is to be fully joined. The stirring events which crowded those years, and which have been so vividly depicted by Sparks and Bancroft and Frothingham, — to name no others, — are too familiar for repetition or reference. Virginia, through the clarion voice of Patrick Henry, nobly sustained by her House of Burgesses, leads off in the grand remonstrance. Massachusetts, through the trumpet tones of James Otis, rouses the whole Continent by a demand for a General Congress. South Carolina, through the influence of Christopher Gadsden, responds first to the demand. "Deep calleth unto deep." In October, 1765, delegates, regularly or irregularly chosen, from nine Colonies, are in consultation at New York; and from South Carolina comes the watch-word of assured success: "There ought to be no New England man, no New Yorker, known on the Continent; but all of us Americans."

Meantime, the people are everywhere inflamed and maddened by the attempt to enforce the Stamp Act. Everywhere that attempt is resisted. Everywhere it is resolved that it shall never be executed. It is at length repealed, and a momentary lull succeeds. But the repeal is accompanied by more declaratory resolutions of the power of Parliament to tax the Colonies "in all cases whatsoever;" and then follows that train of abuses and usurpations which Jefferson's immortal paper charges upon the King, and which the King himself unquestionably ordered. "It was to no purpose," said Lord North in 1774, "making objections, for the King would have it so." "The King," said he, "meant *to try the question* with America." And it is well added, by the narrator of the anecdote, "Boston seems to have been the place fixed upon to try the question."

Yes, at Boston, the bolts of Royal indignation are to be aimed and winged. She has been foremost in destroying the Stamps, in defying the Soldiers, in drowning the Tea. Letters, too, have reached the government, like those which Rehum the Chancellor and Shimshai the Scribe wrote to King Artaxerxes about Jerusalem, calling this "a rebellious city, and hurtful unto Kings and Provinces, and that they have moved sedition within the same of old time, and would not pay toll, tribute, and custom;" and warning His Majesty that, unless it was subdued and crushed, "he would have no portion on this side the River." In vain did our eloquent young Quincy pour forth his burning words of remonstrance. The Port of Boston is closed, and her people are to be starved into compliance. Well did Boston say of herself, in Town Meeting, that "She had been stationed by Providence in the front rank of the conflict." Grandly has our eloquent historian, Bancroft, said of her, in a sentence which sums up the whole matter "like the last embattelling of a Roman legion": — "The King set himself and his Ministry and his Parliament and all Great Britain to subdue to his will one stubborn little town on the sterile coast of the Massachusetts Bay. The odds against it were fearful; but it showed a life inextinguishable, and had been chosen to guard over the liberties of mankind!"

Generously and nobly did the other Colonies come to our aid, and the cause of Boston was everywhere acknowledged to be "the cause of all." But we may not forget how peculiarly it was "the cause of Boston," and that here, on our own Massachusetts soil, the practical question of Independence was first tried and virtually settled. The brave Colonel Pickering at Salem Bridge, the heroic minute men at Lexington and Concord Bridge, the gallant Colonel Prescott at Bunker Hill, did their part in hastening that settlement and bringing it to a crisis; and when the Continental Army was at length brought to our rescue, and the glorious Washington, after holding the British forces at bay for nine months, had fairly driven them from the town, — though more than three months were still to intervene before the Declaration was to be made, — it could truly and justly be said that it was only " the declaration of a fact which already exists."

Indeed, Massachusetts had practically administered " a government independent of the King" from the 19th of July, 1775; while on the very first day of May, 1776, her General Court had passed a solemn Act, to erase forthwith the name of the King, and the year of his reign, from all civil commissions, writs, and precepts; and to substitute therefor " the Year of the Christian Era, and the name of the Government and People of the Massachusetts Bay in New England." Other Colonies may have empowered or instructed their delegates in Congress, earlier than this Colony, to act on the subject. But this was action itself, — positive, decisive, conclusive action. The Declaration was made in Philadelphia; but the Independence which was declared can date back nowhere, for its first existence as a fact, earlier than to Massachusetts. Upon her the lot fell " to try the question ; " and, with the aid of Washington and the Continental Army, it was tried, and tried triumphantly, upon her soil. Certainly, if Faneuil Hall was the Cradle of Liberty, our Old State House was the Cradle of Independence, and our Old South the Nursery of Liberty and Independence both ; and if these sacred edifices, all or any of them, are indeed destined to disappear, let us see to it that some corner of their sites, at least, be consecrated to monuments which shall tell their story, in legible lettering, to our children and our children's children for ever!

Thanks be to God, that, in His good providence, the trial of this great question fell primarily upon a Colony and a people peculiarly fitted to meet it ; — whose whole condition and training had prepared them for it, and whose whole history had pointed to it.

Why, quaint old John Evelyn, in his delicious Diary, tells us, under date of May, 1671, that the great anxiety of the Council for Plantations, of which he had just been made a member, was " to know the condition of New England," which appeared " to be very independent as to their regard to Old England or His

Majesty," and "almost upon the very brink of renouncing any dependence on the Crown!"

"I have always laughed," said John Adams, in a letter to Benjamin Rush, in 1807, "at the affectation of representing American Independence as a novel idea, as a modern discovery, as a late invention. The idea of it as a possible thing, as a probable event, as a necessary and unavoidable measure, in case Great Britain should assume an unconstitutional authority over us, has been familiar to Americans from the first settlement of the country, and was as well understood by Governor Winthrop, in 1675, as by Governor Samuel Adams, when he told you that Independence had been the first wish of his heart for seven years." "The principles and feelings which produced the Revolution," said he again, in his second letter to Tudor, in 1818, "ought to be traced back for two hundred years, and sought in the history of the country from the first plantations in America." The first emigrants, he maintains, were the true authors of our Independence, and the men of the Revolutionary period, himself among them, were only "the awakeners and revivers of the original fundamental principle of Colonization."

And the accomplished historian of New England, Dr. Palfrey, follows up the idea, and says more precisely: "He who well weighs the facts which have been presented in connection with the principal emigration to Massachusetts, and other related facts which will offer themselves to notice as we proceed, may find himself conducted to the conclusion that when Winthrop and his associates (in 1629) prepared to convey across the water a Charter from the King, which, they hoped, would in their beginnings afford them some protection both from himself and, through him, from the Powers of Continental Europe, they had conceived a project no less important than that of laying on this side of the Atlantic the foundations of a Nation of Puritan Englishmen, — foundations to be built upon as future circumstances should decide or allow."

Indeed, that transfer of their Charter and of their "whole government" to New England, on their own responsibility, was an act closely approaching to a Declaration of Independence, and clearly foreshadowing it. And when, only a few years afterwards, we find the magistrates and deputies resisting a demand for the surrender of the Charter, studiously and systematically "avoiding and protracting" all questions on the subject, and "hastening their fortifications" meantime; and when we hear even the ministers of the Colony openly declaring that, "if a General Governor were sent over here, we ought not to accept him, but to defend our lawful possessions, if we were able," — we recognize a spirit and a purpose which cannot be mistaken. That spirit and that purpose were manifested and illustrated in a manner even more marked and unequivocal, — as the late venerable Josiah Quincy reminded the people of Boston, just half a century ago to-day, — when under the lead of one who had come over in the ship with the Charter, and had lived to be the Nestor of New England, — Simon Bradstreet, — "a glorious Revolution was effected here in Massachusetts thirty days before it was known that King William had just effected a similar glorious Revolution on the other side of the Atlantic." New England, it seems, with characteristic and commendable despatch, had fairly got rid of Sir Edmond Andros, a month before she knew that Old England had got rid of his Master!

But I do not forget that we must look further back than even the earliest settlement of the American Colonies for the primal Fiat of Independence. I do not forget that when Edmund Burke, in 1775, in alluding to the possibility of an American representation in Parliament, exclaimed so emphatically and eloquently, "Opposuit Natura — I cannot remove the eternal barriers of the creation," he had really exhausted the whole argument. No effective representation was possible. If it had been possible, England herself would have been aghast at it. The very idea of James Otis and Patrick Henry and the Adamses arguing the great questions of human rights and popular liberty on the floor of the House of Commons, and in the hearing of the common people of Great Britain, would have thrown the King and Lord North into convulsions of terror, and we should soon have heard them crying out, "These men that have turned the world upside down are come hither also." One of their own Board of Trade (Soame Jenyns) well said, with as much truth as humor or sarcasm, "I have lately seen so many specimens of the great powers of speech of which these American gentlemen are possessed, that I should be afraid the sudden importation of so much eloquence at once would endanger the safety of England. It will be much cheaper for us to pay their Army than their Orators." But no effective representation was possible; and without it Taxation *was* Tyranny, in spite of the great Dictionary dogmatist and his insolent pamphlet.

Why, even in these days of Ocean Steamers, reducing the passage across the Atlantic from forty or fifty or sixty days to ten, representation in Westminster Hall is not proposed for the colonies which England still holds on our continent; and it would be little better than a farce, if it were proposed and attempted. The Dominion of Canada, as we all know, remains as she is, seeking neither independence nor annexation, only because her people prefer to be, and are proud of being, a part of the British empire; and because that empire has abandoned all military occupation or forcible restraint upon them, and has adopted a system involving no collision or contention. Canada is now doubly a monument of the greatness and wisdom of the immortal Chatham. His military policy conquered it for England; and his civil policy, "ruling from his urn," and supplemented by that of his great son, holds it for England at this day; permitting it substantially to rule itself, through the agency of a Parliament of its own, with at this moment, as it happens, an able, intelligent, and accomplished Governor-General, whose name and blood were not without close affinities to those of that marvellous statesman and orator while he lived.

It did not require the warning of our example to bring about such results. It is written in the eternal constitution of things that no large colonies, educated to a sense of their rights and capable of defending them, — no English or Anglo-Saxon colonies, certainly, — can be governed by a Power three thousand miles across an ocean, unless they are governed to their own satisfaction, and held as colonies with their own consent and free will. An Imperial military sway may be as elastic and far-reaching as the magnetic wires, — it matters not whether three thousand or fifteen thousand miles, — over an uncivilized region or an unenlightened race. But who is wild enough to conceive, as Burke said a hundred years ago, "that the natives of Hindostan and those of Virginia could be ordered in the same manner; or that the Cutchery Court and the grand jury at Salem could be regulated on a similar plan"? "I am convinced," said Fox, in 1791, in the fresh light of the experience America had afforded him, "that the only method of retaining distant Colonies with advantage is to enable them to govern themselves."

Yes, from the hour when Columbus and his compeers discovered our continent, its ultimate political destiny was fixed. At the very gateway of the Pantheon of American Liberty and American Independence might well be seen a triple monument, like that to the old inventors of printing at Frankfort, including Columbus and Americus Vespucius and Cabot. They were the pioneers in the march to Independence. They were the precursors in the only progress of freedom which was to have no backward steps. Liberty had struggled long and bravely in other ages and in other lands. It had made glorious manifestations of its power and promise in Athens and in Rome; in the mediæval republics of Italy; on the plains of Germany; along the dykes of Holland; among the icy fastnesses of Switzerland; and, more securely and hopefully still, in the sea-girt isle of Old England. But it was the glory of those heroic old navigators to reveal a standing-place for it at last, where its lever could find a secure fulcrum, and rest safely until it had moved the world! The fulness of time had now come. Under an impulse of religious conviction, the poor, persecuted Pilgrims launched out upon the stormy deep in a single, leaking, almost foundering bark; and in the very cabin of the "Mayflower" the first written compact of self-government in the history of mankind is prepared and signed. Ten years afterwards the Massachusetts Company come over with their Charter, and administer it on the avowed principle that the whole government, civil and religious, is transferred. All the rest which is to follow until the 4th of July, 1776, is only matter of time and opportunity. Certainly, my friends, as we look back to-day through the long vista of the past, we perceive that it was no mere Declaration of men, which primarily brought about the Independence we celebrate. We cannot but reverently recognize the hand of that Almighty Maker of the World, who "founded it upon the seas and established it upon the floods." We cannot but feel the full force and felicity of those opening words, in which the Declaration speaks of our assuming among the powers of the earth, "that separate and equal station to which the laws of Nature and of Nature's God entitled us."

I spoke, Mr. Mayor, at the outset of this Oration, of "A Century of Self-Government Completed." And so, in some sort, it is. The Declaration at Philadelphia was, in itself, both an assertion and an act of self-government; and it had been preceded, or was immediately followed, by provisions for local self-government in all the separate Colonies; — Massachusetts, New Hampshire, and South Carolina, conditionally, at least, having led the way. But we may not forget that six or seven years of hard fighting are still to intervene before our Independence is to be acknowledged by Great Britain; and six or seven years more before the full consummation will have been reached by the adoption of the Federal Constitution, and the organization of our National System under the august and transcendent Presidency of Washington.

With that august and transcendent Presidency, dating, — as it is pleasant to remember, — precisely a hundred years from the analogous accession of William of Orange to the throne of England, our history as an organized Nation fairly begins. When that Centennial Anniversary shall arrive, thirteen years hence, the time may have come for a full review of our National career and character, and for a complete computation or a just estimate of what a Century of Self-Government has accomplished for ourselves and for mankind.

I dared not attempt such a review to-day. This Anniversary has seemed to me to belong peculiarly, — I had almost said, sacredly, — to the men and the events which rendered the Fourth of July so memorable for ever; and I have willingly left myself little time for any thing else. God grant, that, when the 30th of April, 1889, shall dawn upon those of us who may live to see it, the thick clouds which now darken our political sky may have passed away; that wholesome and healing counsels may have prevailed throughout our land; that integrity and purity may be once more conspicuous in our high places; that an honest currency may have been reëstablished, and prosperity restored to all branches of our domestic industry and our foreign commerce; and that some of those social problems which are perplexing and tormenting so many of our Southern States may have been safely and satisfactorily solved!

For, indeed, Fellow Citizens, we cannot shut our eyes to the fact, that this great year of our Lord and of American Liberty has been ushered in by not a few discouraging and depressing circumstances. Appalling catastrophes, appalling crimes, have marked its course. Financial, political, moral, delinquencies and wrongs have swept over our land like an Arctic or an Antarctic wave, or both conjoined; until we have been almost ready to cry out in anguish to Heaven, "Thou hast multiplied the nation, but not increased the joy!" It will be an added stigma, in all time to come, on the corruption of the hour, and on all concerned in it, that it has cast so deep a shade over our Centennial Festival.

All this, however, we are persuaded, is temporary and exceptional, — the result, not of our institutions, but of disturbing causes; and as distinctly traceable to those causes, as the scoriæ of a volcano, or the débris of a deluge. Had there been no long and demoralizing Civil War to account for such developments, we might indeed be alarmed for our future. As it is, our confidence in the Republic is unshaken. We are ready even to accept all that has occurred to overshadow our jubilee, as a seasonable warning against vain-glorious boastings; as a timely admonition that our institutions are not proof against licentiousness and profligacy, but that "eternal vigilance is still the price of liberty."

Already the reaction has commenced. Already the people are everywhere roused to the importance of something higher than mere partisan activity and zeal, and to a sense that something besides "big wars" may be required to "make ambition virtue." Everywhere the idea is scouted that there are any immunities or impunities for bribery and corruption; and the scorn of the whole people is deservedly cast on any one detected in plucking our Eagle's wings to feather his own nest. Everywhere there is a demand for integrity, for principle, for character, as the only safe qualifications for public employments, as well as for private trusts. Oh, let that demand be enforced and insisted on, — as I hope and believe it will be, — and we shall have nothing to fear for our freedom, and but little to regret in the temporary depression and mortification which have recalled us to a deeper sense of our dangers and our duties.

Meantime, we may be more than content that no short-comings or failures of our own day can diminish the glories of the past, or dim the brilliancy of successes achieved by our Fathers. We can look back upon our history so far, and find in it enough to make us grateful; enough to make us hopeful; enough to make us proud of our institutions and of our country; enough to make us resolve never to despair of the Republic; enough to assure us that, could our Fathers look down on all which has been accomplished, they would feel that their toils and sacrifices had not been in vain; enough to convince other nations, and the world at large, that, in uniting so generously with us to decorate our grand Exposition, and celebrate our Centennial Birthday, they are swelling the triumphs of a People and a Power which have left no doubtful impress upon the hundred years of their Independent National existence.

Those hundred years have been crowded, as we all know, with wonderful changes in all quarters of the globe. I would not disparage or depreciate the interest and importance of the great events and great reforms which have been witnessed during their progress, and especially near their end, in almost every country of the Old World. Nor would I presume to claim too confidently for the closing Century, that when the records of mankind are made up, in some far-distant future, it will be remembered and designated, peculiarly and preëminently, as The American Age. Yet it may well be doubted, whether the dispassionate historian of after years will find that the influences of any other nation have been of farther reach and wider range, or of more efficiency for the welfare of the world, than those of our great Republic, since it had a name and a place on the earth.

Other Ages have had their designations, local or personal or mythical, — historic or pre-historic; — Ages of stone or iron, of silver or gold; Ages of Kings or Queens, of Reformers or of Conquerors. That marvellous compound of almost every thing wise or foolish, noble or base, witty or ridiculous, sublime or profane, — Voltaire, — maintained that, in his day, no man of reflection or of taste could count more than four authentic Ages in the history of the world: 1. That of Philip and Alexander, with Pericles and Demosthenes, Aristotle and Plato, Apelles, Phidias and Praxiteles: 2. That of Cæsar and Augustus, with Lucretius and Cicero and Livy, Virgil and Horace, Varro and Vitruvius: 3. That of the Medici, with Michel Angelo and Raphael, Galileo and Dante: 4. That which he was at the moment engaged in depicting, — the Age of Louis XIV, which, in his judgment, surpassed all the others!

Our American Age could bear no comparison with Ages like these, — measured only by the brilliancy of historians and philosophers, of poets or painters. We need not, indeed, be ashamed of what has been done for Literature and Science and Art, during these hundred years, nor hesitate to point with pride to our own authors and artists, living and dead. But the day has gone by when Literature and the Fine Arts, or even Science and the Useful Arts, can characterize an Age. There are other and higher measures of comparison. And the very nation which counts Voltaire among its greatest celebrities, — the nation which aided us so generously in our Revolutionary struggle, and which is now rejoicing in its own successful establishment of republican institutions, — the land of the great and good Lafayette, — has taken the lead in pointing out the true grounds on which our American Age may challenge and claim a special recognition. An association of Frenchmen, under the lead of some of their most distinguished statesmen and scholars, — has proposed to erect, and is engaged in erecting, as their contribution to our Centennial, a gigantic statue at the very throat of the harbor of our supreme commercial emporium, which shall symbolize the legend inscribed on its pedestal, — "Liberty enlightening the World!"

That glorious legend presents the standard by which our Age is to be judged; and by which we may well be willing and proud to have it judged. All else in our own career, certainly, is secondary. The growth and grandeur of our territorial dimensions; the multiplication of our States; the number and size and wealth of our cities; the marvellous increase of our population; the measureless extent of our railways and internal navigation; our overflowing granaries; our inexhaustible mines; our countless inventions and multitudinous industries, — all these may be remitted to the Census, and left for the students of statistics. The claim which our country presents, for giving no second or subordinate character to the Age which has just closed, rests only on what has been accomplished, at home and abroad, for elevating the condition of mankind; for advancing political and human freedom; for promoting the greatest good of the greatest number; for proving the capacity of man for self-government; and for "enlightening the world" by the example of a rational, regulated, enduring, Constitutional Liberty. And who will dispute or question that claim? In what region of the earth ever so remote from us, in what corner of creation ever so far out of the range of our communication, does not some burden lightened, some bond loosened, some yoke lifted, some labor better remunerated, some new hope for despairing hearts, some new light or new liberty for the benighted or the oppressed, bear witness this day, and trace itself directly or indirectly back, to the impulse given to the world by the successful establishment and operation of Free Institutions on this American Continent!

How many Colonies have been more wisely and humanely and liberally administered, under the warning of our Revolution! How many Churches have abated something of their old intolerance and bigotry, under the encouragement of our religious freedom! Who believes or imagines that Free Schools, a Free Press, the Elective Franchise, the Rights of Representation, the principles of Constitutional Government, would have made the notable progress they have made, had our example been wanting! Who believes or imagines that even the Rotten Boroughs of Old England would have disappeared so rapidly, had there been no American Representative Republic! And has there been a more effective influence on human welfare and human freedom, since the world began, than that which has resulted from the existence of a great land of Liberty in this Western hemisphere, of unbounded resources, with acres enough for a myriad of homes, and with a welcome for all who may fly to it from oppression, from every region beneath the sun?

Let not our example be perverted or dishonored, by others or by ourselves. It was no wild breaking away from all authority, which we celebrate to-day. It was no mad revolt against every thing like government. No incendiary torch can be rightfully kindled at our flame. Doubtless, there had been excesses and violences in many quarters of our land,—irrepressible outbreaks under unbearable provocations,—"irregular things, done in the confusion of mighty troubles." Doubtless, our Boston mobs did not always move "to the Dorian mood of flutes and soft recorders." But in all our deliberative assemblies, in all our Town Meetings, in all our Provincial and Continental Congresses, there was a respect for the great principles of Law and Order; and the definition of true civil liberty, which had been so remarkably laid down by one of the founders of our Commonwealth, more than a century before, was, consciously or unconsciously, recognized,—"a Liberty for that only which is good, just, and honest."

The Declaration we commemorate expressly admitted and asserted that "governments long established should not be changed for light and transient causes." It dictated no special forms of government for other people, and hardly for ourselves. It had no denunciations, or even disparagements, for monarchies or for empires, but eagerly contemplated, as we do at this hour, alliances and friendly relations with both. We have welcomed to our Jubilee, with peculiar interest and gratification, the representatives of the nations of Europe,—all then monarchical,—to whom we were so deeply indebted for sympathy and for assistance in our struggle for Independence. We have welcomed, too, the personal presence of an Emperor, from another quarter of our own hemisphere, of whose eager and enlightened interest in Education and Literature and Science we had learned so much from our lamented Agassiz, and have now witnessed so much for ourselves.

Our Fathers were no propagandists of republican institutions in the abstract. Their own adoption of a republican form was, at the moment, almost as much a matter of chance as of choice, of necessity as of preference. The Thirteen Colonies had, happily, been too long accustomed to manage their own affairs, and were too wisely jealous of each other, also, to admit for an instant any idea of centralization; and without centralization a monarchy, or any other form of arbitrary government, was out of the question. Union was then, as it is now, the only safety for liberty; but it could be only a Constitutional Union, a limited and restricted Union, founded on compromises and mutual concessions; a Union recognizing a large measure of State rights, — resting not only on the division of powers among legislative and executive departments, but resting also on the distribution of powers between the States and the Nation, both deriving their original authority from the people, and exercising that authority for the people. This was the system contemplated by the Declaration of 1776. This was the system approximated to by the Confederation of 1778–81. This was the system finally consummated by the Constitution of 1789. And under this system our great example of self-government has been held up before the nations, fulfilling, so far as it has fulfilled it, that lofty mission which is recognized to-day, as "Liberty enlightening the World!"

Let me not speak of that example in any vain-glorious spirit. Let me not seem to arrogate for my country any thing of superior wisdom or virtue. Who will pretend that we have always made the most of our independence, or the best of our liberty? Who will maintain that we have always exhibited the brightest side of our institutions, or always entrusted their administration to the wisest or worthiest men? Who will deny that we have sometimes taught the world what to avoid, as well as what to imitate; and that the cause of freedom and reform has sometimes been discouraged and put back by our short-comings, or by our excesses? Our Light has been, at best, but a Revolving Light; warning by its darker intervals or its sombre shades, as well as cheering by its flashes of brilliancy, or by the clear lustre of its steadier shining. Yet, in spite of all its imperfections and irregularities, to no other earthly light have so many eyes been turned; from no other earthly illumination have so many hearts drawn hope and courage. It has breasted the tides of sectional and of party strife. It has stood the shock of foreign and of civil war. It will still hold on, erect and unextinguished, defying "the returning wave" of demoralization and corruption. Millions of young hearts, in all quarters of our land, are awaking at this moment to the responsibility which rests peculiarly upon them, for rendering its radiance purer and brighter and more constant. Millions of young hearts are resolving, at this hour, that it shall not be their fault if it do not stand for a century to come, as it has stood for a century past, a Beacon of Liberty to mankind! Their little flags of hope and promise are floating to-day from every cottage window along the roadside. With those young hearts it is safe.

Meantime, we may all rejoice and take courage, as we remember of how great a drawback and obstruction our example has been disembarrassed and relieved within a few years past. Certainly, we cannot forget this day, in looking back over the century which is gone, how long that example was overshadowed, in the eyes of all men, by the existence of African Slavery in so considerable a portion of our country. Never, never, however,— it may be safely said, — was there a more tremendous, a more dreadful, problem submitted to a nation for solution, than that which this institution involved for the United States of America. Nor were we alone responsible for its existence. I do not speak of it in the way of apology for ourselves. Still less would I refer to it in the way of crimination or reproach towards others, abroad or at home. But the well-known paragraph on this subject, in the original draught of the Declaration, is quite too notable a reminiscence of the little desk before me, to be forgotten on such an occasion as this. That omitted clause, — which, as Mr. Jefferson tells us, "was struck out in complaisance to South Carolina and Georgia," not without "tenderness," too, as he adds, to some "Northern brethren, who, though they had very few slaves themselves, had been pretty considerable carriers of them to others," — contained the direct allegation that the King had "prostituted his negative for suppressing every legislative attempt to prohibit or restrain this execrable commerce." That memorable clause, omitted for prudential reasons only, has passed into history, and its truth can never be disputed. It recalls to us, and recalls to the world, the historical fact, — which we certainly have a special right to remember this day, — that not only had African Slavery found its portentous and pernicious way into our Colonies in their very earliest settlement, but that it had been fixed and fastened upon some of them by Royal vetoes, prohibiting the passage of laws to restrain its further introduction. It had thus not only entwined and entangled itself about the very roots of our choicest harvests, — until Slavery and Cotton at last seemed as inseparable as the tares and wheat of the sacred parable, — but it had engrafted itself upon the very fabric of our government. We all know, the world knows, that our Independence could not have been achieved, our Union could not have been maintained, our Constitution could not have been established, without the adoption of those compromises which recognized its continued existence, and left it to the responsibility of the States of which it was the grievous inheritance. And from that day forward, the method of dealing with it, of disposing of it, and of extinguishing it, became more and more a problem full of terrible perplexity, and seemingly incapable of human solution.

Oh, that it could have been solved at last by some process less deplorable and dreadful than Civil War! How unspeakably glorious it would have been for us this day, could the Great Emancipation have been concerted, arranged, and ultimately effected, without violence or bloodshed, as a simple and sublime act of philanthropy and justice!

But it was not in the Divine economy that so huge an original wrong should be righted by any easy process. The decree seemed to have gone forth from the very registries of Heaven:

> "Cuncta prius tentanda, sed immedicabile vulnus
> Ense recidendum est."

The immedicable wound must be cut away by the sword! Again and again as that terrible war went on, we might almost hear voices crying out, in the words of the old prophet: "O thou sword of the Lord, how long will it be ere thou be quiet? Put up thyself into thy scabbard; rest, and be still!" But the answering voice seemed not less audible: "How can it be quiet, seeing the Lord hath given it a charge?"

And the war went on, — bravely fought on both sides, as we all know, — until, as one of its necessities, Slavery was abolished. It fell at last under that right of war to abolish it, which the late John Quincy Adams had been the first to announce in the way of warning, more than twenty years before, in my own hearing, on the floor of Congress, while I was your Representative. I remember well the burst of indignation and derision with which that warning was received. No prediction of Cassandra was ever more scorned than his, and he did not live to witness its verification. But whoever else may have been more immediately and personally instrumental in the final result, — the brave soldiers who fought the battles, or the gallant generals who led them, — the devoted philanthropists, or the ardent statesmen, who, in season and out of season, labored for it, — the Martyr-President who proclaimed it, — the true story of Emancipation can never be fairly and fully told without the "old man eloquent," who died beneath the roof of the Capitol nearly thirty years ago, being recognized as one of the leading figures of the narrative.

But, thanks be to God, who overrules every thing for good, that great event, the greatest of our American Age, — great enough, alone and by itself, to give a name and a character to any Age, — has been accomplished; and, by His blessing, we present our country to the world this day without a slave, white or black, upon its soil! Thanks be to God, not only that our beloved Union has been saved, but that it has been made both easier to save, and better worth saving, hereafter, by the final solution of a problem, before which all human wisdom had stood aghast and confounded for so many generations! Thanks be to God, and to Him be all the praise and the glory, we can read the great words of the Declaration, on this Centennial Anniversary, without reservation or evasion: "We hold these truths to be self-evident, that all men are created equal, and that they are endowed by their Creator with certain unalienable rights; that among these are life, liberty, and the pursuit of happiness." The legend on that new colossal Pharos, at Long Island, may now indeed be, "Liberty enlightening the World!"

We come then, to-day, Fellow Citizens, with hearts full of gratitude to God and man, to pass down our country and its institutions, — not wholly without scars and blemishes upon their front, — not without shadows on the past or clouds on the future, — but freed for ever from at least one great stain, and firmly rooted in the love and loyalty of a United People, — to the generations which are to succeed us.

And what shall we say to those succeeding generations, as we commit the sacred trust to their keeping and guardianship?

If I could hope, without presumption, that any humble counsels of mine, on this hallowed Anniversary, could be remembered beyond the hour of their utterance, and reach the ears of my countrymen in future days; if I could borrow "the masterly pen" of Jefferson, and produce words which should partake of the immortality of those which he wrote on this little desk; if I could command the matchless tongue of John Adams, when he poured out appeals and arguments which moved men from their seats, and settled the destinies of a Nation; if I could catch but a single spark of those electric fires which Franklin wrested from the skies, and flash down a phrase, a word, a thought, along the magic chords which stretch across the ocean of the future, — what could I, what would I, say?

I could not omit, certainly, to reiterate the solemn obligations which rest on every citizen of this Republic to cherish and enforce the great principles of our Colonial and Revolutionary Fathers, — the principles of Liberty and Law, one and inseparable, — the principles of the Constitution and the Union.

I could not omit to urge on every man to remember that self-government politically can only be successful, if it be accompanied by self-government personally; that there must be government somewhere; and that, if the people are indeed to be sovereigns, they must exercise their sovereignty over themselves individually, as well as over themselves in the aggregate, — regulating their own lives, resisting their own temptations, subduing their own passions, and voluntarily imposing upon themselves some measure of that restraint and discipline, which, under other systems, is supplied from the armories of arbitrary power, — the discipline of virtue, in the place of the discipline of slavery.

I could not omit to caution them against the corrupting influences of intemperance, extravagance, and luxury. I could not omit to warn them against political intrigue, as well as against personal licentiousness; and to implore them to regard principle and character, rather than mere party allegiance, in the choice of men to rule over them.

I could not omit to call upon them to foster and further the cause of universal Education; to give a liberal support to our Schools and Colleges; to promote the advancement of Science and of Art, in all their multiplied divisions and relations; and to encourage and sustain all those noble institutions of Charity, which, in our own land above all others, have given the crowning grace and glory to modern civilization.

I could not refrain from pressing upon them a just and generous consideration for the interests and the rights of their fellow men everywhere, and an earnest effort to promote Peace and Good Will among the Nations of the earth.

I could not refrain from reminding them of the shame, the unspeakable shame and ignominy, which would attach to those who should show themselves unable to uphold the glorious Fabric of Self-Government which had been founded for them at such a cost by their Fathers; — "*Videte, videte, ne, ut illis pulcherrimum fuit tantam vobis imperii gloriam relinquere, sic vobis turpissimum sit, illud quod accepistis, tueri et conservare non posse!*"

And surely, most surely, I could not fail to invoke them to imitate and emulate the examples of virtue and purity and patriotism, which the great founders of our Colonies and of our Nation had so abundantly left them.

But could I stop there? Could I hold out to them, as the results of a long life of observation and experience, nothing but the principles and examples of great men?

Who and what are great men? "Woe to the country," said Metternich to our own Ticknor, forty years ago, "whose condition and institutions no longer produce great men to manage its affairs." The wily Austrian applied his remark to England at that day; but his woe — if it be a woe — would have a wider range in our time, and leave hardly any land unreached. Certainly we hear it now-a-days, at every turn, that never before has there been so striking a disproportion between supply and demand, as at this moment, the world over, in the commodity of great men.

But who, and what, are great men? "And now stand forth," says an eminent Swiss historian, who had completed a survey of the whole history of mankind, at the very moment when, as he says, "a blaze of freedom is just bursting forth beyond the ocean," — "And now stand forth, ye gigantic forms, shades of the first Chieftains, and Sons of Gods, who glimmer among the rocky halls and mountain fortresses of the ancient world; and you, Conquerors of the world from Babylon and from Macedonia; ye Dynasties of Cæsars, of Huns, Arabs, Moguls, and Tartars; ye Commanders of the Faithful on the Tigris, and Commanders of the Faithful on the Tiber; you hoary Counsellors of Kings, and Peers of Sovereigns; Warriors on the car of triumph, covered with scars, and crowned with laurels; ye long rows of Consuls and Dictators, famed for your lofty minds, your unshaken constancy, your ungovernable spirit; — stand forth, and let us survey for a while your assembly, like a Council of the Gods! What were ye? The first among mortals? Seldom can you claim that title! The best of men? Still fewer of you have deserved such praise! Were ye the compellers, the instigators of the human race, the prime movers of all their works? Rather let us say that you were the instruments, that you were the wheels, by whose means the Invisible Being has conducted the incomprehensible fabric of universal government across the ocean of time!"

Instruments and wheels of the Invisible Governor of the Universe! This is indeed all which the greatest of men ever have been, or ever can be. No flatteries of courtiers; no adulations of the multitude; no audacity of self-reliance; no intoxications of success; no evolutions or developments of science, — can make more or other of them. This is "the sea-mark of their utmost sail," — the goal of their farthest run, — the very round and top of their highest soaring.

Oh, if there could be, to-day, a deeper and more pervading impression of this great truth throughout our land, and a more prevailing conformity of our thoughts and words and acts to the lessons which it involves, — if we could lift ourselves to a loftier sense of our relations to the Invisible, — if, in surveying our past history, we could catch larger and more exalted views of our destinies and our responsibilities, — if we could realize that the want of good men may be a heavier woe to a land than any want of what the world calls great men, — our Centennial Year would not only be signalized by splendid ceremonials and magnificent commemorations and gorgeous expositions, but it would go far towards fulfilling something of the grandeur of that "Acceptable Year" which was announced by higher than human lips, and would be the auspicious promise and pledge of a glorious second century of Independence and Freedom for our country!

For, if that second century of self-government is to go on safely to its close, or is to go on safely and prosperously at all, there must be some renewal of that old spirit of subordination and obedience to Divine, as well as human, Laws, which has been our security in the past. There must be faith in something higher and better than ourselves. There must be a reverent acknowledgment of an Unseen, but All-seeing, All-controlling Ruler of the Universe. His Word, His Day, His House, His Worship, must be sacred to our children, as they have been to their fathers; and His blessing must never fail to be invoked upon our land and upon our liberties. The patriot voice, which cried from the balcony of yonder Old State House, when the Declaration had been originally proclaimed, "Stability and perpetuity to American Independence," did not fail to add,

"God save our American States." I would prolong that ancestral prayer. And the last phrase to pass my lips at this hour, and to take its chance for remembrance or oblivion in years to come, as the conclusion of this Centennial Oration, and the sum, and summing up, of all I can say to the present or the future, shall be:—There is, there can be, no Independence of God: In Him, as a Nation, no less than in Him, as individuals, "we live, and move, and have our being!" GOD SAVE OUR AMERICAN STATES!

PEABODY EDUCATION FUND.

ADDRESS AT THE ANNUAL MEETING OF THE TRUSTEES, AT THE WHITE SULPHUR SPRINGS, VIRGINIA, AUGUST 3, 1876.

GENTLEMEN OF THE BOARD OF TRUSTEES OF THE PEABODY EDUCATION FUND:

AN Annual Meeting of this Board was clearly contemplated by our illustrious founder, and was expressly recognized in the original resolutions by which the organization and proceedings of the Trustees were arranged, in March, 1867. We have, therefore, never failed to hold one. But the times and places of these Annual Meetings have hitherto been somewhat casually and capriciously appointed.

One of them has been held in January; two of them in February; one in June; two in July; and the last two in October.

Four of them have been held in the City of New York. One of them has been held in Baltimore; one in Washington; one in Philadelphia; and one in Boston.

Meantime there have been four Special Meetings of the Board, besides that at Washington, at which it was first established, in February, 1867. Two of these Special Meetings have been held at New York; one of them at Richmond, Virginia; and one of them at Newport, Rhode Island. Other Special Meetings have been conditionally appointed, both for Memphis and for Nashville, Tennessee; but, owing to intervening circumstances, have been given up.

The Trustees have repeatedly evinced a disposition and a purpose to fix the time and place of their Annual Meetings definitely and positively. In 1869 they voted that Washington and the third Thursday of January be the place and time of our Annual Meetings, until otherwise ordered. In 1870 this vote was repealed, and the City of New York and the third Wednesday of February were adopted as the place and time, except when otherwise ordered. In 1872 it was voted that " the Annual Meeting shall hereafter be held in the City of New York, in the month of July in every year, the precise day to be fixed by the Chairman and General Agent, after due consultation with the Trustees individually." In 1873 the second Wednesday in October was fixed for the day of the Annual Meeting; and, in 1874, the first Wednesday in October was substituted for the second: New York, however, still being named as the place.

As the result of all these various and varying votes, I think it may fairly be inferred that New York has peculiarly commended itself to the Board as the most eligible and appropriate place for our Annual Meeting, and October as the most convenient month; and I cannot help feeling that it would be wise for us to establish this place and this time by a by-law, which should henceforth be changeable, if at all, only by a two-thirds, or even a unanimous, vote.

Holding our charter from the State of New York, it seems fit that our Annual Meeting should be held within the limits of that State. Our Treasurer, too, with his books and vouchers and the greater part of our securities, has had from the first, and probably will continue to have to the last, an abode in the great commercial metropolis of the Union; and there only can his accounts and books and evidences of property be conveniently examined. Meantime, both for our financial reports and for those of our General Agent, it is extremely desirable that the time of the Annual Meeting should be so regulated, that these reports should cover as nearly as possible the exact term of twelve months; and that we should thus be able to form a full and correct impression, year by year, of our work in the past and of our ways and means for the future. The embarrassments and uncertainties which have been experienced or brought to my knowledge officially, now and heretofore, in view of a midsummer meeting at an unusual place, have concurred with the considerations I have already suggested, in inducing me to urge upon the Board to adopt a rule, which shall be beyond easy reversal, for holding our Annual Meetings regularly in the City of New York, and in the month of October.

At our meeting in 1873, a discretionary authority was given to the Chairman to call the next Annual Meeting thereafter at these White Sulphur Springs in Virginia; but on consultation with the Trustees, as the time approached, it was found best to relinquish the idea. At our meeting, last October, the proposal to meet here was renewed in a more positive form; and we are here to-day in conformity with the express order of the Board.

We have come at length to this celebrated Watering Place of the Old Dominion, which was so dear to Mr. Peabody himself, and where he spent not a few of the last and happiest weeks of his life, in the months of August and September, 1869, after his great plans of philanthropy and beneficence had all been arranged, and when nothing remained for him but to enjoy — so far as his failing strength allowed him to enjoy any thing — the respect and gratitude and affectionate attentions of the troops of Southern friends by whom he was here surrounded.

More than one of our number were witnesses to what occurred here during those weeks. Our Secretary, Mr. Russell, was here. Our second Vice-President, Governor Aiken, was here. Our General Agent, Dr. Sears, was here, and received the last counsels and instructions, in regard to the prosecution of our work, from lips which were so soon to be closed.

The associations of this place cannot fail, I am sure, to exercise a wholesome influence over our deliberations and doings, and to impress upon us all a renewed sense of the importance and responsibility of the trust which has been committed to us. We may not forget that nearly one full third of the time prescribed by Mr. Peabody for the positive continuance of the trust has already been completed. We may well rejoice that so much has been accomplished in the cause of free schools in the Southern States during these nine or ten years; and I think we shall all agree that we have a special cause for gratitude to

God, that the life and health of our General Agent have been spared, and that our work, during the whole period, has thus had the consistency and efficiency which could only have come from a single directing mind, devotedly pursuing a policy which had been carefully considered and deliberately adopted.

But while our General Agency has so happily remained unchanged, the Board itself, by whose appointment and with whose authority every thing has been done, has enjoyed no such exemption. In the little photograph group of the original Trustees, taken in March, 1867, there were twelve standing figures and five sitting figures, including that of our illustrious founder himself. Of the sitting figures, but two are now figures of the living; of the standing figures, only six. At almost every Annual Meeting, we have had sad reminders that the tenure of our service was not dependent alone on Mr. Peabody's appointment, and that but few of those who took part in the organization of our work could expect to be in the way of watching over it to its close.

Such a reminder comes to us most impressively to-day. In a letter from our late esteemed and beloved associate, Governor Clifford, written to me from Italy, last September, and a part of which, it may be remembered, was read at the opening of our last Annual Meeting, he said of Governor Graham, the tidings of whose death had just reached him: "He was not one of those who, when we last met, I had any forebodings might be *starred* on our fast-diminishing roll of Mr. Peabody's original appointments, before the Board assembled again. But it will not be long before that roll will bear more of these sad and impressive signs of our common mortality. Already the little band of sixteen counts but one more among the living than it does of those who have joined the venerated founder of the trust in that spirit-land to which we are all rapidly hastening."

He little dreamed, when he was writing these words in a foreign land, and while he was enjoying the raptures of a first visit to the Alps, of which his letter was full, that a star against his own name, in our very next Annual Report, would have eliminated that "one more" from his reckoning; and that his own death would be the means of leaving Mr. Peabody's original appointments just equally divided, as they are to-day, between the living and the dead!

Returning home from this first visit to Europe, not many months after that letter was written, re-invigorated in health, as was thought by his friends and by himself, — seemingly with a new lease of life, as was hoped by all who knew him, — he was suddenly prostrated by a disease of the heart, and died at his residence, in New Bedford, on the second of January last.

Born in Rhode Island, in 1809, and educated at the University of that State, of which our General Agent was so long the President, he became a citizen of Massachusetts in his earliest manhood; and was successively a Representative in her Legislature, a member of her Senate and President of that body, District-Attorney, Attorney-General, and, in 1853, Governor of the Commonwealth. In all these relations he acquired high distinction, and acquitted himself in a manner to win universal respect and confidence. He had no passion, however, for public office, and assumed it only from a sense of duty. He refused more candidacies than he ever accepted, and it is no secret that he declined more than one offer of foreign appointment during the very last year of his life. He had great capacities for public usefulness, and would have adorned any position in the gift of the people or the President, at home or abroad. But he preferred the quieter and more independent walks of life, and only abandoned his professional labors at last, to preside over one of those great Railroad Corporations whose business demands so much both of legal skill and of practical tact.

It is, however, mainly in his connection with our own Board that I would speak of him on this occasion. From only two of our thirteen meetings, Annual and Special, has he been absent; — the very first, at Washington, when he had hardly received notice of his appointment; and the very last, at New York, while he was still on the other side of the ocean. No one has taken a more active, earnest, intelligent, efficient part in all our deliberations and in all our doings. No one has contributed more to the harmony of our councils. No one has added more to our social satisfactions and enjoyments.

His genial temperament, his generous impulses, his ready and felicitous words, his always kind and conciliatory tone and manner, together with his wisdom and judgment, have rendered him one of the most valuable and important members of our Board; and there is hardly any other loss which could be felt more deeply than his, by those who have been associated with him here.

For myself, certainly, accustomed as I have been, from the first, to enjoy his friendly companionship in coming on to our meetings, wherever they were held, and to rely, as I always could and did, on his advice and co-operation in all that related to our proceedings, I can hardly express too strongly the personal sorrow I feel in being called on to announce his death. I leave it to others to prepare and propose such formal Resolutions as may secure for his name such a place on our records, as, I am assured, his memory will always hold in our hearts.

COLONEL THOMAS ASPINWALL.

REMARKS AT A MEETING OF THE MASSACHUSETTS HISTORICAL SOCIETY, OCTOBER 12, 1876.

We have had a long vacation, Gentlemen. In the whole history of our Society, running through more than eighty years, I doubt whether there has ever been so long an interval between our meetings. We met last on the 11th of May; and it is now the 12th of October, — five months and a day.

When Dr. Ellis made the motion for so long a suspension of our customary proceedings, he certainly exhibited a wise forecast. The intense heat of the past summer was, indeed, enough of itself to dissolve any good purposes of literary or historical labor. But when we remember, also, the varied and distracting avocations of not a few of us during this Centennial Year, we may well be satisfied that we had been exempted in advance from any positive obligations in this quarter. We return to those obligations, I trust, with a refreshed sense of their interest and importance, and with a renewed purpose to discharge them punctually and faithfully.

But we may not forget this morning, Gentlemen, that during our long vacation we have lost a distinguished and venerable name from the roll of our living Resident Members.

Hardly three years have elapsed since, in speaking of the late Colonel Thomas Aspinwall, in the new Town Hall of his native place, I was able to say that, "until a few weeks past, he had exhibited so little of old age, except its experience, its wisdom, and its venerableness, that no one was ready to give credit to the tale which he sometimes told of a birthday in Brookline eighty-six or eighty-seven years ago."

Later still, at our monthly meeting in June, 1873, our associate, Mr. Sibley, in referring to the aged graduates of Harvard University, made a graceful allusion to the personal presence of Colonel Aspinwall, a graduate of the year 1804.

But that was his very last appearance among us. He could no longer contend against the infirmities of mind and body which weighed upon him so heavily. He might still be seen, even to the last week of his life, taking his occasional exercise, and threading his way along our crowded sidewalks, with a sturdy step and something of the old martial air, but recognizing no one out of his own family, and remembering little or nothing of matters or things either recent or remote.

He died on Friday, the 11th of August, at his residence in Hancock Street in this city, at the age of ninety years two months and nineteen days, having been born in Brookline on the 23d of May, 1786. His funeral took place on the following Monday afternoon at Brookline; and nothing but absence from the State prevented me from attending it. Both personally and officially I should have felt bound to be present, had it been in my power.

He had been connected with our Society longer than any other member at the time of his death. He was chosen a Corresponding Member in July, 1833, while he was American Consul in London; and soon after his return home, in April, 1855, he was elected a Resident Member. He was on our Standing Committee for four years, and on the Publishing Committee for three volumes of our Collections. From 1862 to 1870, he was one of our Vice-Presidents.

During his resident membership, he made valuable communications at our meetings and important contributions to our Historical Collections. His Papers on the Narragansett Patent, and on William Vassall, and his admirable tribute to his friend General Winfield Scott, on the death of the old hero, will be remembered by us all.

But the ninth and tenth volumes of the Fourth Series of our Collections, both printed in 1871, furnish a still more recent and more adequate memorial of his labors in our behalf. Entitled "The Aspinwall Papers," and supplied wholly from the materials gathered by himself in England, they will keep his name fresh and fragrant where he would most desire that it should not be forgotten. We have no other volumes, I think, and may never again have, edited and annotated by one who had already reached his eighty-fifth year!

Colonel Aspinwall was a man of the highest integrity and the most ardent patriotism. On the first breaking out of the war of 1812, he abandoned his profession as a lawyer and took a commission as Major in the Army of the United States. He was brevetted a Lieutenant-Colonel for his gallantry at Sackett's Harbor in 1813, and a Colonel for his courage and conduct at Fort Erie in 1814, where he lost his left arm in battle. On the restoration of peace, though offered the position of Inspector-General, he preferred civil service, and was soon afterwards appointed Consul at London. In that capacity he served his country diligently and faithfully until 1853, — a term of thirty-eight years. During this period he formed the intimate friendship of such men as Joshua Bates, the benefactor of our Boston Public Library, and Washington Irving, whose publishing contracts were made through him, and to whom he paid a most interesting tribute at one of our meetings, in 1859.

I will dwell no longer on the details of his career, which may well form the subject of a formal Memoir, according to our custom. It is enough to say of him that he had the respect, esteem, and affection of all who knew him. A braver and more independent spirit has hardly ever dwelt among us. He measured his patriotism by no party standard. Always for his country, its constitution, and its union, he was as sincere and earnest in its cause when it was assailed from within, as when he was personally combating against a foreign foe. But he had his own opinions as to men and measures, and never flinched from the responsibility of avowing them and acting upon them.

I can close this brief notice in no way more appropriately than by reading a portion of a letter lately received from our worthy Honorary Member, Mr. Grigsby,[1] who illustrates Colonel Aspinwall's acuteness in historical inquiries as follows: —

[1] The Honorable Hugh Blair Grigsby, LL.D., President of the Virginia Historical Society, and Chancellor of William and Mary's College.

"How well-timed my visit to Boston in 1867! I saw Ticknor, and Jeffries Wyman, and good Mr. Folsom, and Colonel Aspinwall, who has just gone. Let me give you a reminiscence of Colonel Aspinwall. I was introduced to him in the hall of the Historical Society, on my visit in June, 1867. A short time before, I had written a letter, which appeared in 'The Proceedings,' relating to the origin of the name of Newport News, and endeavored to show that the true name was Newport Newce, in honor of Sir William Newce, the Marshal of the Virginia Colony in 1621. I would add that I believe there did not then exist half-a-dozen men in the United States who knew that such a man as Sir William Newce ever appeared upon the stage in Virginia or elsewhere. You may imagine, then, my surprise, when Colonel Aspinwall, almost immediately after my introduction to him, said to me, with an evident sense of interest in the question, 'Mr. Grigsby, why do you believe that the name of Newce was taken from Sir *William*, instead of from his brother *George?*' I was so struck with the question, coming from an old gentleman, then in his eighty-third year, and known to me only as one of the heroes of the war of 1812, and as the Consul at London, that I answered playfully, 'To tell you the truth, Colonel Aspinwall, I did not know that Sir William had a brother.' When I had thus expressed my admiration of his minute historical knowledge, I assigned the obvious reasons, that Sir William Newce had been largely endowed by the Virginia Company, that he was the most distinguished military and naval officer in the colony, and that he was the only one who had attained to the dignity of knighthood.

"The venerable patriot must have had a happy life: — military fame; forty years in the leading foreign consulate; and an old age of competence, respect, and honor; and the only one, out of the hundred thousand of his fellow-beings who began life with him, who passed beyond the milestone of ninety; while Macaulay went off in the fifties; Scott, Prescott, Choate, in the sixties; Folsom and Everett in the seventies; Ticknor almost, and Savage quite, in the eighties."

THE UNVEILING OF THE STATUE OF DANIEL WEBSTER.

AN ADDRESS DELIVERED IN THE CENTRAL PARK, NEW YORK, NOVEMBER 25, 1876.

I AM here, Mr. Mayor, fellow-countrymen and friends, with no purpose of trespassing very long on your attention. I was doubtful almost to the last moment whether I should be able to be here at all to-day, and I am afraid that I have neither voice nor strength for many words in the open air.

But, indeed, the Address of this occasion has been made. It has been made by one to whom it was most appropriately assigned, and who had every title and every talent for making it. It was peculiarly fit that this grand gift to your magnificent Park should be acknowledged and welcomed by a citizen of New York, — one of whom you are all justly proud, an eminent advocate and jurist, a distinguished statesman and public speaker, with the laurels of the Centennial Oration at Philadelphia still fresh on his brow.[1] The utterances of this hour might well have ended with him.

I could not, however, find it in my heart to refuse altogether the repeated and urgent request of your munificent fellow-citizen, Mr. Burnham, that I would be here on the platform with Mr. Evarts and himself, to-day, to witness the unveiling of this noble Statue, and to add a few words in commemoration of him whom it so vividly and so impressively portrays.

Mr. Burnham has done me the honor to call me to his assistance on this occasion, as one who had enjoyed some peculiar opportunities for knowing the illustrious statesman to whose

[1] The Hon. William M. Evarts.

memory he is paying these large and sumptuous honors. And it is true, my friends, that my personal associations with Mr. Webster reach back to a distant day. I recall him as a familiar visitor in the homes of more than one of those with whom I was most nearly connected, when I was but a schoolboy, on his first removal to Boston, in 1817. I recall the deep impressions produced on all who heard him, and communicated to all who did not hear him, by his great efforts in the Constitutional Convention of Massachusetts, and, soon afterward, by his noble Discourse at Plymouth Rock, in 1820. I was myself in the crowd which gazed at him, and listened to him with admiration, when he laid the corner-stone of the Monument on Bunker Hill, in presence of Lafayette, in 1824. I was myself in the throng which hung with rapture on his lips as he pronounced that splendid eulogy on Adams and Jefferson, in Faneuil Hall, in 1826. Entering his office as a Law-Student, in 1828, I was under his personal tuition during three of the busiest and proudest years of his life. From 1840 to 1850 I was associated with him in the Congress of the United States; and I may be pardoned for not forgetting that it was then my privilege and my pride to succeed him in the Senate, when he was last called into the Cabinet, as Secretary of State, by President Fillmore.

I have thus no excuse, my friends, for not knowing something, for not knowing much, of Daniel Webster. Of those who knew him longer or better than I did, few, certainly, remain among the living; and I could hardly have reconciled it with what is due to his memory, or with what is due to my own position, if I had refused, — I will not say, to bear testimony to his wonderful powers and his great public services; for all such testimony would be as superfluous as to bear testimony to the light of the sun in the skies above us, — but if I had declined to give expression to the gratification and delight with which the Sons of New England, and the Sons of Massachusetts and of Boston especially, and I as one of them, cannot fail to regard this most signal commemoration of one, whose name and fame were so long and so peculiarly dear to them.

Neither Mr. Evarts nor I have come here to-day, my friends, to hold up Mr. Webster, — much as we may have admired or loved him, — as one with whom we have always agreed, as one whose course we have uniformly approved, or in whose career we have seen nothing to regret. Our testimony is all the more trustworthy, — my own certainly is, — that we have sometimes differed from him. But we are here to recognize him as one of the greatest men our country has ever produced; as one of the grandest figures in our whole national history; as one who, for intellectual power, had no superior, and hardly an equal, in our own land or in any other land, during his day and generation; as one whose written and spoken words, so fitly embalmed "for a life beyond life" in the six noble volumes edited by Edward Everett, are among the choicest treasures of our language and literature; and, still more and above all, as one who rendered inestimable services to his country, — at one period, vindicating its rights and preserving its peace with foreign nations by the most skilful and masterly diplomacy; at another period, rescuing its Constitution from overthrow, and repelling triumphantly the assaults of nullification and disunion, by overpowering argument and matchless eloquence.

Mr. Webster made many marvellous manifestations of himself in his busy life of threescore years and ten. Convincing arguments in the Courts of Law, brilliant appeals to popular assemblies, triumphant speeches in the Halls of Legislation, magnificent orations and discourses of commemoration or ceremony, — are thickly scattered along his whole career. I rejoice to remember how many of them I have heard from his own lips, and how much inspiration and instruction I have derived from them. To have seen and heard him on one of his field-days, was a privilege which no one will undervalue who ever enjoyed it. There was a power, a breadth, a beauty, a perfection, in some of his efforts, when he was at his best, which distanced all approach, and rendered rivalry ridiculous.

And if the style and tone and temper of our political discussions are to be once more elevated, refined, and purified, — and we all know how much room there is for elevation and refinement, — we must go back for our examples and models at least as far as the days of that great Senatorial Triumvirate, — Clay, Calhoun, and Webster. There were giants in those days; but none of them forgot that, though "it is excellent to have a giant's strength, it is tyrannous to use it like a giant."

Among those who have been celebrated as orators or public speakers, in our own days or in other days, there have been many diversities of gifts and many diversities of operations. There have been those who were listened to wholly for their intellectual qualities, for the wit or the wisdom, the learning or the philosophy, which characterized their efforts. There have been those whose main attraction was a curious felicity and facility of illustration and description, adorned by the richest gems which could be gathered by historical research or classical study. There have been those to whom the charms of manner and the graces of elocution and the melody of voice were the all-sufficient recommendations to attention and applause. And there have been those who owed their success more to opportunity and occasion, to some stirring theme or some exciting emergency, than to any peculiar attributes of their own. But Webster combined every thing. No thoughts more profound and weighty. No style more terse and telling. No illustrations more vivid and clear-cut. No occasions more august and momentous. No voice more deep and thrilling. No manner more impressive and admirable. No presence so grand and majestic, as his.

That great brain of his, as I have seen it working, whether in public debate or in private converse, seemed to me often like some mighty machine, — always ready for action, and almost always in action, evolving much material from its own resources and researches, and eagerly appropriating and assimilating whatever was brought within its reach, producing and reproducing the richest fabrics with the ease and certainty, the precision and the condensing energy, of a perfect Corliss engine, — such an one as many of us have just seen presiding so magically and so majestically over the Exposition at Philadelphia.

And he put his own crown-stamp on almost every thing he uttered. There was no mistaking one of Webster's great efforts. There is no mistaking them now. They will be distinguished, in all time to come, like pieces of old gold or silver plate, by an unmistakable mint-mark. He knew, like the casters or forgers of yonder Statue, not only how to pour forth burning words and blazing thoughts, but so to blend and fuse and weld together his facts and figures, his illustrations and arguments, his metaphors and subject matter, as to bring them all out at last into one massive and enduring image of his own great mind!

He was by no means wanting in labor and study; and he often anticipated the earliest dawn in his preparations for an immediate effort. I remember how humorously he told me once, that the cocks in his own yard often mistook his morning candle for the break of day, and began to crow lustily as he entered his office, though it were two hours before sunrise. Yet he frequently did wonderful things off-hand; and one might often say of him, in the words of an old poet, —

> "His noble negligences teach
> What others' toils despair to reach."

Not in our own land only, Mr. Mayor and fellow-countrymen, were the pre-eminent powers of Mr. Webster recognized and appreciated. Brougham, and Lyndhurst, and the late Lord Derby, as I had abundant opportunity of knowing, were no underraters of his intellectual grasp and grandeur. I remember well, too, the casual testimony of a venerable prelate of the English Church, — the late Dr. Harcourt, then Archbishop of York, — who said to me, thirty years ago, in London, "I met your wonderful friend, Mr. Webster, for only five minutes; but in those five minutes I learned more of American institutions, and of the peculiar working of the American Constitution, than in all that I had ever heard or read from any or all other sources."

Of his Discourse on the Second Centennial Anniversary of the Landing of the Pilgrims on Plymouth Rock, John Adams wrote, in acknowledging a copy of it, "Mr. Burke is no longer entitled to the praise of being the most consummate orator of modern times." And, certainly, from the date of that Discourse, he stood second, as an Orator, to no one who spoke the English language. But it is peculiarly and pre-eminently as the Expounder and Defender of the Constitution of the United

States, in January, 1830, that he will be remembered and honored as long as that Constitution shall hold a place in the American heart, or a place on the pages of the world's history.

Mr. Webster once said, — and perhaps more than once, — that there was not an article, a section, a clause, a phrase, a word, a syllable, or even a comma, of that Constitution, which he had not studied and pondered in every relation and in every construction of which it was susceptible.

Born at the commencement of the year 1782, at the very moment when the necessity of such an Instrument for preserving our Union, and making us a Nation, was first beginning to be comprehended and felt by the patriots who had achieved our Independence, — just as they had fully discovered the utter insufficiency of the old Confederation, and how mere a rope of sand it was; born in that very year in which the Legislature of your own State of New York, under the lead of your gallant Philip Schuyler, at the prompting of your grand Alexander Hamilton, was adopting the very first resolutions passed by any State in favor of such an Instrument, — it might almost be said that the natal air of the Constitution was his own natal air. He drank in its spirit with his earliest breath, and seemed born to comprehend, expound, and defend it. No Roman schoolboy ever committed to memory the laws of the Twelve Tables more diligently and thoroughly than did he the Constitution of his country. He had it by heart in more senses of the words than one, and every part and particle of it seemed only less precious and sacred to him than his Bible.

John Adams himself was not more truly the Colossus of Independence in the Continental Congress of 1776, than Daniel Webster was the Colossus of the Constitution and the Union in the Federal Congress of 1830.

For other speeches, of other men, it might perhaps be claimed that they have had the power to inflame and precipitate war, — foreign war, or civil war. Of Webster's great speech, as a Senator of Massachusetts, in 1830, — and of that alone, I think, — it can be said, that it averted and postponed Civil War for a whole generation. Yes, it repressed the irrepressible conflict itself for thirty years! And when that dire calamity came upon us at last, though the voice of the master had so long been hushed, that speech still supplied the most convincing arguments and the most inspiring incitements for a resolute defence of the Union. It is not yet exhausted. There is argument and inspiration enough in it still, if only they be heeded, to carry us along, as a United People, at least for another Century. In that Speech "he still lives;" and lives for the Constitution and the Union of his Country.

Why, my friends, not even the Dynamite and Rend-rock and Vulcan powder of your scientific and gallant Newton were more effective in blasting and shattering your Hell-Gate reef, and opening the way for the safe navigation of yonder Bay, than that speech of Webster was in exploding the doctrines of nullification, and clearing the channel for our Ship of State to sail on, safely, prosperously, triumphantly, whether in sunshine or in storm!

Beyond all comparison, it was *the Speech* of our Constitutional Age. "*Nil simile aut secundum.*" It was James Madison, of Virginia, himself, who said of it in a letter at the time: "It crushes nullification, and must hasten an abandonment of secession." Whatever remained to be done, in the progress of events, for the repression of menacing designs or of overt acts, was grandly done by the resolute patriotism and iron will of President Jackson, whose proclamation and policy, to that end, Mr. Webster sustained with all his might. They were the legitimate conclusions of his own great Argument.

Of other and later efforts of Mr. Webster, I have neither time nor inclination to speak. There are too many coals still burning beneath the smouldering embers of some of his more recent controversies, for any one to rake them rashly open on such an occasion as this. I was by no means in full accord with his memorable 7th of March speech, and my views of it to-day are precisely what he knew they were in 1850. But no differences of opinion on that day, or on any other day, ever impaired my admiration of his powers, my confidence in his patriotism, my earnest wishes for his promotion, nor the full assurance which I felt that he would administer the Government with perfect integrity, as well as with consummate ability. What a President he would have made for a Centennial year! What a tower of strength he would have been, to our Constitution and our Country, in all the perplexities and perils through which we have recently passed, and are still passing! "Oh! for an hour of Dundee"!

No one will pretend that he was free from all infirmities of character and conduct, though they have often been grossly exaggerated. Great temptations proverbially beset the pathway of great powers; and one who can overcome almost every thing else, may sometimes fail of conquering himself. He never assumed to be faultless; and he would have indignantly rebuked any one who assumed it for him. We all know that, while he could master the great questions of National Finance, and was never weary in maintaining the importance of upholding the National Credit, he never cared quite enough about his own finances, or took particular pains to preserve his own personal credit. We all know that he was sometimes impatient of differences, and sometimes arrogant and overbearing towards opponents. His own consciousness of surpassing powers, and the flatteries,—I had almost said, the idolatries,—of innumerable friends, would account for much more of all this than he ever displayed. I have known him in all his moods. I have experienced the pain of his frown, as well as the charms of his favor. And I will acknowledge that I would rather confront him as he is here, to-day, in bronze, than encounter his opposition in the flesh. His antagonism was tremendous. "Safest he who stood aloof." But his better nature always asserted itself in the end. No man or woman or child could be more tender and affectionate.

And there is one element of his character which must never be forgotten. I mean his deep religious faith and trust. I recall the delight with which he often conversed on the Bible. I recall the delight with which he dwelt on that exquisite prayer of one of the old Prophets, repeating it fervently as a model of eloquence and of devotion: "Although the fig-tree shall not blossom, neither shall fruit be in the vines; the labor of the olive shall fail, and the fields shall yield no meat; the flock shall be cut off from the fold, and there shall be no herd in the stalls: yet I will rejoice in the Lord, I will joy in the

God of my salvation." I recall his impressive and powerful plea for the Religious Instruction of the Young, in the memorable case of Girard College. I have been with him on the most solemn occasions, in Boston and at Washington, in the midst of the most exciting and painful controversies, kneeling by his side at the table of our common Master, and witnessing the humility and reverence of his worship. And who has forgotten those last words which he ordered to be inscribed, and which are inscribed, on his tombstone at Marshfield: —

"'Lord, I believe; help Thou mine unbelief.' Philosophical Argument, especially that drawn from the vastness of the universe, in comparison with the apparent insignificance of this globe, has sometimes shaken my reason for the faith which is in me; but my heart has always assured and re-assured me that the Gospel of Jesus Christ must be a Divine Reality. The Sermon on the Mount cannot be a merely human production. This belief enters into the very depth of my conscience. The whole history of man proves it. — DANIEL WEBSTER."

I cannot help wishing that this declaration, in all its original fulness, were engraved on one of the sides of yonder monumental base, in letters which all the world might read. Amid all the perplexities which modern Science, intentionally or unintentionally, is multiplying and magnifying around us, what consolation and strength must ever be found in such an expression of faith from that surpassing intellect!

I congratulate you, my friends, that your Park is to be permanently adorned with this grand figure, and that the inscription on its massive pedestal is to associate it for ever with the great principle of "Union and Liberty, one and inseparable." Nor can I conclude without saying, that, from all I have ever known of Mr. Webster's feelings, nothing could have gratified him so much as that, in this Centennial Year, on this memorable Anniversary, nearly a quarter of a century after he had gone to his rest, — when all the partialities and prejudices, all the love and the hate, which wait upon the career of living public men, should have grown cold or passed away, — a Statue of himself should be set up here, within the limits of your magnificent

City, and amid these superb surroundings. Quite apart from those personal and domestic ties which rendered New York so dear to him, — of which we have a touching reminder in the presence of the venerable lady who was so long the sharer of his name and the ornament of his home, — quite apart from all such considerations, he would have appreciated such a tribute as this, I think, above all other posthumous honors.

There was something congenial to him in the grandeur of this great Commercial Metropolis. He loved, indeed, the hills and plains of New Hampshire, among which he was born. He delighted in Marshfield and the shores of Plymouth, where he was buried. He was warmly attached to Boston and the people of Massachusetts, among whom he had lived so long, and from whom he had so often received his commissions as their Representative and their Senator in Congress. But in your noble City, as he said, he recognized "the commercial capital, not only of the United States, but of the whole continent from the pole to the South Sea." "The growth of this City," said he, "and the Constitution of the United States are coevals and contemporaries." "New York herself," he exclaimed, "is the noblest eulogy on the Union of the States." He delighted to remember that here Washington was first inaugurated as President, and that here had been the abode of Hamilton and John Jay and Rufus King. And it was at a banquet, given to him, at your own Niblo's Garden in 1837, and under the inspiration of these associations, that he summed up the whole lesson of the past and the whole duty of the future, and condensed them into a sentiment, which has ever since entered into the circulating medium of true patriotism, like an ingot of gold with the impress of the eagle: "One Country, One Constitution, One Destiny."

Let that motto, still and ever, be the watchword of the hour, and whatever momentary perplexities or perils may environ us, with the blessing of God, no permanent harm can happen to our Republic.

In behalf of my fellow-citizens of New England, I thank Mr. Burnham for this great gift to your Central Park; and I congratulate him on having associated his name with so splendid a tribute to so illustrious a man. A New Englander himself, he long ago decorated one of the chief Cities of his native State with a noble Statue of a venerated father of the Church to which he belongs.[1] He has now adorned the City of his residence with this grand figure of a pre-eminent American Statesman. He has thus doubly secured for himself the grateful remembrance of all by whom Religion and Patriotism, Churchmanship and Statesmanship, shall be held worthy of commemoration and honor, in all time to come.

[1] A bronze Statue of the Rt. Rev. Thomas Church Brownell, D.D., — for more than forty years the Bishop of Connecticut, and, at his death, in 1865, the presiding Bishop of the Protestant Episcopal Church in the United States, — was presented to Trinity College, Hartford, of which he was the Founder, by his Son-in-law, Mr. Burnham, and was unveiled in the College Grounds, on the 11th of November, 1869.

OLYMPIA MORATA.

REMARKS AT A MEETING OF THE MASSACHUSETTS HISTORICAL SOCIETY, FEBRUARY 8, 1877.

THE paper which has just been read has carried us back a hundred years, and given an interesting account of one whose name was probably known to but few of us, until we listened to it. Meantime, I will venture to go back more than three hundred years, and to call attention to a name which may be even less familiar to most of those present.

It will be remembered, perhaps, that I have more than once made reference to an old manuscript volume, which seems to have been a kind of Commonplace-Book of Adam Winthrop, the father of our Governor. From that little *farrago libelli*, as it might well be called, I have, at one time, derived a contemporaneous account of the execution of Mary Queen of Scots; and, at another time, a detailed description of the last sad scene in the life of Sir Walter Raleigh, with the words which he uttered on the scaffold.

There are a few other passages in the same miscellaneous scrap-book not unworthy of notice; and one of them I propose to deal with briefly this morning. It will at least afford me the opportunity of relating one of those little incidents or accidents of travel by which my visit to Europe, two or three years ago, was diversified.

In looking at this ancient manuscript book, I had more than once observed, on some of the most closely and crabbedly written pages, a name with which I had no associations whatever;

and I had turned over the leaves again and again, without feeling any impulse to decipher or copy them. The name alone had lingered in my memory, and that somewhat faintly and flickeringly. But, in driving through the streets of Heidelberg, in the autumn of 1874, after having just come down from a visit to the magnificent ruins of Heidelberg Castle, I passed the Church of St. Peter, — an old Lutheran church, on the walls of which, it was said, Luther himself had affixed one of his famous Theses; and, on asking the friend who accompanied me whether there was any thing within the church of special interest, I was told that there was nothing except a monument to a remarkable woman named OLYMPIA MORATA. The church was closed, and it was too late for me to obtain an entrance. But, feeling sure that Olympia Morata was the name I had once or twice spelt out in Adam Winthrop's Commonplace-Book, I requested my friend to send me a copy of the inscription on the monument, with a reference to any account of her life which might be extant. It appeared that a careful biography of her had been written in French, not many years ago, by M. Jules Bonnet, of which I have now here the fourth edition, and which has been thought worthy of being "crowned," as the phrase is, by the French Academy. A most interesting little volume it is, which might well be translated, and find a place among our literary and religious biographies.

A more remarkable woman, certainly, has seldom lived, in any age or land, than Olympia Morata. Born in Ferrara, in 1526, about the time of the great Revival of Letters, she seems to have exhibited in her earliest years a most precocious and marvellous talent for the languages of ancient Rome and Greece; and, under the tuition of her father and other professors, she soon mastered the works of Virgil and Cicero and Homer. Before she had completed her sixteenth year, she had composed a defence of Cicero against some of his critics and calumniators. About the same time she wrote observations on Homer, and translated parts of the Iliad, "with great strength and sweetness." Meantime, she composed many and various poems herself, with great elegance, and dialogues in Greek and in Latin, in imitation of Plato and Cicero. "I have heard her at court," writes Curio, "declaiming in Latin, speaking Greek, and answering questions, as well as any of the females among the ancients could have done. Do not feel a doubt respecting the Sapphic Ode, in which she celebrates the praises of the Most High." This ode or hymn was even compared with those of Pindar.

She of course became celebrated far beyond the immediate circle in which she moved, and was chosen as the special companion and friend of the eldest daughter of the Duke of Ferrara.

But the Revival of Letters, as we know, was the immediate precursor of the great Reformation in Religion. It was the age of Luther; and his doctrines and writings speedily found their way to the parts of Italy in which Olympia resided, agitating the whole mass of Italian as well as German society. Her young heart soon caught the spirit of the reformers, and she became absorbed in the new religious movement. She was discharged from the Duke's household, and compelled to fly from Ferrara. Meantime, she had found a protector in Professor André Grunthler, a distinguished physician, whom she married, in 1550; and together they went first to Augsburg, and afterwards to Schweinfurt. Then came the civil wars, with the terrible siege of Schweinfurt, which lasted fourteen months. Escaping from there at great peril, they at length reached Heidelberg, where her husband was made a Lecturer in the University. But, two years afterwards, the plague broke out there, with great fury; and on the 26th of October, 1555, she fell a victim to it, and died at twenty-nine years of age.

The inscription on her tomb affords contemporaneous testimony to the exalted estimation in which she was held at Heidelberg; while, at Schweinfurt, the house in which she had lived for three years was ordered by the municipality to be restored at the public expense, and inscribed as follows: —

"A POOR AND HUMBLE MANSION, BUT NOT WITHOUT GLORY; IT WAS INHABITED BY OLYMPIA MORATA."

The tidings of her death, it is said, spread deep distress through the Reformed Churches in Germany, Switzerland, and France; and the warmest and most unqualified testimonies to her extraordinary genius and accomplishments were paid by De Thou, Beza, Melchior Adam, and others of the most distinguished writers of the time. There is a brief notice of her in the "Crudities" of the old pedestrian traveller, Thomas Coryat, first printed in 1611; and the "Itinerum Deliciæ" of Chytræus, printed in 1594, contains the inscription on her monument in Heidelberg.[1]

All of her writings which had been saved from the siege of Schweinfurt were carefully collected and printed by Celius Secundo Curio, Professor of Roman Eloquence in the University of Basle, to whom she had bequeathed them on her death-bed. The first edition was printed at Basle, in 1558; and a second, in 1562, which was dedicated to Queen Elizabeth.

Of her printed letters, one was in Greek, two in Italian, and forty-five in Latin. I know not how early any of them were printed in English; but here, in the old Commonplace-Book of Adam Winthrop, I find two of them carefully written out in English,[2] — whether translated by himself or not I have no means of knowing. This old manuscript volume must have been familiar to his son, and perhaps was prepared for his edification and instruction.

It is, then, hardly too much to say, that Olympia Morata was one of the characters from which some of our Puritan ancestors drew their examples; and I confess, as I have cursorily reviewed her career in this little volume, the figure of this young Italian girl, of whom, I regret to say, there is no adequate or authentic likeness, has seemed to rise before me from the dust, — I had almost said from the oblivion, — of centuries, to claim a place and a memory among those who, by their genius and fortitude and piety, animated and inspired the men and women who planted the land, which her great compatriots, Columbus, Vespucius, and Cabot, had discovered.

It is in this relation only that I have ventured to introduce her name here to-day.

[1] These volumes are in the library of Mr. Charles Deane, to whom I am indebted for the references.

[2] See next page.

Olympia Morata, the wife of Andrew Grunthler, unto her sister Victoria Morata, sendethe greetinge.

Deare Sister, — Wee are yet (throughe the love of God towards us) safelie escaped out of the great shipwracke of our wedded countrie: for wch you also, sister, are bounde to render thanckes to the almightie & good God, who hathe preserved us, beinge plucked from the fire & sworde, & even out of the jawes of utter distruction. If I shoulde declare to you the dangers & miseries of warre wch wee have suffered, I shoulde rather compile a greate volume than an epistle: ffor wee were xiiij monethes full, whilst the citie was beeseeged, in great distresse, & night & daie amonge the shotte of gunnes: so as if I shoulde tell you the number of shotte that battered the walles in one daie, ꝑchance it woulde seeme incredible. But God woulde have the citie holde out so longe that he might reduce the people to goodnes, ffor whilest wee were beeseeged fewe of ours were slaine; & the citie was impregnable, though it was not very greate, nor sufficientlie defended against so great force & munitions of the enymie. But at lengthe, when we thought they had bin gonne (as the Empero^{r} himselfe & other princes of the Empire had comanded), & that all thinges now had bin quiet, see, upon the suddaine, & not wthout treacherie, they rushe into the citie, & when they had rifeled it, they set it on fire. This sore wounde did Germanie (otherwise happie) receive in her bowelles throughe civil dissention of the princes. In this so grete feare & astonishment, when, as my husbande & I were even thinckinge to get us into the Churche as into a sanctuary, a souldio^{r}, whom we knewe not, came runninge, & advized us forthwth to flie out of the cittie, or otherwise wee shoulde be burned wth it. And trulie, if we had bin in the Churche, the very smoke had stifeled us, as it did others, who fled thether. Therefore we obeied his warninge, whosoever he was; wh^{ch} whilest wee doe, we fall amongst the soldiours, who spoile us; and my husbande also is twice taken of them, wch I tooke most heavilie of all: who, if hee had bin any longer detained, & God had deferred his helpe (for God did give him to mee at my petition), I had surelie died throughe the bitternesse of my greefe. The losse of all other thinges I easily endured (for I had only my smocke lefte to cover my bodie), but the losse of my most deare husbande I coulde no waie have borne. But God our father hearde my sobbes, not onlie at that present time, but after also. ffor he beinge our guide, wee came to divers Counts (as nowe a daies they call them, beinge lordes of townes & castelles), of whom we were honorablie received, & had bestowed uppon us clothes & other necessaries: amonge whom there is one whose wife is the daughter of one of the most noble Dukes of the Germans, who are called Palsgraves. This Ladie entertained mee wth suche love & godlie affection, beinge brought verie lowe, that when I was sicke shee ministred to me wth her owne handes; & besides that shee gave me a faire gowne, worthe about five powndes. An other noble man, whom we had not so muche as hearde of before, sent us, whilst wee were in o^{r} iournie, a good supplie of monye. By their liberalitie, wee were sustained in so great straightes untill my husbande was called to Heidelberge (where wee nowe bee) by the most illustrious prince Pallatine, one of the seven Electors of the Empire, to be the publicke reader of Phisicke there, for it is one of the Univ^{r}sities of Germanie, & not the meanest of them. Althoughe in this calamitous & turbulent time, there is more preparinge for armes than for artes. The Bisshops have a greate armye, & the others have the like, so as they spoile, rifle, & burne all thinges. Also in Englande the godlie are greevouslie afflicted. I heare that Bernardino Ocello, of Iene, a true Xtian man, is fled to Geneva. So that every where he that wilbe a Christian must beare his Crosse. And truelie for my part I had rather suffer, so it be wth Christ, than to inioie the whole earthe wthout Christ. Neither do I desire any thinge more but him. Althoughe I am not ignorant that our forepassed sufferinges shall not be the last, many other thinges abide us to be suffered hereafter if wee live; nay, not at this very time are wee free from troubles. One thinge I pray for, that God will give me faithe & constancie unto the ende, wch I also trust that he will doe, for he hathe promised to heare my prayers, as often as I call uppon him. And I doe dailie powre oût my soule before him. Neither is it in vaine, for I feele myselfe so strengthened & confirmed that I have not given place to his adversaries who abounde in all places, no not a haires breadthe, in the cause of religion. Neither in any thinge doe I consent wth those Epicures, who pretende the sacred name of the Gospel, to cover their filthie lustes. Thus thou seest (Deare Sister) that no place is cleare of enemies, the worlde, the Devil, & the fleshe. But it is farre better to suffer afflictions wth the Churche of God, in this most short life, then to be condemned wth the adversaries to everlasting sorrow, where the eyes are closed up to eternal night. Wherefore I earnestlie pray thee (good sister) to have respecte to thy salvation, & to feare him more, who wth one worde created all thinges, who hathe made you, who hathe saved you, & heaped so many benefites uppon you, then a fewe unprofitablé burthens of the earthe, then the shadowe of the worlde allthoughe it threaten, or ells smile & fawne uppon you. ffor all thinges that you looke uppon, what are they but a thynne vapour, or vanishinge smoke, or as stubble & haie, suddenlie to be consumed by fire. If so be that you feele yo^{r}selfe weake in this waie that leadeth to heaven, take heede that you excuse not yor weakenes; for the concealinge of a disease makes it the greater, & it is displeasinge unto God: for this cause the prophet David (Psa. cxli. 4) praiethe that God woulde not suffer his heart to incline so muche, as that he shoulde pretende an excuse for his sinnes. What must you doe then? Confesse yo^{s} disease unto the lorde, the true physition: beseche him that he would applie some medicine to you; that he woulde adde strengthe to yor weakenes; & that he woulde cause you to love & feare him more then men, ffor therfore in the psalmes he is so often called the God of our strengthe, to the ende that he may fortifie us & make us stronge, so that wee will knowe ourselves, & aske it of him; for he wilbe prayed to continually that he may be intreated. And be assured that he heareth thy praiers, & will doe what thou desirest; yea, & above thy request, seinge he is liberall, & bountifull towardes all those that seeke him heartelye. But take heede (my sister) that you despise not the voice of the gospell & saie, if, indeed, if I bee one of those that bee chosen, & appointed to salvation, I cannot perishe, for this were to tempt God, who willeth us, by the obedience of the gospel, & praier, to obtaine salvation. ffor albeit election be certaine, & the salvation of those who be p̃destinate be sure, wch such as are Christes doe feele in the inner man; yet is it not wthout Christ, & those thinges wch doe adorne the Christian profession. Paul tells us, that faithe is by hearinge, & hearinge by the worde of God. The same he writes also in the epistle to the Galathians, & in the Actes of the Apostles it appeares by the very place, that those were endued wth the holy Ghost wch had hearkened to the voice of the gospel. Let that also never be forgotten of you, wch both Paul & James doe affirme, that the faith is approved of the lorde wch is lovelie & workinge by love, & not that wch is idle & unprofitable. If it be so that you want libertie to heare, yet let no daie passe wthout readinge the holy scripture & prayer; that God woulde inlighten yor mynde, to und^{r}stande & gather out the thinges wch may further you to live well & happilie. But if also you have little spare time from yor mistres buysines, arise somewhat the more earlie in the morninge, & goe a little the later to bed in the eveninge, & so in yor private bedchamber ꝑforme those duties that serve for yor salvation. ffor the lorde comandes us to seeke his kingedome & the righteousnes thereof, before all thinges. Those duties ꝑformed, intende yor m^{res} service wth that willingnes & faithefulnes, wth that respecte & hono^{r} wch may well beseeme a Christian maiden wel brought up. Speake to Lavinia yor mistres that shee also may seeke ease of her griefes & vexations from Christian philosophie, together wth rest from all cares. Wee shall shortlie arive in the wished haven. Time passeth swiftelie, as wel in adversitie, as in prosperitie. But if her sufferinges seeme longer & harder, let her consider that shee suffers wth the citizens of heaven & of Christ, yea, wth Christ himselfe. ffor even that noble woman, whom I mentioned before, dothe beare her Crosse, & that no light one neither. And thoughe she be borne of a roial race & stocke, of w^h^ there have also bin some Emperors, yet shee is as content w^h^ this meaner condition, wch hathe befallen her. This ladie, in xix yeares space, had scarse one daie free from sicknes; yea, nowe also shee is & hathe bin many daies so dangerouslie sicke, that it is gretlie doubted of her life. Shee is a woman most religious & continuallie talketh of God, and of the life to come, wth an ernest desire & fervencie of spirite to be there. Her husbande & shee have bin oftentimes brought into the hazarde of their lives & goodes for the gospels sake. O my deare sister, praye you wth Moses in the 90 Psalme. Teache me, O Lorde, to number my dayes, & to have alwaies before myne eyes the fewnesse of them; that contemninge this vaine lyfe, I may wholy addicte myselfe to wisdome, & to the contemplation of eternitie. Seeke the lorde whilest he may be founde, pray to him continually, when you take yor foode give him thanckes; resigne yo^r^selfe wholly to his love. Walke not in the waie of the wicked. Keep yor harte pure & chaste; that at lengthe overcoming you may receive y^r^ rewarde. Salute hartilie in my name those matrons & damselles that be wth you. Write unto me a large letter of all yor afaires. The l^res^ of your deare Ladie Lavinia (whose name I hono^r^) I do greatlie desire: hir sweete behaviou^r^ & godlines are never out of my mynde. I sent hir some little bookes, but chefelie of Celius Secundus makinge. I longe to knowe whether shee received them, & if they were welcome unto her. My husbande & brother Emilius doe kisse & most hartilie salute you. ffarewell, my deere & sweete sister Victoria.

ffrom Hidelberghe, 6 Aug. 1554.

An Epistle of Olympia Morata, unto Celius Secundus Curio.

I suppose, well-beloved Celius, I neede not nowe to use any excuse to you why I have not answered your l^res^, delivered unto me longe since, for that the warre itselfe doothe sufficiently cleere me, wherew^th^ for the space of xiiij monethes we were so vexed, that by it we received all maner of calamities. For so sone as Marquis Albert, by reason of the fitnesse of the place, had placed his hoste in Swynforde, then his enymies wch were many, began to beseege the cittie, & to assaulte it, & daie & night wth their gunnes to beate the walles on all sides, when neverthelesse wee were also afflicted w^th^in the walles by the Marquesses soldiers wth many injuries, neither was any man safe ynoughe in his owne house. Beesides so often as their wages was not paide them, when it was due, they did threaten to take awaye all from the citizins, as thoughe they had been sent for, & hired by us. In so muche as the cittie, by maintaininge so many soldiours, was nowe utterlye consumed. By whose infection also so grevous a disease did welneere invade all the citizins that many, through greefe, & trouble of mynde being afflicted, died thereof, wherew^th^ also my moste lovinge husbande was taken, so that there appeared no hope of his life, whom God having pittie of mee most afflicted, w^th^out any medicine applied, did heale. For in the towne ther was not any salves.

But as Seneca saieth, the goinge out of one evil is the steppe to another that will come; for beinge delivered by God from that disease, wee were by & by beseeged wth a greater bande of enymies, wch daie & night did throwe fire into the cittie, that oftentimes in the night you woulde have thought the whole towne had bin on fire. And all that time wee were constrained to lie hidde in wine cellars. But at lengthe when wee looked for a happie ende of the warre, throughe the departure of the Marquis, who was about to leade awaie his hoaste by night to another place, wee fell into greater miserie. ffor he was scarcelie goune out of the cittie wth his hoaste, when the next daye the soldiers of the Bisshops & of the Noringbers rushed into the cittie, & after they pilled it they sett it on fire. But God tooke us out of the middest of the flames, when one even of the enymies had admonished us to depart out of the cittie before it burnt in every parte; whose counsel obeyinge, wee went forthe, being spoiled & made naked of all thinges, so that wee might not be suffered to carry awaye a halfepeny. Nerelie in the middest of the market-place o^r^ garmentes were plucked from us, neither was there any thinge lefte mee, but my smocke to cover my bodie w^th^all. And when wee were goune out of the cittie, my husband was taken by the enymies, whom I coulde not ransome wth a smal thinge; but when I sawe him lead out of my sight, I prayed to Almyghty God wth teares & sighes, who presently sent him freed to me againe. But nowe beinge goune out of the cittie, wee knewe not whether to goe. At last wee tooke o^r^ iournye towards Hamelburgh, unto wch towne I was scarse able to creepe. ffor that towne was distant three Germaine miles from Swinforde. And the townsmen were unwillinge to receive us; for that they were forbidden to intertaine or harbour any of us. But I, amongst the poore women, seemed of all the beggers to bee a queene: I entered into that towne barefoote, my haire ruffeled, wth a torne coate, wch indeede was not myne owne, but was lent mee of another woman. And through the wearysomenes of that iournie, at lengthe also I fell into an ague, wch held me all the time of my travaillinge. ffor when the Hamelburghs feared that it was not safe for them to let us abide w[th] them any longe time, wee were forced, though I was sicke, w[th]in fowre daies after to depart from thence. But there againe whilst wee were compelled to passe by a certaine towne of a Bishop, my husband was apprehended by the Bishops chefe officer, who saide that his most mercyfull lorde comanded him to kill all ꝑsons that fled thether out of Swinforde. Therfore we were holden captives there betwene hope & feare until wee were let goe by the Bishops letters. And then at length God began to looke mercifully upon us; & brought us first to the noble Earle of Rinecks, & afterwardes to the most honorable Countes Erbacks, who for the Christian religion have often ventured their lives & the losse of their estates & goodes, of whom wee were bountifully intertained, & wth many giftes. Also we taried wth them many daies, until I was wel amended, & my husband chosen to reade the phisicke lecture publickly in the Universitie of Heidelbergh.

Inscription on the Tomb of Olympia Morata at Heidelberg.

DEO IMM. S.

Et virtuti ac memoriæ Olympiæ Moratæ Fuluii Morati Mantuani, viri doctiss. filiæ, Andreæ Grunthleri Medici conjugis lectissimæ: fœminæ, cuius ingenium, ac singularis vtriusq; linguæ cognitio; in moribus autem probitas, summumq; pietatis studium, supra cōmunem modum semper existimata sunt. Quod de eius vita hominum iudicium, beata mors, sanctissimè ac pacatissimè ab ea obita, divino quoque confirmavit testimonio. Obiit mutato solo à salute D. L. V. supra millesimū, suæ ætatis xxix. Hîc cum marito, & Æmilio fratre sepulta. Guilielmus Rascalonius M.D. B.B. MM. P P.

EMORY WASHBURN.

REMARKS AT A MEETING OF THE MASSACHUSETTS HISTORICAL SOCIETY, APRIL 11, 1877.

A PURE, earnest, upright, and singularly useful life was brought to a close, to the sorrow of us all, by the death of our Second Vice-President, the Hon. EMORY WASHBURN, on Sunday, the 18th of March last. The tributes which have already been paid to his memory by the daily journals, by the American Antiquarian Society, by the American Peace Society, and other philanthropic associations, by members of both branches of the Legislature of Massachusetts, and by those who officiated at his funeral, have left little for any one to say here to-day. Yet we cannot meet this morning, for the first time since the sad event occurred, without recalling the loss we have sustained as a Society and as individuals, nor without placing on record some expression of our deep sense of the excellence of his character and of the eminence of his career.

It was my good fortune to know Governor Washburn, more or less intimately, for hardly less than half a century. I remember him as a frequent guest at my father's table when I was just leaving college, and when he was one of the youngest members of the Legislature of Massachusetts, as the representative of his native town of Leicester. The cordial, amiable, and attractive disposition and manner which characterized him at that early day were unchanged to the last. No cares or casualties of life, no occupations of business or study, no official elevation, no professional engrossments, ever seemed to impair the warmth of his friendships, or to disturb the genial current of his social intercourse. He was a willing worker in every good cause, and was never weary of doing obliging things for others. His accomplishments as a lawyer, his successes at the bar, his faithful services on the bench, his able discharge of the duties of Governor of the Commonwealth, his devoted labors as Professor of the Harvard Law School, — will not be forgotten or overlooked by any one.

It happened to me, as President of the Old Whig Convention, in 1853, which nominated him for the chief magistracy of the State, to know how little that nomination was expected by him, and how entirely unsought for it had been. He was still on the ocean, returning from a visit to Europe, when the Convention was held and the nomination made. Indeed, it may be justly said of him that he never sought any thing, in the way of public office certainly, for himself; while he was always ready to serve his fellow-citizens in any station which might be assigned to him.

In the pursuits of our own Society he took a lively interest, and often made communications of importance at our meetings. No one can examine our published volumes without finding ample evidence of his labors in our service for many years past. The amendment to our Charter, which we accepted at our last meeting, was carried through the Legislature by him as a representative of Cambridge; while the new serial number of our "Proceedings," on the table this morning, contains an interesting Memoir from his pen. His very latest efforts were thus in our behalf. Meantime, his History of his native town, and his sketch of the Judicial History of Massachusetts, will co-operate with his elaborate legal essays on "Real Property" and on "Easements and Servitudes," in securing for his name an enviable remembrance as an author.

He died at a good old age, having entered on his seventy-eighth year on the 14th of February last. Yet the idea of advanced years was never associated with him, so young was he in heart, so vigorous in step, so full in the enjoyment and so free in the exercise of every intellectual and physical faculty. The mortal malady struck him while in the active performance of his duties at the State House, as a member of the Legislature of Massachusetts.

WEDNESDAY EVENING CLUB.

ADDRESS AT THE CENTENNIAL COMMEMORATION OF THE CLUB, MAY 9, 1877.

I HAVE been hoping, Mr. Secretary, sincerely hoping, that I might be excused altogether this evening; and now, that I have been so kindly — I had almost said so cruelly — called on, I must be pardoned if all that I attempt to say shall take the form of an apology, rather than of an address.

I left New York only an hour before noon *to-day*, rather than miss this meeting; and I could not help thinking, as I came along, that if the nine men — our sacred Nine — who founded this Club just a hundred years ago, could have had it predicted to them that two of their successors — for my friend Mr. Mason was with me — should come all the way from New York to Boston, in seven hours, to celebrate their Centennial, they would, one and all, have pronounced it as incredible and fabulous as any thing in the Arabian Nights. And I am not quite sure, sir, that our successors, a hundred years hence, will have seen any thing in this line more remarkable. There must be a practical limit to the speed of human locomotion, and I sometimes doubt if it has not been almost reached.

Such a journey, however, has not been without fatigue; and absent as I have been from home for nearly a month past, and having returned thus rapidly only two hours ago, I am afraid I shall find it impossible to collect my scattered and jaded thoughts, and to deal, as I could wish to deal, with the only topics befitting this occasion.

But, indeed, sir, were it otherwise with me, I should hardly know how to add any thing worth adding to what has been already so impressively said by yourself, and by the other gentlemen who have followed you.

And then, too, Mr. Secretary, all the associations, all the traditions, all the usages, of this Club seem to rise up in judgment before me at this moment, and to protest against my attempting any thing like a formal speech. Why, sir, the great peculiarity and the great charm of our meetings, from first to last, has been their purely unceremonious and unconventional character. We have come together, from week to week, always and only, to exchange words and thoughts and feelings in the most social and conversational way — "dextræ jungere dextram, ac veras audire et reddere voces." In our whole hundred years, there has hardly been such a thing as a formal address heard at our meetings until to-night; and one almost instinctively shrinks from celebrating our Centennial Anniversary by a direct defiance and violation of a custom, which has held us together in unity and harmony so long. My own tongue, certainly, would cleave to the roof of my mouth, were I to attempt — malice aforethought — any thing rhetorical to-night. I fear it is beginning to do so already.

And yet, my friends, I should in vain endeavor to repress some acknowledgment, — feeble and faltering though it may prove to be, — of the satisfactions and enjoyments which I have derived, in common with you all, from my relations to this Club.

In looking back, indeed, over the forty years since I was elected a member of it, I find that I have been a terrible truant, and that long, long gaps have occurred in my attendance at its meetings. Nearly twelve years of public service at Washington, and repeated visits to Europe, have made a large deduction from my enjoyment of the opportunities and privileges which belong to our membership. Yet enough, and more than enough, has been left for the most grateful remembrance. The mere consciousness that once in every week, on a stated night, we were privileged to go — if we were in the way of going — to the house of a friend, to meet familiar faces, and to learn the latest word in all the departments of law or medicine, of theology or science, of commerce or politics, from the chosen representatives of every profession and calling, has been, I venture to say, for all of us, — as I know it has been for myself, — a source of gratification and pleasure not easily exaggerated, and one quite apart from the enjoyments of the meetings themselves.

But the meetings themselves, I need not say, have never been wanting in materials of entertainment of almost every variety. I have more than once wished, since we began to contemplate this Centennial commemoration, that there could have been kept some continuous record of these weekly meetings. What a story it would have told of men and of events! Even now, it may not be too late to gather up the reminiscences and traditions of our meetings, and to make them into a little book of remembrance, a little volume of "Memorabilia of the Wednesday Club," with sketches and photographs, perhaps, of persons and places. There may be diaries from which facts may be gleaned, — like the diary of our illustrious member John Quincy Adams, from which we have just heard. A group of this very Centennial gathering would be a fit frontispiece for such a volume.

From such a record, the distinguished guests we have so often had with us could not be omitted. I recall the occasional presence at my own house, or at others' houses, not merely of such men as Webster and Everett, and good Bishops Fitzpatrick and Eastburn, and Governor Clifford and Governor Washburn, and Agassiz, of our own State and neighborhood; but of Lyell and Thackeray, of William C. Rives and Thomas H. Benton, of George Peabody and Dr. Barnas Sears. I am particular in recalling this last name, because I cannot but remember that the accident — I should rather say the Providence — of Dr. Sears's presence at one of our meetings determined the whole direction and success of the Peabody Trust for Southern Education. It was at this Club, ten or eleven years ago, that I first communicated to him the great endowment of Mr. Peabody, and took the first step towards securing his inestimable advice and counsel in its administration.

And from that little volume of Memorabilia, as made up by

our excellent Secretary, who alone could do it justice, he would not willingly omit, I am sure, an account of some of our anomalous and exceptional meetings: — That, for example, at the Café de Paris, in 1868, when six or seven of our number, of whom he and I were two, had so humorous and so charming a reunion in a foreign land. And I should be sorry to have him forget a meeting at Brookline, too, when the Club did me the favor and honor to come out to my suburban villa, where I was passing a winter; — their first and only meeting in the country, I believe, and the only one at which the visible presence of ladies was welcomed at our repast.

Of the men with whom we have been associated as members, not a few have been already named with peculiar interest and affection, — Judge Davis, James Savage, Ephraim Peabody, and Charles Mason; the Curtises, Dr. Homans, and Dr. Hayward. But I confess I have no stronger or more vivid personal association, to-night, than with Francis C. Gray, — so genial, so accomplished, so quick-witted, with such a marvellous memory, with such an exhaustless fund of information and anecdote. The Club has had no more devoted member, certainly, in my day, nor any one more worthy of respectful and affectionate remembrance on this occasion.

But I dare not trespass longer on the closing hours of our festival, lest I should be held responsible for the ice-cream being melted, or for the stewed oysters being cold. Let me only remind you how striking a contrast our Century Club — for so it must henceforth be called — presents to that which I have just visited in New York, with its five or six hundred members and all its sumptuous apartments and appointments!

That Club, which owed its name, I believe, to the original number of its members, is a comparatively modern creation of the wealth and culture of the great Commercial Metropolis of our country. No one who has experienced the charm of its hospitality so recently as I have done, can fail to recognize it as a grand institution, worthy of the noble city it adorns, and fitly presided over, at one time by the late genial Gulian C. Verplanck, and now by the veteran poet, William C. Bryant. But what a contrast it presents to that on which Time, rather than any caprice or choice of our own, is now casting the same or a similar title!

Founded in the darkest hours of our revolutionary struggle, with only nine members at the outset, and hardly more than three times nine now, our little Club has gone along quietly and prosperously for a hundred years. Quietly and prosperously, I trust, it will not fall short of a second century; and we all hope and predict that it may live a thousand years. It is peculiarly a Home Club, not dependent on costly buildings or onerous assessments, and without any popular element which could be affected by accidental circumstances. It will not be permitted to die out; and we may confidently send down our greetings and good wishes — as we hereby all do — to those who shall celebrate its successive Centennials, in a far, far remote futurity, with our heartiest hopes and prayers that they may be in the enjoyment of all, and more than all, the social and political advantages in which we now rejoice; and that they may remember our names as kindly and as proudly as we, this night, recall those of George Richards Minot, and John Eliot, and John Quincy Adams, and John Thornton Kirkland, and the rest, — whom we look back upon so reverently as our forerunners and founders!

QUINCY AND MOTLEY.

REMARKS AT A MEETING OF THE MASSACHUSETTS HISTORICAL SOCIETY, JUNE 14, 1877.

OUR first thoughts to-day, Gentlemen, are of those whom we may not again welcome to these halls. We shall be in no mood, certainly, for entering on other subjects this morning, until we have given some expression to our deep sense of the loss — the double loss — which our Society has sustained since our last monthly meeting.

When our valued associate, Mr. EDMUND QUINCY, took his seat at this table for the first time as our Recording Secretary, on the 10th of May last, there was hardly one of our number, I think, for whom many years to come might have been more reasonably hoped, or more confidently predicted. Active, cheerful, vigorous, without an infirmity which betrayed itself to the most observing eye, he seemed to promise as protracted an old age as that of his honored father, who was so long the Nestor of our Society. We all counted on a long continuance of his services, and of his cherished companionship, as a matter of course, and without the slightest misgiving.

In the providence of God, however, a single week sufficed to complete his earthly career. Returning to his pleasant residence at Dedham, after a day of various occupation in the way of duty at Cambridge and in Boston, he was struck by a sudden illness on the afternoon of the 17th ultimo, and reached his home only to die. Many of us had the sad privilege of attending his funeral on the 21st, and it only remains for us now to pay a parting tribute to his memory, and fill his place as best we may.

It is not for me to attempt any sketch of his life or character. Yet I may not forget that my acquaintance with him was not of yesterday. Indeed, I can hardly remember a time when I did not know him. We were friends in our earliest boyhood, as we were friends in our latest manhood. Nearly sixty years ago, I think, the houses of our fathers and mothers were next door to each other, and we were mingling often in the same sports and preparing for the same pursuits, if not attending the same schools. And though he entered college a year before I did, there was hardly one of my own class with whom I was more intimate than with him. With common tastes and common friendships, we were long members of the same household, and always of the same Clubs.

I recall especially a journey to the White Hills which we made together during one of the college vacations. It was no ordinary or easy expedition at that day. Much of it was to be made on foot, and there were not a few hardships to be encountered along the route. There were thick woods to be traversed; there were swollen streams to be waded; there was a night to be passed in the open air. And then the disappointments! Though we had rainbows beneath our feet, and glorious glimpses of sky above our heads, when we were half-way up, — we reached the summit of Mount Washington only to find ourselves enveloped in a drenching mist which cut off all our view. Thus early and impressively were we both admonished that the loftiest climbings do not always lead to sunshine, and that he who takes "Excelsior" for his motto, in its true spirit, must look higher than any earthly mountains. It was the very season of a most memorable landslide, and the rains were already descending which were to wash down hills and forests and human habitations. I cannot but remember that we passed some hours in the well-known Willey House, hardly a fortnight before its inmates were to fly from the avalanche, and not a few of them to perish in their flight.

During all that trying trip, which I recall the more vividly from having myself been prostrated by the fatigue, Quincy never lost his patience or endurance, or that sort of philosophical equanimity which so peculiarly characterized him both as boy and man. He was the same brave, cheery, charming companion when we were clambering over those rocks, or confronting those pelting rains, as he was here last month in these historical halls, — where he had endeared himself so much to us all, — when he laid down the pen, which had just been committed to him, with a characteristic pleasantry, and looked forward confidently to resuming it this morning.

I have said that we were friends in our earliest boyhood and in our latest manhood. But I may not forget, in justice to him, if not to myself, that there was a long interval during which our ways of life were quite apart, and our associations and sympathies interrupted. I am not aware, however, that we ever indulged in mutual reproaches for our different views of social or political or sectional questions. At any rate, we happily lived long enough to come back to a complete rejuvenescence of our old relations of cordial regard and friendship, and to find out that, after all, our views of measures and of men had not been so widely different as they seemed to have been, either to others or to ourselves. Certainly, there are few persons who had a higher appreciation of his sterling qualities of mind and heart than I had, or who more sincerely lament his loss, personally, socially, and as a most valuable member of this and many other Associations. One could not but feel that he had capacities still unused, and that he had reached a vantage-ground where his great reading, his classical scholarship, his ready wit and racy humor and graceful pen, might have won new honors for himself, and accomplished valuable results, for biography or history, in our own or some other service.

But he had done enough to secure a pleasant and enduring remembrance of his name, as one of a family which has rarely been without a distinguished representative since the earliest Edmund Quincy came over to New England with John Cotton in 1633. His little novel, "Wensley," was said by Whittier to be the most readable book of the kind since Hawthorne's "Blithedale Romance." His contributions to the anti-slavery press for many years were pungent and powerful. His Life of his father, prepared in co-operation with an accomplished sister, will always have a place among our choicest American biographies; and it was fitly followed by a volume of his father's remarkable speeches in Congress. The little Memoir of Charles Sprague which he contributed to our own volumes of Proceedings will not be forgotten, nor his very recent Lecture delivered in aid of the fund for the preservation of the Old South.

There is no room for repining — on his own account, certainly, — at the release of one who had entered his seventieth year with such a record made up, more especially when that release came in a form which had often called forth from him expressions of envy, when it had been mercifully vouchsafed to others. Spared alike from the infirmities of age and from the pangs of disease, he was permitted to pass, without a struggle, from the things which are seen and temporal to the things which are unseen and eternal.

I have said, Gentlemen, that we had a double loss to deplore to-day, and I turn to a brief notice of another.

The death of our distinguished associate, JOHN LOTHROP MOTLEY, can hardly have taken many of us by surprise. Sudden at the moment of its occurrence, we had long been more or less prepared for it by his failing health. It must, indeed, have been quite too evident to those who had seen him, during the last two or three years, that his life-work was finished. I think he so regarded it himself.

Hopes may have been occasionally revived in the hearts of his friends, and even in his own heart, that his long-cherished purpose of completing a History of the Thirty Years' War, as the grand consummation of his historical labors, — for which all his other volumes seemed to him to have been but the preludes and overtures, — might still be accomplished. But such hopes, faint and flickering from his first attack, had well-nigh died away. They were like Prescott's hopes of completing his

Philip the Second, or like Macaulay's hopes of finishing his brilliant History of England.

But great as may be the loss to literature of such a crowning work from Motley's pen, it was by no means necessary to the completeness of his own fame. His "Rise of the Dutch Republic," his "History of the United Netherlands," and his "Life of John of Barneveldt," had abundantly established his reputation, and given him a fixed place among the most eminent historians of our country and of our age.

No American writer, certainly, has secured a wider recognition or a higher appreciation from the scholars of the Old World. The Universities of England and the learned Societies of Europe have bestowed upon him their largest honors. It happened to me to be in Paris when he was first chosen a corresponding member of the Institute, and when his claims were canvassed with the freedom and earnestness which peculiarly characterize such a candidacy in France. There was no mistaking the profound impression which his first work had made on the minds of such men as Guizot and Mignet. Within a year or two past a still higher honor has been awarded him from the same source. The journals not long ago announced his election as one of the six foreign associates of the French Academy of Moral and Political Sciences, — a distinction which Prescott would probably have attained had he lived a few years longer, until there was a vacancy; but which, as a matter of fact, I believe, Motley was the only American writer, except the late Edward Livingston, of Louisiana, who has actually enjoyed.

Residing much abroad, for the purpose of pursuing his historical researches, he had become the associate and friend of the most eminent literary men in almost all parts of the world, and the singular charms of his conversation and manners had made him a favorite guest in the most refined and exalted circles.

Of his relations to political and public life, this is hardly the occasion or the moment for speaking in detail. Misconstructions and injustices are the proverbial lot of those who occupy eminent position. It was a duke of Vienna, if I remember rightly, whom Shakspeare, in his "Measure for Measure," introduces as exclaiming, —

> "O place and greatness, millions of false eyes
> Are stuck upon thee! Volumes of report
> Run with these false and most contrarious quests
> Upon thy doings! Thousand 'scapes of wit
> Make thee the father of their idle dream,
> And rack thee in their fancies!"

I forbear from any application of the lines. It is enough for me, certainly, to say here, to-day, that our country was proud to be represented at the courts of Vienna and London successively by a gentleman of so much culture and accomplishment as Mr. Motley, and that the circumstances of his recall were deeply regretted by us all.

His fame, however, was quite beyond the reach of any such accidents, and could neither be enhanced nor impaired by appointments or removals. As a powerful and brilliant Historian we pay him our unanimous tribute of admiration and regret, and give him a place in our memories by the side of Prescott and Irving. I do not forget how many of us lament him, also, as a cherished friend.

He died on the 29th ultimo, at the house of his daughter, Mrs. Sheridan, in Dorsetshire, England; and an impressive tribute to his memory was paid, in Westminster Abbey, on the following Sunday, by our Honorary Member, Dean Stanley. Such a tribute, from such lips, and with such surroundings, leaves nothing to be desired in the way of eulogy. He was buried in Kensal Green Cemetery, by the side of his beloved wife.

One might well say of Motley, precisely what he said of Prescott, in a letter from Rome to our associate, Mr. William Amory, immediately on hearing of Prescott's death: "I feel inexpressibly disappointed — speaking now for an instant purely from a literary point of view — that the noble and crowning monument of his life, for which he had laid such massive foundations, and the structure of which had been carried forward in such a grand and masterly manner, must remain uncompleted, like the unfinished peristyle of some stately and beautiful temple on which the night of time has suddenly descended. But, still, the works which his great and untiring hand had already thoroughly finished will remain to attest his learning and genius, — a precious and perpetual possession for his country."

THE ORIGIN AND PROGRESS OF THE PEABODY EDUCATION TRUST.

ADDRESS AT THE ANNUAL MEETING OF THE TRUSTEES, NEW YORK, OCTOBER 3, 1877.

GENTLEMEN OF THE BOARD OF TRUSTEES OF THE PEABODY EDUCATION FUND:

THE day and the place of our Annual Meetings were fixed by the By-Law proposed by Chief Justice Waite, and unanimously adopted by the Board, at the White Sulphur Springs in Virginia, last year. Agreeably to that By-Law, we meet on this first Wednesday of October, in the city of New York, to receive the Report of our General Agent, to examine our Treasurer's accounts, and to shape our policy and make our appropriations for the year to come.

The first Wednesday of October has happened to fall this year on the third day of the month, and our meeting has thus assumed something of an Anniversary character, — in my own thoughts, certainly, if not in those of others, to whom the circumstances are less familiar. To some of the Board they are, perhaps, wholly new.

I cannot forget that it was on the same day of the same month, eleven years ago, — the 3d of October, 1866, — that our illustrious founder, Mr. Peabody, came to spend a few days with me, at my summer residence in Brookline, Massachusetts, to communicate to me confidentially the great American benefactions which he was proposing to bestow, and to consult and advise with me in regard to the arrangement and organization of this, the greatest and noblest of them all. I recall him, at this moment, seated in my own hall, under a portrait, as it happened, of our world-renowned philanthropist, as well as philosopher, diplomatist, and statesman, — Benjamin Franklin, — taking from his capacious wallet a budget big enough for a chancellor of the Exchequer or a chairman of the Committee of Ways and Means, and reading to me privately that long schedule of appropriations for Education, Science, and Charity, which soon afterwards delighted and thrilled the whole community. "And now I come to the last," said he, as he drew forth yet another roll with a trembling hand. "You may be surprised when you learn precisely what it is; but it is the one nearest my heart, and the one for which I shall do the most, now and hereafter." And he then proceeded to read the crude sketch of that endowment for Southern Education of which we are the Trustees, and of which the formal instrument bears date, Feb. 7, 1867.

I dare not attempt to describe the emotions of astonishment and admiration with which I listened to his declaration of a purpose to devote successive millions of his money to the children in those Southern States which had just been impoverished and desolated by the war. I am not ashamed to say that a sense of the sublime in action was never more forcibly brought home to my heart.

I would not willingly have this picture lost from the history of our Trust, and I know not where it could more appropriately be preserved than in these introductory remarks on this Anniversary of the occurrence. It was the earliest signal manifestation of a spirit of reconciliation towards those from whom we had been so unhappily alienated, and against whom we, of the North, had been so recently arrayed in arms. I may not forget that it came from a man born in Massachusetts, and who sought and secured, first of all, the sympathy and co-operation of Massachusetts men, in carrying out his munificent design.

And now, as we witness and realize to-day the change which has come over the spirit of the people in all quarters of the land, — as we exult in the renewed harmony of North and South, and in the restored and reassured unity of the Nation,

— we may well be allowed to remember how largely the organization of this little Board and the noble spirit of its founder were concerned in initiating that "era of good feeling" which is so auspicious of the future welfare of our whole Country. We may well be allowed to remember that the very earliest amicable consultations of leading men of Virginia and Louisiana, of North Carolina and South Carolina and Maryland, with those of New York, Pennsylvania, and Massachusetts, for devising means to build up again the waste places which the war had left behind it, and to institute measures for the moral reconstruction of the desolated States, was when this Board assembled for the first time in a little upper chamber of Willard's Hotel, at Washington; and having inaugurated its proceedings with prayer by our lamented associate, Bishop McIlvaine, received its credentials and its Trust Securities from the hands of George Peabody himself.

With his memory, therefore, and with the memory of that particular scene in his life, must always be associated the dawn of that restoration of national concord, which, we thank God, seems now approaching its meridian, if, indeed, it has not already reached its culmination.

Ten years were completed on the 28th of May last, since our Board, at a special meeting in this city, convened for the purpose, received and accepted the Act of Incorporation which had been granted to us, at our request, by the State of New York. With the adoption of that Act our work may be fairly held to have commenced; and I am glad to say that the Report of our General Agent to-day will furnish us with a summary view of all that has been attempted, and all that has been accomplished, during this first decennial period of our existence. You will learn from that Report, which I have been privileged to see in advance, that, while rigidly adhering to our original policy of not encroaching on the principal sum entrusted to us, we have been able during this period to appropriate from our income little less than a million of dollars towards the encouragement and support of education in the various States to which our work was limited by Mr. Peabody. And, as almost all our contributions have been conditioned on the appropriation of much larger sums by those who have been aided, it would be safe to say that the action of this Board has involved an expenditure of at least ten millions of dollars in the cause of Southern Education during the past ten years.

But no mere pecuniary tables or estimates will afford any adequate impression of what has been accomplished by the judicious efforts and devoted energy of our General Agent. The service which he has rendered by correspondence and by personal visits and addresses, in the various States within the sphere of our Trust, — bringing his accomplishments, and his invaluable experience in the work of teaching, directly to bear upon the Schools and School Boards, upon the Superintendents of Education and upon the Legislatures of these States, — has far outweighed in value and importance any contributions he has been empowered to communicate from our treasury. The one thing needful for these States, under the changed social condition resulting from the War, was an enlightened public opinion on the subject of education, and a deeper impression of the essential importance of Free Schools for their whole population, under regulations of their own establishment, together with examples of such schools of the highest character, and of Normal Schools for the training of Teachers.

I think it will abundantly appear from the Report, which will presently be submitted to you, that such examples of the best sort have been established, and that such a public opinion has been created in many of the States, if not quite yet in all. The visit of Dr. Sears to Texas during the last winter, agreeably to the instructions of the Board, was welcomed in many parts of that great and powerful State; and there is every reason for hoping that the interest which it awakened will not be without important results. This visit to Texas having been accomplished, we may feel that no portion of the field assigned to us has failed to receive the attention of our General Agent, or to recognize the beneficent influence of the Trust committed to us.

You will not have forgotten, Gentlemen, that, on motion of Mr. Evarts, at our last Annual Meeting, I was requested to have designed and executed "a testimonial Medal to be distributed as an incentive to proficiency in qualifications for teaching among the pupils of the Normal Schools, which shall be approved by this Board." I was at first in hope that the National Gold Medal presented by Congress to Mr. Peabody himself, in the name of the People of the United States, might furnish a design suitable to our purposes. But that Medal was too elaborate a work of art to be multiplied or copied, and must for ever remain, in its cabinet at Mr. Peabody's birthplace, as unique as the benefactions which it commemorates. The Medal which I now submit to you, in bronze and in silver, is of a simpler character, and fitter to be included in a series of historical medals. It has been struck at the United States Mint from dies executed by an experienced artist. The profile head on its front was copied under my own supervision from the admirable bust by Hiram Powers, now in the possession of the Massachusetts Historical Society, and which has always been considered one of the very best likenesses of Mr. Peabody in existence. The legend, on the reverse, was from Mr. Peabody's own lips or pen, on the occasion of his earliest gift to the cause of Education.[1] You have already authorized the distribution of these Medals to those to whom they may be awarded by our General Agent, under the direction of the Executive Committee, and that course will be pursued until the further orders of the Board.

Nothing remains for me, Gentlemen, except to express the sincere regret we all feel at again finding a vacant place at our Board. The Honorable Samuel Watson died at Nashville, soon after his return home from our last Annual Meeting. He was the earliest of our elected members, having been chosen a Trustee in 1869, on the death of our lamented associate, the Honorable William C. Rives, of Virginia. Though a New Englander by birth and education, Mr. Watson had long been a citizen of Tennessee, and had been prominently associated with important institutions of that State. He had been particularly active and zealous in the cause of education, and to his efforts we owe not a little of the success of the Free School

[1] "Education. — A debt due from present to future generations."

system in that quarter of the country. He was a most earnest and devoted co-operator with our General Agent, and no member of the Board has been more serviceable to the work in which we are associated. It is due to the memory of so worthy — and, I may add, so modest and unassuming — a man, that, before filling his place, as Mr. Peabody's Trust Letter requires us to do, we should put on our records some formal expression of our respect for his character and of our gratitude for his services.

GEORGE T. DAVIS.

REMARKS AT A MEETING OF THE MASSACHUSETTS HISTORICAL SOCIETY, OCTOBER 11, 1877.

AT our November meeting, in 1871, a letter was read from the Hon. GEORGE T. DAVIS, who had been one of our associate members for thirteen years, announcing that he had become a permanent resident of Portland, in the State of Maine, and had thus, according to our rules, ceased to be a member of this Society.

At our monthly meeting in the February following, Mr. Davis, having been nominated in January, was elected one of our Corresponding Members, and continued such until his death in June last. His contributions to our work had not been numerous. In April, 1869, he communicated a journal of a tour made by his uncle, Samuel Davis, in 1789; and, in May following, a brief Memoir of another uncle, the late excellent Isaac P. Davis, so long our Cabinet-keeper. In the following May, he made a longer and very interesting communication on the "St. Regis Bell," in which he furnished abundant reasons for discrediting the old story of the Deerfield Church-bell having been carried off by the Indians, in 1704, to be hung in an Indian church at St. Regis.

He has left no other trace, I believe, on our records, except that of an occasional presence at our meetings. Yet we had few more interested, sympathetic, or loyal members, nor one whom we should have been more sure to meet whenever we assembled, had not his residences, alike in Maine and in Massachusetts, been so remote from Boston. And, certainly, there was no one whose presence was more heartily welcome to us all.

Mr. Davis was the son of Wendell Davis, Esq., one of the sons of that Thomas Davis of Plymouth, who was the father, also, of our late President, Judge John Davis, and of our late Cabinet-keeper, Isaac P. Davis, as well as of Thomas, the old Treasurer and Receiver-general of the Commonwealth, of William, and of Samuel, the Antiquary. No family has done more, if any so much, towards illustrating the history of the Plymouth Pilgrims. They seemed always the chosen guardians of the Rock and its sacred memories, and no one could meet them without thinking and talking of the "Mayflower."

Mr. George T. Davis, our lamented friend, was born in Sandwich, not far from Plymouth, on the 12th of January, 1810; was graduated at Harvard with the distinguished class of 1829; was admitted to the bar in 1832; was a member of the Senate of Massachusetts in 1839 and 1840, and a Representative in Congress, from the Connecticut River District, from 1851 to 1853.

He resided in Greenfield, in the county of Franklin, for the greater part of his life, and until, on his second marriage, he recently removed to Portland, Maine. The law was his chosen profession, and he devoted himself to the practice of that profession assiduously and successfully. Now and then he made good speeches at political meetings. Now and then he delivered good addresses at agricultural or other festivals. But he had no particular taste for public efforts or appearances, except in the line of his profession.

It is as a great reader, and a singularly agreeable and entertaining converser, that he will be longest remembered by all who had the good fortune to enjoy his friendship. He was eminently a wit, in the sense in which that word was used in good old Queen Anne's time. He had an eager eye for every thing quaint and racy. He had Thackeray's and Dickens's works almost by heart, and was well acquainted with their authors during their visits to this country. But Boswell and Johnson and Goldsmith and Sterne and Swift, and all the great wits and humorists of the olden time, were his favorite companions; and all the anecdotes of their lives and times were familiar to him as household words. He might have rivalled the *Causeries* of Sainte-Beuve, had he been as willing to use his pen as he was his tongue; and he could have held his own among the best *raconteurs* of this or any other land. He was one of those men who leave an impression, when they die, of how much more they might have been, and how much more they might have done. But he did enough, and was enough, to be remembered with respect and affection by all who knew him; and his death has made a gap in many circles, which cannot easily be filled.

THIERS.

REMARKS AT A MEETING OF THE MASSACHUSETTS HISTORICAL SOCIETY, OCTOBER 11, 1877.

THE death of M. ADOLPHE THIERS has not only deprived France of her most eminent citizen, but has hardly left a living name in either hemisphere associated with a public service so long and so conspicuous.

Born at Marseilles, of the humblest parentage, on the 16th of April, 1797, his native energy, untiring industry, and extraordinary intellectual vigor had carried him on through a varied career of political and literary celebrity, until, at his death, on the 3d of September last, in the eighty-first year of his age, he was the most interesting and most important person in the land which gave him birth, — "the central figure, certainly, of French politics."

The details of his public life would fill a volume. They belong to his biographer. They will doubtless be brilliantly and lovingly sketched, as no one else could sketch them, by his accomplished and eloquent contemporary and friend, Mignet, if his own life and health be spared, as we earnestly trust they may be, for another of his annual *Éloges* before the Institute of France, of which Thiers had become the senior member.

But nothing less circumscribed than a History of France during the period of his mature life would afford room for the full development of his many-sided capacity and marvellous activity.

There is a most characteristic story told of his earliest literary triumph. While he was a very young man, it seems, he had entered into competition for a prize offered by the Academy of Aix for the best essay on some historical subject, — a prize like one of our Bowdoin prizes at Harvard University. The essay of Thiers was found to be the best; but a majority of the judges being Royalists, and holding the young Thiers to be little better than a Jacobin, the trial was postponed to the following year. Thiers at once resolved to outwit them. He sent back his original production, without a word of change, for the postponed competition, but prepared a second discourse on the same subject, and had it transmitted by post from Paris, as if it had come from another hand. The result was that the first prize was awarded to his new discourse, and the second prize to his old one. Thiers had won them both, to the ridicule of the Academy of Aix; and had proved, thus early, that he was not only capable of the first best and of the second best, but that he had wit and cunning enough to checkmate those who would wrong him, and that he was as ready in expedients as he was remarkable in resources.

Very soon we find him established in Paris as a journalist, and wielding a pen as prolific as it was powerful. Politics, literature, the fine arts, the drama, were the varied subjects of articles which were the talk of Paris at the time, and many of which were not long afterwards included among the contents of permanent volumes.

And now he betakes himself to serious History; and between 1823 and 1827 ten volumes are to be found bearing his name, entitled the History of the French Revolution, from 1789 to the 18th Brumaire, — 9th November, 1799. But the arbitrary ministry and despotic designs of Polignac, in 1829, arrest his historical studies just as he is embarking on a voyage of circumnavigation with a view to prepare himself for writing a more general history. He forthwith unites with Mignet and others in founding the "National," and in devoting its columns to the single and avowed purpose of overthrowing the Bourbons. It was in these columns that he first gave utterance to a memorable *mot*, which, with the article in which he developed it, was itself an event, rousing up an irrepressible spirit of resistance to the government: "Le Roi règne, et ne gouverne pas."

On the fall of Charles X., Thiers was at once recognized among the founders of the new dynasty, and was nominated to the Council of State, as Under-Secretary of the Finances, by Louis Philippe. He had already been chosen a member of the Chamber of Deputies; and from that date, 1830, his career is too much a part of the history of France to be followed on such an occasion as this. He became Minister of the Interior in 1832, on the death of Casimir Périer, and soon afterward Minister of Commerce and Public Works. He was President of the Council and Minister of Foreign Affairs, for a short time, in 1836; and again, for several months, in 1840.

He now resumes his historical labors; and, as the result of them, between 1845 and 1857, at least seventeen volumes of his great work, "L'Histoire du Consulat et de l'Empire," are published, in which the genius and exploits of the First Napoleon are portrayed with so much brilliancy and power.

During the early part of these twelve years, however, great changes had occurred in France, of which he had been by no means a silent witness. He had been a sturdy opponent of Guizot's Ministry, in the Chamber of Deputies, on more than one great issue; and when, in 1848, a new revolution was at hand, the last act of Louis Philippe was to summon Thiers to the Tuileries, in February, 1848, to form a new ministry with Odillon Barrot. But it was too late. The Republic was proclaimed; and he at once gave in his adhesion to it. Taking a place again in the new Chamber of Deputies, he votes for the dictatorship of Cavaignac, and afterwards for the Presidency of Louis Napoleon. But, in 1851, he was one of the victims of the *Coup d'État*, and was sent to the prison of Mazas. From there he was exiled to Frankfort, but soon obtained permission to return to Paris, where he lived for many years in retirement, devoting himself to the completion of his great historical works.

In 1863 he appears again in the Representative Assembly, or Corps Législatif, of France, and is heard opposing, in unequivocal terms, many of the most noted measures of the

Emperor, — the Italian War, the Mexican War, and, finally, the fatal declaration of war against Prussia. He stood almost alone in deprecating and denouncing this last declaration. His greatest services to France were rendered on the fall of the Second Empire. His mission to all the European courts to solicit intervention; his negotiations with Bismarck for an armistice; his election by twenty-six Departments simultaneously as a member of the National Assembly; his election by that assembly as first President of the Republic; and his liberation of the territory of France from foreign occupation, by a wise submission to irreparable events, and a masterly provision for the immediate payment of the indemnity imposed by the conqueror, — have impressed his name on the historic roll of France, where it can never be overlooked or obliterated.

The rebuilding of his own house at the cost of the Nation, after it had been destroyed by the Communists, will take its place on the same page with the restoration of the Napoleon Column in the Place Vendôme, — the final completion of which I witnessed in 1875, — among the most significant and striking events of the period in which he lived.

Failing at last in his favorite policy of consolidating what he called a Conservative Republic by legislative enactment, Thiers resigned his Presidency, in May, 1873; and the office was conferred on the gallant Marshal MacMahon. During the four years which have since elapsed, he has been regarded as the Nestor of the Republican Party, if not of the Republic. All its friends have deferred to his counsel, and waited on his words. Maintaining resolutely to the last that the Republic was the only form of government now possible for his country, he has striven to encourage and animate its supporters, and, at the same time, to repress and restrain those who might be disposed to lead it into extravagant and radical courses. "The Republic must be conservative," he continually declared, "or it will cease to be;" and he enjoined on his friends to show that "the Republic is a government of order, peace, and liberty." And so, up to the very last hour of his life, the friends of the Republic were looking to him — past fourscore as he was — to resume the helm, and steer the Ship of State, if the pending elections should result, as some of them hoped, in rendering it necessary for the Marshal-President to withdraw before the end of his Septennate. There is authority for saying that he himself was dreaming of a near triumph, and did not scruple to say to at least one who conversed with him, only a few days before his death, "I shall die President." But death got the start of him; and his dreams, so far at least as they were personal, died with him.

It was my good fortune to know M. Thiers personally, in Paris, thirty years ago. Even before that time, I may be pardoned for remembering that some utterances of mine in the House of Representatives of the United States had attracted his notice, and been the subject of complimentary remark in the Chamber of Deputies. The earliest recognitions of a young man are ever the most gratefully cherished, and the last to be forgotten, as one becomes an old man. My opportunities of meeting him were, indeed, but rare and at long intervals; and the difference of language — for he could not, or certainly would not, speak a word of English — was always a serious impediment. But no one could be with him for a moment without perceiving the nervous energy, the intellectual agility, the sparkling wit, and the determined will, which animated his little frame, almost giving to a pigmy the proportions of a giant. Like Humboldt and the great Napoleon, he allowed himself but few hours of sleep or rest. The wonder was that a nature so electric and intense could sleep or rest at all. If his formal speeches were sometimes conversational in their form and tone, his conversation, when I had the privilege of listening to it, had all the animation and eloquence of a formal speech. I cannot forget that I was a witness and a delighted hearer of one of his most remarkable exhibitions in the Corps Législatif; and I have in my hand a pamphlet copy of the Speech to which I listened, with one of his latest photographs, kindly sent me by himself. It was in December, 1867, when, interrupting M. Émile Ollivier, he exclaimed: "We are here, sometimes Italians, sometimes Germans: we are never Frenchmen. Let us be French!" That ejaculation, twice repeated, — "Soyons

Français!" — was uttered with an emotion — I might call it an explosion — which cannot be described; and it produced an impression which convulsed the Chamber, and even shook Paris itself to its centre. It recalled to me some of those scenes in the House of Representatives of the United States at Washington, when John Quincy Adams, who had so many elements, physical and intellectual, in common with Thiers, turned upon some Southern — or it may have been some Northern — assailant, and carried the House and the country by storm.

My last interviews with Thiers were but two years ago, when I was repeatedly at his temporary residence, the Hôtel Bagration, and dined with him, in company with his cherished friend, our Minister, Mr. Washburne. He had then lately received his certificate of membership of our American Academy of Arts and Sciences, signed by our Vice-President, Mr. Adams, and an invitation to our Bunker Hill Centennial, which seemed particularly to gratify him. He had been chosen one of the Honorary Members of this Society many years before. In the course of conversation, he alluded to having read something of Professor Dana's of Yale College,[1] asked whether I knew him, and begged me to present to him his compliments and respects. His mind had evidently been engaged on some of the materialistic theories of modern philosophy, from which it revolted; and he used language to me not very unlike that which he is reported to have used in his literary Will, where he says "he has thought much about religion in his retirement, and has become convinced that it is the basis of every organized society. He will die, therefore, believing in God, one and eternal, the Creator of all things, whose mercy he implores for his soul."

In this cursory account of the career of M. Thiers, I have attempted no delineation of his character. He has been called an adventurer; a man of expedients, without fixed principles;

[1] Professor James Dwight Dana, a Corresponding Member of the French Academy of Sciences, as well as of many other foreign Academies, and to whom the Royal Society of London has recently awarded "The Copley Medal," the highest honor in their gift, "for his biological, geological, and mineralogical investigations, carried on through half a century, and for the valuable Works in which his conclusions and discoveries have been published."

a man of many inconsistencies, — now for a Monarchy, now for an Empire, now for a Republic, — only to be accounted for by a vaulting ambition, and a selfish seeking of opportunity and power for himself. I dare not contest such imputations; but, certainly, I am unwilling to concur with them. I leave them all for those who can pronounce upon them with authority, from points of view not commanded by one at so great a distance.

For myself, I prefer to think of him, and to speak of him, as a grand example of a self-made man, who filled up the long measure of his protracted life with strenuous labors for literature, for history, for the fine arts, and for his country; overcoming the obstacles of humble birth and adverse fortune by indomitable courage and perseverance; yielding neither to the blandishments nor to the menaces of kings or emperors, of conquerors or communes; and achieving at last his greatest glory by inestimable services to his native land.

One attribute of Thiers will, indeed, never be disputed by anybody, — his intense attachment to his own country, his ardent and passionate love of France. In that we may all recognize a golden thread binding together all his inconsistencies into a grand whole of Patriotism, and giving ample justification to at least one part of the enviable inscription which was engraved on the plate of his coffin, —

"PATRIAM DILEXIT, VERITATEM COLUIT."

THE EARL OF ST. GERMANS.

REMARKS AT A MEETING OF THE MASSACHUSETTS HISTORICAL SOCIETY, NOVEMBER 8, 1877.

THE interesting remarks of Mr. Winsor in regard to the old Bradford manuscript volume in the library of the Bishop of London, at Fulham, recall to me the consultations on that subject which I held, many years ago, — long before Mr. Motley was our minister in England, — with Archdeacon Sinclair, with Sir Henry Holland, and with the Earl of St. Germans, and which resulted in the conviction that nothing less than an Act of Parliament would be considered as authorizing its transfer to America.

The venerable Archdeacon died in 1875, and Sir Henry somewhat earlier. The death of Lord ST. GERMANS has just been announced, and I cannot mention his name without referring briefly to our obligations to him as a Society. He was not one of our members, either Corresponding or Honorary; but we were primarily indebted to his kindness, some years ago, for a most interesting communication. He was a lineal descendant of the noble-hearted Sir John Eliot, who died in the Tower of London, as a martyr to free speech in Parliament, in 1633; and from his family papers were obtained the invaluable materials for the Life of that great English statesman and patriot by the late John Forster.

In that Biography, a brief reference was made to a correspondence between Sir John Eliot and the famous John Hampden on the subject of emigrating to New England. By the favor of

Lord St. Germans, in answer to an application of my own, the correspondence thus referred to was examined; and it proved, as I felt sure it would prove, that the "Conclusions or Reasons for planting New England," which were prepared by Governor Winthrop before he left England, had been communicated to Eliot while in the Tower, and had been the subject of consultation between him and Hampden.

We had often heard before, that the English patriots of the Commonwealth period were, many of them, in intimate association and correspondence with our Puritan leaders. But such authentic evidence that two of the foremost of them all, — whose lives, had they been spared, would have influenced the course of events in England so prominently and pre-eminently, — were in immediate consultation with the founders of the Massachusetts Colony, had never before been produced.

It was well said by John Forster, in his note to me communicating the papers: "The questions raised by this curious discovery are, indeed, full of striking interest." . . . "I am not without hope of what a closer examination of the papers may bring. Were the matter to end here, however, resting where it does, there is a new and striking interest contributed to a transaction which, more largely than any other in history, has affected the destinies of the human race."[1]

I am not aware that either Lord St. Germans or Mr. Forster himself ever found time for that "closer examination of the papers." Something may still be hoped for, now that the papers have passed into the possession of a younger generation. Meantime, I am glad of an opportunity of reminding the Society of their indebtedness to Lord St. Germans, and of expressing the high respect and affectionate regard I had for him. He was one of my oldest and most valued English friends, and one with whom I had exchanged occasional letters for a full term of thirty years. This friendly correspondence gave me an opportunity, more than once, during the progress of our late Civil War, to make informal explanations and suggestions, which were sure of being turned to the best account

[1] These papers may be found in the Proceedings of the Massachusetts Historical Society, for July, 1865.

for the cause of the Union. Lord St. Germans was, during a part of that time, associated with the British Ministry, as Lord High Steward of her Majesty's household. He had been, moreover, one of the little party which accompanied the Prince of Wales to America, and remembered with gratitude the attentions he had received here. He had been Postmaster-general in Sir Robert Peel's Cabinet, and afterwards Lord-lieutenant of Ireland. But his most memorable service, while he was known as Lord Eliot, was in 1835, when, as Ambassador to Spain, during her civil wars, at great risk of his own safety and life, he succeeded in negotiating and enforcing a Convention — entitled "The Eliot Convention" — for the merciful treatment and exchange of prisoners. Within the last ten years, he has published a monograph of that Mission, parts of which have an almost romantic interest, and which secures for him the enviable credit of having saved scores of human lives by his persevering and chivalric intervention.

A hardly less interesting incident of his early life is found in Gleig's Life of the Duke of Wellington, where Lord St. Leonards describes the escape of the Duke from a mob, in the days of the Reform Bill (1832), from which Lord Eliot and Lord Granville Somerset protected him on the one side and on the other.

Lord St. Germans married a grand-daughter of the first Marquis Cornwallis, — better known to our Revolutionary history as Earl Cornwallis; and I remember his showing me, at his own house, the sword which Cornwallis captured from Tippoo Saib; adding, pleasantly, that the Marquis's Yorktown sword was not in his possession.

He was a fine old English gentleman, dignified and stately, full of kindness and courtesy, bearing a long illness with Christian resignation, and dying, in his eightieth year, with the respect and warm regard of all who knew him, from the Queen and the Princes downward.

THE BOSTON PUBLIC LATIN SCHOOL.

SPEECH FROM THE CHAIR, AT THE FESTIVAL OF THE ALUMNI OF THE SCHOOL, NOVEMBER 15, 1877.

It was not without many misgivings, my friends, that I accepted the invitation of your Committee of Arrangements, and agreed to come here to preside over your festivities this evening. I am sincerely and deeply conscious that younger blood than mine would have been better adapted to the demands and duties of such an occasion. But I have not forgotten the line of Juvenal, which I learned at the Latin School under good Master Gould, more than half a century ago: "Galeatum serò duelli pœnitet." Doubts and misgivings belong before the trumpet sounds. They are quite out of place after that tocsin of the soul, as Byron calls it — the dinner bell — has rung; and, more especially, after the dinner itself has been eaten. I dismiss them all now, therefore, and proceed, without further apology or preamble, to the service which has been assigned to me.

And, first, let me present my credentials. Let me hold up before you the unimpeachable documentary evidence of my title to be with you at all. It is a printed broadside, somewhat soiled and scratched and time-worn, but still entirely legible and intelligible, which has been in my own cherished possession from the time of its date. Its caption reads as follows: "Catalogue of Scholars at the Public Latin School, Boston, 1821." It gives the names of two hundred and six pupils, arranged in five classes, and most of these classes in several divisions. And here, in the first division of the second class, a name confronts me, to which I have always answered, boy and man, — a name which I could not disown if I would, and would not if I could. There is no appeal from such a record.

I did not enter this School, as most of my classmates did, in 1818; and I had thus no experience of its lower forms. But after three years under the worthy Deacon Samuel Greele, and three more under Dr. John Carlton Fisher, a most accomplished teacher, who had been brought over from England under the auspices of Edward Everett — that prince of good scholars — on the alleged idea that there was at that time no adequate instruction in the classics to be obtained in Boston, — I came here at last in 1821, and remained till I entered Harvard College in 1824.

Fifty-six years have thus elapsed since I became a Latin School boy; and that is certainly long enough to give one, not merely a title to be here to-night, but a license to indulge in some reminiscences of the past, which might savor of pretension in a younger person. I dare say there is a duplicate of this old broadside in the library of our Association. If not, this one shall certainly go there. But I cannot find it in my heart to part with it, to that library or to any other, without yielding to some of the associations which it revives, and making it the text of all I have to say on this occasion.

It carries me back to my boyhood, as hardly any thing else could do; and, as I glance over the roll of my early companions — so many of them lost to sight, but still to memory dear — the old school-house, which stood then and long afterward on the very spot on which we are assembled,[1] rises freshly to my view, with all its dingy walls, and notched and dented desks and benches, — and I almost hear the voice of my old Master, calling on me to stand up and recite my lesson, or speak my piece.

[1] The precise site of the old school-house is now occupied by "The Parker House," in which this Festival was held.

It recalls to me the pride with which I saw my name for the first time in print, as a Latin School boy, and carried home the catalogue to be preserved as a precious relic, as it is this day.

It recalls the time when we Boston boys were learning to swim, where the Public Garden and its grand Statues now are; and when, in our games of football or cricket, we were joint occupants of the Common with the cows.

It recalls the not infrequent mornings, when, coming out of my father's house in Hamilton Place, I was privileged to walk along, arm in arm, or, it may have been, hand in hand, with the late venerable Josiah Quincy, who lived next door, — then in his mature middle age, — he on his way to the City Hall as Mayor of Boston, and I on my way to school; sometimes, as I well remember, without his speaking a word to me the whole way, so absorbed was he in the meditation of those municipal duties which he discharged so long and so faithfully.

It recalls to me the prizes I contended for, and sometimes gained. Others won more than I did, and I am not here to boast of any thing. But I have not forgotten a little gold medal for a Latin poem, or a larger silver Franklin medal, or a set of books from Master Gould, or another set "Ab Urbe pro meritis Datum," which are among my most cherished treasures to this hour.

It recalls to me the occasion when those prizes were bestowed, and when I achieved my earliest rhetorical success by drawing tears from the eyes of young ladies in my audience, while I was paying my juvenile tribute to poor Lord Byron, who had just died in Greece.

It recalls to me most vividly and most gratefully the Masters, to whom I owed so much of instruction and of kindness, — the accomplished and thorough Dr. J. Greely Stevenson, who died early, more than forty years ago; the late laborious Dr. Joseph Palmer, who lived to be a painstaking journalist and one of the Necrologists of Harvard College; but above and before all others, the excellent and true-hearted Benjamin Apthorp Gould, as genial as he was gifted, who swayed even the ferule, which he rarely used, with singular dignity and grace, — more often patting the hand lovingly with it by way of warning, than dealing blows by way of punishment, — an admirable Head-Master, to whom we were all attached and whom we all respected. Of each one of these Masters, indeed, we could say with Goldsmith, —

> "Yet he was kind, or if severe in aught,
> The love he bore to learning was in fault."

But it recalls to me, before all else, more than one endeared playmate and schoolmate, afterward classmates, and one of them my chum, at Cambridge, but called away long, long ago — Charles Chauncey Emerson and James Jackson — who, had their lives been spared, would have added no inferior honors to family names, which are hardly second to any names in our Commonwealth, or in our whole Country. No two young men of my period, certainly, ought to be more tenderly remembered among the Worthies of this School, than the two I have mentioned. For both alike — the one in medicine, the other in literature and law — the most useful and brilliant careers were just opening, when they passed from human sight.

> "Ostendunt terris hos tantùm Fata, neque ultra
> Esse sinunt."

This little faded broadside contains, indeed, but the record of 1821. The name of my friend Mr. Adams is not on it, for he left the School for College just as I was entering it. The name of Ralph Waldo Emerson is not on it, for he was a little farther in advance. And there is one name whose absence from this particular roll I hardly know how to account for. It is the name of one who carried off the highest honors and prizes of my class, both at School and at College. He must have entered a little later, and passed over all our heads at a bound. If our friend George S. Hillard had been able to be with us, I should call on him for an explanation. He could tell us how all this was. He could shoulder his crutch and show us all how fields were won and triumphs achieved. Alas, that he should have any crutch to shoulder! He was one of the leading founders of this Association in 1844, and I am glad of the opportunity to assure him, in his enforced absence, that he is not forgotten at our festival.

But there is another void on this old catalogue, which some of you, perhaps, may regard as an aching void; which is regarded by some persons, certainly, elsewhere if not here, as a *hiatus valde deflendus*. It is the entire absence of the feminine gender! These two hundred and six names are all boys' names; and I know not what would have been thought if the proposal of a mixed school had been suggested at that time. I am wrong. I do know. We all know that such an idea would not have been seriously entertained for an instant. I have no purpose of discussing the subject on such an occasion as this. Mr. Adams, in his brief note, has expressed my views as well as his own, and far better than I could express them in the longest speech. But, after all, my friends, we recognize it as the special prerogative of the ladies to say *No* on all interesting questions; and I hope and believe that a great majority of mothers and daughters would unite in giving an emphatic and unequivocal negative to any such offer, even if it were made, — as does not seem at all likely at present. Let us help them to have Latin Schools and Colleges for themselves. Vassar and Wellesley are theirs already. On neither of them, I believe, is to be found the inscription which Tennyson paints on the college gate of his "Princess," "Let no man enter in on pain of death." Visitors of both sexes have entered them, and found much to admire. Let them study the classics to their heart's content — the *levitas Græca* as well as the *gravitas Romana*. There have been Olympia Moratas, and Lady Jane Greys, and Madame Daciers, and Mrs. Ripleys of Waltham, before now, and there will be again. "They sparkle still the true Promethean fire;" and we are ready to add, as Shakspeare added, nearly three centuries ago, —

> "They are the books, the arts, the academes,
> That show, contain, and nourish all the world;
> Else none at all in aught proves excellent."

But we are persuaded, notwithstanding, that girls and boys both will study better, and learn more, and have fewer distractions, in separate institutions, — until they have studied enough and learned enough to be prepared for the serious duties and responsibilities of life, and are ready to contemplate a different sort of conjugations from any which are to be found in our Latin or Greek grammars.

This little broadside, as I have said, includes only the pupils of a single year. But it is no unfair index of the men who have owed their early education to this School. It contains the names of two who have been Head-Masters of the School itself — Charles K. Dillaway and Epes S. Dixwell. It contains the names of three who have been Chief Justices of our own or other States; of three who have been Senators in Congress; and of many more who have been associated with distinguished services in the pulpit, at the bar, in medicine, in commerce, in agriculture, in philanthropy, in journalism, and in literature. It thus does no discredit, to say the least, to this oldest institution of learning in our land, which has included on its earlier roll such names as Franklin, and Samuel Adams, and Bowdoin, and Hancock, and Robert Treat Paine. I may not attempt to enumerate the celebrities of its later catalogues, living or dead. Their names are familiar to you all.

But pardon me, my friends, for having occupied so much time in these personal and historical reminiscences. Our School has had, indeed, a glorious past. The great question is, What can be done to secure for it a still more glorious, let me rather say, a still more useful, future? What can this Association do, what can any of its individual members do, to promote its honor and welfare, future or immediate? Each one of us owes it a debt. It is difficult to estimate, or certainly to over-estimate, that debt. We can all gratefully recognize our paramount and supreme obligations to the kind Providence which has cast our lot in such pleasant places. But it is by no means easy for any of us to distinguish and part out our respective obligations to parental training, to school teaching, to college education, to self-education, to opportunity, circumstances, and intercourse with our fellow-men.

I may not be quite able to say with one of my friends, that this is the only school which ever taught me any thing. But

I can say sincerely, that, in looking back over my life, among the very last associations which I should be willing to relinquish or obliterate, — always excepting those of home and of the house of God, — are my associations with this Free Public Latin School of my native city. We all owe it an incalculable debt. How can we pay it? How can we discharge any part of it? How can we show our grateful appreciation of it?

We can do something by manifesting our interest and pride in its prosperity and progress. We can do something by helping to enlarge its library and enrich its cabinet. There ought surely to be on its shelves an autograph presentation copy of every good book written by a Latin School pupil. We can do something by giving our personal attendance and attention, from time to time, to its examinations and exhibitions, — not withholding our just admiration for the exact drill and discipline of its military corps, or for the success of its athletic sports. We may be able to do something, one of these days, by founding and endowing a Harvard Scholarship or two for meritorious and needy graduates of the School. We can certainly do something by contributing toward the preparation and publication and illustration of a complete and adequate history of the School, which shall hold up the example of the past as an incentive to the present and the future; such a history as may be found of the great schools of Old England, — Eton, and Harrow, and Charter House, and Rugby.

All this is obvious and easy. But, after all, the most important history of the School is that which the boys on the benches are making for it, and making for themselves, day by day. No patronage or endowments, no gifts or prizes or words of encouragement from us or from others, no new and grander schoolhouse erected by the city, can take the place of thorough, conscientious devotedness on the part of the pupils. This School, and every school, must be what the scholars, under the influence of their masters, make it. There is no substitute for subordination and study. We can only tell them, for ourselves, that we look back with regret on every duty which we left undone, on every lesson which we left unlearned, on every opportunity we neglected or slighted. We can only remind them that their best successes and highest triumphs, in after life, are to be secured or lost by the habits they form, and the efforts they make, or omit to make, here and now. We can only entreat them, for the character of the old School, for the credit of the old City of which it has so long been the pride, for the hopes of the Commonwealth and the Country, to make the most of their advantages, — to respect their teachers, to respect themselves, and to reverence the great obligations which rest upon them, and the great expectations which are rightfully formed of them. The Future of our country is in its Schools.

In journeying through Northern Italy many years ago, I remember being struck by an inscription over the gateway of one of the schools of the University of Padua, — that ancient University at which — if there be no mistake, as I shrewdly suspect there is, in a printed record which I obtained at Padua[1] — no less illustrious an Englishman than Oliver Cromwell received a part of his education, and which prides itself justly on its associations with the birthplace of the great Roman historian, Livy. I wish the same inscription could be emblazoned where it might be read, day by day and every day, by Latin School boys or Hârvard College men. It might be engraved over the entrance of that new school-house, for which, it is said, the piles have just been driven. I quote it, as I procured it at the time, as the conclusion of all I have said, and of all I have to say, on this occasion: —

"Sic ingredere, ut te ipso quotidie doctior: Sic egredere, ut in dies Patriæ Christianæque Reipublicæ utilior evadas: Ita demum Gymnasium a te feliciter ornatum existimabitur."

If I could borrow for a moment the pen of my friend, President Eliot, which has recently signalized itself by the inscriptions on the Memorial Hall at Cambridge, and the Soldiers' Monument on Boston Common, I might be able to give you a terser translation. But I venture to offer the best that occurs to me: —

"So enter here, that you may daily add something to your

[1] See note on the next page.

own learning: So go forth, that you may be more and more useful to your Christian Commonwealth and Country: Thus at last you shall be esteemed as having been an ornament to this School!"

I will only detain you longer, Fellow Students, while I propose as a sentiment:—

"Continued prosperity and honor to the old Boston Public Latin School, — *in secula seculorum!*"

NOTE.

At Padua, in May, 1860, I found a little work with this title: "Della Università di Padova Cenni ed Iscrizioni: 1841;" and in the Preface I read as follows:—

"Non è necessario ricordare che numerosi rampolli d' illustri famiglie d' ogni nazione frequentarono le nostre scuole, e che alumni di questo tanto celebre stabilimento furono ed il Principe Gustavo di Svezia, e Stefano Battoreo, e Giovanni Sobieski poscia Re di Polonia, ed *Oliviero Cromvell protettore o tiranno dell' Inghilterra,* e Francesco Bernardo Visconti."

Again, in section IV. of the work, in the list of celebrities associated with the University, "*Un Protettore d' Inghilterra*" is distinctly named.

A recent correspondence with my friend the Hon. George P. Marsh, our Minister in Italy for so many years, — who kindly consulted the distinguished Professor Villari, of Florence, — confirms my doubts of the accuracy of this record. Yet one would almost as soon suspect a mistake in one of Mr. Sibley's Triennial Catalogues of Harvard University. Such a fact, however, could hardly have escaped the exhaustive research of Oliver's great biographer, Carlyle. Possibly, Thomas Cromwell, the Earl of Essex, whom Shakspeare has rendered familiar to us in "Henry VIII.," and who is known to have obtained most of his education on the Continent, may have been at the University of Padua in the previous century; and this may prove to have been the origin of the mistake, if it be one. But this is only a conjecture of my own.

THE PEABODY MUSEUM OF AMERICAN ARCHÆOLOGY AND ETHNOLOGY.

INTRODUCTORY ADDRESS ON THE OPENING OF THE NEW BUILDING, CAMBRIDGE, MASSACHUSETTS, FEBRUARY 18, 1878.

OUR Annual Meeting, Gentlemen, has been postponed for several weeks, in order to allow our Curator more leisure for preparing these apartments for our reception. We meet now, for the first time, in our permanent home, over the entrance to which — carved legibly on the free-stone block above the door — is the Inscription: "Peabody Museum of American Archæology and Ethnology." We meet, too, by a somewhat fortuitous, but certainly a most auspicious, coincidence of dates, on the birthday of our illustrious Founder. Mr. Peabody was born at South Danvers, in this State, on the 18th of February, 1795, and would have been entering to-day, had he lived, on his 83d year.

I am unwilling that our meeting on this Anniversary, and in this new Hall, should pass off without a few informal words, on my part, as the permanent Chairman of the Board, which seem to be due to the memory of Mr. Peabody, if not due to myself, and which belong indeed to the history of this Institution. If our Museum shall fulfil its promise, and shall become, as I think it rapidly is becoming, one of the most interesting and important Scientific Departments of the University, a day may arrive, in some far distant future, when it shall itself be the subject of archæological research, and when its small beginnings may furnish matter for eager investigation. Let me recall, then, some dates and facts which are probably within my own knowledge only, and which may at least serve to help the future inquirer.

It was on the 1st of June, 1866, as I find by my notes at the time, that I first met Mr. Peabody, at his own request, at the Tremont House in Boston, to consult with him on his proposed endowment for Harvard University. On the 4th of June, three days afterwards, Professor O. C. Marsh, of Yale College, and Mr. George Peabody Russell, both of them nephews of our Founder, called on me at the rooms of the Massachusetts Historical Society, for further consultation on the subject. On the 17th of June following, Mr. Peabody spent an hour with me at Brookline, solely in reference to this plan for Harvard. At this interview he placed in my hands a rough sketch of our Institution, and gave me permission to consult confidentially with one or two of the friends of the University in regard to it.

For this consultation I selected, before all others, the late President Walker, and I am not sure that I sought serious counsel of any one else. Dr. Walker took the matter into consideration in his calm, wise, common-sense way, and was ready, after a few days, to pronounce a deliberate judgment. He saw, as I did, that, in confining his liberality to this one scientific object, Mr. Peabody would disappoint not a few hopes and expectations at Cambridge. There were peculiar needs there at that time. The Library was greatly in need. The Museum of Comparative Zoölogy was not less in need. The general finances of the University were sadly deficient. Meantime, the idea of such an Institution as this had never occurred to any one, and pre-historic science was too much in its infancy to have enlisted any ardent votaries.

But Dr. Walker soon reached a conclusion, in his own mind, on these and all other points of doubt. I remember how emphatically he said to me, substantially, as the result of his deliberations: "Mr. Winthrop, I have always been of opinion that when a generous man, like Mr. Peabody, proposes a great gift, we should accept it on his own terms, and not on ours. Even if we could persuade him to change his plans, and endow some other branch of the University, he would never take the same interest in it, or regard it so much as his own. We had better take what he offers, and take it on his own terms, and for the object which he evidently has at heart. That object may not impress the College or the community, at first sight, as one of the highest interest or importance. There may be, and will be, as you say, disappointments in some quarters. But the branch of Science, to which this endowment is devoted, is one to which many minds in Europe are now eagerly turning, and with which not a few of the philosophical inquiries and theories of the hour are intimately associated. It will grow in interest from year to year. This Museum, too, will be the first of its kind in our country, and will have the best chance of securing those relics of our Indian tribes, which are now scattered in so many private collections. It is, moreover, precisely one of those institutions which must necessarily owe its foundation to private liberality. We could never hope to make it the subject of a public subscription or contribution. But if Mr. Peabody will make it his own, and endow it handsomely; and if we can get a safe, sound, accomplished person, like Jeffries Wyman, to take the charge of it, — there can be no doubt of its ultimate success."

Dr. Walker, as you all know, was not a man of many words, and I may have amplified in some degree the views he expressed in our repeated comparisons of opinion. But such were his conclusions; and I should be wanting to his memory, if I did not place him foremost among those whose advice and counsel led to the unqualified acceptance of Mr. Peabody's offer, and to the establishment of this Museum.

On the 6th of July I was able to communicate to Mr. Peabody, by letter, the result of our consultations. But it was not until the 24th of September that his plan was sufficiently matured to be communicated to others. On that day he met me again, at the Historical Rooms, together with his nephews, Prof. Marsh and Mr. Russell; and, after arranging the details of our organization, I was authorized to call a meeting of the gentlemen designated as Trustees. On the 28th of September, a primary and provisional meeting was accordingly held, — the late Francis Peabody, of Salem, Professor Asa Gray, Professor Jeffries Wyman, Hon. Stephen Salisbury, and Mr. George

Peabody Russell being in attendance, and making, with myself, all the Trustees except Mr. Adams, who was still in London, as American Minister.

On the 18th of October Mr. Peabody signed the Instrument of Trust, which was published in the Boston "Daily Advertiser" of the next morning, and on the 3d of November, 1866, the first formal meeting of the Trustees was held. The Board was organized on that day, agreeably to the terms of the Instrument; and I then proceeded, with Mr. Salisbury and Mr. Francis Peabody, to the office of Blake Brothers & Co., in State Street, where we received the Massachusetts Bonds for one hundred and fifty thousand dollars, counted them and sealed them up, and then deposited them temporarily in the safe of the Massachusetts General Hospital Life Insurance Company. From that time to this our proceedings have been a matter of record.

I have referred to the early and emphatic suggestion, by Dr. Walker, of JEFFRIES WYMAN, as the man of all others for the Curator of our Museum; and I find that, on the 1st of December following our organization, Dr. Walker spent an hour with me in my library in earnest enforcement of this suggestion. It needed no enforcement, so far as I was personally concerned; and it soon proved that our whole Board was of one mind on that point. The Curatorship was unanimously assigned to Professor Wyman, who was also one of our Trustees; and he continued to discharge the duties of that office for the eight remaining years of his life.

His death, on the 4th of September, 1874, occurred while I was in Europe; and I cannot forget the deep sorrow with which I saw its announcement, accidentally, in a copy of "Galignani's Messenger," while I was passing a few days at Heidelberg. As my absence from home deprived me of the opportunity of uniting with the Trustees in paying him the just tribute which is upon our records, I may be pardoned for dwelling, for a moment longer, upon his signal and pre-eminent services to this Institution. My relations to him, as Chairman of the Board, brought me into very frequent consultation and correspondence with him in regard to the Museum. As we were living so near to each other, the oral consultations were more frequent than the correspondence; but I have brought with me here to-day a large number of his letters, — all of them having reference to his labors in our behalf, and many of them containing interesting and important suggestions as to the work in which we were engaged. These letters, thirty-two in number, seem to me to belong to the history of our Institution, and I propose to deposit them in its archives. The earliest bears date, November 26, 1866; and the last, July 9, 1874, — less than two months before his death. Some of them were written among the White Hills of New Hampshire, some of them in Florida, and some of them in Italy and France, while he was travelling abroad for his health. The last two — as well as a few of the earlier ones — were addressed to me while I, in my turn, was absent from our own country. They all alike bear witness to his devoted interest in this Institution, and to his untiring labors in its behalf. If my own letters to him, of which I kept no copies, shall happen to have been preserved by himself or his family, they will show, in connection with his own, the measures which were taken for securing the Mortillet Collection, the Clement Collection, the Castellani Vases, the Cushing relics from Mexico, and the grand collection of Danish Flints of Mr. Wilmot J. Rose, — all of which were obtained through my intervention, with his counsel and co-operation, for purposes of comparison with the pre-historic specimens of our own land. It may well be doubted whether these collections, or any others at all comparable to them, could have been secured at a later day, or under any other circumstances than those, of which we were so fortunately in the way of taking advantage, at the precise moment when they were obtained. We should seek for them in vain now, either at home or abroad.

No more patient, persevering, skilful, and thoroughly scientific person could have been designated, for the work of founding and building up such a Museum as this, than Jeffries Wyman; and his name deserves to be associated with that of Mr. Peabody himself, in the history of the rise and progress of the Institution. At some future day, it may be hoped that portraits of them both may adorn these walls. The modesty of Professor Wyman was as remarkable as his merits, and he was satisfied with accomplishing his work from day to day, and from year to year, without seeking to display his own labors in organizing and developing the Institution which had been committed to his charge. All the more ought we to take care that his name should be ever remembered, prominently and pre-eminently, in connection with this Museum, and be inscribed on some appropriate part of its inner walls, as its first Curator, — I had almost said, Creator. His personal qualities endeared him to all who knew him, and I count my own relations with him for eight years among the most valued privileges of my life.

Under his superintending care the Institution was rapidly developed, while at the same time the interest in this department of science, in Europe and in our own land, was steadily increasing year by year, as Dr. Walker predicted it would do. The marvellous discoveries of Dr. Schliemann — to name no other name — have given still a new and stronger impulse, of late, to the search for whatever may be found in mounds or burrows, in bogs or glacial drifts, at the bottom of lakes, in caves or in shell heaps, as well as under the débris of ancient cities, to throw light on the history of the past. And thus, at the end of ten years since our organization, Mr. Peabody's foundation is amply justified; and nobody, I think, would now desire it to have been any other than what it was.

In entering our new Hall, to-day, we do not forget our indebtedness to our Associate Trustee, Colonel Lyman, and to our friend Professor Alexander Agassiz, for their devoted attention to the erection of this building, from its inception to its completion. We do not fail, also, to remember gratefully the faithful services of our Treasurer, Mr. Salisbury, under whose care the fund appropriated to this purpose by Mr. Peabody was accumulated, until it had reached the amount prescribed before the edifice should be undertaken.

Nor can we omit our acknowledgments of the diligent and untiring services of our present Curator, Prof. F. W. Putnam, and his Assistant, Mr. Lucien Carr, by whom the laborious work of transferring our collections to this new building, and arranging them in its various apartments, has been so satisfactorily and successfuly performed, and under whose auspices so many valuable additions have been made to the Museum. Happily, these gentlemen are all with us, to enjoy their best reward in witnessing the grand consummation of their labors.

And now, Gentlemen, in taking possession this morning of a Building which, we trust, is not only to outlast us all, but to be the scene of scientific labors and acquisitions in future and far distant generations, I may be permitted to invoke for the Institution not merely the favor of our fellow-men, but the blessing of God, — remembering those words of the great father of modern science, Lord Bacon, who would have had every thing dedicated alike to "the relief of man's estate and to the glory of the Creator."

There are but few passages more striking among the voluminous writings of Bacon which are left to us, than the little "Student's Prayer," as he entitled it, which he seems to have composed while he was engaged on his "Novum Organum" and his "De Augmentis Scientiarum." After some formal opening phrases, he proceeds: "This also we humbly and earnestly beg, that human things may not prejudice such as are Divine; neither that from the unlocking of the gates of sense, and the kindling of a greater natural light, any thing of incredulity or intellectual night may arise in our minds toward the Divine Mysteries; but rather that by our mind thoroughly cleansed and purged from fancy and vanities, and yet subject and perfectly given to the Divine Oracles, there may be given unto Faith the things that are Faith's. Amen."

Such words — these very words — might well be inscribed on the walls of every student's chamber, and of every hall of Modern Science. They breathe a spirit worthy of being devoutly cherished by all who deprecate any needless conflict, or wanton contention, between Science and Religion.

It was in this spirit, as I well know, that our illustrious Founder endowed this Institution. It was in this spirit, as I remember well, that President Walker advised its acceptance, and urged upon me the appointment of Jeffries Wyman as its Curator. It was in this spirit, as we can all bear witness, that the lamented Wyman himself pursued his work and prosecuted his investigations. And, certainly, it is in this spirit, that, having counselled and co-operated with them all, I shall maintain my relations to the Museum, agreeably to Mr. Peabody's assignment, as long as life and health shall enable me to watch over it. And may the blessing of God rest upon all our counsels and labors!

GENERAL THEOLOGICAL LIBRARY.

REMARKS AT THE ANNUAL MEETING, BOSTON, APRIL 15, 1878.

ON my return, Gentlemen, from a short journey last spring, I found myself most unexpectedly announced as the President of this institution. Had I been at home when the election occurred, I should have excused myself from the office. But I have been unwilling to withdraw hastily from duties which have been rendered so light and easy by the untiring devotion of your Secretary and Librarian, Mr. Farnham. To him the institution is indebted for its earliest suggestion, and for its successful management during the whole period of its existence. Its broad, catholic character — opening its shelves to volumes on all religious creeds, and its doors, at a very small assessment, to all who desire to consult those volumes — commends it to the favor of a Christian community.

This is, I believe, its sixteenth annual meeting, and the Secretary, in his report, will sufficiently inform you of the progress which has been made in accumulating a library, and in obtaining the means for its preservation and usefulness. He will not fail to inform you of the liberal bequest which has recently come to us by the will of a most estimable lady, the late Mrs. James W. Sever.

We remember, also, with gratitude, the large contributions of books and of money which we have received from the late Rev. Dr. Charles Burroughs, of Portsmouth, New Hampshire. He is entitled to be recorded as the founder of the Library and its largest benefactor. He was also its first President, and continued to preside over the institution for nearly six years, and until his death in March, 1868.

For the nine following years, and until the last annual meeting, the office of president was held by the Hon. Edward Brooks, who died on Thursday last, the 11th instant, in the eighty-fifth year of his age. We owe it to ourselves, no less than to his memory, to make respectful and grateful mention this morning of his valuable services; more especially as we had no opportunity of attending his funeral, which took place, without public notice, at Medford, — the old home of his father, and of his kinsman, the late Governor John Brooks, — on Saturday last.

Mr. Edward Brooks, our late President, was the eldest son of the Hon. Peter C. Brooks, so well remembered in this community as one of Boston's wealthiest and most eminent men of business, and of whom an admirable memoir may be found among the writings of his illustrious son-in-law, Edward Everett. He was graduated at Harvard University in 1812, in the class with those beloved pastors, Dr. Henry Ware, Jr., and Bishop Wainwright, and with the venerable Peleg Sprague, who so long adorned the bench of the United States District Court, and who is now one of the few survivors of his associates in college.

Mr. Brooks was one of the Representatives of Boston in the Legislature of Massachusetts forty years or more ago, where, as a member of the same body, I was in the way of witnessing his ability as a debater and his earnest interest in the affairs of our Commonwealth. He was afterwards, I believe, a member of our State Senate.

But the health of his wife compelled him to break off from all pursuits at home, and to spend many successive years in foreign lands. It will not be forgotten that on his return he presented a very striking original portrait of Franklin to our Public Library, which is among the gems of that noble establishment.

He was a man of vigorous intellect, of great reading, and of many varied accomplishments. He took a warm interest in this Library, and made repeated contributions to it of books and of money. There are those present who will bear witness with me to his punctuality, fidelity, and courtesy in presiding over its administration. The infirmities of advanced age constrained him to resign his relations to us little more than a year ago, and he has now followed to the grave, after an interval of only a few weeks, his younger brother, the late amiable and excellent Mr. Sidney Brooks.

The Secretary of our institution, or some one of our Directors, who has been a sharer of his labors in our behalf for more years than I have been, will present Resolutions for your adoption, which I am sure will meet with your unanimous acceptance.

WILLIAM C. BRYANT.

REMARKS AT A MEETING OF THE MASSACHUSETTS HISTORICAL SOCIETY, JUNE 13, 1878.

THE death of the venerable WILLIAM C. BRYANT has been announced in the public papers this morning, at too late a moment before our meeting, to allow any of us to speak of it, or to speak of him, as we should desire to speak. But as we are not likely to hold another meeting for several months, I am unwilling to postpone all notice of so impressive an event.

A native of our own State, and long an honorary member of our own Society, his death may well find its earliest mention here, even though our tribute be brief and inadequate.

As a poet, as a journalist, as a patriot, as a pure and upright man, living to an almost patriarchal age, yet never losing his interest, or relaxing his efforts, in whatever might advance the honor or welfare of his fellow-men, he has won for himself an imperishable remembrance on the page of history.

No one, certainly, as long as our language shall be read or spoken, will forget the author of "Thanatopsis," "The Waterfowl," and "The Land of Dreams," — to name no others of his poems, — or ever cease to be grateful for those inspiring and exquisite strains.

His loss is, indeed, primarily and peculiarly that of our great sister City and State, with whose interests and renown he has been for so many years identified. But his name and fame have long ceased to be local, and his death is nothing less than a national bereavement.

I forbear from attempting any sketch of his life or labors, lest I should fail at such short notice to do justice to his memory. But as there has been no opportunity for a meeting of the Council, from whom such a notice should come, I venture, on my own responsibility, to offer the following Resolutions: —

Resolved, By the Massachusetts Historical Society, that, in the death of our distinguished honorary member, William Cullen Bryant, our country has lost a patriotic and noble citizen, the press an accomplished and powerful journalist, and American literature one of its earliest, purest, and most enduring ornaments.

Resolved, That, while we remember with pride that he was born in Massachusetts, and educated at one of our own Colleges, our warmest sympathies in this bereavement are due, and are hereby offered, to the scholars and to the whole people of New York, with whom he has been so long and so eminently associated, and to whom his genius and his fame have been ever so justly dear.

Resolved, That these Resolutions be communicated to the New York Historical Society, with the assurance that our hearts are with them in lamenting the loss, and in doing honor to the memory, of their illustrious associate and Vice-President.

SEMI-CENTENNIAL OF THE CLASS OF 1828.

ADDRESS AT THE DINNER OF THE ALUMNI, JUNE 26, 1878.

I AM greatly honored, Fellow Students of Harvard, by this kind reception. I thank you, Mr. President, for the complimentary words with which you have called upon me. I hardly know how to make any adequate acknowledgment. But, indeed, my friends, I cannot help feeling that I have already contributed my full share to this entertainment in having secured for it, by a most fortunate intervention, the presence and assistance of our illustrious guest, the Governor-General of Canada.[1] I must, certainly, be pardoned for indulging in all the pride of the sexton in the old story, who, while his congregation were in raptures with an impressive and eloquent discourse, was heard boasting that he had, at least, pulled the bell for it. We all knew something about the felicity of the noble Earl's speeches, in more languages than one, before to-day. We were all familiar with his inimitable Latin speech at an Icelandic dinner, as reported by himself in one of his charming "Letters from High Latitudes." And many of us had not failed to observe, very much more recently, that when he received a degree at Montreal, like that which has been conferred on him here this morning, he made his acknowledgments in the choicest Greek. But now we have been privileged to hear him in that dear mother tongue of New England as well as of Old England, which is fast becoming the common speech of both hemispheres;

[1] The Earl of Dufferin.

which has just achieved a new triumph in being employed by Bismarck, as well as Beaconsfield, at the Berlin Congress; and which, though it may not quite yet have reached the dignity of being the court language of the world, must always be the language for those who would study, in the original, the great principles of liberty and law, and the glorious history of free institutions and free men,—the language of Washington and Franklin and Webster, as well as of Chatham and Burke and Fox and Sheridan. God grant that it may ever be a bond of love and a pledge of peace between the nations which are alike privileged to call it their own!

But I must not be betrayed into any random utterances or miscellaneous discourse on this occasion, or into following any train of thought which may have been suggested by those who have preceded me. I am here in special trust, charged to represent the class of 1828, and to say such few words as I may be able to say at all, in strict reference to our Golden Wedding, on this fiftieth anniversary of our marriage to the Muses, whom we had courted for four years previously in the shades of Harvard, and from whom we won, after all, on that occasion, only a Bachelor's Degree!

I am here to represent a class of fifty-two members, of whom eighteen or nineteen only are still living. I may not forget that I had no original claim to the distinction of being their spokesman, as my rank was No. 3, not No. 1. But, of the two who were above me, one has long been sleeping in his early grave,—the brilliant and excellent Charles Chauncy Emerson; while the other—my accomplished friend, Mr. Hillard—is, to the regret of us all, too much of an invalid to venture here to-day.

Let me recall that Commencement, on the 27th of August, 1828, in a few words, that you may be able to contrast it with the one we are enjoying at this moment. It comes back to me as vividly as if it had occurred but yesterday. There was no President of the University on that occasion. What should we have done without our young and vigorous President to-day! The revered and beloved Kirkland had resigned a few months before, and Josiah Quincy—of whom, I rejoice to say, we are at last to have Story's charming statue to adorn these halls — had not yet been chosen to succeed him. The venerable Henry Ware, the Hollis Professor of Divinity, sat in the antique Holyoke chair, looking almost as old as the chair itself, and with a shaking head and trembling hand delivered to us our diplomas, which bore his signature as Vice-President of the College. Around him were the veteran Professors, Hedge and Popkin and Farrar and Channing and Willard and the rest, and the old members of the Corporation, Dr. Porter and Judge Story and Dr. Bowditch, with Levi Lincoln, as Governor of Massachusetts, and all the other notables of the Commonwealth and the neighboring city.

But if we had no President of the University, we had a President of the United States to grace our Commencement, — our own John Quincy Adams, then in the last year of his Presidential term, though, as I rejoice to remember, with many grand years of public service still opening before him. And with him on the stage that day was the Hon. Andrew Stevenson, of Virginia, then the Speaker of the House of Representatives of the United States. These were the two most distinguished guests at our Commencement, — the two principal figures which filled my eye then, and which fill my eye again to-day, as I turn it back upon that well-remembered scene. How little could either of them have dreamed that, before twenty years had passed away, a certain young man, who shall be nameless, whom they then heard speaking somewhat disparagingly of "Public Station," should be occupying the same high chair which one of them then held, while the other, full of years and of honors, should fall in addressing him, and die in his official chamber at the Capitol![1]

That Commencement was a day of prolonged literary exercises, beginning at ten, and hardly ending before four o'clock. Here is the original printed order of performances, the same which I held in my hand fifty years ago. There were no less than thirty-two parts, only two of which were excused. We had but nine speakers, in all, this morning. Good Dr. Pierce, so long

[1] Winthrop's Addresses and Speeches, Vol. I. p. 614.

the secretary of the Overseers, and the liner of the psalm at the dinner table, was at his post, with his note-book and pencil, to jot down, according to his wont, the precise number of minutes taken by each performer, and to record them all in his diary. And I remember, with compunction and remorse, his telling me at the time that I had delivered the longest oration of which he had kept the reckoning, on that or any other Commencement Day! It might well become me to make all the amends in my power by being brief, or even by saying nothing, on this occasion. The truth was, that I had been a little nettled at being allowed only twelve minutes, while others were allowed fifteen; and I here make humble confession that I wilfully disregarded all limit, in defiance of the Faculty, and occupied more than half an hour. What was my astonishment, many years ago, at finding this juvenile performance, with one other of the orations of my class, printed in a volume among the selected models of academic exercises![1]

Pardon me, I pray you, Mr. President and Fellow Students, for these personal allusions. It is the special privilege of us fifty-years' men to indulge to-day in reminiscence and retrospect; and even egotisms like these may not be wholly unpalatable or unpardonable. Let me hasten towards a conclusion by saying that our class has better things to boast of than any thing of my own. We may not claim to have been one of the great classes, like that of 1802, or that of 1811, or that of 1817, or that of 1829. Early deaths took away from us not a few of our most promising scholars. And then we had no poet, like the class which succeeded us; no Oliver — I had almost said Goldsmith, but you all know whom I mean — to sing to us, and sing of us, at our occasional meetings. *Carent vate sacro* must be accepted as our legend; and, if not unwept and unhonored, we must be content to pass away unsung. Our "*Morituri Salutamus*," unlike that exquisite farewell at Bowdoin three years ago, has already been uttered in stern prose. We had no Holmes or Longfellow in our ranks, to give expression to our emotions.

[1] Parker's "Aids to English Composition," p. 354.

Yet I may not forget that we have given a Hillard to literature, a Bowditch to medicine, a Barnard to philanthropy, a Gilchrist to the chief-justiceship of New Hampshire, a Babbidge to be the first volunteer chaplain of the first volunteer regiment, and a Major-General James S. Wadsworth to be one of the last and most lamented victims of our late war for the Union. If any public offices or honors have attached themselves to any other names on our roll, they may all be thrown into the scale for whatever they are worth, to swell the aggregate claims of the class of 1828 to the kind consideration and remembrance of those who may take an interest in its record, now or hereafter.

Let me not, however, wholly omit one other name. While, as a class, we have only contributed our little accumulation of twelve or fifteen hundred dollars to the grand fund of the Alumni, it is not to be forgotten that a contingent bequest, which has since been realized, and which has added a round sum of fifty thousand dollars to the much needed resources of the College library, is credited to Charles Minot, of the class of 1828.

And now our half-century is closed. Its account is made up. There is no re-opening it for amendment or alteration of any sort. It must stand as it is, for better or for worse. We are not ashamed of it. If, indeed, on that bright August day, in 1828, we could have looked forward to the present hour, and been privileged to catch a glimpse of the triennial catalogue as it is made up to-day, with a few names on our roll in italics, and fewer still in capitals, and with the fatal asterisk against two-thirds of our number, — if we could have foreseen how many of our brightest and best were to be starred within a few years of their graduation, — we might have pressed each other's hands more closely as we parted, and might have had a deeper sense of the great responsibilities of life and death. But, as the old poet tells us, —

> "Heaven from all creatures hides the book of fate,
> All but the page prescribed — their present state.
> Oh, blindness to the future, kindly given,
> That each may fill the circle marked by Heaven!

It only remains for us who linger a little longer to remember affectionately those who are gone before; to thank God for sparing our own lives; and to resolve to continue doing whatever it may still be in our power to do, for the honor of our Class, for the good of our fellow-men, and for the prosperity and welfare of our beloved Alma Mater. Let us hope that we may never be counted among her unworthy or ungrateful children!

TWO HUNDRED AND FIFTIETH ANNIVERSARY OF ENDICOTT'S ARRIVAL AT NAUMKEAG.

SPEECH AT THE SALEM BANQUET, SEPTEMBER 18, 1878.

I THANK you, Dr. Wheatland, Ladies and Gentlemen, for so friendly and flattering a reception. I was greatly honored and obliged by the early summons which was served upon me by the Essex Institute to be present here on this occasion. But their Committee will bear me witness that in accepting it, as I did at sight, I expressly declined to be responsible for any formal address. I came to hear others; and especially to listen to the worthy and distinguished descendant of him whose arrival here, two hundred and fifty years ago, you are so fitly commemorating to-day.

But I cannot find it in my heart to be wholly silent. And let me say at once, Mr. President, that this is not the first time I have participated in celebrating the settlement of Salem under the lead of John Endicott. I cannot forget that I was here fifty years ago to-day. It was my well-remembered privilege to accompany my honored father, who came, as Lieutenant Governor of the State, to unite in representing Massachusetts on that Two Hundredth Anniversary of its small beginnings. There were no railroads in 1828, and we drove down together from Boston that morning, and drove back again at night, having retired early from the dinner table to allow time for getting home before dark.

I was thus in the way of hearing the eloquent Oration of Judge Story, in company with Webster and Everett and Quincy and the other illustrious guests of that occasion, and of being in close proximity to the venerable Dr. Holyoke, who had already completed the hundredth year of his age. I recall him at this moment, as I saw him, coming out of his own door, with an unfaltering step, to join the procession on its march to the Hall. And here, in his own handwriting, is the very Toast which he gave at that Dinner, — a precious autograph presented to our old Historical Society by our associate Mr. Waterston, and which, by the favor of Dr. Deane, I am able to exhibit at this festival.

Here it is, with the autograph verification of Judge Story beneath it, — and my distinguished friend next to me, the Dean of Westminster, will bear witness, while I read it, to the clearness and firmness of the writing: — "*The Memory of our Pilgrim Forefathers*, who first landed on this spot on the 6th of September, 1628 (just two centuries ago this day), who forsook their native country and all they held dear, that they might enjoy the liberty of worshipping the God of their fathers, agreeably to the dictates of their consciences."

The Dean, in his admirable "Historical Memorials" of the world-renowned Abbey over which he presides, has made special record of the "Monuments of Longevity," including, of course, "the gravestone of the olde, olde, very olde man," Thomas Parr, "the patriarch of the seventeenth century," who is said to have lived to the age of 152.[1] But I doubt whether Thomas Parr, or anybody else of later date, could have executed a piece of penmanship as fair and steady as this, after the authenticated completion of his hundredth year.

And now, Mr. President, I could hardly have excused myself, had I failed to come here again to-day, — not merely to revive the pleasant associations of 1828, but to manifest in maturer years my sense of the intrinsic interest of the occasion. My coming to your Two Hundredth Celebration was only and altogether an act of filial duty. I was then a mere Law Student, just out of College. I come now to your Two Hundred and Fiftieth Anniversary, after a half century of observation and experience, as a recognition, both official and personal, of

[1] Memorials of Westminster Abbey, by Arthur Penrhyn Stanley, D.D. Fourth Edition, p. 327.

its significance and importance. I say official, — for I certainly could not have reconciled it with my duty, as President of that old Massachusetts Historical Society of 1790, which you have just toasted, to absent myself from an occasion which carries us back so close to the very cradle of our Commonwealth. And I say personal, — because I should have felt myself disloyal to the memory of my venerated New England progenitor, had I not been here, as his representative, to bear testimony to one, who hastened on board the "Arbella" to welcome him, on his own arrival with the Charter, in this same "Haven of Comfort," less than two years afterwards, and who so kindly refreshed him and his Assistants, as he was careful to record in his Journal at the time, "with good venison pasty and good beer"; — a bill of fare which might well make some of our mouths water at this moment.

Nor could I have been held guiltless by any of you, if, by my own delinquency, the name and blood of Governor Winthrop had been missing from the representative group of the old Fathers of Massachusetts, which lends so signal a lustre, and so peculiar an historical interest, to this scene and its surroundings. Conants and Cradocks and Endicotts and Higginsons and Dudleys and Saltonstalls, — not one of them, I believe, is without a lineal descendant here, to do honor to his memory! Well may the words of the Psalmist of the old original Salem come back to us with new force: "Instead of thy fathers shall be thy children: — The children of Thy servants shall continue, and their seed shall be established before Thee."

But this day, Mr. President, belongs peculiarly and pre-eminently to old Naumkeag and to John Endicott. We are not here to discuss historical conundrums, — if there be any still unsolved, after the exhaustive, judicial analysis which was made by your accomplished Orator this morning, — but we are here to recognize and commemorate historical facts. I rejoice to remember that Endicott and Winthrop were always friends. No question of priority or precedence, titular or real, was ever heard of in their day. They understood perfectly the respective parts they were called on to play in founding Massachusetts, and they performed those parts with entire harmony and concord. It was my good fortune, not many years ago, to bring out from my old family papers more than twenty original letters from Endicott to Winthrop, — twice as many as had before been known to exist, — which had most happily been preserved for two centuries and a quarter, and which make up a large part of the best illustration of his character and career. They are all printed in our Historical Collections, and they all bear witness to the confidence, friendship, and affection, which the two old Governors entertained for each other, and which nothing ever interrupted or disturbed.

Endicott lived fifteen or sixteen years longer than Winthrop, and during the latter part of his life was associated with troubles and responsibilities from which we all might wish that he had been spared. He was a man of impulsive and impetuous temper, and sometimes too summary and severe in his views and acts. But no mild or weak nature could have contended with the wilderness trials he was called to encounter. As Palfrey well says, in his excellent History of New England, "His honesty, frankness, fearlessness, and generous public spirit had won their proper guerdon in the general esteem." Or we may adopt the words with which Bancroft introduces him into his brilliant History of the United States: "A man of dauntless courage, and that cheerfulness which accompanies courage; benevolent, though austere; firm, though choleric; of a rugged nature, which his stern principles of non-conformity had not served to mellow, — he was selected as a fit instrument to begin this wilderness work."

As the Founder of this oldest town of Massachusetts proper, whose annals contain the story of so much of early commercial enterprise and so much of literary and scientific celebrity, — including such eminent names as Gray and Peabody and Derby, and Silsbee and Pickman and Pickering and Putnam, and Saltonstall and Bentley and Bowditch and Story, and Peirce and Prescott and Hawthorne, — his own name could never be forgotten. While, as the Governor of the pioneer Plantation which preceded the transfer of the whole Massachusetts Government from Old England to New England, — without either predecessor or successor in the precise post which he was called on to fill from 1628 to 1630,[1] — he must always hold a unique place in Massachusetts History. Nor will it ever be forgotten, that, when he died, in 1665, he had served the Colony in various relations, including the very highest, longer than any other one of the Massachusetts Fathers.

All honor, then, to the memory of John Endicott, and may he never want a distinguished and eloquent descendant, like my friend to whom we have listened this morning,[2] to illustrate his name and impersonate his virtues!

May I be pardoned, Mr. President, for trespassing a moment longer on the indulgence of the company, while I give one more reason for my unwillingness to plead either avocations, distance, or age, for not being here on this Anniversary? There seems to be a disposition, in some quarters, to deal disparagingly, and even despitefully, with some of the Puritan Fathers of Massachusetts. There is a manifest eagerness to magnify their errors of judgment and to exaggerate their faults of character or conduct. Men find it easier to repent of the offences of their forefathers, than of their own offences. I trust that we of Massachusetts may be betrayed into no recriminations. We can never exhibit any thing but respect for the chivalrous planters of the Old Dominion; or for the brave Dutchmen of New Netherlands; or for the pure-hearted Quakers of Pennsylvania or New Jersey; or for that grand impersonation of Soul-Freedom which our sister Rhode Island recognizes in her illustrious founder. And, certainly, we can entertain nothing but the profoundest admiration and reverence for the Pilgrims of Plymouth Colony, — so long independent of our own Commonwealth. But all this is consistent with holding, as we of Salem and Boston all do hold, I trust and I believe, at this hour, that the fathers and founders of Massachusetts proper are to be accounted as second to none of them, either in themselves, or in the institutions which they established. We are not called on to defend their bigotry or superstitions. We may deplore their occasional eccentricities and extravagancies. But no other characters than theirs could

[1] See Life and Letters of John Winthrop, Vol. I. pp. 342–352, Vol. II. pp. 23–32.

[2] The Oration had been delivered by the Hon. William C. Endicott, an Associate Justice of the Supreme Court of Massachusetts.

have made New England what it is. Indeed, the prosperity and freedom which our whole land has enjoyed for a century past have had no earthly source of greater influence and efficacy than what is called the Puritanism of the Massachusetts Fathers.

I have no serious fear for the future welfare and glory of our Country. Out of all the crime, and corruption, and political chaos, which are appalling us at this moment, light and virtue and order will reappear again, — even as the dense and protracted fogs which darkened the whole North last week have broken away into the glorious sunshine of this day; or as the terrible fever which is at this moment desolating the whole South, exciting all our sympathies and receiving all our succors, will soon, by the blessing of God, be followed by renewed health and happiness. New England may never, perhaps, recover her lost ascendency. But her power has passed to those in the Great West, who do not forget the old hives from which they swarmed, and who will not wholly renounce the memories or the principles of their Puritan ancestry.

Let me once more thank the Essex Institute for the privilege of taking part in this interesting Festival, and assure them of the best wishes of the old Massachusetts Historical Society, over which I have the honor to preside, for their continued prosperity and welfare.

BENJAMIN F. THOMAS.

REMARKS AT A MEETING OF THE MASSACHUSETTS HISTORICAL SOCIETY, OCTOBER 10, 1878.

THE tidings of the serious illness of our Associate Member, the Honorable BENJAMIN FRANKLIN THOMAS, took us all by surprise not many weeks ago. It terminated fatally on the 27th ult., at Beverly Farms, in this State, where he had his summer residence; and his funeral took place at the First Church, in this city, on Tuesday, the 1st inst. I regretted sincerely to be compelled to go to New York at the very hour for which it was appointed. But our Society was amply represented by Mr. Adams, Dr. Ellis, and others, in the throng of mourners on that occasion.

The numerous and just tributes which have already been paid to his character and services, by the Press and by the Pulpit, by the American Antiquarian Society, of which he was the Vice-President, and by the Bars both of Worcester and of Suffolk, of which he was so distinguished a member, have left little, if any thing, to be added here to-day. Nothing more, certainly, is needed to his own commemoration. But we owe it to ourselves, if not to him, that one of such eminent ability and excellence, who has been associated with us for eighteen years, and whose genial tributes to his friends Governor Clifford and Governor Washburn have so recently found a response in all our hearts, should not go down to his grave himself without some immediate expression of our respect and of our sorrow.

A Boston boy by birth, yet having been removed at six years of age to the old home of his grandfather, — the patriot printer and historian of printing, and the founder of the American Antiquarian Society, at Worcester, — and having been graduated, eleven years later, at Brown University, of which he was Chancellor at the time of his death, — he owed no part of his education to Boston schools or Massachusetts colleges. The public services, too, and the professional practice of his earlier life, were in the heart of the Commonwealth. He represented the town of Worcester in the State Legislature in 1842, and was for several years afterwards the Judge of Probate for Worcester County. But, at forty years of age, he took his seat on the bench of the Supreme Court of Massachusetts, and his labors and reputation thenceforth ceased to be local. After six years' service in this high office, he established himself in the neighborhood of Boston, now a part of it, for the practice of the law, and was soon afterwards sent to Congress to represent the West Roxbury District, within which he then resided, as the successor of our Vice-President, Mr. Adams, on his appointment as Minister to England. A nomination to the Chief Justiceship, which met the approval of the community though not of the Executive Council, completes the record of his relations to public office.

But a good and great man is, in some sense, never without office. "Nulla vitæ pars vacare officio potest." Judge Thomas was of a peculiarly independent spirit, and, having ample occupation in his own profession, had little concern for the favors or the frowns of those by whom public station is bestowed. With a strong sense of duty to himself and to his fellow-men, to his country and to his God, he never swerved from his own conscientious convictions, in order to conciliate popular support. He was a zealous member of the old Whig party of Massachusetts, as long as that party had any existence; and I should hardly be excused for not remembering that it was from his hand, as President of the Whig Convention, in 1851, that I received the nomination for Governor. He said to me playfully, not many months ago, that the only time he was ever angry with me, was when I refused to run a second time. His service in Congress was during the earlier years of the Civil War; and after the close of that service, and his failure to be re-elected, he published a volume of more than two hundred pages, containing all his speeches, in Congress or out of Congress, during the period of his holding that position. He had not yielded to the idea, that the support of the war, and the support of the country, necessarily involved the support of all the measures of the actual Administration; and he had been bold in criticising and opposing some parts of its policy. In speaking of his principles, in the Preface to this volume, he says: "That they are unpopular at this moment, does not disturb me: the more imperative is the duty of standing by and upholding them. The citizen owes to the country, in the hour of her peril, honest counsel, calmly given, but with the 'love that casteth out fear.' Never were freedom of thought and of the lips and pen so necessary as now. They have become not only the most precious of rights, but the most religious of duties."

He had an earnest and deep conviction that under the exigencies and strains of Civil War we were drifting away from the Constitution, — not for the moment only, not exceptionally, but permanently and irrecoverably.

That conviction was by no means wholly changed in later years; and he told me, not long ago, that he was meditating, and, as I understood him, preparing, a history of parties in their relation to the Constitution, to vindicate this view. It will be the subject of deep regret if such a work is to be entirely lost. A political history of this sort, written by an eminent lawyer and a sincere patriot, would be hailed with interest and eagerness, even by those who might differ from its conclusions.

The last formal discourse of Judge Thomas was his Centennial Oration at Worcester, on the 4th of July, 1876, which abounds in expressions of patriotic and fervent hopefulness for the future of our land, and maintains that we have no right and no cause to despair of the Republic.

I will not prolong this announcement. Of his efforts and successes in the Courts of Law, to which his life was mainly devoted, others have spoken most felicitously elsewhere. I have said enough to show the appreciation which we all have of the excellent qualities of our departed friend, and to manifest our sense of the great loss, not only to the institutions and associations with which he was connected, but to the whole community, which such a death involves. Younger than most of us, he seemed to have a physical as well as mental vigor and vivacity which promised to outlast us all. There was an energy, too, in his nature, which would never have allowed him to be idle or unprofitable while his life and health were spared. There is no measurement for such a loss, coming, as it has come, when our Commonwealth and our Country can least afford to bear it. He would have been less missed at other periods of our history.

It only remains for me, as the organ of the Council, to submit the customary Resolution: —

Resolved, That we have heard with sincere sorrow of the death of our able and accomplished associate, Benjamin Franklin Thomas, and that the President be requested to appoint one of our number to prepare a Memoir for our Proceedings.

APPENDIX.

APPENDIX.

I.

HON. JOHN J. CRITTENDEN AT WEST POINT.

A LETTER TO HIS DAUGHTER.[1]

Boston, Dec. 26, 1870.

My Dear Mrs. Coleman, — I have not forgotten my promise to give you some account of what happened at West Point, when I had the good fortune to meet your excellent father there, during one of the early years of our late civil war. I had enjoyed his friendship, and not a little of his confidence, as you well know, while I was in Congress with him many years before; and I had always admired the generous and noble qualities of his mind and heart. But the occasion to which I refer was one which left the deepest impression on my memory, and I am, perhaps, the only one left to tell the story.

It was on the 8th day of August, 1862. I had stopped at West Point on my way from Niagara, to pay a little visit to General Scott; and while I was with him, at Cozzens's Hotel, Mr. Crittenden came in. He told me at once that he had come there for a special purpose, in which he was deeply interested; and that he wished me to accompany him to the camp of the Cadets, and be a witness to whatever might occur. Not long afterwards we went to the camp together, and, after a brief preliminary interview with the commanding officer (Colonel Bowman, if I remember rightly), Mr. Crittenden explained to him and to myself his precise view in coming. He said that the cadets from many of the Southern States had exhibited a disposition to leave the Academy with the purpose of taking sides with their own States in the contest which was then in progress. Some of them, as I understood, had gone already; and he was in great concern lest the Kentucky cadets should be induced to follow their example. He thought that his personal influence might possibly do something to arrest such a design, should it exist in any quarter; and, after consulting with General Scott, he asked leave of the

[1] Life of John J. Crittenden, Vol. II. p. 350.

commanding officer to have an interview with each one of the Kentucky cadets in succession.

The leave was readily granted, and they were accordingly sent for in turn. To each one of them, as he came up, Mr. Crittenden made an informal, but most earnest, appeal. He seemed to know the personal history and family connections of them all. More than one of them, I believe, had received their appointments on his own recommendation. One of them had already distinguished himself, though a mere boy, by brave services as a volunteer, and his appointment had been made in recognition of his youthful gallantry.

I shall not forget how your father's eye kindled, and his voice trembled with emotion, as he spoke to them of the Union cause, and of his ardent desire that Kentucky should be true to the Union flag. He spoke, as he always spoke best, from the inspiration of the moment, and out of the fulness of his noble and patriotic heart. No one of those cadets can have failed to remember that most impressive scene. There was nothing of ostentation or formality about it. He told me he had come to West Point without previous consultation with anybody, and he evidently did not wish to have his intervention spoken of at the time. I think that he did not even enter his name on the books of the hotel, and left West Point as soon as he had accomplished the object for which he had come. He was unwilling to have it supposed that he had any distrust of the cadets of his own State, and assured me that he felt none. But he said he should sleep more easily after he had done what he could to make his young friends feel that his whole heart was concerned in their loyalty to the Government. I have never seen a man more in earnest than he was on that day, and he seemed to excite an electric sympathy in all whom he addressed, and in all by whom he was surrounded. For myself, I have rarely been more moved; and I could not resist the impulse, at a recruiting meeting on Boston Common, not many weeks after my return home, even at the risk of his displeasure, to make the following brief allusion to what I had witnessed: —

"At West Point, too, I met the generous and true-hearted Crittenden. I accompanied him to the camp of the cadets, and saw the emotion with which he grasped the hands of the young Kentuckians who clustered around him. One of them was a son of the noble preacher and patriot, Robert J. Breckinridge, of Danville; and another, whose name I am ashamed to have forgotten, but which history will not forget, was a young Kentuckian of only sixteen years of age, who, having been already wounded, while serving as a volunteer at the battle of Shiloh, had now come to prepare for future responsibilities by studying the science of war."[1]

[1] Winthrop's Addresses and Speeches, Vol. II. p. 532.

I am not aware that any other public allusion to the scene I have thus described has ever before been made; but, since the death of my lamented friend, I have felt that it was due to his memory that so significant and characteristic an illustration of his devoted patriotism should not be wanting to the biographical sketch which you are preparing.

Believe me, dear Mrs. Coleman, very sincerely yours,

ROBERT C. WINTHROP.

Mrs. A. M. COLEMAN.

II.

THE PEACE JUBILEE.

A LETTER TO REV. JAMES B. MILES.

BROOKLINE, Sept. 20, 1871.

MY DEAR SIR, — It will not be in my power to attend the meeting of the American Peace Society on the 26th inst., to which you so urgently and so kindly invite me. Most heartily, however, do I concur in the general views with which that meeting has been called.

It is indeed a subject for devout thankfulness, and for special rejoicing among Christian men throughout the world, that a treaty has been made and ratified for the final and amicable settlement of all existing questions of dispute between Great Britain and the United States. It is even more a subject for rejoicing that the great principle of *Arbitration* has been so signally recognized and sanctioned by two of the leading Powers of the world.

I may be pardoned for recalling to remembrance, in this connection, the following Resolutions, which I had the honor to offer in the House of Representatives of the United States, on the 19th of December, 1845, when the Oregon Question was so seriously threatening to involve us in war with England: —

"*Resolved*, That if no other mode for the amicable adjustment of this question remains, it is due to the principles of civilization and Christianity that a resort to arbitration should be had; and that this Government cannot relieve itself from all responsibility which may follow the failure to settle the controversy, while this resort is still untried.

"*Resolved*, That arbitration does not necessarily involve a reference to crowned heads; and that, if a jealousy of such a reference is entertained in any quarter, a Commission of able and dispassionate citizens, either from the two countries concerned, or from the world at large, offers itself as an obvious and unobjectionable alternative."[1]

In the heat of political animosity and party rivalry which prevailed at that period, these Resolutions failed to secure the assent of the American

[1] Winthrop's Addresses and Speeches, Vol. I. p. 499.

Government. But I cannot forget that they were made the subject of special allusion, as an evidence of progress, in the French Chamber of Deputies at the time, by that eminent historian and statesman (M. Thiers) who is now attracting all our best wishes in his trying responsibilities as the Chief Executive Magistrate of France. I thank God that an example of such "a Commission of able and dispassionate citizens," in the interests of peace and justice, has now emanated from the Capital of our own country. It is an event to give character to the period in which we live, and to reflect imperishable honor on the men and on the nations by whose co-operation it has been accomplished.

I dare not indulge in dreams of perpetual peace, foreign or domestic. I am not quite yet a convert to any general doctrine of disarmament, abroad or at home. But I cannot doubt that a step, and a great step, has been taken, by the negotiation and ratification of this treaty, towards that long-expected, often-predicted, and always devoutly-desired day, when disputed rights and wrongs, disputed boundaries, disputed claims of all sorts, shall be settled by means less abhorrent and less barbarous than war.

Thanking you once more for your obliging invitation, I am, dear Sir, respectfully and truly,

Your obedient servant,

ROBERT C. WINTHROP.

Rev. JAMES B. MILES,
Secretary of the American Peace Society.

III.

THE EVANGELICAL ALLIANCE.

A LETTER TO REV. WILLIAM ADAMS, D.D.[1]

BROOKLINE (BOSTON), Oct. 11, 1873.

MY DEAR DR. ADAMS, — I owed to your kindness the first invitation, which I received some months ago, to be present at the meeting of the Evangelical Alliance, and which I was obliged to decline. More recently I gave my consent, most gladly, that my name should be included in the organization of the meeting, with the full understanding that it would be out of my power to be present. But as I have read, from day to day, the stirring reports of what has been said and done during the past week, I have regretted sincerely that I could not have broken away from a complication of engagements at home, and have run on, even at the eleventh hour, to manifest my sympathy in the objects and in the utterances of the occasion.

I should have eagerly embraced the opportunity to offer my most grateful acknowledgments to those who had thought me worthy to be named in your list of Vice-Presidents, — an honor which I could not but hold all the more distinguished and all the more dear, as associating me, in some humble measure, with the venerable President of your Assembly, — Dr. Woolsey, — whose signal and most successful labors in every good cause, whether religious, literary, educational, or international, have given him a deserved pre-eminence, which I should rejoice to have publicly recognized. I confess that my heart burned within me to be at his side, when those thrilling words of his opening address came leaping over the telegraphic wires: "We are here, each one of us, whatever our form of worship, whatever our discipline, whatever our old recollections derived from our Christian forefathers, — we are here as one body; with separate badges and banners, it may be, to mark our national or denominational differences, but all recognizing our supreme allegiance to one great standard of the Cross." This was the substance, if not the exact language, of an Address which gave the key-note to all which followed.

[1] Evangelical Alliance Conference, 1873, p. 724.

I cannot but feel, my dear sir, that there has been something of unspeakable impressiveness and grandeur in this multitudinous gathering from all quarters of our country and of the world, which New York has been privileged to witness. We have been accustomed, of late years, to vast assemblies, here and elsewhere. We have been entertained, almost to satiety, with what have been called "monster meetings," in almost all regions of the earth, and especially in our own region. We have seen grand Expositions of Art and Industry in the principal cities of Europe and America, — in Paris, in London, in New York, in Boston, and more lately in Vienna. We have seen the votaries of Agriculture, on our own and other soils, rallying together to exhibit the triumphs and to advance the interests of their own pre-eminent department of labor. We have seen, almost annually, British Associations and American Associations of Science meeting to compare opinions, to proclaim results, and to encourage investigation and research. Grand Musical Jubilees, too, for which the most accomplished and renowned artists, and the most gigantic chorus-bands, have been enlisted, are no strangers to our own or other lands. Almost every interest among worldly occupations and pursuits, — civil and military, political, literary, scientific, and mechanic, — has heretofore had its Mass Meetings or Conventions, and has challenged and chained the attention and sympathy of mankind by appeals to the eye or to the ear.

But the wonderful gathering at New York, which is just now about to separate, has been, I need not say, of a different sort, and in a different spirit. It was convened to discuss no mere secular subjects, to advance no mere material interests. It assembled in no pride of human invention or human intellect. The learning of Germany, the piety of Switzerland, the roused religious inquiry of France or Spain or Italy, the scholarship and eloquence of English Universities or Cathedrals or Independent Churches, — met for no purpose of competition or rivalry, and with no view to ostentatious display. No contests were to be waged, no triumphs to be achieved, no prizes to be won, save only that "prize of the high calling of God in Christ Jesus," toward which the great Apostle represented himself as so eagerly pressing. All, all came together to lay aside for a time the differences which had so long separated them, and to remember only the better and higher things in which they agreed. They met to give public and united recognition of the truth, that Religion is above all dogmas, precious as some of those dogmas may be; that Faith is above all forms, dear as many of those forms may be; that postures and vestments and prayer-books are secondary matters, strongly as those prayer-books may be cherished, and justly as they may be prized; that unity and uniformity are two different things; that there may be separation without estrangement; antagonism, even, without alienation; and that the cause of Christ and his Kingdom, and his Church Universal, — "which is the blessed company of all faithful people," — is to be preferred far, far above the cause of any particular church, however venerable its history, or however valuable its organization.

Who can over-estimate the importance and the influence of such a meeting, — even if its only effect were to draw men out, for a time, from the narrow circles of their own denominations; to impress upon them that those circles are, after all, concentric circles, whose radii reach back alike to one and the same great Sun of Righteousness; and thus to give them a broader margin and a wider circumference for their Christian charity and their Christian fellowship!

"Surely it is a strange fact," wrote an Episcopal clergyman of an English church to me, not many weeks ago, "and one pregnant with hope for the yet unchristianized portions of the earth, that, in the good providence of God, the Sultan of Turkey, the Khedive of Egypt, ambassadors of Japan, and the Shah of Persia — potentates heretofore shut up in their unapproachable exclusiveness — should be moved by a desire to visit the nations of Europe. But how should it shame us that we are unprepared, by our unhappy divisions, to exhibit the oneness of the 'truth as it is in Jesus,' and so render nugatory our blessed Lord's prayer that his disciples may 'all be one, that the world may believe that Thou hast sent me'!"

And how just and forcible were the words of the excellent Archbishop of Canterbury, in the letter brought over by our friend the learned and liberal Dean of that cathedral, whose presence has added so much to the occasion: "Never," says the Primate of all England, — "never since the Reformation has it been more important that Christian men should learn to labor with one another; that they should, by the manifestation of their union in faith and good wishes, offer effectual opposition to the growing purposes of superstition and infidelity. And never," he adds, "has this union been more earnestly longed for than in the present day."

I owe you an apology, my dear Dr. Adams, for so long a letter, recapitulating what is so familiar to you already. But as you had more than once most kindly urged my attendance at the meeting, you will know how to pardon my trespassing upon you. I desired to show you how deeply the meeting has impressed me as a churchman and as a layman; and to give you, too, the text upon which I should have ventured to offer a few words, if I could have succeeded in getting to New York even in season for the closing exercises to-morrow night.

It was my good fortune to see Professor Christlieb for a few moments before he went on to New York, and I have read his masterly essay with the greatest interest. The Dean of Canterbury passed a day with me.

Let me only hope, in conclusion, that the spirit which has animated the delegates may be kindled in millions of other hearts; and that to this great meeting in New York may be traced, hereafter, the lighting up anew of a flame of Christian faith and hope and charity, which may catch and spread throughout the world, and which neither superstition nor infidelity shall be able to extinguish or withstand.

Believe me, reverend and dear sir, with the highest respect and regard, yours sincerely,

ROBERT C. WINTHROP.

REV. WILLIAM ADAMS, D.D.

IV.

PEABODY EDUCATION TRUST.

A LETTER TO THE GENERAL AGENT.

BERNE, SWITZERLAND, Sept. 1, 1874.

MY DEAR DR. SEARS, — It is with sincere reluctance that I have at last relinquished the expectation of being present at the next Annual Meeting of the Peabody Trustees. Having come abroad, however, wholly for the health of others, I am not at liberty to yield to inclinations and impulses of my own, which would have certainly carried me home in October.

Be good enough to make my apologies to our associates, and to assure them of my great regret at finding myself unable to meet with them next month, and to participate in the important deliberations and duties which will again devolve upon the Board.

Be good enough, also, to remind them that I did not overlook the discretionary power which was given to me, as Chairman, in regard to holding our Annual Meeting at the White Sulphur Springs in Virginia. But after corresponding with a large number of the Trustees individually, I found a general concurrence in the opinion that it was inexpedient to change the time and place which had been provisionally fixed at the last Annual Meeting.

You will further oblige me by bringing formally to the attention of the Board the Volume of our Proceedings, which was prepared by their order, and of which a copy for examination and correction was transmitted to each one of the Trustees some months ago.

In the preface to that volume, I have sufficiently recalled the purposes for which it was ordered, and the views with which it was prepared. I hope that this preface may be read at our Meeting, and may be considered as a part of this letter.

It will now be for the Board to decide on the number of copies to be printed at once, and on the mode of distributing them among the Public Libraries of the country. As the volume is stereotyped, it will be in our power to order additional copies, as they may be wanted, from year to year; and I should think that fifteen hundred, or even a thousand, would be quite enough to begin with. The Proceedings of the Annual Meeting of the present year may well be included in the volume, under your own supervision, before it is finally made up.

I cannot forget that a vacancy has been created in our Board since we last met, by the death of our esteemed and respected associate, Charles Macalester, Esq. He was, as you know, an old and valued friend of Mr. Peabody, and was included by him in the original nomination of his Trustees. And, certainly, no one of us all has been more diligent and devoted in the discharge of the duties thus devolved upon him.

His long practical experience in business affairs commended him at once to Mr. Peabody, and to ourselves, as a member of our Finance Committee; and, in that capacity, he has rendered invaluable service to the work which has been intrusted to us.

We have all confided in him, as a man of sound judgment, of scrupulous integrity, of exemplary life, and of Christian principle. We have all been warmly attached to him, as an associate and friend, whose companionship and counsel were ever welcome at our Meetings.

Born in Philadelphia, on the 17th of February, 1798, and dying in the same city on the 9th of December last, he had almost completed his seventy-sixth year. But it was only at our very last meeting that the vigor of his frame and the cheerfulness of his spirit seemed in any degree impaired. We parted from him then, and he from us, with little expectation, on either side, of his living to be with us again.

His faithful services, I need hardly suggest, deserve an honorable mention in our records, and I would gladly have paid a more adequate tribute to his memory.

The composition of our Board is gradnally undergoing serious changes. The names of Rives, Farragut, Bradford, McIlvaine, and Macalester have already disappeared from our little original roll. But I rejoice to remember that the policy which we adopted during the lifetime and in the immediate presence of our illustrious Founder, is unchanged; and I heartily hope that under your faithful supervision it will be pursued systematically and successfully to the end.

Once more begging you to remember me cordially and affectionately to our associates, I remain, dear Dr. Sears, with the warmest regard and respect, Sincerely yours,

Robert C. Winthrop.

The Rev. Barnas Sears, D.D.,
General Agent of the Peabody Education Fund.

P. S. Before closing this letter, I have learned with sincere sorrow that our friend Mr. Eaton died suddenly in Edinburgh, more than a month ago, and that a second vacancy has thus been created in our Board. We can hardly be surprised that one so feeble and suffering, as he has been for several years past, has at length been released to his rest. He has made heroic efforts to come to our Annual Meetings more than once, while in a condition of physical prostration which gave us warning that the end could not be far off. But we all remember the zeal and energy with which he originally entered on our work, and the valuable assistance which he rendered us during the earlier years of our organization. Meantime, his great amiability and excellence have endeared him personally and warmly to us all. We shall all, I am sure, cherish his memory, as a friend and associate, with respect and affection; and others will pay him the tribute which he has so well deserved, and for which I have no opportunity.

V.

THE LEXINGTON CENTENNIAL.

A LETTER TO THE COMMITTEE OF INVITATION.

ROME, March 17, 1875.

GENTLEMEN, — I dare not longer delay an acknowledgment of your most obliging communication. It reached me when I was just quitting the quiet retreat on the shores of the Mediterranean to which I had resorted, during the early winter, for the health of one of my family.

It renewed, I need hardly say, the deep regrets which I had already expressed to my valued and venerable friend, your Chairman, that unavoidable absence from home and country would deprive me of the privilege of taking part in your great Centennial Celebration of the 19th of April.

I thank you sincerely, Gentlemen, for counting me worthy to be remembered again, at so great a distance, in a foreign land, among those whom you would be pleased to welcome to your festive board. The occasion is one full of interest and attraction for every American heart; and your programme gives promise of a celebration from which no one would willingly be absent.

Most gladly would I have paid my humble tribute to the memory of the men who perilled their lives, and poured out the first blood, in the cause of American liberty. Even here, where I am surrounded with the monuments of so many grand and heroic acts, and where so large a part of the history of the Old World is written on the magnificent ruins which confront me on every side, I turn to Lexington and Concord for examples of deliberate valor in a just cause, which are not surpassed by any thing of Greek or Roman fame.

Here, too, where so many of the earlier local glories are merely legendary, and where, through the relentless investigations of modern archæologists and antiquaries, so many of the most cherished and charming legends are fast fading into fables, I cannot but appreciate, more highly than ever before, the value of our own authentic records, and rejoice, with a new fervor, that there is nothing of uncertain tradition or doubtful testimony about the glory of your village heroes.

It seems only yesterday, — but you will know how much less than half a century ago it was, — that, after following their hallowed remains from the humble graves in which they had originally reposed, to the vault beneath the monument where they now rest, I was listening to their story with all its thrilling incidents, as it fell from the lips of one who told it as no other man could tell it. And, if any detail of the day and its events were omitted by Edward Everett, it has been more than supplied in the admirable town history of your Chairman, to whose fidelity and ability I was so long a witness, both in the Legislature of Massachusetts and in the Congress of the United States.

The annals of Lexington, and of the men who have made its name famous for ever, are indeed safe; and the lapse of ages can only increase the veneration in which the memories of those men are held by the lovers of liberty throughout the world.

For ourselves, who have inherited the freedom which was purchased for us at so great a price, we can never be too grateful either to those who planted our colonies, or to those who achieved their independence. Other and later struggles and triumphs, however important, must never be suffered to blind us to the magnitude of those which crowd the early pages of our colonial and national history. Writing at this moment from an apartment which overhangs the site of the old gardens of Sallust, the words which that great historian puts into the mouth of Cæsar, and which were familiar to me as a school-boy, come back with renewed vividness, and find fresh illustration and force in events at home which have recently filled so many hearts with apprehension: —

"*Profectò virtus atque sapientia major in illis fuit, qui ex parvis opibus tantum imperium fecēre, quam in nobis, qui ea bene parta vix retinemus.*"

Let me not seem, however, to imply a doubt, even under the cover of a dead language, that we shall still hold fast and for ever to the Union and Liberty which were won for us by the wisdom and valor of our fathers. This very Centennial Period comes round most opportunely for recalling the whole people of the country from divisions, contentions, and estrangements which have too long poisoned our peace, and for fixing their minds and hearts once more on the common glories which belong to them as a nation, and on the great first principles which were contended for so nobly on every battle-field of the Revolution.

Let us, then, pay to the heroes of those battle-fields the full honor which belongs to them, — beginning at Lexington and Concord, and ending only with Cowpens, and Eutaw Springs, and Yorktown. The memory and example of our fathers may thus do almost as much in these latter days in helping us to uphold and maintain our free institutions, as their wisdom and valor did, a hundred years ago, in founding and establishing them.

Once more thanking you for your most friendly and flattering invitation, and with sincere wishes for the success of your celebration,

I am, Gentlemen, your obliged fellow-citizen,

ROBERT C. WINTHROP.

Hon. CHARLES HUDSON,
M. H. MERRIAM,
WILLIAM H. MUNROE,
Esquires,
Committee of Invitation.

VI.

THE BUNKER HILL CENTENNIAL.

A LETTER TO THE PRESIDENT OF THE ASSOCIATION.

PARIS, May 17, 1875.

DEAR MR. WARREN, — I have not forgotten my promise to write to you before the great Centennial, over which you are privileged to preside, just a month hence.

And where could I write more appropriately, in regard to any thing which concerns our Revolutionary struggle, than here, in the Capital of France, to whose generous aid we owed so much of our final success, — now a Republic herself, our younger sister!

I cannot but recall, too, how greatly the presence of the noble-hearted Lafayette contributed to the interest of the Fiftieth Anniversary of Bunker Hill. I can hardly realize that fifty years have passed away since I saw him in the throng of that great celebration, "the observed of all observers," and listened to the incomparable eloquence of Webster in addressing him.

Of all the omissions with which we are chargeable, in the way of commemoration, I know of none which calls more emphatically for reparation, at this Centennial Period, than the omission to place a statue of Lafayette in some one of the public squares or halls of Boston. Such a statue might well be seen by the side of Washington in the State House, or by the side of Warren at Bunker Hill, or by the side of Franklin in front of the City Hall.

Agreeably to your request, that, as one of the vice-presidents of our Association, I would invite some appropriate guests to our Centennial Festival, I called on one of the grandsons of Lafayette, a few days ago, and assured him how peculiarly welcome would be the presence, on the occasion, of one bearing the name and blood of the great and good Marquis. I fear, however, that it will not be in the power of any of the family to leave France for such a purpose.

I have also found an opportunity to express to M. Thiers, the veteran historian and statesman, — the first President of the existing French Republic, — how cordially and enthusiastically he would be received at Bunker Hill, and everywhere else, during our Centennial Period. I dare not encourage a hope that he can be induced to cross the Atlantic, though our worthy minister, Mr. Washburne, — in whose company I recently dined with M. Thiers, — loses no occasion of urging him to make the effort.

The new volume of Bancroft's history of the United States, which I have been reading of late, brings freshly to mind our indebtedness to France; and my accomplished friend, Count Adolphe de Circourt, who is preparing a translation of Bancroft's volume into French, will accompany it with documents, never before printed, which will throw new light on that memorable Alliance of 1778.

But I must not trespass longer on your indulgence. You know already how deeply I regret being absent from your great celebration; and I need not repeat what I have said in previous letters. Let me only offer to the Association, and to yourself, my best wishes for the brilliant success of the occasion, and my ardent hope that the influence of all that is said and done at Bunker Hill, on the 17th of June, 1875, may be as effective for the harmony and union of our beloved country, as were the acts and suffering of our fathers, on that consecrated height, a hundred years ago.

Believe me, dear Mr. President,

Very faithfully yours,

ROBERT C. WINTHROP.

Hon. GEORGE WASHINGTON WARREN,
President B. H. M. Association.

VII.

THE GEOGRAPHICAL CONGRESS IN PARIS.

REPORT TO THE AMERICAN ACADEMY OF ARTS AND SCIENCES, BOSTON, NOVEMBER 10, 1875.

It has seemed to me proper, Mr. President, that I should make some brief report of what I did, and of what I left undone, under the commission with which the Academy honored me, some months ago, to represent them at the International Congress of Geography in Paris.

Agreeably to a suggestion which I ventured to make to the Secretary, on receiving my own appointment, Mr. Ingersoll Bowditch, then abroad, was afterwards associated with me in the delegation. But I am sorry to say that neither of us found it practicable to be in Paris during the week in which the sessions were held. For myself, I reached there only on the evening of the day on which they were formally closed. It was an occasion of public ceremonial, which I was sincerely sorry to have missed. I regretted much less that I was unable to attend the opening ceremonies, as they took place on Sunday; and, though I do not care to associate myself with too sanctimonious a sabbatarianism, I have always been offended, when abroad, by the habitual selection of Sunday, particularly in Paris, for spectacles and shows of all sorts. Such a course seems almost like an insult to Protestantism, and might well be the subject of remonstrance where the occasion is not of a local character.

I had reported myself, as a delegate from the Academy, previously to my arrival, and my name had been duly entered on the roll of the Congress. Nothing remained, however, for the members to do, except to make a visit to the Sewers of Paris, — a geographical exploration from which I was willing to excuse myself during the heats of last August, — and to pay their respects to the Préfet of the Seine, at a formal reception arranged for that purpose.

This latter service I performed, and found a large and brilliant assembly at the palace of the Luxembourg, quite in Imperial style, notwithstanding the Republican element which has recently entered into the institutions of France. The staircase was lined with *gens d'armes* in uniform, a mounted police guarded the gateways, and one of the regimental bands played national airs within the palace. Nothing could have been more cordial and gracious than the welcome given me as a representative of the American Academy by the Préfet, M. Ferdinand Duval; and I had an opportunity of meeting not a few of the literary and scientific celebrities of France, as well as the delegates from other countries.

The next day I proceeded, with my card of membership, and under the escort of my accomplished friend, Colonel Perraud, to visit the *Exposition Géographique*, which had been arranged in those parts of the palace of the Tuileries which had escaped the torches of the Commune. A marvellous and most multitudinous exposition it was, and one which reflected the highest credit on the Geographical Society of France, under whose auspices it was prepared. I could not have believed it possible that any thing so dry, and so little æsthetic, as geography, could furnish the materials for so really interesting and brilliant a show. It was, indeed, an exhibition of many other things besides such as might be supposed to belong to geography proper. Geology, archæology, ethnology, antiquities of every sort, historic and pre-historic, were gathered there, side by side with maps and memorials of the most recent researches of modern travellers and explorers.

My eye lighted, for instance, on a photographic *fac-simile* of the "Mappamondo di Frà Mauro" of 1459, and on copies or originals of not a few other maps, on which there was no America. It was a relief to turn from these and see, as I did, the beautiful chart, published by our Coast Survey, of Boston Harbor, hanging at the very entrance of the little American department.

I remember seeing, too, the War Map used by the heroic Charles XII. of Sweden, and not far off the manuscript notes and maps of the not less heroic Livingston and Speke and other recent explorers of Africa.

A cast of the wonderful Meteorite of Greenland, weighing (the original) twenty thousand kilos, if I remember right, occupied a whole corner of one apartment. *Fac-similes* of Domesday Book and of the black-letter Prayer Book of 1636 attracted my eye in the English division.

This will give a sufficient indication of the somewhat heterogeneous things which were gathered together from all quarters under the banners of Geography, recalling that comprehensive, all-embracing description of Cicero: "Omnes etenim artes quæ ad humanitatem pertinent habent quoddam commune vinculum, et quasi cognatione quâdam inter se continentur."

The archives of all countries, and the museums of all learned societies, had indeed been made tributary, without reserve, to this Exposition; and things old and new had been brought forth from private cabinets and public collections to enrich and adorn it.

But I must not leave the impression that Geography proper, so to speak, was without its full representation. Such an array of globes and maps and photographic illustrations of earth and sea and sky could never have been congregated anywhere before. The Russian department was exceedingly rich, and surpassed all others in the number and perfection of the geographical works with which it was crowded. The Prussian or German department was hardly less striking; while the Austrian, Spanish, Portuguese, Italian, Danish, Norwegian, Dutch, Belgian, and Swiss departments contained many most interesting and valuable contributions. England was hardly there in full force, and the American department was small and poorly supplied.

When I alluded to this, however, as I did with regret, the Préfet of the Seine, with true French politeness, replied, "Yes, but we know you are fitly and fully engrossed with your grand Centennial Exposition at Philadelphia next year, which is well worthy of all your attention; and we shall all be interested in its success."

I lay upon the table a printed Catalogue of this remarkable Exhibition, with a few other pamphlets relating to it, which may give the Academy a better idea of its character than I have been able to convey in these cursory remarks.

Before resuming my seat, however, I may be pardoned for alluding to the monument of Count Rumford, which I visited in company with the American Minister, Mr. Washburne. It received some not very considerable damage from a shell which struck it, or exploded near it, during the siege of Paris. It was understood, before I left Paris, that this Academy had passed a resolution for its repair, and such a measure would certainly be a graceful act to be performed by this or some other American instrumentality. Our Minister was anxious to superintend such a repair, if authority should be given him to do so; and I promised to bring the subject to the renewed consideration of the friends and guardians of Count Rumford's memory.[1]

[1] I was soon afterwards authorized to empower our American Minister to have the Monument of Count Rumford repaired, at the joint expense of the American Academy and Harvard University; and it was done accordingly.

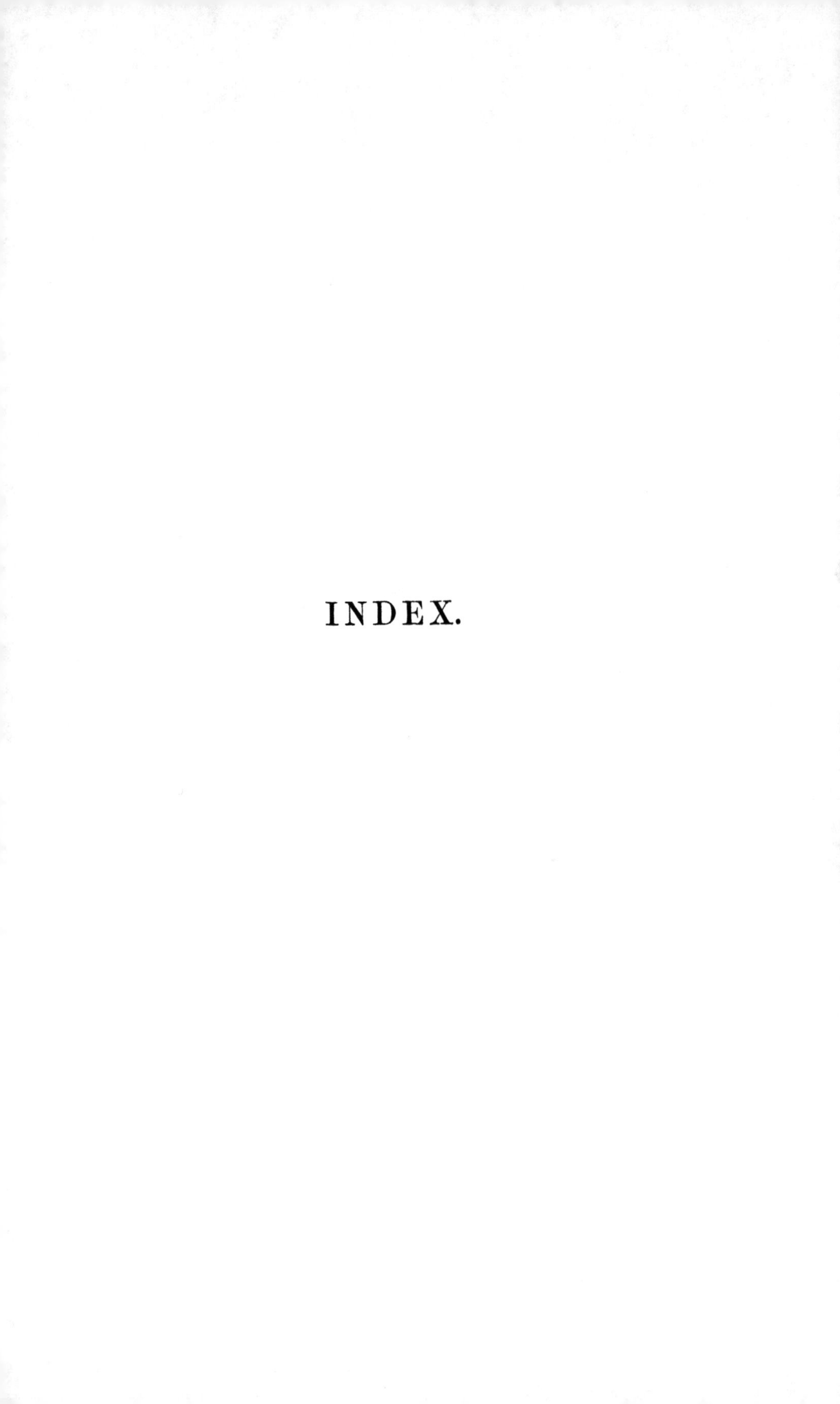

INDEX.

INDEX.

A.

B.

H.

I.

J.

K.

L.

M.

N.

O.

P.

Q.

R.

S.

T.

U.

V.

W.

Cambridge: Press of John Wilson & Son.

www.ingramcontent.com/pod-product-compliance
Lightning Source LLC
LaVergne TN
LVHW021226110826
845150LV00002B/254

* 9 7 8 1 4 2 5 5 6 3 7 1 4 *